Making Black History

Making Black History

THE COLOR LINE,
CULTURE, AND RACE
IN THE AGE OF JIM CROW

Jeffrey Aaron Snyder

The University of Georgia Press
Athens

A Sarah Mills Hodge Fund Publication
This publication is made possible in part through a grant
from the Hodge Foundation in memory of its founder,
Sarah Mills Hodge, who devoted her life to the relief and
education of African Americans in Savannah, Georgia.

© 2018 by the University of Georgia Press
Athens, Georgia 30602
www.ugapress.org
All rights reserved
Set in 9.5/13.5 Miller Text by Kaelin Chappell Broaddus

Most University of Georgia Press titles are
available from popular e-book vendors.

Printed digitally

Library of Congress Cataloging-in-Publication Data

Names: Snyder, Jeffrey Aaron, author.
Title: Making black history : the color line, culture, and race in
the age of Jim Crow / Jeffrey Aaron Snyder.
Description: Athens, Georgia : University of Georgia Press,
[2018] | "A Sarah Mills Hodge Fund Publication." |
Includes bibliographical references and index.
Identifiers: LCCN 2017024960| ISBN 9780820351834
(hardback : alk. paper) | ISBN 9780820352831
(pbk. : alk. paper) | ISBN 9780820351841 (ebook)
Subjects: LCSH: African Americans—Segregation—History. |
Woodson, Carter Godwin, 1875–1950. |
Association for the Study of Negro Life and History, inc.
Classification: LCC E185.61 .S658 2018 |
DDC 323.1196/073—dc23
LC record available at https://lccn.loc.gov/2017024960

For my father,
Melvin Leroy Snyder
(1946–1990)

CONTENTS

Acknowledgments   ix

A Note on Racial Terminology   xi

Introduction   1

PART 1: THE COLOR LINE, 1915-1926

CHAPTER ONE "The Cause"   19

CHAPTER TWO "Reverse the Stage"   46

PART 2: CULTURE, 1922-1941

CHAPTER THREE Heritage: Anthologies and the Negro Renaissance   73

CHAPTER FOUR The New Negro Goes to School   94

PART 3: RACE, 1942-1956

CHAPTER FIVE "A Revision of the Concept of Race and of Racism"   123

CHAPTER SIX "Look to the Roots": History Lessons for the Present   147

Epilogue   165

Notes   171

Bibliography   209

Index   233

ACKNOWLEDGMENTS

The origins of this book reach back to the spring of 2005, when Julie Reuben introduced me to the wonders of the history of American education. I was a graduate student enrolled in an educational psychology program. Julie's seminar "The Elusive Quest for Equality: Historical Perspectives on American Education" turned me into a budding historian. Soon after, Ellen Condliffe Lagemann convinced me that I could take my interest in educational history and turn it into a career. My experience as her research and then teaching assistant was a tour-de-force introduction to the rigorous, invigorating work of top-notch scholarship and teaching.

Ellen, who has been both an outstanding mentor and dear friend, introduced me to Jonathan Zimmerman. Jon would become my thesis adviser, and without his generous and unflagging support, this book would not have been possible. (Like many history monographs, this book started out as a dissertation.) Over the past decade, through graduate school and beyond, Jon has been helpful, kind, and upstanding—in short, a real mensch. I have benefited enormously from his incisive feedback on my work. I consider myself lucky to have been one of his students.

At New York University, professors James Fraser, Joan Malczewski, Michele Mitchell, Jeffrey Sammons, Nikhil Singh, and Harold Wechsler provided valuable guidance on my research project. I am also indebted to my peers in the NYU History of Education Writing Group—Zoë Burkholder, Diana D'Amico, Erich Dietrich, Ansley Erickson, Natalia Mehlman Petrzela, John Press, and Afrah Richmond—all of whom offered constructive criticism on my dissertation chapters.

I received vital financial support to fund archival research from Emory University's Manuscript, Archives and Rare Book Library (MARBL) and the Steinhardt School of Culture, Education, and Human Development. A Faculty Development Endowment grant from Carleton College afforded me the time to revise and prepare my manuscript for publication. I was fortunate to have received the help of librarians and archivists at Duke University's Rare Book, Manuscript and Special Collections Library, Emory University's MARBL, the Harvard University Archives, the Library of Congress Manuscript Division and Howard University's Moorland-Spingarn Research Center (MSRC). Joellen El Bashir and Ida Jones at MSRC both deserve special mention for their expert assistance.

I am grateful to all of the people at the University of Georgia Press who helped turn a rough manuscript into a polished book, including Christina Cotter, David Des Jardines, MJ Devaney, Rebecca Norton, Bethany Snead, and Mick Gusinde-Duffy. A special note of acknowledgement to Mick, executive editor of the press, who helped me navigate the novel terrain of academic publishing with his wealth of knowledge and characteristic good humor.

My academic home at Carleton is in the Educational Studies Department, and I have been fortunate to have the support of my colleagues Deborah Appleman, Anita Chikkatur, and Annie Larson. As chair of the department when I first arrived, Deborah helped me find my footing on campus and has been nothing short of remarkable in her commitment to helping me develop as a teacher and a scholar ever since.

I am deeply grateful to my wife, Alene Tchourumoff, for her abiding support. Without her patience, dedication, and love, not to mention her strategic browbeating, I would still be in graduate school, laboring over my footnotes—and this book would have amounted to nothing more than a wistful daydream. Our two beautiful boys, Nime and Naran, make my world go round. Looking over my shoulder as I typed, they would wonder why Dada's book had so few pictures. Special thanks to my mother-in-law, Dorie Tchourumoff, and sister-in-law Elsa Tchourumoff for helping out with childcare when I faced a pressing deadline.

My parents, Bonnie Lawlor and Melvin Snyder, imparted to me their love of books and their passion for teaching. Every time I teach, I strive to recreate the enthusiasm, creativity, and wonder that I saw in my mother's elementary school classrooms. This book is dedicated to my father, a social psychologist who never had the chance to write all the books he held in his mind's eye.

A NOTE ON RACIAL TERMINOLOGY

Racial terms are inherently flawed, as imprecise as they are mercurial. In the pages that follow, I use the terms "black" and "African American" interchangeably. I also use the term "Negro" for the purposes of historical fidelity. "Negro" may sound hopelessly outdated (even to the ears of practiced historians), but it was the most commonly used word by blacks and whites alike to describe people of African descent in the first half of the twentieth century. Moreover, "*the* Negro," an expression with no modern analog, is the only term that adequately conveys the distinctive racial logic of the Jim Crow period.

Making Black History

Introduction

As a graduate student, I was astonished to learn that there were over one hundred historically black colleges and universities. The names of the schools—Spelman, Tougaloo, Wilberforce—sounded like faraway cities that I had vaguely heard of but would never be able to place. Howard, I discovered from Zora Neale Hurston's autobiography, was the "capstone of Negro education," symbolizing to black Americans in the Jim Crow era "what Harvard was to the whites."[1] Reading about the history of Howard, I encountered pioneering African American academics such as Kelly Miller, Alain Locke, and Carter G. Woodson for the first time. They belonged to the American Negro Academy, wrote articles for publications such as the *Baltimore Afro-American*, *Crisis*, and the *Journal of Negro Education*, and delivered lectures at African Methodist Episcopal churches, "colored" YMCAs, and black fraternities.

This book emerged out of an interest in the parallel society that African Americans developed during the Jim Crow era. "At the turn of the twentieth century," Leon Litwack explains, "in the face of growing white hostility, violence and both legal and extralegal repression, blacks drew inward, constructing in their communities a separate world with its own businesses, fraternal organizations, churches, schools, newspapers and community institutions— in many ways, a replica of the society that excluded them."[2] Along with their own churches, schools, and newspapers, African Americans also had their own history.

The study and celebration of black history became an increasingly important part of African American life over the course of the early to mid-twentieth century. It was the glue that held African Americans together as "a people," a weapon with which to fight racism, and a roadmap to a brighter future. *Making Black History* focuses on the engine behind the early black history movement: Carter G. Woodson and his Association for the Study of Negro Life and History. It offers the first extended account of how this movement reflected, refracted, and sometimes even shaped broader trends in African

American thought and culture. In my analysis, I line up the trajectory of the early black history movement with the wider arc of African American history, an undertaking that enhances our understanding of some of the signal institutions and developments in twentieth-century black life such as segregated black schools, the Harlem Renaissance, and the emerging modern civil rights movement.

Carter Godwin Woodson (1875–1950) was born in the hardscrabble town of New Canton, Virginia.[3] Because he spent part of his adolescence working in West Virginia coal mines, he did not graduate from high school until he was twenty-two years old. Woodson received a BA from Berea College in 1902, a master's degree from the University of Chicago in 1908, and a PhD in history from Harvard in 1912. The first and only professional historian whose parents had been born into slavery, Woodson pursued the vocation of black history as if it were, in his words, a "life and death struggle."[4] Woodson was exceptionally prolific, producing no fewer than four monographs, five textbooks, five edited collections of primary source materials, five coauthored sociological studies, and hundreds of articles, essays, book reviews, and newspaper columns.[5] He founded the Association for the Study of Negro Life and History, which was designed to collect and publish "historical and sociological material bearing on the Negro," in 1915.[6] From its humble beginnings as a fledgling society organized around the *Journal of Negro History*, the association became the nucleus of a movement. By the late 1920s, the association had established a clear institutional structure, centered around a professional journal, a publishing house (Associated Publishers), annual conventions, yearly Negro History Week celebrations, and a national network of devoted educators. It was in fact three organizations wrapped into one: a scholarly body devoted to the advancement of black history as a professional field, a curriculum and instruction network for black educators, and a clearinghouse for community-based engagement with black history that provided schools, churches, social welfare, and civic groups with pamphlets, posters, photographs, and books.

Making Black History takes an expansive view of the historical enterprise as one that includes not just the production of history but also its dissemination, consumption, and reception as well as its study, celebration, and performance.[7] Among the many different groups of people who contributed to the early black history movement were professional historians, lay historians, scholars in other disciplines, schoolteachers, schoolchildren, bibliophiles, librarians, archivists, "race women," "race men," journalists, and artists. No matter their backgrounds, each individual affiliated with the association grappled with a set of interrelated questions: Who and what is "Negro"? What is the relationship of black history to American history? And, most broadly, what are the purposes of history? I track the different answers to these ques-

Portrait of Carter G. Woodson as a young man.
(Scurlock Studio Records, Archives Center, National Museum of American History, Smithsonian Institution)

tions in an attempt to recover the public discourse of the early black history movement and show what made it distinctive and resonant. This public discourse took shape in journals, monographs, and textbooks and sprang to life in the pages of the black press, the classrooms of segregated schools, and annual celebrations of Negro History Week. It did not, as a general rule, cross the color line. In spite of the association's eagerness to reach the white public, its white audience was more imagined than real. The overwhelming majority of whites had little to no exposure to "Negro history" during Woodson's lifetime.[8] It was not until the 1960s that the civil rights and Black Power movements brought black history into white consciousness.[9] Even so, a prospective white readership loomed large in the minds of association authors, a fact that is vital to take into account. As James Weldon Johnson declared in 1928, the black author's audience was "*always* both white America and black America." It was "impossible for a sane American Negro to write with total disregard for nine-tenths" of the U.S. population.[10]

Remarkable educational gains in African American literacy and education supported the development and growth of the early black history movement, expanding the ranks of the black reading public and the number of classrooms where black history could find a home. An estimated 5 percent of the black population was literate in 1860. Nearly a third was literate in 1880, and by 1910, more than two-thirds of African Americans had acquired at least basic literacy skills. At the turn of the twentieth century, only 36 percent of black children between the ages of five and fourteen attended school in the southern states. By 1940, the figure was 78 percent. (The figures for white children were 55 percent and 79 percent, respectively.) The first third of the twentieth century saw "a crusade" for black common schools across the rural South. Thousands of schools were constructed, fueled by black southerners' "enduring beliefs in universal schooling and their collective social actions," as well as the support of northern philanthropies such as the Anna T. Jeanes Foundation and the Julius Rosenwald Fund. Higher education for blacks likewise saw a significant, if not quite as dramatic, expansion during this same period. In 1915, some twenty-five hundred students were enrolled in black public and private colleges in southern states and the District of Columbia—in 1935, the number was close to twenty-nine thousand.[11] It was during this same period that the study of black history was incorporated into the growing course offerings in history at schools such as Hampton, Tuskegee, Atlanta, and Howard.[12] (The black academy was a stronghold for *Journal of Negro History* subscriptions.)

The association was one node among the network of institutions that supported black communities in the age of Jim Crow. While dozens of black colleges and universities had been founded in the wake of the Civil War, the turn of the twentieth century witnessed the creation of scores of new black associations, organizations, and institutions devoted to racial uplift. Harriet Tubman, Ida B. Wells, and Mary Church Terrell helped to found the National Association of Colored Women in Washington, D.C., in 1896. Booker T. Washington launched the National Negro Business League in 1900. The *Chicago Defender* printed its first issue in 1905, while Alpha Phi Alpha, the inaugural black fraternity, held its first meeting at Cornell in 1906. Catalyzed by a race riot in Abraham Lincoln's hometown of Springfield, Illinois, the NAACP was established in 1909. The next year, sociologist George Edmund Haynes and colleagues founded the National Urban League.

Embraced by the small fraction of educated blacks at the turn of the twentieth century, racial uplift ideology was a response to the "suffocating realities" of the United States under Jim Crow. "Lifting as We Climb," the National Association of Colored Women's motto, is the quintessential expression of this ideology, which was predicated on an ethic of service and the belief that the improvement of blacks' moral values and material circumstances would provide a pathway to full citizenship. A capacious ideology characterized by "tensions and contradictions," racial uplift comfortably encompassed both Booker T. Washington's philosophy of self-help and Du Bois's missionary vision of the talented tenth. With a steadfast commitment to "education as the key to liberation," racial uplift was designed to build bridges between black elites and the black masses. Emphasizing bourgeois morality and patriarchal authority, it was often circumscribed by class and gender hierarchies. But it could also be more expansive and democratic, reaching for a "positive black identity in a deeply racist society, turning the pejorative designation of race into a source of dignity and self-affirmation."[13] While Woodson clearly espoused middle-class virtues such as industry, thrift, and respectability, the association's brand of racial uplift stressed race pride, the development of racial solidarity across class lines, and the transformative power of education.

Association members referred to the early black history movement as "the cause," and as is the case with all causes and crusades, this one was grounded in a set of common values, starting with a commitment to a "usable past."[14] They also believed in historical truth, the power of history to change hearts and minds, racial integration, and the basic integrity of American democracy. These fundamental assumptions proved to be remarkably stable over the course of Woodson's lifetime, coalescing to form a loose association worldview.

The association firmly rejected a cloistered, ivory tower approach to the historical enterprise in which any attempt to make history relevant was seen as a bastardization of "pure" history. "History," Woodson declared, "has no value unless it shows the bearing of the past upon the present and that of the present upon the past."[15] "A sane presentation of the past of the Negro" was the antidote to the poisonous polemics about the so-called Negro problem.[16] It provided a means by which to discuss contemporary events, issues, and trends in a more evenhanded fashion, injecting a desperately needed sense of perspective into a field filled with diatribes and vitriol. The association was not interested in converting everyday people into brainy drips who spent every waking hour with their heads "plunged into books," but rather in providing the public with a foundation of historical facts that was solid enough to inform constructive responses to the most urgent problems of the present. As Mary McLeod Bethune put it, the mission of the association was to "arm us with the facts so that we may face the future with clear eyes and a sure vision."[17]

With respect to the history of the Negro, association members saw a profound discrepancy between "what has *actually* happened and what those who have written the history have *said* has happened."[18] The association endeavored to close this gap, bringing the narratives of black history into closer alignment with "the facts" of black history. At the association's twentieth anniversary celebration in Chicago in 1935, Bethune said its most important contribution to society was "the discovery, the interpretation and the dissemination of truth in the field of Negro life." The association's investigators were "pioneers, trailblazers, [and] adventurers in handling facts," deftly separating them from "the admixtures of prejudice, passion and selfish interest" in order to arrive at "objective and precise" information.[19]

"Facts are not important for their own sake," Bethune went on to say in her address. "They are important," she maintained, "only as a basis for human action."[20] Facts guided human behavior not only by supplying the building blocks for abstract ideas and intellectual frameworks but also by shaping basic human psychology, including identity, attitudes, and self-esteem. Teaching the wrong facts could have devastating, even fatal, consequences.[21] The most dangerous so-called fact taught in black and white schools alike was "the inferiority of the Negro."[22] "To handicap a student by teaching him that his black face is a curse and that his struggle to change his condition is hopeless is the worst sort of lynching," Woodson explained:

> It kills one's aspirations and dooms him to vagabondage and crime. The crusade against such propaganda, then, is much more important than the anti-lynching movement, because there would be no lynching if it did not start in the schoolroom. Why not exploit or enslave a class that everybody is taught to regard as inferior?[23]

Propagating the racial inferiority doctrine was a double injustice, saddling blacks with an "inferiority complex" and licensing whites to treat blacks as second-class citizens or worse. The only way to rectify this wrong, from the association's point of view, was to promote "self-respect" and "tolerance" by teaching the "whole truth" about black history.[24]

The "whole truth" rested on the bedrock assumption that black people are not racially inferior. Indeed, this premise is the crux of black history. It might seem like the inclusion of black people in historical accounts is black history's essential feature. On further reflection, though, it becomes clear that representation is a necessary but not sufficient component of black history. The first historical accounts of Reconstruction, for instance, not only included African Americans but also assigned them starring roles, demonizing them as the main culprits responsible for "the decline" of southern civilization and virtue. The source of black history, as Woodson suggested in *The African Background Outlined*, was the following conviction: "The author considers the Negro as human, responding very much as others do to the same stimuli, advancing when free to go forward and lagging behind when hindered by obstacles not encountered by others." Or, as W. E. B. Du Bois lyrically proclaimed in *Darkwater*: "All men, black and brown and white, are brothers, varying through time and opportunity, in form and gift and feature, but differing in no essential particular and alike in soul and the possibility of infinite development."[25]

The association aimed to provide a winning combination of facts and inspiration, striving "to mirror the past as accurately as possible" while also attesting to the Negro's intrinsic worth. Association publications highlighted prejudice and discrimination—"to provide *all America* with a lesson" on the "wickedness of human exploitation and injustice that have characterized too much of this nation's past."[26] They also foregrounded achievements and victories—"the peak that was scaled, the foe that was vanquished, the deep river that was crossed."[27] For African Americans, black history was an injection of hope, a stimulus to do better and reach higher. "If you teach the Negro that he has accomplished as much good as any other race," Woodson averred, "he will aspire to equality and justice without regard to race." For whites, meanwhile, black history was a kind of vaccination shot, inoculating them against the disease of race prejudice. Expose whites to black history and "the Negro [would] enjoy a larger share of the privileges of democracy as a result of the recognition of his worth."[28] That ignorance was the root cause of racial antagonism was one of the association's basic precepts.[29] As a high school teacher, Woodson would exhort his students with the well-known biblical phrase "Ye shall know the truth and the truth shall make you free."[30] Too many people, Woodson elucidated, were "victims of falsehoods" simply because they did not have an opportunity to hear the truth unvarnished.[31] Although it required an enormous investment of time and energy, the association held fast to the belief that the majority of the world's people could ultimately be depended on to heed "the teachings of the truth." "Facts," as Bethune put it, "have a ruthless way of winning the day sooner or later."[32]

Convinced that facts ultimately prevail, the association invested history instruction with extraordinary power, to the point that Woodson's proclamations sometimes strayed into the territory of wishful thinking. "The distortion of facts has been the cause of our present plight," Woodson wrote in 1928. "The teaching of the truth of history as it is, therefore, will remove the evils from which we now suffer," he concluded. This is an arresting statement. According to this logic, it was not, for instance, that slavery *itself* was the wellspring of continued black suffering but rather the misrepresentation of the historical facts *about* slavery. However quixotic, the notion that just getting the facts straight could straighten out the "race problem" was part of the association's DNA. This emphatically did not mean it was the job of historians to take on the mantle of "professional race leaders." "The Association," Woodson said, "always makes a sharp distinction between the study of the Negro and the agitation of the race problem." This was not, Woodson stressed, to minimize "the importance of the agitation for the rise of the Negro to the level of citizenship." Rather it was a declaration of the historian's duty "to serve the truth." Striving to remain above the fray of partisan political battles, Woodson proclaimed that the Association "has no special brand for the solution of the race problem except to learn to think."[33]

Regarding activism, the association's unofficial credo is summed up nicely by John Hope Franklin's judgment that there was a place for advocacy on the part of African American scholars as long as they recognized when they were playing the role of advocate and when they were playing the role of scholar.[34] As politically engaged individual citizens, members of the association tended to gravitate toward the NAACP. Woodson and many of his colleagues—including Luther Porter Jackson, Rayford Logan, and John Hope Franklin—were active NAACP members. Woodson was a strong proponent of expanding economic opportunity for blacks and supported black-owned businesses and the interests of black workers. (He backed the nearly decade-long "Don't Buy Where You Can't Work Campaign" that used boycotts and picketing to boost black employment.) Woodson had some contact with the Popular Front in the 1930s, primarily through A. Philip Randolph's National Negro Congress, but he regarded the revolutionary visions of Marx-inspired "radicals" with deep skepticism. Writing in the throes of the Great Depression, Woodson dismissed the calls for a planned collectivist economy as "pleasant dreams," asserting that "a social program based on competition" was the best available economic model.[35] As a body, the association paid close attention to socioeconomic issues, but unlike, say, the adherents of the "Amenia ideal" (including Abram Harris, E. Franklin Frazier and Ralph Bunche in the 1930s), it never came close to endorsing the analytical position that "class had to be considered at least as strongly as race as a causative factor in blacks' degraded position in American life."[36] The cause of the proletariat was effectively absent from the association's purview.

Eschewing direct involvement in politics, the work of the association was nonetheless deeply informed by a mainline racial integrationism committed to blacks' "full participation in American life on equal terms with any other citizen."[37] Woodson, like many of his peers (including Du Bois, Locke, and Charles H. Thompson), believed that the only way to address the bleak facts of Jim Crow segregation was through a strategic pragmatism animated by racial solidarity and supported by black institutions. In 1932, Woodson declared that he had "never advocated the separation of the races" but that nevertheless as a teacher, he had to serve his "people in their separate schools or permit them to grow up in ignorance." Working in segregated institutions was not an endorsement of the racial status quo—it was a necessary means of economic and cultural survival. Not only that, black institutions, in fact, served as the main staging grounds for assaults against Jim Crow. "Isolation and segregation are terrible evils," Woodson clarified, "but they offer at the same time an unusual opportunity for us to organize efficient agencies for our own uplift." "If segregation is forced upon us," Woodson said, "let us take it and make the most of it."[38] Distilled to a slogan, here is how Woodson described this racial uplift strategy in *Miseducation of the Negro*: "Use segregation to kill segregation."[39]

The association's broad commitment to racial integration reflected a deeper faith in American liberal democracy and the "American Creed." In spite of searching, often searing, critiques of the United States, Woodson and his colleagues never abandoned their faith that African Americans would eventually be brought into the fold of "American justice, American liberty, [and] American civilization."[40] The quintessential expression of this faith is found in Rayford Logan's 1954 monograph *The Negro in American Life and Thought*, in which he introduced the term "nadir" to describe the precipitously declining status of African Americans from 1877 to the turn of the century. After charting in painstaking detail the rise of "Exploitation, Disenfranchisement, Segregation, Discrimination, Lynching [and] Contempt," Logan concluded that none of the many enemies of the Negro—from southern demagogues to social Darwinists—could "exorcise from the Declaration of Independence the assertion that 'All men are created equal.'"[41] Woodson and his colleagues wrote about America, not Amerikkka. It was not until the late 1960s that a more militant strand of black history declared that the founding ideals were a sham and that the country was rotten to its core.

Trained at the country's leading research universities, including Chicago, Columbia, and Harvard, the top black scholars in the age of Jim Crow "lived, worked and most frequently published from behind the line of segregation."[42] In the Harvard class of 1908 *Twenty-Fifth Anniversary Report*, Howard University philosopher Alain Locke lamented the "comparative isolation that separates Negro life and institutions from even academic and cultural interests at large."[43] Toward the end of his life, Du Bois expressed a similar sentiment with a sharper edge:

> So far as the American world of science and letters was concerned, we never "belonged"; we remained unrecognized in learned societies and academic groups. We rated merely as Negroes studying Negroes, and after all, what had Negroes to do with America or science?[44]

"Segregated scholars," to borrow Francille Rusan Wilson's apt phrase, not only had to challenge the deep-seated notion that the life of the mind was not for black people—they also had to contend with a host of practical barriers that could stymie their careers. In the South, blacks were excluded from research libraries, scientific laboratories, and local learned societies. Moreover, segregation by law and by custom prevented black scholars from attending the conferences of national scholarly organizations in almost all southern and some northern cities.[45] No matter how many credentials they had, black scholars could not escape the "indignities of Jim Crow America."[46]

In John Hope Franklin's estimation, the "world of scholarship" was nearly as racially "partitioned" as any other public sphere. The history discipline was no exception in this regard.[47] Black historians were on the periphery of the mainstream historical associations, conventions, and journals throughout the Jim Crow era. While Du Bois participated in the 1891 and 1909 American Historical Association (AHA) conventions and published an article in the *American Historical Review* (*AHR*) in 1909, African American scholars would remain on the sidelines of the profession for decades thereafter. In fact, Du Bois's 1909 essay was the only article published by a black scholar in the *AHR* until Franklin's AHA presidential address appeared in 1979. With respect to AHA conventions, in 1929, Monroe Work became the first black scholar to make an appearance on the podium there since Du Bois. A session titled "The Negro in the History of the United States" for the 1940 convention, chaired by Du Bois and featuring Charles Wesley and Rayford Logan, was a rare acknowledgment of the existence of black history. With the exception of occasional reviews of books released by Associated Publishers and the odd mention of Negro History Week, the work of the association rarely attracted the attention of the mainstream historical profession.[48] In a blunt assessment, August Meier and Elliott Rudwick conclude that, until the 1960s, black history was a "Jim Crow specialty ignored by nearly the entire profession."[49] With a touch more nuance, it is fair to say that black historians "struggled to be heard beyond their professional homes" in the black academy and that their scholarly contributions and innovations were largely confined to "racial spheres."[50]

Isolation from the professional networks, financial resources, and prestige of white academe, of course, had devastating effects. ("The world of the Negro scholar," Franklin wrote in 1963, "is indescribably lonely.")[51] At the same time, though, there were arguably some advantages to operating on the edges of the history profession. In *Women and the Historical Enterprise in America*, Julie Des Jardins presents a compelling argument that disciplinary margins are "sites of disempowerment and limitation" but also "spaces of opportunity, experimentation and perspective." Turn-of-the-century women historians, for example, were able to perceive intricacies of societal power relations that most male historians were blind to, according to Des Jardins. Consequently, they were more likely to focus on understudied topics such as local history, family history, and Native American history; they were also more open to using innovative primary sources such as material artifacts, oral testimony, and folklore.[52] The idea that writing history from the margins could be liberating is borne out by the work of the association. Woodson and his colleagues demonstrated a strong commitment to recovering "the hidden lives of the poor, the oppressed, and the disenfranchised."[53] Consequently, they produced a disproportionately large share of the most avant-garde scholarship, work that anticipated some of the most significant modern developments in the profession such as the rise of "new history" and the transnational turn.[54]

In addition to significant hardships and benefits, the life of the black scholar also came with serious responsibilities. Surveying how Jim Crow segregation influenced black scholars, Jonathan Scott Holloway and Ben Keppel conclude that pioneering African American academics viewed intellectual pursuits as a kind of vocation. "Much as ministers respond to a call to faith in the church," they write, "early black thinkers responded to a call to service in their scholarship."[55] Given the severe crises black America faced in the early twentieth century, some black scholars perceived service to "the race" as compulsory rather than voluntary. As Woodson argued in *The Negro in Our History*, the most highly educated African Americans—including the likes of Du Bois and Kelly Miller—had been "impressed into the service" of fighting the "ordeal" of Jim Crow at the turn of the century. They took it as their obligation, Woodson said, to expose "the folly of the reactionaries promoting the return to medieval civilization in proscribing the citizenship of Negroes."[56] Foolishness on the race question ran rampant. In a 1932 newspaper article called "Why We Should Publish Truth in Self-Defense," Woodson lamented the regular appearance of books slandering the Negro, rendering it "necessary for scientifically trained persons to write a dozen or more books to counteract the disastrous effect of that particular misrepresentation."[57]

Twenty-five years later in the pages of *Crisis*, John Hope Franklin took up this theme of self-defense to characterize Woodson's own career. In an essay called "The New Negro History," Franklin said the work undertaken by Woodson and the association was arguably "the most far-reaching and ambitious effort to rewrite history that has ever been attempted in this country." "It was," Franklin wrote,

> a remarkable attempt to rehabilitate a whole people, to explode racial myths, to establish a secure and respectable place for the Negro in the evolution of the American social order, to develop self-respect and self-esteem among those who had been subjected to the greatest indignities known in the Western world. Finally, it was a valiant attempt to force America to keep faith with herself, to remind her that truth is more praiseworthy than power, and that justice and equality, long the stated policy of this nation, should apply to all its citizens and *even* to the writing of history.[58]

Franklin's assessment underscores the extent to which he viewed race vindication—that is, the "defense of black humanity against racist disparagement"—as the association's core mission.[59] Indeed, echoing Woodson, Franklin maintained that defending the race was an unavoidable responsibility for the first generation of professional black scholars. In his well-known 1963 essay "The Dilemma of the Negro Scholar," Franklin argued that the most talented early black academics—including Locke, Du Bois and Woodson himself—had "felt compelled" to address "contentions of Negro inferiority." Franklin emphasized how unrewarding it must have been for black scholars to declare, "I am indeed *not inferior*." "They made their argument simply and directly," Franklin said. "It was as though whites had said they could not count and Negroes then counted from one to ten to prove that they could."[60]

Franklin had enormous respect for his predecessors, and he clearly saw the achievements of the early black history movement in heroic terms. Even so, the strong emphasis he placed on race vindication had the potential to reduce the work of Woodson and the association to a "byproduct of American racism."[61] It would be historically inaccurate, even irresponsible, to temper the awesome power that the "infinitely varied and resourceful racism of white America" exerted on black intellectual life in the age of Jim Crow.[62] At the same time, though, it is imperative to recognize that the early black history movement was not merely a reactive enterprise, mechanically and predictably responding to racial insults. The key point here is that the work of the association was shaped but not determined by the racism that pervaded the historical profession and the broader society. While Woodson and his colleagues *had* to confront the racist theorems that littered the U.S. history field, they did so as imaginative research scientists, probing for weaknesses in reigning interpretations, generating alternative hypotheses, and searching for different kinds of evidence—at times formulating wholly new paradigms. Intellectual self-defense, then, elicited innovations at every stage of the historical research enterprise. With respect to evidence, for example, to demonstrate, rather than merely assert, that the "contented slave" was a caricature with no basis in fact required the identification and excavation of novel primary source sites. Beyond the standard plantation records, Woodson and his colleagues turned to previously unexamined materials, including advertisements for runaway slaves, slave narratives, and letters written from ex-slaves to their former masters. Investigations like these not only supplemented conventional interpretations of slavery—they transformed the extant accounts, changing our understanding of the very nature of slavery as an institution.

As I explored the primary sources generated by Woodson and his colleagues, I found that three key concepts were nearly always implicated in the association's work: the color line, culture and race. Resonating on multiple registers, these protean concepts provided a basic lexicon for the world of Jim Crow. Woodson and his colleagues confronted the "color line" as a literal dividing line—you could point to it on a map of virtually any American city or town—as well as a figurative expression for the exclusion of blacks from full participation in the life of the nation. They engaged with "culture" as a synonym for "civilization" and as an anthropological concept, signifying a "way of life." With respect to "race," at the same time that Woodson and his coworkers had to reckon with "race" as a biological category, they also used "*the* race" to signify African Americans as a social group or a people.

Intersecting, overlapping, and reinforcing one another, the three ideas of the color line, culture, and race defined Jim Crow's logic and texture. Take miscegenation, for instance, a specter that haunted the imagination of white folks from the first days of Reconstruction. It was based on the "scientific" premise that whites and blacks represented two biologically distinct racial groups; consequently, "racial admixture" posed a grave reproductive peril in that children born of interracial unions would necessarily suffer from serious physical and mental defects. Miscegenation was also deeply informed by the assumption that blacks and whites constituted two separate cultural groups. Hence the anxiety surrounding so-called social equality, in which blacks would be able to mingle with—even marry—whites. Lurking behind concerns about "social equality," of course, was the fear that political equality would follow soon on its heels. Take away the scientific, legal, and moral prohibitions against interracial sex and interracial marriage and you had a cultural revolution on your hands; a revolution that would ultimately erase the previously sacrosanct boundaries of the color line, bringing white supremacy to an ignoble end. Notions of race (biology), culture (social arrangements and social mores), and the color line (power hierarchies) were all intertwined.

Although it is impossible to completely disentangle the ideas of the color line, culture, and race from one another, each one came to the forefront for a particular phase of the early black history movement. To help demarcate the major shifts that characterized the study and celebration of black history in the Woodson era, I have divided this study into three sections: the first explores the color line in the years between 1915 and 1926; the second takes up culture from 1922 to 1941; and the third considers race from 1942 to 1956.

Woodson called "segregation" the "most far-reaching development in the history of the Negro since the enslavement of the race." "In fact," he said, "it is a sequel of slavery."[63] The defining features of Jim Crow—disenfranchisement, lynch law, segregation in public accommodations, and so on—had only recently crystallized by the time Woodson founded the association in 1915. The modern color line, in short, was a recent invention, and Woodson and his colleagues endeavored to wrap their heads around it. They were particularly interested in exploring what freedom and citizenship meant for black people in a world where the Reconstruction Amendments (1865–70) coexisted with the Supreme Court's 1896 *Plessy v. Ferguson* decision. Woodson conducted a multipronged historical analysis of the color line's origins, striving to understand how its boundaries were created and maintained. This prompted him to investigate topics such as miscegenation and the "one drop" rule, racial violence, and Supreme Court rulings relating to black citizenship. Working on the periphery of a lily-white profession, Woodson and his coworkers challenged the notion that progress was the primary law governing U.S. history. This challenge was closely tied to the association's creation of a black archive that assembled scores of primary source documents—including diaries, letters, and speeches—presenting African American testimony, with an emphasis on blacks' interior psychological experience. As one white native of Mississippi put it, most southern whites did not have "the faintest comprehension of the inner lives of Negroes," which, he suggested, were "forever secret and alien to them."[64] As a result of cultural isolation and a lack of education, many blacks too had remained unaware of the full range of black experiences across the country—the black archive would hold up a mirror to black communities, allowing them to see both commonalities and differences reflected through the historical record.

In the 1920s and 1930s, the work of the association took a clear cultural turn, anchored around Negro History Week, which was inaugurated in 1926. In decades of scholarship on the Harlem Renaissance, historians and literary scholars alike have all but ignored the association. Similarly, the renaissance is all but absent from the scholarly literature on the early black history movement. If mentioned at all, the movement is portrayed as running in parallel to the renaissance, partaking of the same "spirit of race pride" but not directly interacting with or contributing to it in any significant way.[65] I maintain that the early black history movement was an integral part of the renaissance, providing a foundation for the self-conscious awakening of African Americans as "a people" knit together by a shared struggle and a common culture. Two major questions animated the association's historical production in the renaissance period. First, what is Africa to me? And second, what are black Americans to America? Anthologies of black art, music, and literature as well as Negro History Week celebrations at segregated black schools provided the most important venues to address these questions.

From the early 1940s through the mid-1950s, the work of the association was in dialogue with two big trends: a major revision of the race concept and the emerging civil rights movement. Anthropologists, psychologists, and sociologists arrived at a strong consensus on the intellectual bankruptcy of "scientific" racism. Even as they asserted that innate racial inequality was a "myth," they struggled to explain the profound inequalities evident in the world with respect to the social status of different racial groups. Woodson and his colleagues asked what might account for the uniquely unequal status of African Americans and sought to understand the nature of racial prejudice and discrimination and "race" itself. Beginning in the World War II years, cracks in the Jim Crow racial order that had been consolidated in the early 1900s began to appear, and it was split wide open when the Supreme Court outlawed segregated schools with the *Brown* decision in 1954. Building on its longtime commitment to a "usable past," the association oriented its public mission around racial equality and the push for racial integration. With an unbiased history curriculum as its source, the association imagined that justice would flow out from the classrooms to the surrounding society.

PART ONE

THE COLOR LINE
1915–1926

Du Bois's 1903 statement in *The Souls of Black Folk* that the "problem of the twentieth century is the problem of the color line" is the most famous invocation of the "color line" term. It was not the first. In 1881, Frederick Douglass published a penetrating essay called "The Color Line" in the *North American Review*. The color line, Douglass said, emerged out of the "depths of slavery" and the association of "ignorance ... servility, poverty [and] dependence" with color. The "insidious influence" of the color line confronted blacks in "nearly every department of American life." As Douglass explained, "The workshop denies him work, and the inn denies him shelter; the ballot box a fair vote and the jury-box a fair trial."[1] It took two decades, but the color line eventually became the central metaphor for the racial divide that prevented African Americans from fully participating in the political, economic, social, and cultural life of the country.[2]

Woodson grew up alongside Jim Crow, his formative years coinciding with the advent, spread, and hardening of the color line. He was born in 1875, the year the Civil Rights Act passed, the last-ditch attempt to ensure the enforcement of the Reconstruction Amendments. When the last northern troops departed the South, he was not yet two. Woodson was eight years old when the U.S. Supreme Court decreed the Civil Rights Act unconstitutional in 1883. He was fourteen in 1890 when the Louisiana legislature passed "An Act to Promote the Comfort of Passengers," which decreed that rail travel within the state must be racially segregated. (Fourteen too when Mississippi instituted the South's first poll tax and literacy requirement.) When Booker T. Washington delivered his Cotton Exposition speech in 1895, Woodson was twenty years old and still attending high school. He was twenty-one the following year when the Supreme Court advanced the "separate but equal" doctrine in *Plessy v. Ferguson*. By Woodson's twenty-fifth birthday at the turn of the century, more than twenty five hundred blacks had been lynched during his lifetime.[3] This was the "nadir," in the famous formulation of Rayford Logan, when "Jim Crow was everywhere, instructing blacks as to where they could legally reside, walk, sit, rest, eat, drink, work, seek entertainment, be hospitalized, and be buried."[4]

As August Meier and Elliott Rudwick emphasize, Woodson founded the association at a time of unprecedented "popular and scientific racism in Western thought."[5] Between 1880 and 1920, tens of thousands of racist images and artifacts circulated throughout the United States, ranging from Sambo and Mammy images on toaster and teapot covers to the graphic and enormously popular lynching postcards, which featured grainy photographs of mangled bodies swinging from trees.[6] During this era, which saw the rise of "spokeservants" such as Aunt Jemima and Uncle Ben, "Niggerhead" became a common product name used to sell everything from tea and tobacco to canned oysters.[7] As the color bar extended its power and reach, the "black subject, the black body and the black voice" saturated popular culture, forming a "great deal of the basis of a truly national culture."[8]

Racial oppression in this era, Leon Litwack reminds us, was not only the work of racial demagogues but of "the 'best people'—the most educated, the most refined, the most respected."[9] Professional historians were no exception in this regard, treating African Americans no better than the purveyors of commercial foodstuffs, as they cranked out lurid and contemptuous depictions of black people. Indeed, history played a crucial role in fortifying the color line. Southerners and northerners settled their regional differences by hammering out a "nationalist and racist historiographical consensus" with respect to the Civil War and Reconstruction. The crux of this consensus was the denunciation of Reconstruction's "criminal outrages."[10] D. W. Griffith's blockbuster film *Birth of a Nation* amplified this professional consensus into a kind of racist gospel, which damned blacks as eternally inferior, venerated the Klan as saviors of civilization, and glorified a nation revitalized by the decisive return to white supremacy.

The major scholarly works on Woodson have provided valuable insight into the ways in which racist historiography and the racism of the historical profession shaped the advent of the association.[11] These same works have duly noted that the "racism," "prejudice" and "segregation" of the broader society influenced its development, but this more global racial climate is rarely examined in any real depth.[12] I seek to weave together an "internalist" analysis, which focuses on history as a discipline and profession, with an "externalist" investigation, which concentrates on the larger racial landscape.[13] Regarding this more expansive racial terrain, Woodson's effort to build a movement around the pursuit of black history should be seen as part of a larger movement of "black intellectual reconstruction" during which black authors and scholars attempted to shift the "new century's image of the black away from the stereotypes scattered throughout plantation fictions, blackface minstrelsy, vaudeville, racist pseudo-science and vulgar Social Darwinism."[14]

Covering the years spanning from the foundation of the association in 1915 to the release of the Associated Publisher's *The Mind of the Negro as Reflected in Letters* in 1926, the two chapters that follow outline the most significant reference points for the association's creation and evolution as well as its early accomplishments. Chapter 1 ("The Cause") explores the different strands of racism that Woodson was forced to confront as a budding black scholar living in the Jim Crow United States—they include the reflexive racism of Woodson's graduate studies advisers at Harvard and the larger American historical profession, the virulent racism of Reconstruction historiography, the epic racism of *Birth of a Nation*, and the "racism in the nation's service" of the Woodrow Wilson administration.[15] It also examines the wellsprings of the association, which were deep and various, reflecting Woodson's unique personal background as the only professional historian born to former slaves, his knowledge of vibrant nineteenth-century traditions of African American historical writing and freedom festivals, his involvement with turn-of-the-twentieth-century black literary and historical societies, and his commitment to scientific history, especially the ideal of objectivity. With the overarching objective to build black pride and reduce white prejudice, the association continued the mission of earlier communal, lay, and scholarly forms of the black history enterprise. The association institutionalized the black history pursuit, providing a home for the development of the study and celebration of black history as a movement.

Chapter 2 ("Reverse the Stage") explores how Woodson addressed the fatal flaw of mainstream accounts of U.S. history, which he saw as their "failure to fathom the Negro mind."[16] Imagine American history performed as a pageant. African Americans had the nonspeaking roles, visible only in the background, as caricatures and stereotypes. How do bit parts get transformed into protagonists, people with hearts and minds of their own? By reversing history's stage—turning it around 180 degrees—so that the stock figures such as the slave in chains now appear in the foreground. The publication of primary source documents was at the crux of this process of historical reorientation. In the pages of the *Journal of Negro History*—and in anthologies such as *Negro Orators and Their Orations* (1925) and *Mind of the Negro*—Woodson presented materials in which African Americans spoke on their own behalf. The construction of a new, multifaceted archive of African American experiences was one of the association's first major achievements.

With the appearance of *The Negro in Our History* in 1922, the black history movement had a flagship publication. Woodson's textbook—and other race histories written by his colleagues—foregrounded topics such as racial violence that conventional textbooks avoided. Woodson and his colleagues did not merely write "contributionist" histories, which inserted their own "heroes into the American story"; they also retold the story by placing the African American experience at the center of the narrative.[17] If adding black faces to the pantheon of national heroes changed the complexion of U.S. history, the insistence that black history was American history reshaped its trajectory and transformed its larger themes. With the integration of African Americans into the nation's history, the color line emerged as a principal theme, calling into question the fundamental assumption that the United States was the land of freedom and opportunity for all her peoples.

CHAPTER ONE

"The Cause"

History, for Woodson, was personal before it was ever academic. Woodson's father, James Henry Woodson, was "owned as a slave" by a man called Jack Toney in Fluvanna County, Virginia, about sixty-five miles west of Richmond. In the summer of 1864, Toney had hired James out to a Mr. Stratton who set him to work digging ditches. When Stratton discovered that James was using his leisure time to make furniture and fish traps that he sold for pocket change, Stratton threatened to whip him for taking advantage. Woodson's father, however, "turned the scales" and whipped Stratton. Fearing for his life, he fled toward Richmond in search of Union soldiers, eventually encountering a Union cavalry under the command of General Philip H. Sheridan. James waved a white handkerchief and the Union troops took him on as a local guide. He served with the Union army until the close of the war.[1]

HISTORY AT HOME

Slavery, the Civil War, and emancipation were integral parts of Woodson's immediate family history, and his upbringing was filled with stories about black life that would take on iconic historical significance. Among the most dramatic of all the personal stories was the harrowing experience of Woodson's mother who had spent several days on an auction block in Richmond when she was only eleven years old, where she was "examined as one does a cow or mare for sale."[2] From his father and other veterans, Woodson learned about the "trials and battles of the Negro for freedom and equality." He said that his "interest in penetrating the past of my people was deepened and intensified" during these conversations.[3]

Woodson met hundreds of veterans but his relationship with one in particular was especially important. As a young man in Huntington, West Virginia, during the 1890s, Woodson grew close to Oliver Jones, a former soldier who had been poised in battle formation to attack Lee's army in Appomattox the morning he surrendered. Jones was "a well educated man but he could neither read nor write." As he did for his father, Woodson would read aloud to Jones and his friends from books and newspapers.[4]

In Huntington, Woodson read about and discussed the issues of the day—the gold standard, monopolies, populism, and the like—while digesting the first historical accounts of the Civil War with men who had themselves been on the battlefields. The wide-ranging discussions, according to Woodson, provided him with an invaluable education. Jones's home was "all but a reading room," filled with copies of black papers such as the *Mountaineer*, the *Pioneer*, and the *Richmond Planet* as well as books on the "achievements of the Negro," including W. J. Simmons's *Men of Mark* (1887), George Washington Williams's *Negro Troops in the War of the Rebellion* (1888) and J. T. Wilson's *Black Phalanx* (1890).[5] Simmons, Williams, and Wilson had all fought in the Civil War. Reading their books introduced Woodson to powerful models of African American contributionist historiography, which emphasized black contributions to the United States, highlighting their credentials as full-fledged Americans. "Beating down prejudice and upholding the national cause at the same time," Wilson affirmed in the dedication to *Black Phalanx*, black soldiers "have inscribed upon their banners every important battle from April, 1863 to April, 1865." In Williams's estimation, the heroic exploits of black troops spoke not only to "the proud and priceless heritage of a race but the glory of a nation."[6]

In the nineteenth century, most African Americans learned more about their "priceless heritage" from emancipation celebrations than they did from books. Free blacks in the North pioneered emancipation celebrations with the commemoration of the abolition of the Atlantic slave trade in 1808. Great Britain's abolition of slavery in its West Indian colonies on August 1, 1834, added another date to the freedom festivals calendar. After the Civil War, blacks across the country eagerly participated in a range of emancipation holidays, including Juneteenth, the Fourth of July and, most importantly, January 1 (or "National Freedom Day"), the day Lincoln issued the Emancipation Proclamation in 1863.

Veterans of the Civil War had the "privilege of occupying the front ranks" of Emancipation Day parades in the postbellum years. Some of the veterans Woodson came to know almost certainly participated in these processions. Woodson himself likely attended one or more emancipation celebrations in Virginia or West Virginia in his youth or as a young man. These festivals of freedom were a staple of African American community life in the postbellum era, and so even if Woodson had not participated in one, he would have been familiar with their basic elements through newspaper or word-of-mouth accounts.[7]

Featuring processions, music, poetry, picnics, amusements, and stemwinding orations, these public ceremonies became the "preeminent forum in which blacks displayed their recalled past," enabling "vast numbers of blacks to learn, invent, and practice a common language of memory." Parades were transformed into "mobile living history exhibits" that traced the history of African Americans from slavery to freedom. These events engaged a large and diverse black audience, from "the college-trained preacher to the illiterate day laborer, from the battle-scarred veteran to the impressionable schoolchild." In Norfolk, Virginia, celebrations regularly attracted tens of thousands of black participants.[8]

If some of their particulars varied, freedom festivals shared two essential characteristics. First, they invariably aimed to demonstrate black fitness for citizenship through "paeans to black progress and achievement" and "ripostes to the shibboleths of white supremacy."[9] Second, they served as rituals "of self-definition and legitimation for a people in the process of becoming." Out of the "simultaneous pain and pride" inherent to the African American experience, freedom festivals fostered a powerful sense of collective identity and racial solidarity.[10]

While African Americans celebrated emancipation and the Union victory as glorious triumphs, many white southerners obviously interpreted these events in a radically different way. This fact was exemplified by James Henry Woodson's experience working at the Chesapeake and Ohio Railway in Huntington during the late 1890s. James's foreman was a Confederate veteran. During a heated discussion of the Civil War, they came to blows after the foreman trumpeted the "Lost Cause" and "defended slavery too boldly."[11] This altercation must have reinforced Woodson's sense that blacks and whites often had different perspectives on the same historical events and that history was worth fighting over.

HISTORY AT HARVARD

In the fall of 1908, Woodson sat at a seminar table inside Robinson Hall, a stately brick building tucked into the northeast corner of Harvard Yard. Edward Channing, the distinguished professor who had delivered the first paper at the inaugural meeting of the AHA in 1884, was holding forth on the origins of the American Revolution.[12] Woodson interjected that Crispus Attucks had been the first patriot to die in the Boston Massacre, drawing on the knowledge he had gained from reading books such as *Negro Troops*. (Herein, George Washington Williams referred to Attucks as "the first martyr of the Revolutionary War—a Negro whose blood was given for liberty.") Responding to this comment, Channing dismissed Attucks and his companions as "idlers" who had found themselves facing off against British soldiers only by happenstance. "The professor laughed," Woodson recollected, "at the idea of Negroes who referred to the incident as an important contribution to the independence of this country." Indeed Channing found the whole idea of black history laughable, as he subscribed to the "mulatto hypothesis," which stipulated that blacks had no chance of rising "above savagery" without an infusion of white blood.[13]

Woodson was only in residence at Harvard for a single academic year, 1908–9. It was several decades after a pioneering generation of scholars with PhDs from German universities had established the first history departments in the United States, and the discipline had gained a firm toehold in universities. (There were scarcely two dozen history faculty members in 1886, but by 1910, there were nearly six hundred.)[14] While the academic identity of history had crystallized by the time Woodson arrived in Cambridge, the field was still relatively young, and the architects of professional history continued to evangelize the idea of history as a modern, data-driven science.

Along with Johns Hopkins and Columbia, Harvard boasted one of the oldest, most prestigious, and highly influential history programs.[15] Woodson had the most extensive contact with the three members of his dissertation committee, Channing, Albert Bushnell Hart, and Frederick Jackson Turner. He took classes in American and European history, including three seminars with Channing.[16] Deeply committed to original research, the seminar method, and the growth of the AHA, Hart, Turner, and Channing ranked among the giants of the emergent historical profession. The story of U.S. history, for these three men, was one of "freedom realized and stabilized through the achievement of national solidarity."[17] Woodson's Harvard mentors regarded the rise of an exceptional United States through a powerful racial filter. Reflecting the point of view of the larger historical profession, they depicted American history as a chronicle of progress, propelled forward by the genius of the Anglo-Saxon race. Their intersecting positions on race and the nation inevitably attracted Woodson's close attention.

Hart (1854–1943), the eldest of Woodson's three Harvard mentors, was a founding member of the *AHR* in 1895, edited the monumental twenty-six-volume *American Nation* series (1904–7), and served as president of the AHA in 1909. He was committed to advancing a "genuinely scientific school of history, which shall remorselessly examine the sources." "Every assertion must rest upon a source," Hart said, "as every scientific result rests upon experiment."[18]

While Channing (1856–1931) is most well known for his Pulitzer Prize–winning six-volume *History of the United States* (1905–25), he also published several textbooks including the best-selling *A Student's History of the United States*. Channing's belief in progress was extraordinary. "I have tried to see in the annals of the past," he announced in volume 1 of his *History*, "the story of living forces, always struggling onward and upward toward that which is better and higher in human conception."[19]

Turner (1861–1932), of course, is famous for his epochal 1893 essay "The Significance of the Frontier in American History," arguably the single most important paper in American historiography. For Turner, the frontier was a crucible for mobility, rugged individualism, and democracy. "Society progressed through stages," in Turner's view, "moving from wilderness or savagery to advanced civilization."[20]

Trumpeting the three core themes of liberty, opportunity, and progress, the textbooks that Hart, Channing, Turner and many of their colleagues wrote were in the main "celebratory accounts" that reflected the "conventional pieties and prejudices of the era."[21] Assuming that "oppression or exploitation was never central to any part of the American story," their interpretations expressed the WASPish point of view of the "possessing classes."[22] "Great has been the progress of the American nation in the past," Channing averred in the 1913 edition of *A Student's History of the United States*. "The chief causes of our prosperity in the past," he wrote, "have been the frugality, energy, and personal independence of our people;

> the rapid development of invention; equality of all men in the eye of the law; free institutions and the breaking loose from the prejudices of European societies. These qualities, inherent in the races from which the American people has sprung, without the barriers to human activity which surrounded them in their old homes, have been combined in the United States with a good climate, splendid soil, wonderful mineral resources, and free trade over an enormous extent of territory.[23]

Channing's appraisal of the United States underscores the extent to which historians of his generation attributed the success of the American experiment to the natural race genius of Anglo-Saxons. For Channing, Hart and Turner, there was an almost divinely ordained alignment between the innate talent of the Anglo-Saxon race for self-government and the flowering of American democracy.

If personal freedom, representative government, and respect for the rule of law were "the common inheritance of all the members of the Anglo-Saxon race," as Hart, Channing, and Turner maintained, the "inheritance" of the Negro race was far less impressive.[24] Scion of an abolitionist and thesis advisor to W. E. B. Du Bois, Hart was "more energetic in promotion of black advance" than any of his peers, and yet he remained convinced of blacks' innate inferiority, not to mention ambivalent about their status in the American polity. In a chapter titled "Negro Character" in his 1911 book *The Southern South*, Hart arrived at the following conclusion: "Race measured by race, the Negro is inferior, and his part in history in Africa and in America leads to the belief that he will remain inferior in race stamina and race achievement." Moreover, as he lamented in his best-selling *School History of the United States*, the slave trade had brought into America "a strange and then savage race which otherwise would never have come."[25]

Channing, like Hart, was a "liberal racist," offering vital support to Woodson as an emerging scholar, while evincing a matter-of-fact, almost casual, racism.[26] Turner's racism was also transparent, but it tended to have a sharper edge. According to Turner, slavery had afforded blacks the "opportunity for expressing the natural joyousness of the African temperament," and "hardship was felt rather by individuals than by the mass of slaves."[27]

Woodson was continually affronted by his professors' racist views. He also questioned the veracity of the racially tinted progress narrative they all espoused. The work Woodson produced after leaving Harvard served at least in part as a rebuttal to his professors' claims about American opportunity and the degradation of the Negro race. In spite of Woodson's retrospective claim that it took him twenty years to recover from his Harvard education, it seems that the training he received there reinforced his belief in history as a science, especially regarding "the sanctity of primary sources and [the] careful scrutiny of documents." The same might be said of Woodson's conviction that it was the historian's duty to shed light on the present, a belief that Hart especially held dear.[28]

WASHINGTON, D.C.

In the summer of 1909, Woodson quit Cambridge for Washington, D.C., where he completed the research for his dissertation at the Library of Congress. Given Hart, Channing, and Turner's views on "Negro character," it should not be surprising that Woodson's dissertation—a study of the economic forces that led to the creation of West Virginia—largely avoided the subject of race. At the same time he was completing his dissertation, Woodson held down a full-time job at the famed M Street High School, teaching French, Spanish, English, and history to the children of the district's talented tenth. Rayford Logan recalled Woodson as a "serious, stern, almost dour disciplinarian."[29]

The Harvard History Department approved Woodson's dissertation in the spring of 1912. A few months after they had signed their names on the cover page of his thesis, Hart, Channing, and Turner published a book called *Guide to the Study and Reading of American History*. Here is how the three Harvard men summed up the legacy of slavery: "Slavery, which for eighty years was a cause of difference between North and South, has long since come to an end. The people of the United States are constantly coming closer together."[30] From his home in Washington, D.C., Woodson saw very little evidence of "constantly" increasing national unity. Local schools, churches, and businesses were segregated along racial lines, and it would only be a matter of months before the color bar would be extended into the offices of the federal government, following the inauguration of Woodrow Wilson in March 1913.[31]

Inside the nation's capital, Woodson found a thriving "secret city." With Howard University as its anchor, Washington, D.C., was "black America's intellectual center" from the end of the nineteenth century through the 1940s. Given the nearly universal lack of opportunity for black scholars to teach at predominantly white institutions, as the "capstone of Negro education," Howard housed the most elite of the "segregated scholars," including the likes of biologist Ernest Everett Just, philosopher Alain Locke, and political scientist Ralph Bunche. The segregated public school system in D.C. was "the finest in the country," with teachers making up a sizeable contingent of the city's African American middle class. Teachers were some of the main subscribers to the local black newspapers such as the *Baltimore Afro-American*, the *Colored American*, and the *Washington Bee*. They were also avid participants in the some three dozen African American clubs, fraternal and cultural organizations operating in D.C. at the close of the nineteenth century.[32]

Woodson participated in two of the district's leading cultural associations, the Bethel Literary and Historical Society (BLHS) and the American Negro Academy (ANA). African Methodist Episcopal Church bishop Daniel A. Payne founded BLHS in 1881, which remained active through the 1920s. Its membership was drawn from the middle- and upper-class residents of black D.C., and regular participants included D.C. attorney and educator John Cromwell Sr., Howard University sociologist Kelly Miller, and Mary Church Terrell, the first president of the National Association of Colored Women. Bethel Literary and Historical Society events, which often featured poetry, drama, and music recitals in addition to lectures and discussions, sometimes attracted audiences in the hundreds.[33]

Similar societies to the BLHS existed elsewhere, including the American Negro Historical Society of Philadelphia (founded in 1897), the Boston Literary and Historical Association (started in 1901), and the Negro Society for Historical Research (established by Arthur Schomburg and John E. Bruce in New York in 1911).[34] A politics of respectability suffused all of these societies, informed by the belief that "association with literature was one way of definitively asserting a positive, learned identity far removed from the intellectual poverty associated with slavery." With respect to history in particular, these associations promoted "race pride and racial consciousness," embracing the American Negro Historical Society credo that "no country can record its history truthfully until all of its scrolls are unrolled." In addition to holding meetings and sponsoring lectures, these societies often housed small reading rooms or libraries, collected archival materials, and published occasional papers and pamphlets. While these organizations signaled a burgeoning interest in black history, they nonetheless advanced "a refined culture that seldom reached beyond an exclusive audience."[35]

The ANA was by far the most exclusive black intellectual society at the turn of the twentieth century. Founded in 1897 by Alexander Crummell, it was devoted to "the dissemination of the truth and vindication of the Negro race from vicious assaults." With a highly selective and exclusively male membership, the ANA never had more than thirty-nine members at any given time and over the course of its lifetime had only ninety-nine members total. Woodson was elected a member in 1913 or 1914. Some of the more prominent members included Du Bois, minister and founding member of the NAACP Francis J. Grimké, and Clark University professor of Latin and Greek William H. Crogman. Woodson delivered at least two papers before the ANA, including "Educating the Negro before 1860" in December of 1914. This paper appears to have been one of Woodson's first public lectures.[36] The ANA espoused "civilizationist goals," which emphasized "defined indicators of progress and achievement" such as rates of literacy, church attendance, and homeownership.[37] Its philosophy was "unashamedly elitist," and its members were often "savagely critical" of many aspects of black folk culture. As a result, the ANA's influence never reached beyond "a small circle" of the most highly educated African Americans.[38]

Woodson was not only active in the district's African American literary and cultural associations but also political ones. He joined the D.C. chapter of the NAACP when it was founded in 1912 and was a member of the branch's Committee of Fifty, which organized rallies to bring attention to the increasingly hostile racial climate pervading the capital. The Committee of Fifty helped to organize a mass meeting in October of 1913, in which an overflow crowd of seven thousand gathered at the AME Metropolitan Church to protest the segregation of "colored" employees in federal offices. By this time, officially sanctioned segregation had been instituted in several government departments including the Post Office, the Treasury, and the Navy Department. As Woodson would have read in the *Crisis* that fall, one black clerk even had a cage built around him to separate him from his longtime white colleagues. During the Wilson administration, Woodson later reflected, "Washington was southernized by an influx of public functionaries and civil service employees hypocritically parading as promoters of democracy but inalterably attached to the caste of color." He especially resented the lack of black representation in Wilson's program of "New Freedom."[39]

Jim Crow reached its symbolic apotheosis in the nation's capital on February 18, 1915, when President Wilson had D. W. Griffith's *Birth of a Nation* screened in the White House. "It is like history written with lightning,"

Woodrow Wilson is said to have remarked when the lights went up. It was also, of course, history written by Wilson himself, as his 1901 *A History of the American People* (volume 5, *Reunion and Nationalization*) supplied some of Dixon's most important source material. Wilson's account of Reconstruction provided the framework for part 2 of *Birth of a Nation*, which focused on "the veritable overthrow of civilization in the South" during Reconstruction, depicting the era as an orgy of crime and corruption, with the "white South" crushed "under the heel of the black South."[40]

Griffith and Thomas Dixon Jr., whose 1905 novel *The Clansman* gave *Birth of a Nation* its basic plotlines, both maintained that the film was a serious work of history rather than a mere spectacular or entertainment. In an editorial printed in the *New York Globe* shortly after the film's release, Griffith claimed that *Birth of a Nation* depicted "historic events," which told a story "based upon truth in every vital detail."[41] Dixon, meanwhile, promised a reward of $1,000 to anybody who could prove a single historical inaccuracy in the film. *Birth of a Nation* burnished its history credentials by citing sources for many of the historical scenes depicted, including Lee's surrender to Grant at Appomattox, Lincoln's assassination at Ford's Theatre, and a "riot" in the black-majority South Carolina House of Representatives. For Lincoln's assassination, Griffith constructed a stunning replica of Ford's Theatre and had his onstage actors perform *Our American Cousin*, the play that was being performed on the evening of April 14, 1865. (Although you cannot hear them, Griffith's actors even say the precise lines delivered by the real actors in the moments before Lincoln was shot.)[42]

The arc of history described by *Birth of a Nation* was largely faithful to that of the standard Reconstruction historiography of the period. To the historians who wrote it, the message of Reconstruction history was clear—the Negro had shown himself to be unfit for citizenship. William Archibald Dunning, who regarded Reconstruction as an "unspeakable disaster," was the leading historian of Reconstruction at the turn of the twentieth century.[43] From his post at Columbia University, Dunning and his students produced a flood of studies that denounced "Negro rule" and "Negro government."[44] Dunning's publications, while written in a polite tone of scholarly detachment, were nonetheless saturated with antiblack sentiment. As Peter Novick notes, the "most professionally accomplished" scholarship on Reconstruction in the early twentieth century was "viciously racist."[45] Here is how Dunning summed up the prospects of emancipated former slaves: "The freedmen were not and in the nature of the case could not for generations be on the same social, moral and intellectual plane with whites."[46]

Blacks as multidimensional human beings had no place in *Birth of a Nation*. They were caricatured as faithful former slaves in the Uncle Tom and mammy molds, buffoons incapable of exercising the franchise or legislating with any glimmer of intelligence, and dangerous predators, whose lust for white women knew no bounds. Under pressure from censors, Griffith had excised the film's original coda, entitled "Lincoln's Solution," which depicted masses of black people being boarded onto ships destined for Africa.[47] Instead, the film closes with a hopeful tableau of a heavenly "Hall of Brotherly Love." There is not a black face among the crowd.

Woodson regarded *Birth of a Nation* as devastatingly effective propaganda that reinforced the pernicious idea that the United States was a "white man's country." Attracting record-breaking crowds, the film, according to Woodson, "so set the large majority of the people of the United States against the Negro as to bring to a climax a revolution in the thought of the nation." Indelibly marked by ignorance and depravity, the film "proved" that the Negro "was not a white man with a black skin."[48]

THE LINCOLN JUBILEE

Chicago was still feeling the aftershocks of *Birth of a Nation*'s premiere when Woodson arrived in the city at the end of June 1915. He was in Chicago to conduct research and to prepare for the city's Lincoln Jubilee, a three-week exposition designed to commemorate the half century of emancipation and "the achievements of the American Negro in the realms of Art, Science, Religion, Literature, Music, Commerce and Industry."[49] Although *Birth of a Nation* had debuted on June 5, a petition to ban the film continued to work its way through the courts until the middle of July. The *Tribune*, *Herald*, and *Chicago Defender* newspapers all provided regular updates on the controversy engrossing the picture, which involved municipal censors, the Chicago NAACP, the mayor's office, and the Illinois legislature.[50]

The suit to ban *Birth of a Nation* was ultimately unsuccessful, and on July 15, the film was "free to run over the summer to packed houses."[51] Two days later, the *New York Times* reviewed Woodson's first book, *The Education of the Negro*, alongside W. E. B. Du Bois's *The Negro* and a book called *America's Greatest Problem: The Negro* by R. W. Shufeldt.[52] It was a strangely fitting symmetry, as Shufeldt's book advanced the same basic thesis as Griffith's film.

Shufeldt, a major in the U.S. Army Medical Corps, advocated the "complete and thorough separation" of the two races, calling for the mandatory deportation of all blacks as the solution to America's "greatest problem."[53] In defense of this policy, Shufeldt pointed to the impossibility of successfully assimilating blacks into the life of the country, asserting that "the taking of Africans out of Africa and settling them in this country by no means makes Americans of them." "It would be quite as reasonable," he continued, "to expect zebras to become horses when similarly transported." Shufeldt's utmost fear was miscegenation and the degradation of civilization that was sure to follow. "History has already proven," he warned his readers, that the "typical black-skinned Negroes in the United States" had never "contributed a single line to literature worth the printing; a single cog in the machine of invention; an idea to any science; or, in short, advanced civilization a single millimeter since the first Congo pair was placed on this soil."[54]

Woodson must have been pleased with the *Times*'s notice, as the reviewer concluded that Shufeldt's book was so "intemperate and unjust that it defeats its own ends." *Education of the Negro*, in contrast, was praised as a "thorough and intelligent study, with just enough sympathetic spirit to humanize its array of well-ordered facts." These facts, especially those pertaining to the educational attainments of free blacks, controverted in many instances Shufeldt's "sweeping negatives." One week after the publication of the *Times*'s review, Woodson delivered the first of two lectures before Chicago's Negro Fellowship League. Having been invited by Ida B. Wells (president of the league), Woodson used his book as a springboard to deliver a talk entitled "The Uplift of the Negro prior to 1861 and Its Bearing on Problems of Today."[55]

It is worth pausing to delineate the characteristics of *Education of the Negro* that would become hallmarks of Woodson's future historical scholarship. The monograph explored previously uncharted territory, placed the black experience at the heart of American history, outlined a dynamic dialectic between oppression and agency, creatively analyzed traditional as well as more innovative primary sources, and included a sizeable appendix comprised of original documents.

As Woodson explained in the preface, antebellum education for African Americans was a "neglected aspect of our history." His own treatment was far from comprehensive, he noted, declaring his "hope of vitally interesting some young master mind in this large task." The task was large, as Woodson's account demonstrated, because African American education was inextricably linked to critical historical developments such as Revolutionary-era debates about the "rights of man," the hardening of slavery into a cutthroat economic institution, and the advent of common schools. It is telling that Woodson launched his scholarly career with a monograph on education. The subject of education was a leitmotif in virtually all of the work Woodson produced and supported over the course of his career. Moreover, education was, of course, central to the mission of the association and was enthusiastically embraced by Woodson and his colleagues as the most promising means of racial uplift. As Woodson proclaimed in the preface to *Education of the Negro*, education represented "freedom in its highest and best sense."[56]

Serving as a template for all of Woodson's future publications, *Education of the Negro* presented an uncompromising take on prejudice and discrimination. One of the book's main contributions was to outline the pernicious effects of laws prohibiting the instruction of blacks in states across the antebellum South. "American slavery," Woodson declared, "extended not as that of the ancients, only to the body, but also to the mind." It was an institution designed to induce a "state of ignorance and degradation" so profound that slaves would be reduced to the "condition of brutes." A strong crosscurrent of vindicationism always accompanied the waves of oppression that Woodson charted. This vindicationist theme was particularly salient in a chapter called "Learning in Spite of Opposition," which examined how some slaves managed to manufacture an education "here and there," whether in clandestine schools, stolen moments alone with the accounting books, or with the help of willing white children. "The instances of Negroes struggling to obtain an education read like the beautiful romances of a people in an heroic age," Woodson declared.[57]

Presenting short biographical sketches of exemplary black individuals was one of Woodson's preferred vindicationist techniques. In a chapter on the colonial era, for example, Woodson touted the educational accomplishments of Phyllis Wheatley and Benjamin Banneker, referring to them as two of the most renowned "brainy persons of color." On Wheatley's intellectual talents, Woodson said that "men marveled that a slave could possess such a productive imagination, enlightened mind and poetical genius."[58] Complementing Woodson's portraits of exceptional black individuals, *Education of the Negro*, like all of Woodson's publications, emphasized the signal importance of black communities, highlighting the creation and development of black institutions. For example, Woodson documented the "self-educative work" of blacks in Washington, D.C., and Baltimore in a chapter called "Educating the Urban Negro," showing how many of the most important black schools in both cities originated at black churches.[59]

The footnotes and extensive bibliography in *Education of the Negro* reveal the range of primary sources that Woodson used, from conventional sources such as newspapers, government reports, and the proceedings of conventions, organizations, and societies to more inventive sources such as letters, "Books of Travel by Foreigners," and autobiographies (including Frederick Douglass's *Narrative*). To compensate for the dearth of records on the lives of slaves, Woodson had to be resourceful. For instance, he turned to fugitive slave advertisements in newspapers to estimate the level of education among slaves. Advertisements that described slaves as "artful," "smart," or skilled in languages such as French or High Dutch provided "unconscious evidence of [slaves'] intellectual progress."[60]

Education of the Negro signaled what would prove to be an enduring commitment on Woodson's part to the publication of primary sources. It included a sixty-page appendix, which presented some three dozen excerpts from primary source documents that ranged from colonial-era sermons on the proper instruction of servants to Frederick Douglass's 1853 paper "Learn Trades or Starve."[61]

Copies of *Education of the Negro* would have been prominently displayed in Woodson's small booth at the Lincoln Jubilee, which opened in mid-August at the Chicago Coliseum. Combining the spirit of freedom festivals with the grand scale and artifice of a World's Fair, Chicago's Lincoln Jubilee was one of the most elaborate of the thousands of Emancipation semicentennial expos, fairs, and ceremonies held between 1913 and 1915.[62] The domestic arts—including a truly staggering quantity of needlework—were amply represented. So too the industrial arts with inventions like the "friction heater" showcased. Schools such as Wilberforce, Tuskegee, and the Piney Woods School of Braxton, Mississippi, had their own exhibits. The Federation of Women's Clubs had a booth, as did the National Baptist Association, which showcased a large display of "colored dolls."[63] Hawking history books and portraits of Frederick Douglass, Sojourner Truth, and Paul Laurence Dunbar, Woodson's modest stall competed for the attention of the thousands in attendance with all of these exhibits, as well as hundreds of attractions such as a towering display of glass perfume bottles from the Overton Hygienic Co., the thumping bass drums of the famed Eighth Regiment Band, and the table on which General Lee signed his surrender to General Grant.[64]

When the jubilee opened, twenty-two years had passed since African Americans had been infamously excluded from participating in more than a nominal fashion in the 1893 World's Columbian Exposition held in Chicago.[65] The 1895 Atlanta Cotton States and International Exposition was the first major U.S. exposition to give African Americans their own exhibition hall.[66]

Visitors to the "Negro Building" in Atlanta, winding their way through booths displaying the furniture, textiles, and agricultural cornucopia produced at Hampton, Tuskegee, and other industrial training schools, would have seen "the promise of black life in the South ... rooted in conservative ideals of moral uplift, manual labor and a rural existence."[67] They would not have seen very many specific representations of black history. The historical content of the "Negro Building" was nearly as limited as that conveyed by Booker T. Washington in his remarks at the exposition's opening ceremony. In what would come to be known as his epochal "Atlanta Compromise" speech, Washington presented a "truncated genealogy" of African American life that made "no mention of African origins" and barely touched on slavery.[68] (One of the only exhibits in the "Negro Building" that focused on Africa was the

"Uncivilized Africa" booth, which depicted the "crude" life of the contemporary African "heathen.")[69] Slow and steady progress was the main history lesson of Washington's address. This same theme was evident at the entrance to the "Negro Building," the portico of which juxtaposed an illustration of a "decrepit" wooden cabin dating to the Civil War with a depiction of a "sturdy" present-day stone church.[70] Black patriotism was a main subject of Washington's speech as well as an address titled "The Negro as a Soldier" by Christian A. Fleetwood, a black Civil War veteran and federal War Department employee. Fleetwood called on the nation to remember "the gallant deeds done for the country by its brave black defenders."[71]

In the two decades following the Atlanta Expo, black history became an increasingly important dimension of expositions. *Response to the Call to Arms* was the name of one of the fourteen "Negro tableaux" constructed by sculptor Meta Warrick Fuller inside the "Negro Building" at the 1907 Jamestown Tercentennial Exhibition. Featuring more than 130 plaster figures, this series of dioramas presented a chronological survey of the African American experience, starting with a piece titled *The Landing of the First Twenty Slaves at Jamestown* and concluding with one titled *Commencement Day* (which referenced graduation day at Howard University). Steeped in the values of "middle-class respectability" and advancing an overarching narrative of "linear historical progress," Fuller's dioramas incorporated "the lives and concerns of African Americans into the saga of civilization." Among the most prominent hallmarks of advanced "civilization" in the dioramas were representations of religion, education, and a "stable, decorous, bourgeois family life." Occupying "prime exhibit space," it is possible that Fuller's fourteen tableaux presented a more robust picture of black history than all of the exhibits at the Atlanta Exposition combined.[72]

Emancipation celebrations held in the North between 1913 and 1915 had a different character from the "Negro Buildings" in the South. They were less preoccupied with the Bookerite strategy of "deferential accommodation" and more attuned to the life of urban blacks in the North as well as broader questions of ethnic pluralism. Agricultural and industrial progress remained important themes, to be sure, but a more expansive vision of African American history began to emerge, one that foregrounded a distinctive black cultural heritage. The expositions in New York and Chicago, for example, publicized a "cultural history of the Negro that was both a collective memory drawn from enslavement and a pan-African history that tied its audience to black peoples from the African continent and the Caribbean." A striking architectural feature of the New York National Emancipation Exposition was an Egyptian-style "Temple of Beauty," which was adorned with silhouettes of Egyptian deities and flanked by four towering obelisks covered in hieroglyphics. Meanwhile, at the Lincoln Jubilee in Chicago in 1915, Woodson may have had the chance to see—or at least hear—the Grand Jubilee Chorus of Five Hundred Voices perform a production called *Historical Tableau and Pageant of Negro History*. The pageant opened in Egypt and concluded in "the modern Negro home," with stops along the way for the issuing of the Emancipation Proclamation, the siege at Fort Sumter, and highlights from Supreme Court rulings on segregation.[73]

Unlike earlier expositions in the South, with their separate "Negro Buildings" that were often located on the margins of the grounds, northern semicentennial expositions focused squarely on African Americans. The organizers of these events, including Du Bois (who spearheaded the 1913 New York Emancipation Exposition) and Locke (who codirected the 1913 Golden Jubilee Celebration in Atlantic City), had more autonomy in terms of designing their programs. Although whites were welcome to attend these expositions, they tended to be largely "intraracial affairs." As such, they represented what Mabel Wilson calls the black counterpublic sphere, which comprised "places where different agendas for [black] social advancement, cultural identity, and national belonging could be presented, seen, and debated publicly." The black counterpublic sphere provided an alternative to the larger public sphere where racial prejudice and discrimination predominated, especially with respect to cultural representations of African Americans.[74]

Woodson's presence at the Lincoln Jubilee was one of his first efforts to promote black history to a wider audience. It was a fitting setting in that almost all of his future work would be carried out in black spheres, including the black academy, black schools, and the black press. Sitting inside his stall, Woodson might have remarked on the startling contrast between an exhibition designed to showcase "the remarkable progress made by the race in fifty years" and the vehement denial by the likes of Dixon, Griffith, and Shufeldt that such progress was even possible. Perhaps he was inspired by a positive reception at the coliseum or the way the *Times* had offered a glimmer of hope that a "dispassionate monograph, done in the modern scientific spirit" could counteract "intemperate and unjust" fulminations on the "Negro problem."[75] Whatever he may have felt, Woodson wrote to his friend Jesse Moorland toward the end of August, announcing his plans to establish an organization called the "Historical Alliance," which would house a "Bureau of Research" and a "Quarterly Journal of Negro History" in order to save "the records of the Negro that posterity may know the whole truth."[76] At the same time, Woodson was in constant conversation about *Birth of a Nation*, the jubilee, and black history with his friends and acquaintances at the Wabash Avenue "colored" YMCA. On the evening of September 9, Woodson suggested to his YMCA compatriots that they, as one of those present recollected, "form an organization which would offset the attacks made by whites upon blacks and that this organization set forth the true nature of their past through specialization in Negro history."[77]

THE ASSOCIATION

The Association for the Study of Negro Life and History was officially incorporated in Washington, D.C., on October 3. In January of the new year, Woodson brought out the first issue of the *Journal of Negro History*, borrowing $400 against his own life insurance policy to cover publishing costs. His decision to print the first issue of the journal with nothing in the treasury provoked one of the members of the executive council to "throw up his hands in disgust and resign, while others threatened to do likewise."[78]

"Excepting what can be learned from current controversial literature, which either portrays the Negro as a persecuted saint or brands him a leper of society," Woodson explained in the journal's first issue,

> the people of this age are getting no information to show what the Negro has thought and felt and done. The Negro, therefore, is in danger of becoming a negligible factor in the thought of the world. In centuries to come when white scholars after forgetting the prejudices of this age will begin to make researches for truth, they will have only one side of the question if the Negro does not leave something to tell his own story. The aim of the Association is to raise the funds to employ several investigators to collect all historical and sociological material bearing on the Negro before it is lost to the world. . . . Our purpose then is not to drift into the discussion of the Negro problem. We shall aim to publish facts, believing that facts properly set forth will speak for themselves.[79]

Woodson modeled the *Journal of Negro History* after pioneering journals such as the *AHR* (started in 1895) and the *Mississippi Valley Historical Review* (launched in 1914). In its second issue, Woodson printed some two dozen testimonials in an article titled "How the Public Received the *Journal of Negro History*," featuring fulsome praise from the likes of Du Bois, Edward Channing, and Frederick Jackson Turner as well as the *Boston Herald*, the *AHR* and *Southern Workman*. Woodson clearly intended to send a strong message regarding the journal's "excellent scientific quality," which conformed "in every way to the highest standards of modern historical scholarship."[80]

The litany of endorsements Woodson included in the journal's scholarly bona fides must be seen in the context of the "objectivity question." In his authoritative survey of the American historical profession, *That Noble Dream*, Peter Novick maintains that objectivity was "the founding myth of the historical profession; the pursuit of the objective truth its sacred mission and raison d'etre." Woodson and the association embraced the ideal of historical objectivity, subscribing to its main tenets, including, following Novick, that facts exist "independent of interpretation," patterns in history are discovered, not invented, the quality of an interpretation is assessed by "how well it accounts for the facts," and the role of a historian is that of a neutral judge, not "that of advocate or, even worse, propagandist."[81]

The issue of "objectivity" was especially fraught for black scholars. The professionalization of history at the turn of the twentieth century was a gendered process, as scholars such as Bonnie Smith and Julie Des Jardins have shown.[82] Scientific history was constructed, claimed, and defended as a masculine domain. (The academy, the archive, and the seminar room were effectively off-limits for women.) Professional history was defined in contrast to "amateur" history through a set of male-female dichotomies: "the *objective* and *biased*, ... *official* and *personal*, ... *empirical* and *intuitive*, *trained* and *untrained*, ... *omniscient* and *parochial*."[83] The same terms that were used to describe an amateur or feminine approach to history were often applied to African American scholars. Guided by emotion rather than reason, mired in a provincial, racial perspective, blacks were imagined to have certain disabling character flaws that disqualified them from joining the exclusive guild of professional historians.

Woodson frequently underscored the importance of "the facts," "objectivity" and a "scientific" approach to history.[84] These declarations not only affirmed Woodson's genuine commitment to the ideals of professional history but also served a rhetorical purpose. Throughout Woodson's lifetime, it was widely assumed that black scholars were "incapable of being impartial or objective," especially with respect to writing about their own history.[85] For example, after Milo M. Quaife, the editor of the *Mississippi Valley Historical Review*, perused a copy of the inaugural Negro History Week pamphlet, he felt compelled to address the work of the association in his next official editorial. The association circular, Quaife said, "supplies food for grave reflection." He was particularly alarmed that the eminent men in American life and letters who supported the association were lending their tacit approval to its insistent claims of racial equality. He quoted with evident disdain the following line from the circular: "Let us teach the whole world that, according to science, there is no such thing as superiority or inferiority of races." Quaife then reported that he was forced to conclude that some of the association's work was "animated by a spirit of propagandism which ill accords with the spirit of true scholarship."[86]

Even if they were to be expected, comments like these must have infuriated Woodson. While Quaife and other academics charged the association with failing to meet the highest standards of scholarship, Woodson repeatedly critiqued the mainstream historical profession for trafficking in "propaganda," as far as the history of the Negro was concerned. Woodson worried about two kinds of propaganda in particular. The first was the propaganda of neglect—American history was simply incomplete when "the achievements and status of such a large portion of the human family" were ignored.[87] The second was the propaganda of condemnation—in the few instances where African Americans were included in historical accounts, they were caricatured, ridiculed, and maligned. According to Woodson, conventional history was flawed because of its anti-Negro bias. In the view of his critics, Woodson's history was distorted because of his pro-Negro bias. However paradoxical, both sides claimed the high ground of objectivity, accusing the other of manufacturing propaganda disguised as history.

Woodson is frequently referred to as the "father of black history." While the title is not without justification, it can convey the misleading impression that Woodson conjured black history out of thin air. As we have seen, however, Woodson "swam in a sea of black intellectual discourse."[88] Indeed, as Stephen Hall incisively observes, the founding of the association represented the "culmination of a century-long effort to legitimize the study of the African American experience."[89] A quick perusal of the bibliography to *Education of the Negro* reveals the extent to which Woodson relied on his nineteenth-century predecessors as sources. Among the many works he cited were H. H. Garnett's *The Past and Present Condition and the Destiny of the Colored Race* (1848), George Washington Williams's *History of the Negro Race* (1883), and Wilbur H. Siebert's *The Underground Railroad from Slavery to Freedom* (1898).[90]

Woodson did not only turn to his predecessors for "the facts." The spirit of nineteenth-century African American historical traditions was at the very heart of the association's mission. The twin overarching goals of the association—building black pride and reducing white prejudice—had propelled black history forward since its inception. William C. Nell, whom Woodson regarded as "the first Negro to take seriously the writing of the history of the Negro race," made the following declaration in an 1841 speech: "Let light be shed to dispel the mist of ignorance and it will be remembered that we are Americans." Ignorance was an affliction of whites and blacks alike. "I have met with not a few colored persons who held historical views as prejudicial to the truth in our case as the whites do," James W. C. Pennington wrote in the first chapter to his 1841 *A Textbook of the Origin and History of the Colored People*. Pennington maintained that historical work was valuable as the means by which "prejudices are to be uprooted" and "false views are to be corrected." Truth, he declared, "must be unveiled and permitted to walk forth with her olive branch."[91]

The transformative power of truth was similarly pivotal to Frederick Douglass's philosophy of history. Often featured as the keynote speaker at freedom festivals in the latter half of the nineteenth century, Douglass delivered an address on August 1, 1857, to commemorate the emancipation of slaves in the West Indies on August 1, 1834. These annual celebrations "bring our people together," Douglass said, and "afford an opportunity of presenting salutary truths before the American people." Echoing Douglass's sentiments several decades later, George Washington Williams said that "history would give the world more correct ideas of the Colored people, and incite the latter to greater effort in the struggle of citizenship and manhood."[92]

None other than Booker T. Washington, in the preface to his 1909 *The Story of the Negro*, announced that he would consider the book a success if it inspired "any Negro to make himself useful and successful in the world" or caused "any individuals, not members of my own race, to take a more generous and hopeful view of the condition and prospects of the Negro."[93] By the time Woodson founded the association, then, it had long been an article of faith among the most prominent black thinkers and leaders of all political persuasions that the pursuit of black history could advance the race by appealing to white and black audiences.

Building on the texts, objectives, and community-building ideals of nineteenth-century black historical writing and commemoration, the association distinguished itself from previous African American historical endeavors in two main ways. First, it transformed the production, study, and celebration of black history into a coherent movement. And second, it moved toward a modern, scientific conception of history in which the pursuit of "secular truth" was preeminent.[94]

While the pre-Woodson historical tracts, textbooks, seminars, and societies had only engaged relatively small and rarefied audiences, Woodson's association greatly expanded black history's scope and influence. It was able to do so because Woodson succeeded in establishing a stable organizational configuration, consisting of the *Journal of Negro History*, Associated Publishers, annual meetings, a network of dedicated educators and, starting in 1926, annual Negro History Week celebrations. I suspect that Woodson designed the association to avoid what he regarded as the shortcomings of earlier literary, historical, and scholarly societies, including their indifference to the importance of appealing to broader audiences. Unlike the leadership of most organizations such as the BLHS and the ANA, Woodson was not an "aristocrat of color," and his vision of educational outreach was less constrained by class concerns of not mixing with the masses.

Woodson and the association helped to usher in the modern turn in African American history. The pioneering nineteenth-century authors of African American historical accounts were deeply religious; indeed, many of them, including Hosea Easton, James W. C. Pennington, and George Washington Williams, were ministers. Weaving together the religious, historical, and political, their writing was inseparable from a larger tradition of African American Protestantism.[95] The profound religious convictions that had animated so many of the vital nineteenth-century historical works were mostly absent from the works produced under the auspices of the association. Whereas the first chapter of Williams's *History of the Negro Race* began with a religious defense of the "unity of mankind," Woodson's *The Negro in Our History* treated religion as no different from any other historical topic such as labor or politics.[96] Woodson's 1921 *History of the Negro Church*, meanwhile, offered a stark contrast to the pious house histories of specific denominations that came before.[97] Most broadly, the attenuation of an overt religious framework speaks to a shift in the locus of authority from religion to science, from scriptural evidence to empirical evidence. For instance, while nineteenth-century black chroniclers often celebrated the Union victory as "divinely orchestrated," Woodson relied on secular explanations such as political and military developments.[98]

In spite of the fact that Woodson was fully committed to history as "secular truth," not all of Woodson's coworkers eschewed a religious orientation. In the early years of the association, men such as John Cromwell and C. V. Roman stood as a direct link between the Negro history movement and an older, more Victorian approach to race history. Roman, for example, was a physician, a professor at Meharry Medical College, and a popular "lay preacher" at St. Paul AME Church in Nashville.[99] At the first association meeting in 1917, Roman delivered a talk on "whether or not the Negro has made any contribution to [civilization]."[100] If Roman's past remarks are any guide, he would have answered in the affirmative, emphasizing that civilization "*was* actually cradled in Africa and learning *did* originate in the Dark Continent."[101] In 1921, Roman published a book called *American Civilization and the Negro*, which aimed to "increase racial self-respect and diminish racial antagonism." Maintaining that "we are *all* sinners and have come short of the glories of civilization," Roman declared, "the differences in mankind are the differences between charcoal and diamond—differences of *condition* and not of *composition*."[102] Inspired by religion, racial uplift, and civilizationist ideology, Roman exemplified the strong lay tradition of race history that was amply represented in the first decade or so of the association.

The *Journal of Negro History* is emblematic of how the Association combined modern historiography with a more democratic, community-oriented approach to black history. Woodson's commitment to rigorous scholarship notwithstanding, the *Journal of Negro History* was not a cloistered publication reserved only for the elect few.[103] In addition to the copiously footnoted articles written by Woodson and a small cadre of budding professionals, the journal featured a broad spectrum of black voices, including articles by Leila Amos Pendleton (author of *Narrative of the Negro*), John R. Lynch (former congressman from Mississippi), Mary Church Terrell (civil rights activist) and Alice Dunbar-Nelson (poet turned journalist).[104]

As early as 1917, Woodson referred to "the movement to study Negro life and history" as "the cause," a term that quickly came to enjoy widespread use among the association's members and friends and that would forever be associated with the depth of Woodson's dedication and the force of his personality. Standing "erect as a soldier," Woodson appeared "to be taller than his five feet, eight and a half inches." He was a famously difficult man: irascible, sarcastic, and unforgiving. He had falling-outs—some lasting days, others stretching out into years—with virtually all of his most important colleagues and collaborators. "Worthless to page 58" is how he described a draft report that Charles Wesley and Lorenzo Johnston Greene submitted to him. Association secretary-treasurer Jesse Moorland observed that nobody could write more insulting letters than Woodson. "I am not interested in hearing of headaches, colds, influenza, and nervous prostration," Woodson wrote to the beleaguered association research assistant Alrutheus Ambush Taylor in March 1923. "I am neither a nurse nor a physician," Woodson told Taylor. "I am trying to do a piece of research and since you are not qualified to participate therein and have not the mental capacity to undergo the training necessary thereto, I cannot make any further use of you."[105]

If working with Woodson was often maddening, his dogged commitment to "the cause" could also be invigorating. ("The cause is greater than the man" is how Charles Wesley explained his own dedication to the association.)[106] Woodson lived an "almost Spartan-like existence," with lunch sometimes consisting of nothing more than half a dozen oranges and a glass of water.[107] Known to work sixteen-hour days, his industry was legendary among his colleagues. "Combined with his marvelous capacity for scholarly work," Greene noted, "he cooks, sweeps, scrubs, washes dishes and does every other sort of labor."[108] Langston Hughes, who worked for a short time at the association in 1924, said that Woodson was a paragon of "stick-to-it-tiveness." When Woodson discovered some of his employees playing cards at the office, Hughes remembered that he lectured them on their responsibilities to their "work, to history, and to the Negro race." "And he predicted," Hughes continued, "that neither we nor the race would get ahead playing cards during working hours."[109]

To be fair, Woodson was not uniformly caustic and strict. He could be charming and pleasant company. As Greene recorded in his diary: "Under it all, I believe Woodson is a fine fellow. Comical and very human. Makes an excellent traveling companion." He could also be generous, supporting his sister and brother financially, fund-raising for the NAACP and the YWCA, and helping to obtain funding for promising young scholars to attend graduate school.[110]

Woodson convened the first public meeting of the fledgling association in Washington, D.C., in the fall of 1917. Over the next decade, the association gained strength, and meetings were held in Atlanta, Baltimore, and Louisville, among other cities. Local schools and colleges as well as black churches and colored Ys hosted daily sessions. At any given meeting, one could expect to hear rigorous scholarly papers, stirring speeches on black achievements and progress, and animated discussions about the "status" of the Negro across different arenas such as the Negro in business, the Negro in politics, and Negro welfare work during the First World War. Meetings also featured get-acquainted dinners, music programs, and one or more sessions on the teaching of black life and history.[111] Almost without exception, Woodson and his colleagues would fan out across the host city to visit schools and deliver lectures on the importance of incorporating black history into the official curriculum.

The association attracted a wide range of African American scholars, teachers, and professionals. In Woodson's lifetime, professional historians made up a small fraction of the association's membership. The year the association was founded, Du Bois and Woodson were the only black scholars to hold a PhD in history. As late as 1940, there were not even twenty African American historians with PhD credentials. Given that most mainstream academic societies did not exactly welcome black participation during this period, association conventions provided a vital forum for black scholars across the disciplines to showcase their work. Many black social scientists, for instance, gave their first academic papers at one of the association's annual meetings or published their first articles in the *Journal of Negro History*.[112]

By the end of the 1920s, Woodson had attracted seven younger historians to his "orbit."[113] Affectionately known as "Woodson's boys," Alrutheus A. Taylor, Charles Wesley, Lorenzo Johnston Greene, W. Sherman Savage, James Hugo Johnston, Luther Porter Jackson, and Rayford Logan would eventually form the nucleus of the association alongside Woodson, contributing papers to the *Journal of Negro History*, producing pioneering monographs, participating in Negro History Week celebrations, and delivering papers at the association's annual meetings.[114] Although Woodson's relationships with his "boys" was often contentious, Woodson supported many of their graduate studies and provided a public forum for their scholarship. Representing the first cohort of black PhD historians, they earned their degrees at institutions such as Harvard, Columbia, and the University of Chicago.

Sociologists played a prominent role in the life of the association. Among these were Kelly Miller, longtime professor and dean at Howard University and a vocal proponent of black control of black colleges and universities; Miller's colleague at Howard and trenchant critic of "the black bourgeoisie," E.

Franklin Frazier; Monroe Work, editor of the annual Negro yearbook at Tuskegee; George E. Haynes, founder of the National Urban League; and Charles S. Johnson, race relations guru and champion of the Negro Renaissance.

The association did not neglect literature and the arts, with Alain Locke, Morehouse professor Benjamin Brawley, and poet and professor Sterling Brown all active in the life of the association. Scholars from other disciplines such as political scientist Ralph Bunche and anatomist W. Montague Cobb occasionally enlivened association activities as well.

African American educators formed the backbone of the association, from Mrs. Lucy Harth Smith, principal of Booker T. Washington Elementary School in Lexington, Kentucky, to high school history teacher Herman Dreer of St. Louis and Garnett C. Wilkinson, assistant superintendent of the D.C. public schools. Also among the educators were members of the first generation of black college and university presidents, including John W. Davis of West Virginia Collegiate Institute, Joseph J. Rhoads of Bishop College, and the famously loquacious Mordecai Johnson of Howard University, who said about himself, "The Lord told me to speak, but He did not tell me when to stop."[115]

Businessmen, attorneys, physicians, ministers, clubwomen, and other black professionals made up an important contingent of Woodson's coworkers, stimulating the association to explore the connections between the past and present status of the race, particularly through special panels at annual meetings. Jesse Moorland, social gospel preacher, senior YMCA secretary, and Howard University trustee, played a pivotal role in the early years of the association. Lawyer and activist Archibald Grimké participated in meetings as did Mary McLeod Bethune, president of the National Association of Colored Women and future member of President Roosevelt's "black cabinet."[116]

Whites played various roles in the association. Prominent white scholars such as Franz Boas, Albert Bushnell Hart, and Robert Park served in largely ceremonial roles as members of the *Journal of Negro History*'s executive council. The small number of whites who attended association meetings were typically academics or philanthropists, with interests in studying "race" topics or supporting racial uplift through education. There was, for instance, professor of English R. T. Kerlin, author of the 1923 volume *Negro Poets and Their Poems*; Melville Herskovits, Boas disciple and strong proponent of African "survivals"; Dr. James Dillard, Africa enthusiast and director of the John P. Slater Fund; and Julius Rosenwald, president of Sears and head of the fund bearing his name, which dotted the landscape of the rural South with schools for black children. Although white scholars did not play a large role at annual meetings, they contributed just under half of the articles to the first twenty-five volumes of the *Journal of Negro History*.[117]

BOUNDARY LINES

Woodson's early publications explored a range of historical topics spanning the years from colonial America to World War I, including education, migration, miscegenation, and citizenship. These seemingly disparate subjects were woven together by the thread of the color line.

Woodson's first book, *Education of the Negro*, documented the ways in which race had circumscribed African American educational opportunities. Woodson divided the history of the education of antebellum blacks into two main periods: during the first period, from the introduction of slavery to 1835, the majority of whites considered it prudent to educate slaves; in the second period, from 1835 to the Civil War, whites concluded that education made African Americans too assertive, and many states introduced laws interdicting the instruction of slaves. In short, Woodson tracked the shift from the perception of an educated slave as "useful" to the view that an educated slave was "dangerous." Regarding the latter, the "eternal dread" of slave revolt was fueled by the slave insurrections of Gabriel, Vesey, and Turner as well as news of the Haitian Revolution.[118]

Woodson's second book, the 1918 publication *A Century of Negro Migration*, described African Americans' repeated attempts to escape the strictures of the color line. "The writer," Woodson announced in the book's preface, "has endeavored to present in succinct form the leading facts as to how the Negroes in the United States have struggled under adverse circumstances to flee from bondage and oppression in quest of a land offering asylum to the oppressed and opportunity to the unfortunate." "How they have often been deceived has been carefully noted," Woodson said. Providing an overview of African American migrations from 1815 to the Great War, *Century of Negro Migration* treated colonization schemes, the Exodusters, and the exodus during World War I. In the latter chapter, Woodson described the origins of what would eventually come to be known as "the Great Migration." He presented a prescient analysis of the challenges facing African American migrants to the North, positing that the "maltreatment of the Negroes will be nationalized by this exodus." Indeed the outlines of a formidable color line in the North had already begun to take shape, with restrictions in real estate, discrimination in employment, and "clandestinely segregated" public schools.[119] That the color line was, in effect, "mobile," that it could so readily shift from south to north, was one of the main lessons of *Century of Negro Migration*.[120]

Two of Woodson's most important early *Journal of Negro History* articles examined how legal distinctions helped to both create and fortify the boundaries of the color line. His October 1918 article "The Beginnings of the Miscegenation of the Whites and Blacks" was later reprinted as a stand-alone pamphlet, and whole sections of it appeared nearly verbatim in his 1922 textbook The *Negro in Our History*.[121] "Although science has uprooted the theory," Woodson wrote in the opening line to his miscegenation article, "a number of writers are loath to give up the contention that the white race is superior to others, as it is still hoped that the Caucasian race may be preserved in its purity, especially so far as it means miscegenation with the blacks." "But there are others," Woodson noted dryly, "who express doubt that the integrity of the dominant race has been maintained."[122]

Woodson's concern with miscegenation must be understood in the context of long-standing fears about "racial mixing" and the surge in popularity of race theorists such as Shufeldt, Madison Grant, and Lothrop Stoddard in the 1910s.[123] "Mixed breeding," Grant wrote in 1916, should be regarded as "a crime of the first magnitude." The result, as over a century of racial lore and "science" foretold, was always an insult to the "higher race"—"half-breeds," in the words of Grant. Civilizations rose and fell on the basis of their racial composition, according to the race theorists. Grant, like others possessed by the "Nordic vogue," called for the immediate extension of laws against miscegenation.[124]

"The Beginnings of Miscegenation" presented a brief overview of "race admixture" in the Portuguese, Spanish, and French colonies and followed with an extended discussion of miscegenation, especially antimiscegenation laws, in America. Woodson argued that antimiscegenation laws in America had never been about maintaining bloodlines but rather about maintaining power. These laws, according to Woodson, were intended to "debase to a still lower status the offspring of the blacks . . . and to leave women of color without protection against white men, who might use them for convenience." Explaining what we know today as the "one-drop rule," Woodson said that if the offspring of whites and blacks initially constituted a special class known as "people of color," they ultimately became "classified with all other persons of African blood as Negroes."

In spite of laws to the contrary Woodson showed that "race admixture" had remained common, as a result of both forced, illicit relations and genuine love. Indeed even one of the country's most esteemed founding fathers was implicated here, Woodson noted, referring to "the mulatto offspring" of Thomas Jefferson. With respect to the fantasy of racial purity, Woodson underscored the fact that, according to the most recent census, more than one-fifth of Negroes had some amount of Caucasian blood "in their veins."[125] "Race admixture" between whites and blacks had been an American tradition for a long time. It was absurd to imagine that there had ever been a time without this kind of "intermingling."

While Woodson's miscegenation article helped to explain the origins of the color line, a subsequent article explained how the color line endured. "Fifty Years of Negro Citizenship as Qualified by the United States Supreme Court" appeared in the January 1921 edition of the *Journal of Negro History*. Like "Beginnings of Miscegenation," this article was also published as a stand-alone pamphlet. In addition, the Howard University Law School adopted it as supplementary reading, and a précis of the article appeared in the *Norfolk Journal and Guide* newspaper. "The citizenship of the Negro in this country is a fiction," Woodson declared in the opening line. This article presented a detailed account of the ways in which the Supreme Court had deprived African Americans of "rights essential to freedom and citizenship" in the arenas of transportation, voting, jury service, education, and labor. Woodson argued that with the Fugitive Slave Law of 1850 and the Dred Scott decision of 1857, the federal government had become a "patron of slavery." The result was the advent of "a new sort of nationalism as a defense of [slavery]." With the whole country assigned the job of protecting slave property, every white citizen was now in a position to police the line separating free blacks from slaves.[126]

If blacks briefly enjoyed constitutional rights during Reconstruction, Woodson demonstrated—in a fine-grained analysis of cases such as *Franklin v. South Carolina*, *Plessy v. Ferguson*, and *Cumming v. the Board of Education of Richmond County*—how these rights had been vitiated in the years following Reconstruction. Under "reactionary influence," the Supreme Court had, in effect, decided that there was one set of laws for blacks and another for whites. The Supreme Court, Woodson maintained, had no difficulty finding grounds for jurisdiction where "economic rights" were concerned but was silent when it came to the "human rights" of blacks.[127] With its verdicts on literacy tests for voting, unequal funding for black schools, all-white juries, and so on, the Supreme Court issued ruling after ruling that contributed to the hardening of the color line.

Newly minted in 1912, one of only two African Americans to hold a PhD in history along with Du Bois, Woodson may well have been the only professional historian in the United States who had grown up working with his hands.[128] He stood on the margins of a patrician profession whose members traced their ancestries, literally or figuratively, back to explorers, settlers, and pioneers. Consider the grand coda to Frederick Jackson Turner's 1893 Columbian Exposition address: "Since the days when the fleet of Columbus sailed into the waters of the New World, America has been another name for opportunity."[129] Woodson's historical sensibility was deeply informed by the fact that he could imagine the view from the hull, not just the prow. It was also greatly informed by Woodson's familiarity with nineteenth-century black historical traditions (which foregrounded and celebrated African American contributions to the country) and by his commitment to history as a modern science.

When Woodson founded the association in 1915, apart from the indictment of black people as the main culprits behind the alleged epic failures of the Reconstruction era, "the Negro" was the "invisible man" of U.S. history. The race's invisibility should not be surprising given the egregious racism inside and outside of academe. That African Americans might have been positive, historical actors in the drama of U.S. history was beyond the ken of Turner, Hart, Channing and their professional colleagues, at least in part, because they viewed American history through an Anglo-Saxon racial lens. Black people, by definition, had never had a hand in turning the wheels of progress. So how would they fit into a narrative of opportunity and advancement? To ensure that black people were both seen and heard in American history, Woodson turned his attention to building up a black archive. This effort required the exploration of life, to borrow Du Bois's words, "within the veil." It also entailed challenging the standard forward march of national progress thesis, which was advanced by virtually every standard U.S. history textbook of the late nineteenth and early twentieth centuries.

CHAPTER TWO

"Reverse the Stage"

"For generations in the mind of America, the Negro has been more a formula than a human being." So declared Alain Locke in his tour-de-force introduction to the *New Negro*. A detailed survey conducted in 1934 of the leading U.S. history textbooks published during the 1910s and 1920s found that not a single one included an illustration of an individual African American historical figure. When images of African Americans did appear in the textbooks, they were depicted exclusively in groups or as "types." A generic scene of slaves laboring in a cotton field was by far the most common representation.[1]

The first generation of professionally trained historians who wrote about slavery overwhelmingly cast African Americans as "natural slaves."[2] Indeed the work of U. B. Phillips, who released his landmark study *American Negro Slavery* in 1918, "all but recommended" slavery, in Peter Novick's memorable estimation. A student of William Dunning's, Phillips characterized blacks as innately "submissive," "light-hearted," "amiable," 'ingratiating" and "imitative." His interpretation of slavery "held the field" during the interwar period.[3]

Drawing on a wide range of archival material and including detailed tables and charts, Philips dazzled readers with his quantitative sophistication. Perhaps anticipating that *American Negro Slavery* would make a strong mark on slavery historiography, Woodson reviewed it twice, once for the *Journal of Negro History* and then again for the *Mississippi Valley Historical Review*. While lauding the monograph as a valuable study of the economics of slavery, Woodson said that it fell short of offering a complete history of slavery as an institution. "Very little is said about the blacks themselves," Woodson said, "seemingly to give more space to the history of the whites, who profited by their labor, just as one would in writing a history of the New England fisheries say very little about the species figuring in the industry but more about the life of the people participating in it."[4] "This failure to understand what the Negroes have thought and felt and done, in other words, the failure to fathom the Negro mind, constitutes a defect of the work," Woodson concluded.[5]

American Negro Slavery was an especially jarring example of the larger profession's inability to take into account African American points of view. With blacks neglected, caricatured, or "mentioned only to be condemned" in so much of American history, the effort to recover and offer unprejudiced interpretations of black history had special urgency.[6] The "failure to fathom the Negro mind" not only demeaned black people; it also resulted in a profoundly distorted picture of American history that pushed African Americans outside of its frame. Only by building up a black archive, in Woodson's view, could any semblance of proportionality be introduced into the historical record. In the pages of *Journal of Negro History* and special collections published by Associated Publishers, Woodson set out to gather, organize, and publicize as many primary sources pertaining to black history as he could. The voices represented in this archive testified to dimensions of U.S. history that had been ignored or avoided or that had simply gone unrecognized—slavery through the eyes of slaves, the Great Migration, and the long black freedom struggle, for example. The messages foregrounded in this archive ran against the grain of the contemporaneous historiography, calling into question the triumphalist narrative of U.S. history.

"THE NEGRO MIND"

"In history, power begins at the source." So says Michel-Rolph Trouillot in his brilliant meditation on the historical enterprise, *Silencing the Past: Power and the Production of History*. The "moment of fact creation" (the "making of sources") is the first step in the process of historical production, Trouillot explains. Some facts are recorded; others are not. With respect to an archive, when facts are "collected, thematized and processed," strategic choices are made, choices that are informed by personal, professional and political considerations. Archives therefore always *assemble*, according to Trouillot, rather than merely *collect*. As Trouillot maintains, archival work is "an active act of production that prepares facts for historical intelligibility." Archives, he continues, "convey authority and set the rules for credibility and interdependence; they help select the stories that matter."[7]

The stories that mattered most to professional historians in the early twentieth century revolved around the nation-state. Maintaining a laser-like focus on national politics, academic historians trained their sights on "wars, revolutions and the triumphs of great leaders." As a result, they favored some kinds of evidence over others, privileging "state and court records, legal papers or anything stamped with a government seal." This preference for "official" source materials minimized or erased the historical contributions of common people, especially women, African Americans, the poor and the working class.[8]

From its inception, the association tapped into and expanded the new social history, which "stressed the centrality of previously ignored groups to the drama of the American past." Woodson and his colleagues challenged the conventional notion of history as "past politics," writing "bottom-up" historical accounts that documented the lives of ordinary men and women. Like other proponents of social history, they embraced novel sources such as folklore, oral testimony, and personal letters.[9]

Beginning with its inaugural issue, the *Journal of Negro History* regularly featured a special documents section, which reproduced a wide variety of primary sources.[10] "The collection and printing of primary documents relevant to African American history," Stephen Hall says, "proved one of the crowning achievements of the ASNLH and the *JNH*."[11] By 1930, the journal had printed some two thousand pages of documents. These included materials about African Americans, ranging from slave advertisements and travelers' impressions of slavery" to the letters of George Washington "bearing on the Negro" and Thomas Jefferson's "thoughts on the Negro."[12] More importantly, they also included documents in which, as Luther Porter Jackson put it, "the Negro [is] speaking for himself rather than those in which other persons are speaking for him."[13] From the formal proceedings of black conventions to the letters of sharecroppers, mechanics, and stevedores, the documents printed in the journal represented the voices of both "articulate" and "undistinguished" Negroes. Making its debut in the January 1918 issue, "Some Undistinguished Negroes" was the name of a section of the journal that featured accounts, stories, and family histories of those who would otherwise have been forgotten to history, especially slaves.

Woodson's deep commitment to collecting, cataloging, and publishing primary sources had multiple dimensions. His allegiance to scientific history and his desire to establish the legitimacy of black history were both key factors. Primary sources were the essential building blocks of professional history—the foundation stones on which the entire enterprise was built. (Professional historians derided their "literary" predecessors for relying too heavily on secondary sources and for their clumsy, unsophisticated use of primary materials.) Along with seminar training, archival research was one of the key elements within the "set of practices" that defined professional history.[14] Nobody, Woodson well understood, would take black history seriously in the absence of a black archive.

That different individuals and groups have "unequal access" to the means of historical production is one of the critical overarching arguments Trouillot makes in *Silencing the Past*. Woodson was acutely aware of this fact. It is one reason he considered the pursuit of black history a "life and death struggle." Recall Woodson's declaration in the *Journal of Negro History's* inaugural issue: "In centuries to come when white scholars after forgetting the prejudices of this age will begin to make researches for truth, they will have only one side of the question if the Negro does not leave something to tell his own story."[15] Without a reservoir of original documents pertaining to African American history, there would not be any sources available to construct new arguments, interpretations, and narratives. The loss of the raw materials of historical production would ensure that the truth about the black past remained forever obscure.

Sources, archives, and historical narratives, as Trouillot emphasizes, encode both "presences" and "absences." In standard historical accounts, African Americans were only present in discussions of slavery and Reconstruction. Generally speaking, they were objectified as property in the former case and demonized as unfit for citizenship in the latter. Across the broad sweep of American history, then, black people were conspicuously absent. "Absences," Trouillot insists, often signal "silences," gaps in the historical record that are neither "neutral or natural." ("One 'silences' a fact or an individual as a silencer silences a gun," Trouillot explains.)[16] The "silencing" of the black past in the interwar period reflected the fact that the humanity of people of African descent was not fully recognized by the overwhelming majority of professional historians. African Americans were myths, shells, and shadows—historical pawns rather than historical actors.

Woodson interrupted the silence enveloping the black past with a chorus of voices—an archive of hopes and fears, disappointments and triumphs, and, above all else, dreams. Testimony offered the opportunity to hear African Americans "as they really expressed themselves." Supplying "excellent historical evidence," letters were especially important to viewing black history from an interior angle.[17] By the end of its first decade, the journal had published four large collections of letters—"Letters to the American Colonization Society," "Letters to Antislavery Workers and Agencies," "Letters of Negroes, Largely Personal and Private," and "Letters of Negro Migrants of 1916–1918." Individual letters were often significant in their own right but the true power was in the archive—the curated collection on a specific topic that could reveal, in Woodson's words, the "psychology of the Negro." Writing in 1926, Woodson said that historians had recently come to understand that "the mind of a people" was as significant as and inseparable from "social, political and economic" forces.[18] Through letters and other primary source documents, the association revealed black states of mind, showing how personal testimony illuminated broad historical trends such as abolitionism, emancipation, and migration.

At the heart of African American history, according to Ira Berlin, is the "contrapuntal narrative" of "movement and place." This narrative, Berlin posits, has a powerful psychological dimension, with oscillating experiences of "fluidity and fixity" shaping and reshaping African Americans as a people.

Passages and migrations—homelands lost and found—and the "struggle for place" have been defining features of African American lives. And as Berlin reminds us, place is "not merely a geographic locale, but a social imperative—as in 'stay in your place.'"[19]

The colonization and antislavery movements were crucial developments for nineteenth-century blacks, while the Great Migration was a watershed development for blacks in the century that followed. These three movements speak to the contested and evolving status of African Americans in legal, political, social, and cultural terms. How African Americans participated in conversations about these movements reveals how black people have viewed, navigated, and challenged the boundaries of the color line over time. Colonization was about the place of African Americans, literally and figuratively. What was the status of free blacks in the nation? Was Africa the true "homeland" of African Americans? The abolitionist movement, of course, challenged the fixed status of slaves, calling for a radically reconfigured racial landscape. Post-emancipation, blacks were no longer in chains, but their newfound freedom was tightly, oftentimes violently, circumscribed. The beginning of the Great Migration in the 1910s fused the twin meanings of place, as migrants sought to improve their positions by moving to a new and better location.

In 1926, Woodson published *The Mind of the Negro as Reflected in Letters Written during the Crisis, 1800–1860*, a compendium of several of the correspondence series published in the *Journal of Negro History*, including letters to the American Colonization Society (ACS) and letters to antislavery workers and agencies. Featuring letters from more than two hundred individuals, the *Chicago Defender* heralded *Mind of the Negro* as a "priceless treasure." The *Times* said it made an "arresting contribution" to understanding "the temperament and mentality of the negro during the period of slavery." The main theme of the book, the *Times* reported, was the "ardent desire for freedom and opportunity, the longing to struggle up and out of the overwhelming handicaps the white race had forced upon them."[20]

Part 1 of *Mind of the Negro* presented correspondence of African Americans (including both slaves and free blacks) with the ACS. Gathered from the ACS collection at the Library of Congress, the letters spanned the years from 1818 to 1856, with the bulk of them dating from the late 1840s and early 1850s. The letters, Woodson said, revealed black hopes that were "stimulated" as well as those that were "blasted." Slaves, Woodson's commentary indicated, were more interested in colonization than free blacks. "The Northern Negroes," Woodson wrote, "usually took the position that here their fathers fought, bled and died for their country, here they were born and here they intended to die." Those blacks who did make it to Africa, Woodson asserted, often "went heartbroken to untimely graves."[21]

A long series of letters between Bureel W. Mann of Richmond, Virginia, and the ACS presented, according to Woodson, a representative case of the slave who "struggled in vain" to reach the African promised land promoted by the colonization movement. In the summer of 1847, Mann wrote to the ACS, expressing his desire to go to Liberia to "preach the Gospel to the hethens" and seeking guidance on how he might purchase his freedom. Steamships to Liberia departed and returned as Mann struggled for more than two years to buy himself, his master having capriciously raised the agreed-on price from $150 to $450. With letters of reference testifying to his character lost in the mail, Mann reported that his employer did not allow him "any chants to go among my friends at the churches, to beg a little aid." "The chains of Slavery Do hold me up," Mann wrote, lamenting the "Scattering of my children to the four winds of heaven and the Selling of My beloved Wife!" In the summer of 1849, Mann's fate was still unsettled. Even so, he wrote that he was "not out of patients" and that his "heart is Still fix to go, if I can to Liberia."[22]

Part 2 of *Mind of the Negro* presented letters to antislavery workers and organizations. Woodson introduced the letters by challenging the conventional wisdom that "respectable" colonizationists presented a more objective portrait of antebellum African American life than the "unusually excited" abolitionists. Given that both groups agitated for a particular cause, the idea that one group was truthful and the other disingenuous was a conclusion that could be "supported only by bias and prejudice," Woodson said.[23] The majority of the letters here were reproduced from William Lloyd Garrison's *Liberator* newspaper. Among other topics, the letters presented the stories of escaped slaves, explored the transatlantic abolitionist movement, and documented Frederick Douglass's spectacular falling-out with the Garrisonians.

Echoing his review of Phillips's *American Negro Slavery*, Woodson said that a "neglected aspect of the study of slavery is the mind of the slaves themselves." Observing that most slaves had been "too illiterate to express themselves," Woodson pointed to the significance of the "intelligent testimony" that escaped slaves who had gained some measure of education in the North had to offer. "They have given a picture of the institution from a different point of view," Woodson said. Fugitive slaves, for example, often pushed back against the "nonresistance doctrine" of Garrisonians. In an 1854 letter to Garrison, fugitive slave J. W. Loguen wrote that he hoped Garrison would count him as a "Liberator man." "Whether you will call me so or not, I am with you in heart," Loguen said. "I may not be in hands and head," he explained, "for my hands will fight a slaveholder," something Loguen expected the *Liberator* would be opposed to.[24]

Some of the most poignant letters in *Mind of the Negro* were letters written by escaped slaves to their former masters. Most of them came from the association's own collection of manuscripts. They provide uncommon insight into the existential experience of transitioning from slavery to freedom.

In 1844, Henry Bibb wrote from Detroit to his former master W. H. Gatewood of Trimble County, Kentucky, asking him to pass along his regards to his "aged mother." "My prayer shall be to God that we may meet in heaven," he said. Bibb also appears to have felt an obligation to explain to Gatewood why he ran away, emphasizing his desire to "seek a better home" for his family, free from physical abuse and psychological torment. Mrs. Gatewood, Bibb recounted, frequently flogged his infant child for crying, "until its skin was bruised literally purple." Bibb too could no longer endure Gatewood's merciless beatings of his wife, which were made worse by the helplessness Bibb felt at not being able to afford her protection. He explained to Gatewood that he bore no malice against him. "As it was the custom of your country to treat your fellow men as you did me and my little family," Bibb said, "I can freely forgive you."[25]

Magnanimity was one of the main themes to be found in the letters from ex-slaves to their former owners. In the summer of 1865, Jourdon Anderson of Dayton, Ohio, wrote to his former master, Colonel P. H. Anderson of Big Spring, Tennessee. The colonel had written to Jourdon asking him to return to Big Spring to work, "promising to do better for [Jourdon] than anybody else can." Jourdon responded with a letter that displayed an almost breathtaking graciousness. "Although you shot at me twice before I left you," Jourdon wrote, "I did not want to hear of your being hurt and am glad you are still living." He informed the colonel that he was doing "tolerably well" in Dayton, receiving a salary of $25 a month and living in a "comfortable home" with his wife and children. In Tennessee, Jourdon noted that there had never been "any pay-day for the negroes any more than for the horses and cows," adding that he trusted the "good Maker" had opened Anderson's eyes to "the wrongs which you and your fathers have done to me and my fathers." To test the sincerity of the colonel's offer to treat him "justly and kindly"—and to "forget and forgive old scores"—Jourdon requested that the colonel send him the $11,680 that he owed him in unpaid wages for his thirty-two years of service as well as his wife's twenty years of service. He also wanted assurance regarding the safety of his daughters, now grown up and "good-looking." "You know how it was with poor Matilda and Catherine," Jourdon wrote. "I would rather stay here and starve—and die, if it came to that," Jourdon continued, "than have my girls brought to shame by the violence and wickedness of their young masters." In a stunning closing line, Jourdon wrote, "Say howdy to George Carter and thank him for taking the pistol from you when you were shooting at me."[26]

Letters written by the likes of Henry Bibb and Jourdon Anderson presented a radically different portrait of slavery from that of U. B. Phillips. This kind of correspondence foregrounded the personal rather than the economic dimensions of slavery as an institution, providing a paradigm-shifting perspective through the eyes of the formerly enslaved. These first-person accounts emphasized the brutal violence of slavery, including beatings, sexual assault, and psychological torture. With the slave-master relationship often depicted through stereotypes, these letters also revealed, sometimes in almost bewildering complexity, the multifaceted human beings behind the stock figures. While the former slaves did not hesitate to tell their former owners that they would have to face "a day of reckoning," they often offered their personal forgiveness for the treatment inflicted on them. If many slave owners had wielded absolute power over their slaves, the one power ex-slaves had was that of forgiving their former owners' sins. This remarkable capacity to forgive acknowledged the evils of slavery while simultaneously recognizing the humanity of slave masters.

In the summer and fall of 1919, the *Journal of Negro History* published a two-part series entitled "Letters of Negro Migrants of 1916–1918." Many of the letters were written by black southerners who had responded to recruitment notices in the *Chicago Defender* advertising potential job opportunities in the North. Woodson said the letters expanded awareness of the motives behind the "exodus of the Negroes during the World War, the most significant event in our recent internal history."[27]

"i am in the darkness of the south and i am trying my best to get out," a man from Birmingham, Alabama wrote. "do you no where i can get a job in new york," he wrote, "o please help me to get out of this low down county i am counted no more thin a dog." From Sanford, Florida, another aspiring migrant reported, "The winter is about over and I still have a desire to seek for myself a section of this country where I can poserably better my condishion in as much as beaing assured some protection as a good citizen under the Stars and Stripes."[28] "School has just closed," a girl of seventeen wrote from Alexandria, Louisiana. "I have been going to school for nine months and I now feel like I aught to go to work . . . but there isnt a thing here for me to do:

> What could I earn Nothing. I have a mother and father my father do all he can for me but it is so hard. A child with any respect about her self or his self wouldn't like to see there mother and father work so hard and earn nothing I feel it is my duty to help. I would like for you all to get me a good job and as I havent any money to come please send me a pass and I would work and pay every cent of it back and get me a good quite place to stay . . . I am tired of down here in this _____/ I am afraid to say. Father seem to care and then again dont seem to but Mother and I am tired of all of this I wrote to you all because I believe you will help.[29]

These letters exhibit the potential energy of a taut wire, with desperation pulling from one end and determination pulling the other. Reading them one after the other as a series had a powerful cumulative effect, transforming individual voices into a chorus ringing with the vivid testimony of the hardships in the "darkness of the south" and the fervent desire to improve one's condition. It would be difficult to read these letters without feeling any kind of sympathy for their authors. A basic desire for safety is voiced. So too is the compelling idea that an individual has the right to the fruits of his labor. The importance of family is highlighted in poignant terms. In addition to giving voice to these universal concerns, the letters from aspiring migrants also provided an extraordinary level of detail regarding the specific circumstances facing struggling African Americans in different parts of the South. With this kind of archival reportage, Woodson was effectively documenting history in the present tense.

Letters did not provide the only window into the "Negro mind." In 1925 Woodson published a collection of speeches entitled *Negro Orators and Their Orations*, which compiled, in Woodson's estimation, nearly all of the "extant speeches of consequence" delivered by African Americans.[30] The *Chicago Defender* heralded *Negro Orators* as "a splendid collection of masterpieces. . . . Their fascinating eloquence thrills the soul and captivates the imagination." From one of the first selections, the eighteenth-century "Slavery" by a "Free Negro," to one of the last, "Our Democracy and the Ballot" delivered by James Weldon Johnson in 1923, *Negro Orators* tracked the black struggle for freedom, whether it was the "emancipation of the bond-men," the "liberation from peonage" or the "deliverance from caste."[31]

Negro Orators contained speeches from approximately fifty different people, including abolitionists James Forten, Robert Purvis, and Henry Highland Garnet; African American congressmen John R. Lynch, Joseph H. Rainey, and James T. Rapier; college presidents Booker T. Washington, Robert Russa Moton, and Mordecai Johnson; and activist "race men" Frederick Douglass, Archibald Grimké, and James Weldon Johnson. Given that this was the first anthology of its kind, Woodson's selections proved to be judicious. Woodson featured, for example, what are widely considered two of the most important speeches delivered by African Americans in the nineteenth century—Douglass's 1852 speech "What to the Slave Is the Fourth of July," delivered in Rochester, New York, and Washington's epochal 1895 address at the Cotton States' Exposition in Atlanta.[32]

In the introduction to *Negro Orators*, Woodson outlined a theory of oratory, drawing from the insights of authorities ancient and modern, including Aristotle, Pliny, Pascal, Goethe, and Emerson. Oration, Woodson explained, is "the outgrowth of a conflict between the real and the ideal." The orator was, above all else, a partisan: "His aims are conviction and persuasion." "Charm us, orator," Woodson said, quoting Tennyson, "till the lion looks no larger than the cat." Woodson asserted that "liberty" provided oratory's perennial theme and that "natural oratory" sprang "spontaneously from the breast of patriots inspired to rally the people against the established order of things." Woodson counted Brutus, Patrick Henry, and Frederick Douglass among the most noteworthy patriot-orators.[33]

The testimony contained in the association's publications of speeches, letters, and other primary source documents offered a much sturdier and more nuanced representation of African Americans than the flimsy caricatures presented in mainstream history textbooks. Racist stereotypes flattened the hearts and minds of African Americans to the point where they had no depth at all. The image of the happy-go-lucky slave, for example, denied that black people even had the capacity to feel pain. The archive Woodson constructed in the pages of the *Journal of Negro History* and elsewhere plumbed the depths of, to borrow Du Bois's phrase, the "strange meaning of being black." This process of excavation revealed a panoramic constellation of human emotions, from anger and despair to hope and grace. (*Mind of the Negro* even included a brief section of "love letters," which Woodson referred to as "interesting and valuable sources.")[34] Entering the association archive, like reading *The Souls of Black Folk*, required leaving behind "the white world." Inside the archive, the veil was raised, revealing the inner recesses of African American life, including and especially "the passion of its human sorrow, and the struggle of its greater souls."[35] The association archive presented a fuller, more accurate portrait of U.S. history, one that affirmed black humanity and that revealed some of the broad trends, main themes, and shared common experiences characteristic of the black past. The archive broadcast voices that had rarely—or never—been heard before, and encountering it was both illuminating and gut-wrenching.

THE NEGRO IN OUR HISTORY

The Negro in Our History falls into the category of a watershed text that is frequently mentioned but rarely read. This section offers the most extensive treatment to date of this classic text, placing it in the context of "race histories" written by African American authors as well as the most popular U.S. history survey textbooks of the same period. From the end of the Civil War to 1920, the "race history" was the most popular format for African American historical writing. Several dozen authors—including William Wells Brown, William Henry Crogman, and Anna Julia Cooper—produced notable race histories devoted to the twin themes of civilization and progress. George Washington Williams's two-volume *History of the Negro Race* (1883) was the most well-known text in this genre.[36]

"ONE OF THE GREATEST BOOKS EVER WRITTEN," the *Chicago Defender* trumpeted in all caps in the fall of 1922 about the forthcoming serialized version of *The Negro in Our History*. "A comprehensive review of the part played by the race before, during and following The Days of Bondage," the teaser continued. "You cannot afford to miss a single chapter." A review in the *Baltimore Afro-American* echoed the ebullient language of the *Defender*. "At last it is here," the *Afro-American* declared. "The country has waited long for such a school history."[37]

The first edition of *The Negro in Our History* came out in March 1922. Reviews appeared in, among other places, *Crisis*, *Opportunity*, and the *New Republic*. Tens of thousands of people must have read one or more chapters of *The Negro in Our History* in the *Defender*, which printed the full text of Woodson's book in serialized form over the course of five months, from February to June 1923.[38] By 1927 *The Negro in Our History* had been incorporated into the curriculum of over one hundred schools and colleges in nineteen states and Washington, D.C.[39] It went through ten editions during Woodson's lifetime and was the standard black history textbook for both high school and college students until 1947, the year that John Hope Franklin published *From Slavery to Freedom*. Alain Locke called *The Negro in Our History* "the wedge of the entire [black history] movement," predicting that one day it would be recognized as belonging to "that select class of books that have brought about a revolution of the mind."[40]

Of all the lessons contained in *The Negro in Our History*, the most revolutionary one was as simple as it was profound, namely, the assertion, telegraphed in the textbook's title, that African American history was American history. Woodson shows that the Negro is "interwoven with all phases of American history," *Crisis* declared.[41] Some readers, including Worth Tuttle, reviewer for the *New Republic*, apprehended this basic truth as a kind of revelation. "In reading Mr. Woodson's book," Tuttle wrote, "it is as though we were viewing an historical pageant on the Hippodrome's revolving stage":

> On one side we see the old accustomed march of events from the Mayflower to the Harding administration, with a Negro, backstage in chains during the early scenes, and a Negro, backstage, free of his chains in the latter. Reverse the stage. Here is the Negro up centre enacting a drama within a drama, reaching his own climaxes, arriving at his own dénouement.[42]

Historical episodes that were hastily drawn sketches in other textbooks were presented in great detail in *The Negro in Our History*. "In the twelve chapters devoted to discussion of slavery," Tuttle observed, "one sees more than a semi-nude figure in chains." "One sees," she continued, "the gradual growth of the institution from that early patriarchal system which made a poet out of an African girl in Boston, to the economic system of the nineteenth century which made a chattel out of a man in Louisiana."[43] To borrow the incisive formulation of Ira Berlin, one witnessed the transformation of the country from a "society with slaves" to a "slave society."[44] Images were key to

A SLAVE AUCTION

The Negro in Our History treated the topic of slavery in great depth, using images like this to emphasize its centrality not only to the black past but also to U.S. history writ large.
(Association for the Study of African American Life and History)

Woodson's portrayal of this shift. Illustrations titled "An African Slave Market," "Inspecting a Negro Captive," and "Branding a Negro Woman Slave" depicted the origins of color-coded slavery, while those titled "A Slave Auction" (featuring a white man in a double-breasted suit inspecting a shirtless black man), "The Pursuit of a Slave," and "An Advertisement of a Runaway Slave" showed its institutionalization. The extensive treatment of slavery signaled its centrality not only to the black past but also to U.S. history writ large.

A more comprehensive assessment of *The Negro in Our History* requires comparing Woodson's text to the texts produced at the same time by Woodson's colleagues and professional peers. The following discussion extends from an examination of eight textbooks, four "leading race textbooks of the period" written by black authors (Leila Amos Pendleton's *A Narrative of the Negro* [1912], John Cromwell's *The Negro in American History* [1914], Benjamin Brawley's *A Social History of the American Negro* [1921], and Woodson's *The Negro in Our History*) and four of the era's most popular general U.S. history textbooks, not unexpectedly, all written by white male authors (John Bach McMaster's *A School History of the United States* [1917], Albert Bushnell Hart's *School History of the United States* [1920], David Saville Muzzey's *An American History* [1920], and Lawton B. Evans's *The Essential Facts of American History* [1922]).[45]

The racist extravagancies of early twentieth-century textbooks with respect to the stereotype of the happy-go-lucky slave and the "criminal outrages" of Reconstruction have been ably documented.[46] So too have the revisionist responses of African American scholars to this racist historiography, which stressed the horrors of slavery and the accomplishments of Reconstruction-era governments, especially the dramatic expansion of free public education.[47] Rather than rehearse the familiar subjects of slavery and Reconstruction, then, this analysis focuses on topics that have not received as much attention, including colonization, free blacks, and racial violence.

Before I turn to these topics, a brief overview of the salient differences between *The Negro in Our History* and the other race histories is in order. Woodson was definitely protective of his professional territory. In a lukewarm review of *The Negro in American History*, Woodson applauded Cromwell for producing an "exceptionally well illustrated" book, while chiding him for failing to include sources for the illustrations.[48] He excoriated Brawley, however, for his scholarly failings in a *Journal of Negro History* review of *A Social History of the American Negro*. The book, Woodson said, was an "unscientific" study written by a novice that was wanting in "proportion, style, and accuracy." Cobbled together from an "average knowledge" of American history and race textbooks, the book included many "valuable facts" but nothing in the way of novel interpretation. Dagger flashing, Woodson concluded, "Mr. Brawley does not know history."[49]

Taken together, Woodson's reviews of *The Negro in American History* and *A Social History of the American Negro* underscore his commitment to the conventions of history as a discipline, from using proper citations to advancing original arguments.[50] As the only PhD-credentialed historian among the four African American authors, it should not be surprising that Woodson was more attentive to the standards of professional historical scholarship.[51] Cromwell and Pendleton had a tendency to include lengthy direct quotations and extracts from other texts, a device that Woodson rejected as antiquated. They also organized some of their chapters (or chapter sections) around the biographies of individual figures such as Frederick Douglass and Booker T. Washington. Woodson eschewed this biographical scaffolding as well. In contrast to the occasionally hopscotching back-and-forth-in-time accounts crafted by Brawley, Cromwell, and Pendleton, Woodson's framework was strictly chronological. With respect to tone, Woodson was not as in thrall to the genteel politics of respectability that characterized the work of Brawley, Cromwell, and Pendleton—and most race histories, for that matter. National Urban League executive secretary Eugene Kinckle Jones noted this departure in a review of *The Negro in Our History*, calling Woodson out for his treatment of "miscegenation and fornication," topics that were a "little too salacious for the youthful mind." Finally, with respect to narrative frameworks, *The Negro in American History*, *A Social History of the American Negro*, and *A Narrative of the Negro* were explicitly oriented around the "Negro problem." Indeed, the subtitle of Brawley's book is "Being a History of the Negro Problem in the

United States." *The Negro in Our History*, of course, engaged many questions pertaining to the "Negro problem," but Woodson's book was not designed to offer solutions. This reticence to offer "prognoses for future improvement" was another hallmark of modern historiography.[52]

Colonization, one of the most significant topics in the textbooks produced by black authors, was entirely absent from white authors' texts. Woodson devoted an entire chapter of *The Negro in Our History* to the subject, tracking the development of the American Colonization Society and explaining how the colonization movement was both a method of oppression and a means of uplift.[53] Cromwell similarly argued that colonization could—"paradoxical as it may be"—serve the causes of both slavery and freedom, the former because removing the free people of color would alleviate "the dissatisfaction of the slave with his servile condition," and the latter because the free Negro would be transported to a land where he had "free scope" to pursue his aspirations.[54] All four black authors stressed that there had always been fierce opposition to colonization by free blacks. While acknowledging the role played by African American advocates for colonization such as Paul Cuffe, it was clear that Woodson and his colleagues sided with Frederick Douglass, who had been, in Woodson's assessment, "an uncompromising enemy to colonization."[55]

Regarding "free Negroes," the four white authors either made glancing references to them or ignored them entirely. (It is telling that the entry for "Negroes" in the index to Hart's book instructed the reader to "see Slaves.") In contrast, all of the black authors devoted considerable attention to "free Negroes," emphasizing in particular their relationship with the colonization movement, their participation in the convention movement, and their military service. With respect to the "Negro soldier" and "Negro troops," Evans, McMaster, and Muzzey were silent. Hart, meanwhile, noted that some 186,000 black soldiers served in the Union army, adding almost as an aside that "they probably turned the scale in favor of the North." Black authors, on the other hand, treated black military service in great depth, devoting sections and even entire chapters to black participation in all of the major conflicts, starting with the American Revolution. Crispus Attucks, whose name was not mentioned by any of the white authors, figured prominently in the texts by black authors, showcased as the "first martyr" in the "cause of American freedom."[56]

Harriet Tubman, Sojourner Truth, and Frederick Douglass were among the African American figures routinely ignored by white authors but championed as heroes by black authors. (In several of the black history textbooks, Douglass took pride of place in the frontispiece, occupying the spot typically reserved for George Washington.) This omission reflects the fact that black abolitionists were essentially invisible in mainstream textbooks. Black insurrectionists fared only slightly better. For example, Evans, Hart, and McMaster declined to discuss Nat Turner, while Muzzey devoted a single paragraph to describing Turner's "dreadful deed."[57] All of the black authors, meanwhile, dedicated considerable attention to Turner, discussing his rebellion in the broader context of slave revolts.

John Brown's raid on Harpers Ferry was covered by all of the authors in question. Muzzey called it a "fanatical deed of murder." Evans, Hart, and McMaster emphasized how the North and South came to view the raid quite differently, with the abolitionists and many northerners seeing "something heroic" in Brown's actions. There was no gainsaying among the black authors that Brown was a hero—striking a blow for freedom, he took "his place with the immortals," as Brawley concluded. Woodson even included Brown's "last words" in the appendix to *The Negro in Our History*.[58]

The four white authors did not touch on the subject of rape ("racial admixture" and miscegenation included). Other white authors who did maintained that the rape of a black slave woman by a white man was a rare occurrence. "The lack of chaste sentiment among the female slaves is exhibited by their yielding without objection, except in isolated cases, to the passion of their master," James Ford Rhodes asserted in the 1920 edition of his popular *History of the United States*. "Indeed," Rhodes continued, "the idea of the superiority of the white race was so universally admitted that the negress felt only pride at bearing offspring that had an admixture of the blood of the ruling class."[59] Brawley gently—and obliquely—rebuked this position, asserting that the Negro "has not been chiefly responsible for such miscegenation as has taken place." Woodson was much more forward, describing interracial sex between white men and black women as a "weakness of the white man." While Woodson did not use the term "rape," he maintained that it was the masters—not the female slaves—who had "loose morals."[60] The notion that black slave women solicited advances was rejected out of hand by Woodson, and the brunt of the blame was placed squarely on the shoulders of coercive and lustful white men.

None of the white authors mentioned the lynching of African Americans. In contrast, all four of the black authors devoted considerable attention to the issue, referring to it as "disgraceful," "sinister," "evil," and a form of "cruel persecution."[61] Brawley and Woodson both hammered home two points with respect to lynching. The first was that the "protection of white womanhood" defense of lynching was a canard. Woodson pinned the blame for this misperception squarely on local newspapers, which had successfully appealed to "the race prejudice of the masses," convincing them that "criminal assault" was the general cause of lynchings. Statistics proved, Woodson reported, that ordinary misdemeanors were the "sole excuse" for three of every four lynchings.[62] The second was that the root cause of the lynching epidemic was the desperate effort to resubjugate blacks after the advances they made during Reconstruction.

Cromwell invoked Paul Laurence Dunbar's 1900 poem "The Haunted Oak" to denounce lynching. Using "weird and uncanny imagery," Cromwell explained, the poem told the story "of an oak tree beneath whose shadow [a Negro] was lynched and on which thereafter no leaves grew."[63] Pendleton, meanwhile, quoted a piece from *American Magazine* to convey the "abysmal horror of lynching":

> It is the faces of the spectators [in photographs of lynchings] that shock our very souls. Leave out the grim wreck in the center and the picture might be taken for an ordinary cheerful gathering at a country fair. Leave it in, and oh, my brothers, it is not the dead but the living that terrifies.[64]

While the white authors did not discuss lynching, all four of them did mention the Ku Klux Klan, agreeing that it wielded a "reign of terror" against blacks. For Evans, the "great terror" the Klan instilled in blacks was a "necessity" that "forced the evil ones to behave and made the idle ones work."[65] Hart, McMaster, and Muzzey, in contrast, did not endorse the antiblack violence perpetrated by the Klan; instead they matter-of-factly reported that the Klan's main objectives were to suppress "the Negro vote" and force blacks back into the "humble social position" they held before the war. Brawley and Woodson concurred, discussing the Klan as a "reaction" against black enfranchisement intended to restore "power to the white men of the South."[66] Rather than state their case in the detached language of Hart, McMaster, and Muzzey, however, Brawley and Woodson portrayed the Klan in fire-and-brimstone terms. In a section called "Terrorism," Woodson thundered:

> As hell is never full and the eyes of man are never satisfied, the mere domination [of blacks] did not meet all of the requirements of the degraded class of whites. Slavery had made them brutal. They had been accustomed to drive, to mutilate, to kill Negroes and such traits could not be easily removed. The reign of terror, ostensibly initiated to overthrow the carpet-bag governments by means of the Ku Klux Klan, continued, and it became a special delight for the poor whites to humiliate and persecute the Negroes who had acquired education and accumulated some wealth. The effort was to make the Negro realize that he lives in a white man's country in which law for the Negro is the will of the white man with whom he meets. The Negroes had to undergo punishment for presuming to assume the reins of government during the reconstruction. They had to be convinced that this country will never permit another such revolution.[67]

RISING UP, TRAMPLED DOWN

Brawley, Cromwell, Pendleton, and Woodson covered the decades bookended by the turn of the twentieth century with a profound ambivalence. The chapter titles alone signal this strange combination of hope and despair: "The Vale of Tears, 1890–1910" (Brawley); "Retrospect and Prospect" (Cromwell); "Helps and Hindrances" (Pendleton); and "Finding a Way of Escape" (Woodson). The dichotomous themes of these and other chapters in the books under consideration speak to a basic paradox that most historians have overlooked and that sets early twentieth-century African American history apart from mainstream U.S. history. The authors of race histories—including Brawley, Cromwell, Pendleton, and Woodson—are said to have subscribed to a naïve or conventional narrative of historical progress.[68] While Woodson and his colleagues undeniably presented African Americans as an "eminent, progressive and rising" *people*, their work challenged and ultimately rejected the narrative of progress regarding the United States as a *nation*.[69]

Regarding the evidence of African American progress, Woodson and his colleagues touted black improvement in both moral and material terms. "Negroes are useful citizens," Woodson wrote, "showing little tendency to become peddlers, agents, and impostors who make their living robbing the people." Black authors marshaled mountains of statistical data as evidence of the race's progress. The facts and figures sometimes reached exhaustive, almost comical, levels of specific detail. "It means a great deal," Woodson wrote, "to be able after fifty years of freedom to produce 29,485 teachers, 5,606 musicians and teachers of music, 3,077 physicians and surgeons, 478 dentists, 798 lawyers, 123 chemists, 329 artists, sculptors and teachers of art, 247 authors, editors and reporters, 59 architects, and 237 civil engineers." In addition to advances in the professions, black authors were especially attentive to gains made in the domains of education, religion, benevolent societies, landholdings, and military service. According to Cromwell, the anti-Negro "propaganda" of people like Thomas Dixon, Benjamin Tillman, and J. A. Vardaman deliberately concealed the Negro's "commendable progress" in these arenas.[70]

The images in the textbooks by black authors reinforced this "commendable progress" theme. Here was the stately Howard University Founders Library perched on the hilltop. There were the "typical buildings" at Wilberforce, a "bird's eye view" of Livingstone College and idyllic scenes of industry and domesticity at Tuskegee.[71] Cromwell, Pendleton, and Woodson included copious portraits of prominent black figures, including Paul Laurence Dunbar, Booker T. Washington, and James Weldon Johnson. Woodson and Pendleton both included formal portraits of Du Bois, looking dead serious in a starched white shirt and dark suit jacket.[72] With distinctive features and accomplishments, these "men and women of achievement" embodied the promise of the race.

In spite of the "astonishing progress" in "culture and education" made by African Americans at the turn of the twentieth century, there was "no diminution of race feeling," as Brawley explained. In fact, Brawley reported that this era had witnessed unparalleled "discrimination, crime, and mob violence." It was not enough for the Negro to be "down," Brawley observed. "He was now to be trampled on." This period, as Brawley and his colleagues chronicled, witnessed sharecropping in the South, prejudice and discrimination in labor unions in the North, and an aggressive effort to assert "white supremacy," in Woodson's words, across the country. It was a time, in Brawley's estimation, of "unending bitterness and violence." Disenfranchisement, Pendleton explained, left the Negro's "interests in the hands of his avowed enemies." William Howard Taft's inaugural address in 1909, according to Cromwell, signaled "a complete surrender to the southern view respecting the equal citizenship of the Negro." In too many communities, too "few white men had any conception of the blacks as persons entitled to life, liberty, and the pursuit of happiness," Woodson concluded.[73]

Analyzing African American literature during Reconstruction, literary scholar James Smethurst asserts that black authors emphasized "particularized citizenship and Americanness, whether assumed or questioned, instead of an idealized and unspecified freedom."[74] Similarly, Woodson and his colleagues eschewed abstract discussions of freedom and citizenship, preferring to ground their analyses in historical particulars. In the appendices included in the textbooks under examination, all four white authors included the Declaration of Independence and the Constitution. Cromwell and Woodson's appendices, in contrast, highlighted documents that spoke to natural rights, freedom, and citizenship as subjects of fierce contestation.[75] Cromwell, for example, included summaries of the Somerset case, the "Amistad Captives," and the Underground Railroad. Woodson included a John Adams speech on the Missouri Compromise, the Constitution of the American Antislavery Society (which proclaimed slavery to be "contrary to the principles" espoused in the Declaration of Independence), and the 1865 act to establish the Freedmen's Bureau.[76] All of these documents underscored the extent to which citizenship in the United States had been circumscribed by racial considerations.

Smethurst's examination of late nineteenth-century poetry about black Civil War veterans is useful here. According to Smethurst, this body of poetry written by African American authors challenged the notion that freedom and citizenship were synonymous concepts. African Americans, the poems suggested, might be free in the sense of not being property but they nonetheless were not full-fledged citizens.[77] In *The Negro in Our History*, Woodson elaborated on this idea by examining the black experience during World War I. While emphasizing that blacks "love their native soil and will readily die, if necessary, to defend it," Woodson made sure to note that they did not love the "reactionaries" who denied them the "enjoyment of every right, immunity, and privilege." Underscoring that blacks volunteered for the war effort in numbers exceeding their proportion of the population, he also highlighted the severe discrimination they faced in the ranks. *The Negro in Our History* included two images of all-black units in the armed forces that emphasized the tangled relationship between freedom and citizenship—an illustration of the Fifteenth New York National Guard Regiment and a photograph of the First Separate Battalion of the District of Columbia. Black people were free to fight for their country, but they had to serve in their own segregated ranks.

None of the four white authors mentioned the race riots of the early twentieth century. Cromwell likewise avoided the subject, while Pendleton briefly referred to the 1906 "Atlanta massacre," calling it likely the "most atrocious" of all the "race riots" in the South, North, and West. Brawley and Woodson, on the other hand, devoted a lot of attention to race riots, providing extensive coverage of the 1919 "Red Summer" in particular. In a section called "High Tension: Washington, Chicago, Elaine," Brawley wrote about the grisly racial violence in these three and other cities, including Dyersburg, Tennessee, Shubuta, Mississippi, and Omaha, Nebraska. On the racial terror unleashed in Brooks and Lowndes Counties, Georgia, from May 17 to May 24, 1918, Brawley reported that seven hundred rounds were fired into the bodies of two men shot side by side. He also introduced readers to Mary Turner, the wife of one of the initial victims. When Turner said she would testify if she knew who had killed her husband, she was hung upside down from a tree and doused in gasoline. "While she was yet alive," Brawley wrote, "her abdomen was cut open with a large knife and her unborn babe fell to the ground." "It gave two feeble cries and then its head was crushed by a member of the mob with his heel."[78]

Brawley attributed the heightened racial animosity to the return of black soldiers stateside and to the "hatred aroused by a Negro of independent means who knows how to stand up for his rights." Woodson too saw the escalating violence as a response to the black soldiers returning home, "clamoring for equality and justice." "The very uniform on a Negro," Woodson said, "was to the southerner like a red rag thrown in the face of a bull." Southerners, of course, had no monopoly on racial animus. Mentioning race riots in Youngstown, Ohio, East St. Louis, and Chicago, Woodson observed that "race prejudice" in the North had at times become "more volcanic" than in certain sections of the South.[79]

As he described in *The Negro in Our History*, Woodson himself was caught up in the Washington, D.C., "race war" that started on July 19, 1919, after a rumor spread that some black men had assaulted white women. Whites, including some on leave from the army and navy, formed a mob that stretched from the Capitol to the White House, pulling blacks from vehicles and beating them unconscious. One was assaulted right in front of the White House, where "the President must have heard his groans but has not as yet uttered a word of protest." At the intersection of Pennsylvania Avenue and Eighth

Street, Woodson inadvertently walked into the heart of the mob. He watched an innocent black man shot dead at point-blank range and rushed away from the scene to avoid meeting the same fate.[80]

Referring to race riots, Brawley wrote that horrific racial violence was a "most important matter" that was "regularly ignored or minimized by historians." With the exception of the violence unleashed by the Klan, which was often condoned in mainstream history textbooks, white historians did not address the country's history of antiblack racial violence. This omission may have reflected a basic blindness to the black experience, a casual indifference to the significance of black lives, or a calculated effort to scrub the past clean of some of its most disturbing stains. Whatever the case, Woodson and his colleagues were among the first authors to document and analyze the history of violence against African Americans. Brawley and Woodson, in particular, maintained that racial violence was not an anomaly but rather a concerted—and recurrent—strategy to enforce the boundaries of the color line by any means necessary. This pattern of systematic antiblack violence belied the conventional historical narrative of increasing national comity in the wake of the Civil War.

Woodson and his colleagues had to grapple with a thorny dilemma regarding the status of African Americans. On the one hand, they wanted to show that African Americans were inextricably woven into the fabric of the nation. On the other, they wanted to demonstrate the extent to which African Americans had been prohibited, often forcibly, from full participation in the social, economic, and cultural life of the country. Competing concerns—of inclusion versus exclusion, uplift versus oppression—were in a state of dynamic tension throughout these texts. Striking the right balance between oppression and agency was always a kind of high-wire act for Woodson and other black authors. Place too much of an emphasis on oppression and the danger was that African Americans became nothing more than passive victims. Put too much stress on autonomy, though, and the pitfall was that African Americans would be blamed for their position at the bottom of the American social order. The exceedingly difficult task was to write a compelling and accurate history, populated by black folks who were neither pawns nor superheroes.

Black people exhibited little agency in the accounts of Evans, Hart, McMaster, and Muzzey, a finding that is reflected in the dearth of images of black figures in their textbooks. Muzzey's text did not include a single illustration of African Americans. Neither did Evans's, although he included an illustration of an "old slave market" building in Louisville, Georgia, bereft of any people. The only depiction of black people in McMaster's textbook were the crude caricatures seen on a reproduction of an eighteenth-century slave advertisement where a "parcel" of Negroes was marketed along with a "Quantity of very good Lime-juice to be Sold cheap." Hart's *School History* featured several depictions of blacks, including an illustration of Africans crouching on the Virginia shore "to be sold as slaves" and two illustrations where blacks appeared in the background as well-dressed "house slaves" or servants, one a picture of Thomas Jefferson entertaining friends at Monticello. Hart also included a representation of "old slave huts" in Savannah, Georgia, an illustration of a fugitive slave being unpacked from a crate, and a small reproduction of Augustus Saint Gaudens's Shaw Monument.[81] In sum, across four of the most popular U.S. history textbooks, African Americans were either left out of the visual record or depicted exclusively in the context of slavery. Moreover, after the Reconstruction period, African Americans disappeared from the historical record altogether in these four texts.

In the summer of 1925, copies of *The Negro in Our History* were reportedly confiscated from a Negro Manual Training High School in Oklahoma. The problem was the book's "radical" theme, symbolized by one of its full-page illustrations, a photograph of an interracial jury in the District of Columbia, accompanied by the following caption, "The New Freedom." Positing freedom as the abolition of the color line, this was surely Woodson's sly way of tweaking Woodrow Wilson's doctrine of the same name.[82] With black people in the picture, American history looked very different. It sounded different too, with testimony from the black archive changing the tenor of our history.

If U.S. history were a symphony, according to mainstream textbooks, freedom, opportunity, and progress were the central themes, growing louder and more insistent as the symphony went along. Tone-deaf to the African American experience, Symphony U.S. History 101 ran through a series of pleasing

THE NEW FREEDOM, the first mixed jury in the District of Columbia

Woodson used this photograph in *The Negro in Our History* to draw a connection between freedom and the destruction of the color line.
(Association for the Study of African American Life and History)

harmonies and soaring crescendos, ending on a triumphant note. Woodson and many of his colleagues, however, heard a very different symphony; freedom, progress, and opportunity were important themes, to be sure, but they were accompanied by the contrapuntal melodies of enslavement, exploitation, and segregation. Terrifying crashes, dissonance, and long moments of silence punctuated the symphony's movements, and it ended on an ambiguous note, one filled with melancholy but also hope.

PART TWO

CULTURE
1922–1941

In the aftermath of the Great War, an older and narrower Victorian idea of culture—Matthew Arnold's famous belletristic notion of the "best that has been thought and said"—gave way to a newer and more expansive culture concept, radically reconfigured by the currents of modernism.[1] Before World War I, most cultural elites viewed "culture and civilization [as] indistinguishable." "Those who possessed culture were thought to be civilized," W. Fitzhugh Brundage explains. "Those who lacked it were philistines, or worse, savages."[2] In the 1920s and 1930s, the boundaries between "high" and "low" culture became more permeable, as Boasian cultural relativism began to challenge previously strict hierarchies of aesthetics, morality, and respectability as well as races, peoples, and nations.[3] "Where the older concept [of culture] was hierarchical and normative," John Gilkeson Jr. explains, "the anthropological concept of culture was pluralistic and relativistic."[4] Social scientists and historians were especially receptive to thinking about culture as a "common set of beliefs, values and rituals," embracing the related proposition that culture was learned rather than inherited.[5]

The Harlem Renaissance, as scholars such as Houston Baker, Ann Douglas, and George Hutchinson have demonstrated, was one of the main engines of American modernism.[6] "The aim that united the New Negroes of the twenties, and indeed their white allies," Hutchinson writes, "was in fact an 'attempt to explain America to itself' in a very new way, centering upon the perspectives and experiences and expressive traditions of African Americans, preeminently through the arts."[7] It was not until the 1970s that the term "Harlem Renaissance" superseded "Negro Renaissance" in the scholarly literature. The latter was the preferred term for many of the renaissance's key architects and participants, including Sterling Brown, Alain Locke, and Langston Hughes. I too favor the "Negro Renaissance" term as it more accurately conveys the full scope of the renaissance, which reached well beyond the confines of Harlem. It also more faithfully represents the grand ambitions of the renaissance, which aimed to transform "the race" writ large.

The Negro Renaissance enacted—and elaborated on—the nascent theory of cultural pluralism advanced by Locke, Horace Kallen, and Randolph Bourne in the 1910s. At the core of cultural pluralism was a rejection of the melting pot ideal. Kallen and Bourne were especially worried that the American commercial culture juggernaut—in the form of cheap books and newspapers, popular music, moving pictures, and so on—would run over and flatten whatever cultural diversity still survived on the nation's margins. They looked to the rich cultural traditions of immigrant communities as the answer to the "tasteless, colorless fluid of uniformity" characteristic of middlebrow American society.[8] Kallen famously proposed the metaphor of an orchestra in which each ethnic group would add its own "spirit and culture," just as every type of instrument has its own "specific timbre and tonality."[9] Locke was more concerned about the conspicuous absence of African Americans from the national orchestra than he was about the "leering cheapness and falseness" of American popular culture.[10] For Locke, a genuinely inclusive cultural pluralism would provide a means of reading African Americans into the nation, a way to "re-pot the family tree to include black roots."[11]

While Kallen, Bourne, and Locke all prized cultural diversity, they disagreed on the nature—and sources—of culture. Kallen, for instance, held an essentialist view of culture as something that was passed down intact from generation to generation like an heirloom. "Men," Kallen declared, "cannot change their grandfathers," indicating that an individual's cultural identity was determined by her background.[12] Bourne and Locke, in contrast, shared a more cosmopolitan vision in which culture was viewed as dynamic and composite, and in which cross-cultural pollination and exchange was privileged over an imagined cultural purity.[13] Bourne agreed with Kallen, however, that Europe was the main wellspring of cultural variation, with its wide array of different ethnic groups and their distinctive languages, religions, and artistic traditions. Locke and other African American intellectuals, meanwhile, saw Africa as the fountainhead of cultural diversity.

Africa was a source of inspiration for the renaissance as well as a beacon for the bold journeys of the New Negro. At the turn of the twentieth century, black Americans increasingly looked to the African continent as "a homeland, a site for providential mission, a respite from American racism, a place for self-determination, an inspiration for a new name (Afro-American) and a cause célèbre."[14] This interest in Africa only accelerated after World War I, as many black Americans embarked on a search for "brightest Africa," in the evocative formulation of Jeannette Eileen Jones. In a shift away from the "dark continent" trope of "impenetrable jungles, wild beasts, savages, and primitive governments," African Americans reimagined Africa as the site of a glorious past—with an impressive cultural legacy of firsts (from kingdoms and empires to iron smelting and weaving)—as well as a glorious future in which the continent would be unified and free from colonial rule.[15] This shift was only partial, however, as throughout the interwar period, "dark continent" discourse continued to circulate alongside "brightest Africa" discourse. In Thomas Holt's judgment, African Americans had a complex relationship to Africa that was characterized by a "profound ambivalence built on both engagement and distance." "There was both pride in their African heritage," Holt says, "and condescension toward the putative backwardness of contemporary Africans."[16]

Different varieties of pan-Africanism helped to keep a sustained focus on Africa during the interwar period. In 1919, Du Bois spearheaded the Pan-African Congress, which was held in Paris at the same time as the Peace Conference. The ascendant Universal Negro Improvement Association launched the Black Star line that same year, and Marcus Garvey took on the title of provisional president of Africa the following year in 1920. Throughout the 1920s, artists as diverse as Aaron Douglas, Meta Warrick Fuller, and Claude McKay mined African sources for "artistic ore."[17] The Italian invasion of Ethiopia in 1935 was front-page headlines in the black press and "ushered in a new chapter" in the anticolonialism movement.[18]

Whereas the likes of Bishop Henry McNeal Turner of the African Methodist Episcopal Church had "wanted to shape up the Africans with Christianity, commerce, and civilization," the New Negro generation looked to Africa for inspiration, especially as "a symbolic anchor other than race to ground [their] identity."[19] Countee Cullen's famous "What is Africa to Me?" query reached deep into the black past. Translated into concrete historical terms, Woodson and his colleagues asked where and when black history began. They addressed this question in a variety of venues and media, including Negro History Week pageants, textbooks, and the *Journal of Negro History*. Associated Publishers released its first title on Africa, *African Myths Together with Proverbs*, in 1928, followed by *The African Background Outlined* in 1936 and *African Heroes and Heroines* in 1939.[20] The *Journal of Negro History* published a wide range of articles on Africa such as "The Redemption of Africa," "American Opposition to Slavery in Africa," and "French and British Imperialism in West Africa."[21] Beginning in 1935, the *Journal of Negro History* added two new sections to its notes department: "Books on Africa" and "Articles on Africa in Magazines." Here Woodson kept a running, annotated, and seemingly exhaustive list of the burgeoning scholarship on Africa, including references to books and articles in both German and French.

In the two chapters that follow, I argue that black history was an integral component of the renaissance, providing a foundation for the awakening of African Americans as "a people" with a shared past, a shared struggle, and a shared culture. My analysis, which focuses on the most energetic years of the renaissance, is bookended (literally, in this case) by two anthologies: James Weldon Johnson's *Book of American Negro Poetry* (1922), with its tour-de-force preface, "Essay on the Negro's Creative Genius," which celebrated black literature and a distinctive black cultural heritage, and the *Negro Caravan:*

Writings by American Negroes (1941), a giant compendium that rejected the very concepts of black literature and black culture.

Chapter 3 ("Heritage: Anthologies and the Negro Renaissance") explores the central role that anthologies played in the renaissance. Anthologies set the renaissance's tone and elaborated its logic, stimulating intense debates about the nature of "Negro art" and the relationship between culture and race. The *New Negro* was only one of a flood of anthologies released in the renaissance era. Indeed it was during the 1920s and 1930s that scholars such as Woodson, Locke, and Benjamin Brawley assembled the first collections of African American music, literature, and drama, laying claim to a rich artistic heritage with roots in both Africa and America. Anthologies such as *Negro Poets and Their Poems* (1923), *Book of American Negro Spirituals* (1925), and *Plays of Negro Life* (1927) historicized "the Negro," describing the development of African American art and explaining how it related to larger historical trends. As sources of "facts and inspiration," they also provided a cultural background for the New Negro—a platform for the further development of African Americans as a collective group.[22] Locke, writing in 1926, averred that American culture comprised a "confederation of minority traditions."[23] Historical investigation and analysis were the primary means to recover the African American minority tradition, a heritage that was distinctively black at the same time that it was wholly American.

Chapter 4 ("The New Negro Goes to School") demonstrates that the early black history movement and the Negro Renaissance did not simply run in parallel but intersected and combined in powerful and heretofore unacknowledged ways. The advent of Negro History Week in 1926 should be seen as a landmark development in the history of the renaissance, providing a critical foundation for the cultural awakening of African Americans as a people.[24] Negro History Week celebrations introduced black audiences across the country to renaissance art, ranging from the poems of Langston Hughes to the musical compositions of Harry T. Burleigh. The performance of epic from-Africa-to-the-New-World history pageants stimulated a historically grounded race consciousness, informed by shared struggles and a common cultural heritage. The study and celebration of black history in the form of local research projects, inventive writing activities, and dramatic productions helped to introduce the creative passion of the New Negro into segregated black schools. Central sites of a distinctive black public sphere, segregated schools were vital renaissance staging grounds. With the support of the association, especially the community-minded efforts of African American women educators, large numbers of black people across the country learned that they were not merely spectators to somebody else's history and culture. They had their own heritage to declare.

CHAPTER THREE

Heritage

ANTHOLOGIES AND THE
NEGRO RENAISSANCE

Ask a dozen scholars when the Negro Renaissance started and you will most likely get a dozen different answers, from the 1919 publication of Claude McKay's defiant Red Summer poem "If We Must Die" to the release of Jean Toomer's enigmatic novel *Cane* in 1923 and the inaugural gathering of white literati, Talented Tenth representatives, and aspiring black authors at the Civic Club in March of 1924. If pressed to identify the renaissance's pivotal text, however, these same scholars would in all likelihood unanimously choose *The New Negro*—the renaissance's "definitive text, its Bible," as Arnold Rampersad puts it.[1] Released in November 1925, Locke's edited collection featured the work of thirty of the renaissance's thirty-five stars, according to David Levering Lewis's count, including that of Langston Hughes, Zora Neale Hurston, and Jean Toomer.[2]

History played a prominent, if largely forgotten, role in *The New Negro*, with an entire section devoted to black history. Under the larger heading of "The Negro Renaissance," "The Negro Digs Up His Past" section included an eponymous essay by Arthur Schomburg, an essay titled "The Legacy of the Ancestral Arts" by Locke, an essay titled "American Negro Folk Literature" by Arthur Huff Fauset, two folk tales, and Countee Cullen's poem "Heritage," with the celebrated opening line, "What is Africa to Me?" Schomburg's essay also began with a memorable and frequently quoted line: "The American Negro must remake his past in order to make his future." The Puerto Rican émigré and bibliophile applauded the recent shift in the study of the Negro's past from the vagaries of rhetoric and propaganda—as issued by "the rash and rabid amateur who has glibly tried to prove half of the world's geniuses to have been Negroes"—to a more rigorous and scientific approach. Schomburg believed that an evenhanded and well-documented race history would serve as "a stimulating and inspiring tradition for the coming generations." If "persecution, . . . prejudice, . . . [and] the social damage of slavery" were what ailed the race, a positive race history was a part of the cure. "Already,"

Schomburg avowed, "the Negro sees himself against a reclaimed background, in a perspective that will give pride and self-respect ample scope, and make history yield for him the same values that the treasured past of any people affords."³

Schomburg's comments in *The New Negro* speak to the core of the black history enterprise during the Negro Renaissance years. The archeological metaphor of digging up the past was especially apt. Negro history in the 1920s and 1930s was a process of excavation, an intentional effort to reclaim the cultural background of the race—a background that had been there all along, just waiting to be discovered and interpreted. The phrase "treasured past," meanwhile, signaled the vital importance of fashioning a cultural heritage. A robust heritage, as Schomburg suggested, would help to define African Americans as "a people" and provide a platform for their future development. History would provide the New Negro with "credentials" and a "pedigree."⁴

ANTHOLOGIZING THE NEGRO

The New Negro was just one of many anthologies in a new and unprecedented era of anthologizing African American music, art, literature, poetry, and drama. Two pathbreaking surveys appeared in the 1910s—John Wesley Work's *Folk Song of the American Negro* (1915) and Benjamin Brawley's *The Negro in Literature and Art in the United States* (1918). But the "obsession in anthologizing the Negro," as Gerald Early puts it, did not begin in earnest until the 1920s. The years from 1922 to 1935 witnessed an "astonishing" outpouring of anthologies devoted to African American life and history.⁵ This obsession was related to the broader trend to recover, in Waldo Frank's phrasing, America's "buried cultures." The interwar period saw a "folklore craze," which was later characterized by Margaret Mead as a "search-and-rescue" mission to preserve American folk culture, from the mountain ballads of Appalachia to Negro spirituals in the Deep South.⁶

Pioneering African American anthologists tended to be university men who circulated within the small world of black art and letters and had ties to Woodson and the association. In addition to Woodson, the three most important black anthologists active in the renaissance era were Benjamin Brawley, James Weldon Johnson, and Alain Locke.

Born in 1882 to a prominent family in Columbia, South Carolina, Benjamin Brawley received a BA from Atlanta Baptist College (later Morehouse), an additional BA from the University of Chicago, and a master of arts from Harvard. As a professor of English at his Atlanta alma mater, Benjamin Brawley approached teaching as a "sacred calling." He had exacting standards and was known to return slapdash papers to students with the following comment: "Too carelessly written to be carefully read."⁷ Brawley wrote widely in the fields of art, literature, biography, and history, producing numerous books and scholarly articles as well as essays in popular newspapers and magazines. He published four articles in the *Journal of Negro History*, the first in 1916 and the last in 1934.[8] Brawley's books—including *The Negro in Literature and Art, Women of Achievement,* and *A Social History of the American Negro*— were reviewed in the pages of the *Journal of Negro History* as well.[9] A frequent participant in association meetings, he read a paper on Negro poets at the first annual meeting in 1917.[10]

James Weldon Johnson's professional accomplishments read like those from the CV of a half-dozen different men—he was an attorney, newspaper proprietor, Broadway lyricist, poet, novelist, diplomat, and civil rights activist. Coauthor with his brother Rosamond of "Lift Every Voice and Sing" (1900), author of *Autobiography of an Ex-Colored Man* (1912) and *God's Trombones* (1927), among many other works, Johnson was a U.S. consular representative to Venezuela and Nicaragua and executive secretary of the NAACP.[11] Johnson was not intimately involved with the work of the association, but he participated in at least one of the annual meetings in New York in 1931, delivering remarks at the opening dinner.[12] His "Lift Every Voice and Sing," meanwhile, became the association's unofficial anthem, sung regularly at annual meetings and Negro History Week celebrations.

Locke, arguably the leading writer on black arts and letters during the interwar period, is most well known as the "midwife" to the Harlem Renaissance, plucking out promising artists such as Langston Hughes and Zora Neale Hurston, introducing them to publishers and patrons, and then critically reviewing their work once their names were in print. In addition to and by no means unrelated to his role as the high priest of the "New Negro," Locke was also an important figure in the Negro history movement. Scholars have largely neglected this vital aspect of Locke's career.[13] Locke had a long and productive relationship with Woodson and the association, becoming a lifetime member in 1927. He was a regular participant at its annual meetings during the 1920s and early 1930s, where he frequently spoke about African and African American art. Locke was also a popular lecturer on the Negro History Week circuit, delivering talks at universities, high schools, public libraries, museums, and colored Ys.[14]

Nothing if not erudite, some of the pioneering black anthologists no doubt encountered—perhaps even in the original German, in the case of Locke— Hegel's memorable statement that Africa "had no history in the true sense of the word, . . . no movement or development of its own."[15] "The Negro," Hegel explained in his 1830-31 lectures on the philosophy of history, "is an example of animal man in all his savagery and lawlessness."[16] Locke and his colleagues were also, of course, more well acquainted than they ever wished to be with the thinking of Negrophobes in the Thomas Dixon vein who viewed blacks as "beasts," the "leading" American historians of Reconstruction who portrayed black legislators as incompetent buffoons, and "liberals" on the race question who regarded African Americans as "childlike."[17]

Whether beasts, buffoons, or children, everybody seemed to agree that the Negro race was a "primitive" one. Primitives, as Hegel's analysis suggested, were hopelessly trapped in the present. Driven by instinct, lacking any meaningful cultural traditions, they stood outside of history. "The Negro," Schomburg declared in his contribution to *The New Negro*, "has been a man without a history because he has been considered a man without a worthy culture."[18] The concepts of history and culture, as Schomburg underlined, were inextricably fused. His epigram, then, could just as easily be reversed; that is, one might say a man without a culture is a man without a worthy history. The black architects of renaissance-era anthologies understood this dynamic, contingent, and reciprocal relationship between history and culture. Combine history with culture and the end product is *heritage*. For Brawley, Locke, Johnson, Woodson, and others, the anthology would serve as both declarations of and monuments to a vibrant African American heritage.

Anthologies, by definition, are historical documents. They chart change over time, delineating different movements, trends, and schools. Or they announce a new departure, as in the case of *The New Negro* or a compilation of contemporary African American art. Anthologies always contain "befores" and "afters." Borrowing Hegel's terminology, we might say they show both "movement" and "development." As Brent Hayes Edwards suggests, renaissance-era anthologies positioned "the Negro as paradigmatically modern and up to date, historical and literate." This framing contributed to the "compulsively documentary" nature of the New Negro movement.[19] Consider the richly annotated bibliographies that appeared in so many of the renaissance-era anthologies. *The New Negro*, for example, contained an extensive bibliography, divided into six separate sections, including "The Negro in Literature," "Negro Music," and "The Negro Race Problems." Each bibliographic entry, punctuated by a date, was a marker, a signal that the African American experience did not stanch the flow of time. The "Notable Early Books by Negroes" section compiled by Schomburg listed works by more than eighty authors, from the Revolutionary-era poetry of Phyllis Wheatley to Alexander Crummell's 1891 book *Africa and America*. Here was evidence of a long tradition of African American writing, incorporating jeremiads, slave narratives, and race histories.

The discovery, codification, and publication of an African American cultural heritage, especially in the arts, was one of the signal accomplishments of the Negro Renaissance. Emphasizing texts produced by African Americans, what follows is a survey of the most important anthologies released during the renaissance era. I pay especially close attention to prefaces, agreeing with

Edwards's claim that the "power of the anthology is concentrated in its discursive frame." The preface, Edwards says, is "the very force that animates the book, that opens it for us and shows its contents."[20] I maintain that the anthology was in many respects the quintessential renaissance text. Anthologies embodied the spirit of the renaissance, articulated the renaissance's formal logic, and introduced the terms for vital debates about the definition of "Negro art" and the nature of the relationship between race and culture.

THE BLUEPRINT: FOLK SONG OF THE AMERICAN NEGRO

Folk Song of the American Negro, one of the first major studies of spirituals, was published in 1915.[21] The author was John Wesley Work, composer, professor of Latin and history at Fisk, and director of the famed Jubilee singers.[22] Work was a pioneer in the collection and transcription of black folk songs—Du Bois said he was "the one who began the restoration of the Negro Spiritual to the American people."[23] Interspersed with the lyrics and musical transcriptions of spirituals such as "Balm in Gilead," "Steal Away to Jesus," and "Swing Low, Sweet Chariot," *Folk Song of the American Negro* featured ten chapters, including ones on African song and American song and one titled "A Painted Picture of a Soul."

A labor of love, it took Work more than a decade to bring the book to completion. Because so much that had been written on Negro folk songs was "inaccurate and unreliable," Work turned to the primary sources, the songs themselves and the "makers of the songs." He spent years tracking down sources, traveling from state to state, "hunting in out-of-the-way places" and attending "church services, here, there and yonder."[24]

Highlighting the invaluable work of discovering, preserving, and developing Negro music, Work reported that there were over five hundred documented Negro songs. He dedicated some thirty pages to classifying these songs, constructing a taxonomy with eleven different headings, including "Sorrow Songs," "Songs of Patience," and "Songs of Courage." Work maintained an essentialist view of Negro genius and character, seeing in the spirituals the distinctive expression of Negro emotion and religious fervor. "His pains are poignant, his joys are ecstatic," Work wrote. "He is either on the mountaintop or deep down in the valley."[25]

Folk Song of the American Negro opens in Africa with a discussion of African rhythms and folk songs. The remarkable second chapter ("Transmigration and Transition of Song") transports the reader to the port of Jamestown to witness the arrival of "twenty human beings, dark children of darker Africa." Having passed through the "fires of purgatory," these "children of the tropics" miraculously "chose to sing and not to curse," singing a new song in a foreign land through their "bitter tears." This new song combined the unmistakable rhythm and melody of African tribal songs with the divine inspiration of Christianity. Comparing the "evolution" of the African himself to the corresponding evolution in his music, Work argued that "the process was thorough and both singer and song became American." Indeed, over time, the Negro folk song became America's folk song, the country's "only original music."[26]

Summarizing the significance of the spirituals, Work noted that he tended to regard "this music from a historical and psychological viewpoint":

> It is a reliable account of our people's past. It tells of their suffering and how they bore them, of their joys and how they expressed them, of their lives and how they lived them, how deep and dark were the depths into which they sank, what obstacles they had to surmount. It describes the very tissue of their souls. In short, it tells the stuff of what the Negro is made. With this as a source of facts and inspiration, the author is conscious of a power enabling him to present effectively the cause of his people before the bar of humanity.[27]

Folk Song of the American Negro only receives glancing attention in a handful of renaissance studies.[28] A strong case could be made, though, that Work's book is the original renaissance anthology blueprint. Work's overarching aim in *Folk Song of the American Negro* was to provide a "source of facts and inspiration," an objective embraced by all of the renaissance's African American anthologists. To accomplish this objective, Work and the anthologists that followed him adopted an analytical approach that combined, to borrow sociologist Jon Cruz's terms, a "politics of subjects" with a "science of objects." As Cruz explains, the former approach, favored by the antebellum white abolitionists who championed the value of spirituals, regarded them as a form of "testimony" that provided insight into the subjective experience of slaves. With a "politics of subjects," the main concerns were "moral and political." The latter approach, adopted by the first generations of folklorists and social scientists in the late nineteenth century, saw spirituals as cultural artifacts that could "best be grasped descriptively, taxonomically, and analytically within the larger intellectual schemas of objectification and classification."[29]

Featuring both testimony and taxonomy, *Folk Song of the Negro* advanced a core set of propositions that future anthologists adopted as basic guiding principles. The first was that Africa was a valuable cultural storehouse that had provided African Americans with some of the basic building blocks for the folk traditions and art forms they developed in the United States. The second was that slavery was a crucible through which the African became American. The third was African Americans had the remarkable capacity to transform their unspeakable suffering into art (as Locke put it, to create "beauty instead of ashes").[30] The fourth was that art was a window into the "soul" of the race (which was defined by some in essentialist terms and others in historically contingent terms, a division I address in the "Hokum Versus History" section of this chapter). The fifth was that African Americans were the progenitors of the only original American art. And the sixth was that presenting evidence of an African American cultural heritage and exceptional African American artistic accomplishment would improve the fortunes of the race.

In 1915, Work's *Folk Song of the American Negro* was essentially an anomaly, an innovative cultural history and collection that garnered very little notice in the black press. Within a decade, however, Work's analytical framework and claims about the value of African American art would become part of the basic vocabulary of the renaissance.

MUSIC AND SONG

James Weldon Johnson's 1925 *Book of American Negro Spirituals* was the next major statement on spirituals after Work's *Folk Song of the American Negro*. The success of Johnson's book was "instantaneous," according to the *Philadelphia Tribune*. It sold two thousand copies in two weeks.[31] "At last there appears a satisfactory edition of Negro spirituals," the *New York Amsterdam News* announced, adding that "only one who has waded through many botched editions can appreciate the intelligence with which this book is put together."[32] Not only "music lovers" but "all who are interested in American culture" should applaud the valuable preservation work Johnson had completed, the *Times* enthused.[33] President Calvin Coolidge himself sent Johnson a letter thanking him for the service he had performed in "putting these melodies in permanent form." A review in the *Chicago Defender* cited the glowing assessment of music critic Alfred V. Frankenstein, who suggested that the "enormous popularity" of Johnson's book may indeed have signaled the arrival of the much-touted Negro renaissance.[34]

Johnson cited Work's pioneering efforts, but he did not fully acknowledge the extent to which he had borrowed Work's interpretive framework. The "miracle" of the Negro spirituals "strikes me with increasing wonder," Johnson reported in the book's preface. It was almost unfathomable that "America's only folk music" had emerged out of the horrors of the middle passage and slavery. (The *Journal of Negro History* agreed, reporting that Johnson was "justified in referring to the development of this music as a miracle" and placing it among the "important contributions of modern times"). Johnson cataloged the music's African characteristics, asserting that the Negro brought his innate musical gifts with him from Africa. In America, the Negro discovered the power and the glory of the New World God. According to Johnson, the "spirit of Christianity" fused with the "vestiges" of African music to create the spirituals.[35]

Johnson devoted several pages to debunking the notion that spirituals were not the Negro's "own, original creation." Regarding specious claims that Negro spirituals were derivative of European folk songs, Johnson noted that when the Fisk Jubilee Singers performed in England, Scotland, and Germany in the 1870s, their concerts had caused a "sensation." This would not have been possible, Johnson underscored, if their songs had been "mere imitations" of European folk music. Johnson attributed the skepticism surrounding the black origins of the spirituals to white prejudice, specifically to "an unwillingness to concede the creation of so much pure beauty to a people they wish to feel is absolutely inferior."[36]

Mary White Ovington said that the *Book of American Negro Spirituals* would show Negroes that "their forebears gave this country a great music."[37] Johnson himself explained that it was only in recent years that African Americans had taken a renewed interest in the spirituals. According to Johnson, immediately following emancipation, blacks had revolted against everything connected with slavery, including the spirituals. This attitude of revolt is captured in African Methodist Episcopal minister Theophilus G. Steward's 1876 declaration that "slave history is no history." "Our history," Steward said, "is something to be ashamed of, rather than to be proud of, hence it has no power to unite but great power to divide."[38] Johnson linked the "reawakening" of curiosity in the spirituals to the dawn of "an entirely new phase of race consciousness." It represented, Johnson said, a significant change in the Negro's attitude toward his own artistic products, "the turning of his gaze inward upon his own cultural resources." Johnson saw the influence of this reclamation of the "value and beauty" of the spirituals as having ripple effects, radiating out to influence all of the race's artistic activities. Drawing from this inner reservoir of culture, the world of black art and letters was starting to reach the white world as well. "America," Johnson declared, "is beginning to see in [the Negro] the divine spark which may glow merely for the fanning."[39]

Two additional anthologies of the spirituals appeared in 1925. Distributed by academic presses and produced by white scholars, they highlight a few noteworthy differences in the approach of black versus white anthologists. Dorothy Scarborough's *On the Trail of Negro Folk Songs*, published by Harvard University Press, revealed a collector's mentality. Scarborough devoted the bulk of her book to transcriptions and commentaries of Negro folk songs, with each chapter delineating a different genre of song—"Negro Ballads," "Lullabies," "Work-Songs," and so on. Scarborough, a daughter of the South whose grandfathers had owned large plantations with many slaves (one in Louisiana, the other in Texas), approached her subject with a passion bordering on fanaticism. You must "snatch" a song the first time you hear it, Scarborough informed her readers. Do not let the singer get away. Even if he promises to write it down later, that later rarely arrives, while all the time "he is subject to all the changes of a perilous world, where he may be killed on any street corner, taking the song with him." ("Songs die, too, as well as people," Scarborough said.)[40] If Scarborough aimed to preserve black folk culture, her interest in Negro folk songs, as the title of her book indicates, was also stimulated by the avid collector's "thrill of the chase." Like the butterflies pinned down behind glass by the entomologist, songs were, above all else, specimens to be cataloged and displayed.

Sociologists Howard Odum and Guy Johnson released *The Negro and His Songs: A Study of the Typical Negro Songs in the South* in 1925 as well. Published by the University of North Carolina Press, the book presented the lyrics of Negro songs from northern Mississippi and northern Georgia, along with accompanying commentary; chapters were organized thematically under headings such as "The Religious Songs of the Negro," "The Social Songs of the Negro," and "The Work Songs of the Negro." The work billed itself as an "objective" portrait, which would eschew "cosmic generalizations or ethnic interpretation." In spite of this disclaimer, the authors apparently were not immune to the renaissance zeitgeist, asserting that Negro songs provided vital insights into "the psychic, religious and social expression of the race."[41] The *Journal of Negro History* was not particularly impressed with the quality of the insights drawn by Odum and Johnson. While applauding the editors for attempting to show the public "the world as the Negro sees it," it said the book failed to demonstrate a "clear understanding of the philosophy underlying the life of the Negro."[42]

Locke's "The Negro Spirituals" in *The New Negro* embraced the spirituals as expressions of "the race" without qualification or reservation. The spirituals were, he argued, "uniquely expressive of the Negro," while simultaneously "deeply representative of the soil that produced them": "The song of the Negro is America's folk-song." Underneath an apparent simplicity and naiveté was "an epic intensity and a tragic profundity of emotional experience, for which the only historical analogy is the spiritual experience of the Jews and the only analogue, the Psalms." We must preserve and treasure the spirituals, Locke said, but we must also welcome their contribution to the "music of tomorrow." Locke concluded his essay with the words of Work, who referred to spirituals in *Folk Song of the American Negro* as "the starting point, not our goal; the source, not the issue, of our musical tradition."[43]

The musical transcriptions of two spirituals, "Father Abraham" and "Listen to de Lambs" followed Locke's essay. Transcribing the spirituals into sheet music was not only a form of preservation but also a form of elevation. Unless you were an anthropologist or a folklorist, oral traditions like the sorrow songs did not rate as culture or art. The official music notation system, with its dignified clef, attested to the legitimacy of African American music, endowing it with a kind of weight and substance. Coolidge thanked Johnson for rendering the spirituals in a "*permanent* form." The transformation of folk music into formal music was a form of cultural credentialing. (According to the prevailing civilization pyramid schemes at the turn of the twentieth century, the shift from orality to literacy always marked a cultural advance.) The standard apparatus of anthologies—the critical commentaries, the classification schemes, the copious annotated bibliographies and so on—all served as testimonials to the validity of the Negro's cultural passport. The collection, transcription, and presentation of African American folk music, then, was not simply a process of cultural preservation. It was the *invention*—in the sense of a self-conscious fashioning—of a cultural heritage. The very act of anthologizing the spirituals created the African American folk music tradition, transforming noise into notes and the "wild and barbarous" sounds of slaves into songs.[44]

Collections of spirituals proved to be popular, and a steady stream of new volumes were released starting in 1925 and on through the 1930s, although none of them matched Johnson's *Book of American Negro Spirituals* in its impact. Along with Johnson's own hymnal "Lift Every Voice and Sing," spirituals served as the soundtrack to the Negro history movement.

LITERATURE, POETRY, AND SPEECH

In 1910, Benjamin Brawley privately printed a sixty-page booklet called "The Negro in Literature and Art." Brawley turned this "little work" into a book in 1918. *The Negro in Literature and Art in the United States*, Brawley explained, endeavored to address "more thoroughly than has ever before been attempted the achievement of the Negro in the United States along literary and artistic lines."[45] Woodson concurred, writing in the *Journal of Negro History* that Brawley's purpose was a "lofty one," as he aimed to inform the public that African American artistic production "must be reckoned with in determining the thought of this country."[46]

In the first chapter of the book, significantly titled "The Negro Genius," Brawley said that the Negro's main contributions to "American civilization" had been in the field of aesthetics. The "soul of the race" had an especially artistic character," Brawley explained. It was the "picturesque" things that appealed most to the Negro's "nature."[47] According to Brawley, without suffering, no race could scale "the greatest heights of art." Owing to the race's "background of tragedy," including "the lash," the "child torn from its mother's bosom," and the lifeless, bullet-ridden body "swinging all night from a limb by the roadside," black creative expression resonated with "an unmistakable note of power." Black artistic work also benefited from something "elemental" in the "heart of the race, something that finds its origin in the African forest." If in part a native racial endowment, the "peculiar genius" of the Negro for the arts also had its source in an African heritage and the historical trials and tribulations of slavery and Jim Crow.

To cultivate the Negro's particular artistic gifts was a patriotic duty, according to Brawley, as they would redound "to the glory of the country." Black music, in fact, had already won wide acclaim as the "most distinctive" in the country, and the potential of the Negro in the domains of literature, oratory, sculpture, and painting was "illimitable."[48] Brawley organized his book around exemplary individuals—there were chapters on, among other figures, the poet Phyllis Wheatley, the painter Henry O. Tanner, and the sculptor Meta Warrick Fuller. Although the book was not technically an anthology, Brawley included many excerpts from the work of all of the featured writers (Wheatley, Dunbar, Chesnutt, Du Bois, and Braithwaite) as well as extracts from the speeches of orators Frederick Douglass and Booker T. Washington.

In 1916, Schomburg released *A Bibliographic Checklist of American Negro Poetry*.[49] It proved useful to James Weldon Johnson as he tracked down the materials to include in his *Book of American Negro Poetry*, which was released in 1922 and featured some two hundred poems by thirty-one authors. We now have the "first collected edition of poems by colored authors," the *Afro-American* reported.[50] On the long wait for such a collection, a reviewer for the *New Journal and Guide* said, "We wait a little to open the book, so pleasant is it just to realize its existence."[51] Johnson produced the book, in part, to simply inform the public that black poets existed.[52] A review in the *Journal of Negro History* touted the "historical significance" of the testimony provided by black poets. "It cannot be gainsaid," Woodson wrote, "that the poetry of a race passing through the ordeal of slavery and later struggling for social and political recognition must constitute a long chapter in its history."[53]

Notices in the black press, without exception, called attention to Johnson's striking forty-eight-page-long preface, "The Negro's Creative Genius." The big claim—Johnson himself called it a "startling statement"—that reverberated in the pages of the black press and elsewhere was that blacks had created the only authentic and distinctive American art. They had, in fact, generated four unique "artistic products," as Johnson called them: the Uncle Remus stories, the spirituals, the cakewalk, and ragtime. Literature, song, dance, and music. These four products were indisputable evidence of the "creative genius of the Negro," according to Johnson. They were also incontrovertible proof that black culture had "saturated American life." Originated by black piano players in Mississippi river towns, ragtime—with its "heel-tickling, smile-provoking, joy-awakening, response-compelling charm"—expressed "the blare and jangle and the surge, too, of our national spirit." It was the Negro who had the extraordinary power to "suck up the national spirit from the soil" to create the country's original art.[54]

This power of creative invention was not to be underestimated. In Johnson's view, peoples were judged by the quantity and quality of the literature and art they produced. "No people that has produced great literature and art has ever been looked upon by the world as distinctly inferior," Johnson said. And nothing would do more to raise the Negro's "status" than the production of outstanding literature and art. ("No persons, however hostile, can listen to Negroes singing [the spirituals] without having their hostility melted down," Johnson averred.)[55] In a mere two paragraphs, Johnson sketched the bright outlines of what David Levering Lewis would eventually refer to as "civil rights by copyright," the self-conscious strategy to use art as "the means to change society in order to be accepted in it."[56] Johnson's ideas here, of course, were not sui generis but rather a weaving together—with some additional embroidery around the edges—of ideas from different sources, including Du Bois's notion of the "kingdom of culture," Work's conviction that great art could change hearts and minds, Brawley's elaboration of "Negro genius," and Locke's philosophy of cultural pluralism.[57]

The transition to poetry and the substance of the book was a bit awkward, after Johnson's sensational opening salvos on the black roots of America's most characteristic art forms and the transformative potential of creative self-expression for blacks as a people. In the event, Johnson introduced readers to Phyllis Wheatley, notably "denied her rightful place in American literature" in spite of being one of the first women poets in America and among the first of all American poets to issue a volume. He emphasized Wheatley's patriotism, telling us that General George Washington himself received her and expressed his gratitude for a 1775 poem she had dedicated to him.[58] Dunbar starred alongside Wheatley in Johnson's preface, which concluded with a discussion of poets that would soon make their mark in the Negro Renaissance, including Claude McKay, Fenton Johnson, and Jessie Fauset.

Thomas Talley of Fisk had the misfortune of releasing his book *Negro Folk Rhymes* the same year as the *Book of American Negro Poetry*. With the price "a trifle high," the publisher a bit obscure, and the spirit of the renaissance only flickering in the background, Talley's book was bound to capture less attention than Johnson's anthology.[59] *Negro Folk Rhymes* presented some 350 lyrics, ballads, and rhymes, which had been passed down orally through the generations.[60] The author of the introduction said that Talley was to be commended for the preservation of these "relics." The volume contained an integral part of "the musical and poetic life-records of a people," providing a sympathetic "understanding of the Negro mind."[61]

On this subject of the "Negro mind," the significance of two association anthologies discussed in chapter 2 should be recognized here. *Negro Orators and Their Orations* (1925) and *The Mind of the Negro* (1926) were pioneering collections of black speeches and letters, respectively. The former captured a robust history of African American oratory that reached back to the early republic, while the latter presented the writings of both prominent and "undistinguished" African Americans, dating from 1800 to 1860. With respect to black heritage, both of these anthologies presented evidence of the centrality of the quest for freedom to African American oral and written cultural expressions.

In the vein of formal literature, Associated Publishers released an anthology called *Negro Poets and Their Poems* in 1923.[62] Edited by white author, educator, and social reformer Robert T. Kerlin, the frontispiece, a print of Meta Warrick Fuller's dramatic sculpture *Emancipation Proclamation*, announced Kerlin's intention to situate the anthology squarely in the middle of the unfolding renaissance.[63] "Culture, talent, genius—or something very like it—are theirs," Kerlin announced about the new generation of black poets. They were not wrapping themselves in the mantle of Dunbar but rather in an "unborrowed singing robe, that better fits the 'New Negro,'" Kerlin explained. Their poetry would alert white readers to how oblivious they have been about Negroes, "their real life, their very thoughts, their completely human joys and griefs." Reading Negro poetry offered a powerful rejoinder to the commonplace boast that "I know the Negro better than he knows himself."[64]

Organized thematically by chapter—"Dialect Verse," "The Poetry of Protest," "The Heart of Negro Womanhood," and so on—*Negro Poets* included a similar roster of poets to Johnson's anthology. The second chapter, called "The Present Renaissance of the Negro," highlighted the poems of McKay, Leslie Pinckney Hill, and James Weldon Johnson. "All of a people's history that is permanently or profoundly significant is distilled into poetry," Kerlin averred. Woodson agreed, noting in a review of *Negro Poets* in the *Journal of Negro History* that poetry is "history, too, even if it does not deal with the leadership of armies and the administration of governments," but rather with what "the Negro feels and thinks and dreams."[65] Glossing Johnson's declaration of Negro creative genius, Kerlin argued that the world only really took notice of a particular people when it began to voice its aspirations in poetry. Fortunately, according to Kerlin, the Negro was innately endowed with the "three supreme gifts" of the poet: power of feeling, power of imagination, and power of expression. With these gifts, black bards expressed the arc of black history, *ad astra per aspera*—to the stars through difficulties.[66]

In 1924, Newman Ivey White and Walter Clinton Jackson, self-described "southern white men who desire the most cordial relations between the races," released *An Anthology of Verse by American Negroes*. The authors reported that blacks—"a race unquestionably endowed with humor and music"—had made great strides in poetry since emancipation. From Jupiter Hammon to Pinckney Hill "is a far cry, as far as from the first anonymous slave to the colleges, insurance companies, banks, and business enterprises now operated by and for Negroes," White and Jackson explained. Organized chronologically by individual author, the book had twin aims: first, to bring the attention of white students to a body of American literature that had been largely neglected; and second, to show blacks "evidence of the actual accomplishments of the members of their race."[67] A review in the *Journal of Negro History*, most likely written by Woodson, expressed skepticism that White and Jackson had "properly evaluated" the poems, suggesting they gave too much credit to white influences; at the same time, it celebrated the fact that two gentlemen from the "former master class" had recognized the value of Negro poetry.[68]

Nineteen twenty-seven saw the release of two compilations focusing on present-day black poets. *Four Negro Poets*, edited by Alain Locke, was part of a Simon and Schuster poetry series that sold for a quarter.[69] The four featured poets were McKay, Toomer, Hughes, and Cullen. Cullen himself published a collection of poetry the same year called *Caroling Dusk: An Anthology of Verse by Negro Poets*. With decorations provided by Aaron Douglas, the volume featured the work of "the new voices" associated with the recent "renaissance in art and literature by Negroes."[70] These new voices included poets such as Arna Bontemps, James Weldon Johnson, and Toomer. It is instructive regarding disagreements about the nature of the renaissance to compare the respective introductions to these two volumes. Locke announced that with this new generation of Negro poets, "a folk temperament flowers and a race experience bears fruit." The poems represented, Locke said, "the epic reach and surge of a people seeking their group character though art." This effort involved the reclamation of a previously scorned race heritage. For McKay, for instance, "Africa's past is not an abandoned shambles but a treasure trove." And in Locke's estimation of Toomer's poems, "slavery, once a shame and stigma, becomes a spiritual process of growth and transfiguration."[71]

Cullen, in contrast, one of a handful of black artists who both compiled and appeared in anthologies during the renaissance years, was skeptical of Locke's conception of a "group character." Explaining why the subtitle of the book was *An Anthology of Verse by Negro Poets* rather than *An Anthology of Negro Verse*, Cullen said it was futile to attempt to "corral" the work of all black poets into "some definite mold." Cullen rejected the idea that the work of Negro poets would present any "serious aberration" from the tendencies of their times, asserting that black poets might gain more from the rich background of English and American poetry than from "any nebulous atavistic yearnings toward an African inheritance." This would appear to be a direct rebuke of Locke and his like-minded colleagues. Cullen, like Locke, however, invoked an orchestral metaphor to explain the significance of the work by the new generation of black poets. Cullen described *Caroling Dusk* as a mere prelude to that "fuller symphony which Negro poets will in time contribute to the national literature."[72] Similarly, Locke said the work of Hughes and his colleagues "registered distinctive notes," which were increasingly becoming "orchestrated into our national art and culture."[73]

Anthologies of black poetry entered a fallow period after the appearance of *Four Negro Poets* and *Caroling Dusk*. It was not until 1938 that a collection called *Negro Voices: An Anthology of Contemporary Verse* by Beatrice M. Murphy ended the drought.

Benjamin Brawley's 1935 anthology *Early Negro American Writers* did include poems by Wheatley and Jupiter Hammon but concentrated in the main on prose. Brawley said that the book grew out of his desire to make work previously only available in special collections more widely accessible. Regarding his selections, which included the writings of David Walker, Martin Delany, and Frances E. W. Harper, Brawley said that "what is lacking in literary quality is in general more than made up in social interest." Brawley pointed the reader to what was most important regarding "social interest," providing helpful biographical and critical notes throughout the text. The introduction to *Early Negro American Writers* outlined in close detail three main historical trends that shaped the work of early black writers. They were black participation in American wars, the abolitionist movement, and the "long and contradictory history" of colonization schemes. Antebellum blacks, Brawley noted, faced urgent questions with respect to liberty and freedom—the 1850 Fugitive Slave Law was especially significant—and "there was little time or training for what is called polite literature." Instead of the novel or the drama, black writers produced a kind of protest literature of which the slave narratives were the most significant and influential.[74]

DRAMA

Plays of Negro Life (1927), edited by Alain Locke and Montgomery Gregory, with the telling subtitle, *A Sourcebook of Native American Drama*, was the first ever compilation of plays to focus on African American life. A review in the *New Journal and Guide* heralded the book as a "most remarkable publication," proclaiming that the reading and theater-going publics owed Locke and Gregory "a debt of everlasting gratitude."[75] Aaron Douglas provided the illustrations for *Plays of Negro Life*, which included works by, among others, Eugene O'Neill, Jean Toomer, and Georgia Douglas Johnson. As Locke explained, the collection garnered the yield of an "experimental and groundbreaking decade," which had witnessed two complementary and collaborative developments—the emergence of black playwrights seeking to advance a "Negro drama," on the one hand, and white playwrights' incorporation of "Negro life and folkways" into their plays, the result of their search for new materials for the new "American realism," on the other. Asserting that "Negro experience has been inherently dramatic," Locke quoted Eugene O'Neill, who said "the gifts the Negro can and will bring to our native drama are invaluable ones."[76]

Locke and Gregory's anthology featured twenty one-act plays, the authorship of which was divided roughly evenly between blacks and whites.[77] If black playwrights and actors had the "advantages of greater intimacy of knowledge and feeling" regarding African American life, they should have "no monopoly on the field," Locke declared. Gregory, for instance, described the 1917 New York debut of three plays by white playwright Ridgley Torrence with an all-black cast as a milestone in the development of black drama. The inclusion of white authors in *Plays of Negro Life* is enlightening with respect to Locke's cosmopolitan approach to culture and art, especially regarding art as a vehicle by which to win greater freedom and equality. Locke maintained that every culture was both *distinctive* and *composite*. He rejected the twin ideas of cultural purity and cultural "proprietorship," arguing that these ideas were the poisonous wellsprings of prejudice and discrimination. The modern world demanded "free trade in culture" and the ringing endorsement of "the principle of cultural reciprocity." Culture goods, Locke explained, could not be hoarded as "the exclusive property of the race or people that originated them." Rather than claiming "Negro drama" as the exclusive province of African Americans, Locke maintained that whites could borrow "Negro" themes and idioms, as long as their engagement with "Negro materials" was sympathetic and intelligent.[78]

In a 1927 debate with Lothrop Stoddard, Locke predicted that the widespread recognition of the artistic accomplishments of African Americans was "imminent."[79] The Negro theater was a proof of concept, attesting to the promise of Negro art to attract the world's interest and appreciation.[80] Why was this kind of recognition so urgent? "Cultural recognition," Locke said, "means the removal of wholesale social proscription and, therefore, the conscious scrapping of the mood and creed of 'White Supremacy.'" "It means," he continued, "an open society instead of a closed ethnic shop."[81] *Plays of Negro Life* outlined and documented a rich and mutually beneficial exchange between blacks and whites. As such, it was meant to be a model not only for future artistic exchanges but for race relations writ large. "Free and unbiased" exchanges between the races on the basis of "common interests and mutual consent" was the only viable model for true democracy in the United States, one far superior to the existing system of "inequality based on caste psychology and class exploitation," Locke explained.[82] Locke's approach to the transformative power of art, then, was much deeper and more sophisticated than Lewis's "civil rights by copyright" interpretation indicates. African American art was not simply a product to be appreciated or a vehicle by which to try to change the minds of whites. It was more akin to a pursuit, a staging ground for the meeting of black and white minds. This point of view was evident in the *New Negro* appendix "A Selected List of Modern Music, Influenced by American Negro Theme or Idioms." Selections ranged from George Gershwin's "Rhapsody in Blue" to Antonin Dvorak's string quartettes and Erik Satie's ballet score, "Parade."

Associated Publishers printed the first anthology dedicated exclusively to African American playwrights.[83] *Plays and Pageants from the Life of the Negro* came out in 1930. The plays in this volume, Woodson announced, tell the "simple story of an oppressed but rising people. Despair followed by hope, opposition by assistance, enmity by friendship, defeat by victory and death by life."[84] Edited by Willis Richardson, an exceptionally prolific playwright whose 1923 production of *The Chip Woman's Fortune* was the first "serious drama" written by an African American to open on Broadway, the anthology was intended to be used primarily in schools.[85] (Richardson recalled that it was at one of Georgia Douglas Johnson's famed Saturday night salons that he and Woodson first discussed the potential of drama as a teaching tool.)[86] As such, Richardson explained that he had to cut several promising selections that contained objectionable subject matter, including one play that would have "caused more confusion in the minds of the youthful than a quarrelsome, wide woman in a narrow house."[87]

Handsomely illustrated with woodblock prints produced by James Lesesne Wells, *Plays and Pageants* included eight plays and four pageants and showcased the work of several novice playwrights, including AME minister Edward J. McCoo and D.C. elementary school teacher Dorothy Guinn.[80] McCoo's "Ethiopia at the Bar of Justice" was a model for the popular allegory approach to Negro history dramas in which History is called as the highest court of appeal. Guinn's "Out of the Dark" was an exemplary model of the from-slavery-to-freedom epic pageant. (A more extensive discussion of both of these productions appears in chapter 4.) In 1935, Associated Publishers released another anthology, *Negro History in Thirteen Plays*, which was edited by Richardson and May Miller. Miller, daughter of the legendary Howard University sociologist Kelly Miller and a winner of one of the first writing contests sponsored by *Opportunity*, had four of her own plays included in the volume. Two kinds of plays made up the bulk of the collection: one-act biographies showcasing luminaries such as Crispus Attucks ("The Martyr"), Frederick Douglass, Sojourner Truth, Booker T. Washington, and others and historical dramas—Johnson's "William and Ellen Craft," for example, which presented the Crafts' riveting escape from slavery, with the light-skinned Ellen posing as a white male planter and William playing the part of personal servant.

"Why does not the Negro dramatize his own life and bring the world unto him?" Woodson asked in the introduction to *Negro History in Thirteen Plays*. "His life is the real drama of America." Woodson believed that black playwrights should emulate Molière, who had turned to "country players" to dramatize the life of the French people. Citing the courage it took the Negro to write and perform dramas "in spite of mocking onlookers," Woodson said the book's publication should be considered "another step of the Negro toward the emancipation of his mind from the slavery of the inferiority complex."[89] In a newspaper article released just before the official publication of *Negro History in Thirteen Plays*, Woodson said he was pleased that the collection included two plays focusing on Africa, lest readers think black history started on the American cotton plantation.[90] Woodson was also happy, as he indicated in the pages of the *Journal of Negro History*, that this compilation saw fit to portray "the hovel rather than look eternally to the palace." "In America," Woodson wrote, "we are still exalting the slaveholder rather than the unoffending enslaved."[91]

After *Negro History in Thirteen Plays*, the next black drama anthology did not appear until William Couch Jr.'s *New Black Playwrights* in 1968.[92]

HOKUM VERSUS HISTORY

At the height of the "Negro vogue," the incomparable George Schuyler, who made a career of tweaking the sensibilities of the talented tenth, attempted to single-handedly stem the renaissance's rising tide. In his pungent 1926 essay "The Negro-Art Hokum," Schuyler argued that so-called Negro art gushingly referred to by renaissance boosters as "expressive of the Negro soul" was a sham and a hoax. If art revealed "the psychology and culture" of one's environment, there was no reason for "Negro art" to be anything special, given that the "same economic and social forces" shaping the "actions and thoughts" of whites also molded those of blacks. Blacks and whites, according to Schuyler, smoked the same brands of cigarettes, watched the same Hollywood movies, and read the same "puerile" magazines. "The Aframerican," he concluded, "is merely a lampblacked Anglo-Saxon."[93]

Schuyler granted that the spirituals, blues, and ragtime had "dark-skinned sources," but he roundly condemned their use as an illustration of "Negro genius." They were more regional than racial contributions, Schuyler explained, "no more expressive or characteristic of the Negro race than the music and dancing of the Appalachian highlanders or the Dalmatian peasantry are expressive or characteristic of the Caucasian race."[94] In Schuyler's estimation, the glorification of a racially distinctive art played directly into the hands of the Negrophobes and their claims that there were "fundamental, eternal and inescapable differences" between whites and blacks. The Negro is peculiar and so too must be his art. The renaissance's "Negro-art hokum" only served to prop up the distorted worldview of the scions of slaveholders, Klan members, and "scientists" like Madison Grant and Lothrop Stoddard. Thinking people should reject it with a "loud guffaw."[95]

Renaissance architects, including the leading black anthologists, offered two basic rejoinders to Schuyler's blistering critique. The first was existential, verging on the religious. As Du Bois explained in his meditation on the sorrow songs in *The Souls of Black Folk*, these songs "came out of the South unknown to me, one by one, and yet at once I knew them as of me and of mine."[96] In Du Bois's conception, the spirituals had an ineffable quality that transcended regional boundaries and the variations of personal experience, allowing them to speak for "the race."

The second response, elaborated in the most detail by Locke, was empirical. It was a fallacy—even a dangerous illusion—according to Locke, to think that blacks and whites breathed the same cultural air, as Schuyler contended. In Locke's estimation, blacks shared neither the same sociocultural environment as whites nor, even more importantly, the same history. They had largely avoided the homogenizing crucible of the "melting pot," Locke explained. "Persecution [and] suffering, with their greater discipline and pressure," Locke said, "have intensified the Negro heritage, and caste prejudice has isolated it from the powerful standardizing processes of American life."[97] Unlike in the case of other ethno-racial groups whose folk heritages had withered in the "shallow soil of American materialism"—or been almost completely obliterated in the case of the American Indian—the "Negro folk spirit" remained vital.[98]

Schuyler, like Cullen, ridiculed the proposition that art created by African Americans always expressed the "Negro folk spirit." Locke too rejected this shaky position. In his 1926 essay "The Negro Poets of the United States," Locke made a crucial distinction between "Negro poets" and "Negro poetry." The former, he said, we have had for a century and a half since Phyllis Wheatley, but the latter we have only had since Dunbar, "scarcely a generation." "Negro poetry," according to Locke required a "unity of spirit and sense of tradition." Contemporary black poets had self-consciously turned to "Negro materials as themes and Negro idioms of speech and emotion as artistic inspiration." It was this turn to "the Negro," along with the accompanying desire for "cultural recognition," that brought together different authors with varying styles into a "definite artistic movement."[99]

Schuyler's and Locke's disagreement here must be understood in the broader context of historical tensions between assertions of human sameness and declarations of racial distinctiveness in ideas about African American identity. As Mia Bay argues, "competing claims to equality and difference run through virtually all nineteenth-century black racial thought." On the one hand, black authors contested racist ideas such as polygenesis and racist ideologies such as social Darwinism. ("Of one blood God hath created all nations to dwell on the face of the earth" from Acts 17:29 was one of their preferred rejoinders.) On the other hand, many of these same writers asserted that the "gentle virtues" of African Americans made them morally superior to the "amoral, aggressive, [and] acquisitive" white race.[100] Black intellectuals of the renaissance era likewise espoused contradictory ideas in this regard. While rejecting the rigid racial hierarchies espoused by the likes of Grant and Stoddard, they often did not hesitate to advance claims about the race's unique artistic "gifts."[101]

How did Locke respond to Schuyler's charge that any mention of "Negro art," "Negro genius," or the "Negro soul" would only reinforce white supremacist ideas about ineradicable differences between the races? His answer was subtle, and the logic no doubt would have eluded Negrophobes, not to mention many "friends of the Negro" as well. "It is out of the peculiarity of the [Negro] experience rather than any uniqueness of inherited nature," Locke maintained, that the distinctive features of "Negro art" have arisen.[102] "Negro art," in other words, was racial strictly in a cultural—not a biological—sense. The African American artistic legacy was not simply a matter of birthright. Recall Woodson's Harvard teachers—Albert Bushnell Hart, Edward Channing, and Frederick Jackson Turner—who viewed a talent for self-government as the "common inheritance of all the members of the Anglo-Saxon race."[103] This genius for self-government coursed through the blood. African American heritage, in contrast, was an inheritance that had to be claimed through the self-conscious embrace of a shared history.

The "scheme of our culture is a confederation of minority traditions," Locke wrote in 1926, "a constellation of provinces and not a national sun concentrated in one blazing, focal position."[104] Locke and other black creators of anthologies articulated and advanced their own "minority tradition," staking out the territory of the African American province. This project required a multifaceted engagement with history. First, in collecting material for their anthologies, Locke and his colleagues engaged in historical reclamation. This was history as a process of recovery, as they combed the American Colonization Society archives at the Library of Congress for letters written by slaves or conducted oral histories with rural blacks in the South to collect spirituals. Second, in organizing the material for their anthologies, black anthologists used the tools and techniques of cultural history. They charted genres, schools, periods and transitions, paying close attention to the ways in which black primary sources reflected and shaped larger social forces and trends. Third, in publishing their findings, the African American editors of anthologies turned to history as a form of cultural credentialing. History provided the mark of authenticity for African American expressive traditions. In sum, history was a process, a chain of logic, and a finished product in the renaissance years—discovering, explaining, and announcing the New Negro heritage.

The era of anthologies came to a close in 1941 with the appearance of *The Negro Caravan: Writings by American Negroes*, a door-stopping volume that ran to 1,082 pages. Compiled by Sterling Brown, Arthur P. Davis, and Ulysses Lee, *Negro Caravan* featured eight main sections, including poetry, folk literature, drama, speeches, pamphlets, and letters and biography. (Woodson, Benjamin Brawley, James Weldon Johnson, and Robert Kerlin were all acknowledged for their pioneering anthologizing efforts.) The collection, the preface explained, aimed to "present a truthful mosaic of Negro character and experience in America," emphasizing the key works that had most influenced "American Negroes" and "Americans as a whole."[105]

While the editors were not afraid to discuss "Negro character and experience," they completely disavowed the term "Negro literature." According to Brown, Davis, and Lee, it simply did not exist. Black writers, the editors maintained, wrote "in the forms evolved in English and American literature," having been influenced by broad literary trends such as sentimental humanitarianism, realism, and experimentalism. The "spirit" and "form" of Frederick Douglass's writing, for instance, had much more in common with the writing of William Lloyd Garrison than with the texts written by Phyllis Wheatley or Booker T. Washington. The editors also believed that the term "Negro literature" encouraged critics and readers—black and white alike—to slot writing produced by blacks into "an alcove apart," with the next logical step a "dangerous" double standard of judgment. Ironically, *Negro Caravan* anthologized Alain Locke's introductory essay to *The New Negro*—the quintessential statement of the virtues of a distinctive African American province. So it was an anthology of anthologies and more than large enough to contain contradictions.

CHAPTER FOUR

The New Negro Goes to School

In his 1940 autobiography, *The Big Sea*, Langston Hughes famously summed up the Negro Renaissance as follows: "The ordinary Negroes hadn't heard of the Negro Renaissance. And if they had, it hadn't raised their wages any."[1] Although it would be difficult to argue with Hughes about the wages issue, he was mistaken about the extent to which "ordinary" black folks had been touched by the renaissance. The study and celebration of black history at segregated schools, especially through the vehicle of Negro History Week, broadcast the renaissance far and wide, bringing its poetry, literature, drama, and music to black communities across the country. Far beyond the glittering parties, literary salons, and small journals, the renaissance found its largest audiences, not to mention some of its most eager participants, in schools. Virtually absent from the scholarly literature on the renaissance, schools were in fact key sites of artistic appreciation and expression, and educators, especially women schoolteachers, were some of the renaissance's most important emissaries. By moving the renaissance "beyond Harlem," paying attention to "ordinary" folks (not just cultural elites), and stressing the educational dimensions of the renaissance, this chapter amplifies the findings of the newest scholarship on the renaissance, which has aimed to expand "the frame of the New Negro experience temporally, geographically and conceptually."[2]

"Awakening" was the "key metaphor" of the renaissance, according to Geneviève Fabre and Michel Feith, editors of *Temples for Tomorrow: Looking Back at the Harlem Renaissance*. The "common project" of renaissance artists, Fabre and Feith contend, was an attempt "to control the image of black people in an assertion of pride in the face of political oppression and stereotyping."[3] Race pride, of course, rests on a foundation of race consciousness; more specifically, the identification of individual blacks with African Americans as a people—or, to use the vocabulary of the renaissance era, the identification of individual Negroes with *the* Negro. In celebrating an African American heritage and narrating a shared journey from Africa to the New World, the most important work of the association in the renaissance was its contribution to the self-conscious realization of African Americans as a people, as a group with a unique history and a valuable culture.[4] A burgeoning historical consciousness animated the new race consciousness.

NEGRO HISTORY WEEK

In March 1925, Du Bois wrote to his friend John Hope, president of Atlanta University, to bring Woodson to Hope's attention as a possible candidate for the Spingarn Medal, a prestigious award annually conferred by the NAACP on an outstanding race man or woman.[5] "Woodson is not a popular man," Du Bois stated bluntly at the beginning of his letter. "He is, to put it mildly, cantankerous." Nonetheless, Du Bois asserted that Woodson had carried out "the most striking piece of scientific work for the Negro race in the last ten years of any man that I know," running a historical journal almost single-handedly, founding a publishing association, and bringing out a respected series of scholarly volumes. "At the same time," Du Bois emphasized, "he has maintained his integrity, his absolute independence of thought and action, and has been absolutely oblivious to either popular applause or bread and butter."[6]

Woodson received the Spingarn Medal on June 29, 1926, at the annual NAACP convention in Chicago. The renaissance was in high gear, Langston Hughes having just proclaimed the week before that younger Negro artists "now intend to express our individual dark-skinned selves without fear or shame" in a watershed essay called "The Negro Artist and the Racial Mountain." Prior to the medal ceremony, Du Bois delivered an address devoted to making sense of the cultural politics of the renaissance, outlining a hard-nosed aesthetic philosophy in which truth, beauty, and racial uplift would be inextricably fused. "All art is propaganda," Du Bois famously declared in what would turn out to be an incendiary statement when it was published in the October issue of *Crisis* as "The Criteria of Negro Art." Partway through the speech, Du Bois paused to pay tribute to Woodson. Urging black artists to face their "own past as a people," Du Bois said that Woodson had been hugely influential in helping African Americans take stock of their past, "of which for long years we have been ashamed, for which we have apologized." "We thought nothing could come out of that past which we wanted to remember," Du Bois continued, "which we wanted to hand down to our children." "Suddenly, this past is taking on form, color, and reality and in a half shame-faced way we are beginning to be proud of it."[7]

After Du Bois received an "ovation of the sort rarely yielded by a Chicago audience" and the mayor delivered a few short remarks, John Haynes Holmes conferred the medal. Holmes, Unitarian minister, founding member of the

NAACP, and ardent pacifist, introduced Woodson with a short speech. "We discover today that we are looking into the shining face of the New Negro," Holmes said, "now making his way out there in the fields of science, literature, art, and so on, shoulder to shoulder, heart to heart, with all men everywhere." "Negroes have discovered themselves to be a people and glory in that fact," Holmes announced.[8]

The official Spingarn citation did not mention the recently inaugurated Negro History Week, although Woodson had already written that its invention was "one of the most fortunate steps ever taken by the Association."[9] The precise circumstances surrounding the creation of Negro History Week remain murky, although Woodson claimed that it was his own idea.[10] The designation of certain weeks as, for example, "Cleanup Week" or "Fire Prevention Week" to promote particular issues was not uncommon at the time. Indeed, shortly before he died in 1915, Booker T. Washington helped to launch "National Negro Health Week."[11] In 1920, Woodson had delivered a speech to the black fraternity Omega Psi Phi in Nashville, urging its members to pay more attention to black life and history. Shortly thereafter Omega Psi Phi launched Negro History and Literature Week. Perhaps motivated by the fraternity's decision to replace Negro History and Literature Week with the more present-oriented Negro Achievement Week in 1925, Woodson inaugurated Negro History Week in 1926.[12] Whatever the reason, Woodson had clearly decided that "a more spectacular gesture was needed to reach the large public."[13] He chose the second week of February to honor the birthdays of both Abraham Lincoln (February 12) and Frederick Douglass (who chose Valentine's Day as his birthday).[14] This week must have been a strategic choice, meant to capitalize on the interest surrounding the annual Lincoln-Douglass birthday celebrations held by black cultural, community, and historical organizations, including the Bethel Literary and Historical Society.[15]

In the inaugural Negro History Week pamphlet, Woodson addressed the following question of "why the Negro in history?" at length: "If a race has no history, if it has no worthwhile tradition," Woodson said, "it becomes a negligible factor in the thought of the world and it stands in danger of being exterminated." Consider, Woodson said, the author who writes a book called *New Freedom*, making a thinly veiled reference to President Woodrow Wilson. When somebody asks the author how he can square his anti-Negro policies with his new progressive doctrine of freedom, he replies that "he was not thinking of the Negro when he wrote [the] book." Likewise, consider that when the order is given for the training of "all young men" for military service, a black man applies only to be told that "the principles involved in the war concern only white men" or that a bond issue is passed to improve educational facilities, but the black community is denied its fair share. So what if the Negro is "handicapped, segregated, or lynched," Woodson said, paraphrasing the point of view of the bigot, "for the Negro is nothing, has never been anything, and never will be anything but a menace to civilization."[16] Consequently, according to Woodson, the Negro had to convince the world that his history was equally as glorious as that of any other race or resign itself to a permanent status of subservience. No matter that the greatest scholars were saying that there was "no such thing as race in science" and that there was no scientific evidence to support "such myths as the inferiority and superiority of the races." These truths would have little impact if limited to academic discussions. "There must be an actual demonstration," Woodson said. "The Negro must learn his past and publish it to this prejudiced world."[17]

Race prejudice, Woodson stressed, was not something inherent in human nature but rather a learned response, "the inevitable outcome" of constantly teaching that blacks had not made any meaningful contributions to the advancement of humankind.[18] The Negro, Woodson insisted, must take his rightful place as a race among races, a people among peoples. In a phrasing that Woodson repeated in dozens of articles, essays, and speeches, the study of black history would ensure the recognition of the Negro alongside "the Hebrew, the Greek, the Latin and the Teuton."[19] Recognizing the worth of "the Negro" was as vital for blacks as for whites. According to Woodson, blacks too often had the "attitude of contempt for their own people," as a result of biased textbooks that emphasized black inferiority.[20] Woodson was alert to the potential for black history to replace antiblack bias with a self-aggrandizing black chauvinism. During Negro History Week, Woodson said, "We should emphasize not Negro History, but the Negro in history." "What we need is not a history of selected races or nations," Woodson explained, "but the history of the world void of national bias, race hate, and religious prejudice."[21] Negro History Week, then, was built on a foundation of cultural pluralism in the Lockean vein. Given the "interrelations of the races," learning about different cultures was an essential part of a well-rounded education. Nobody should consider himself educated, Woodson explained, until he "learns as much about the Negro as he knows about other people."[22]

In the inaugural Negro History Week pamphlet, the association suggested that Negro History Week programs emphasize the history of prominent laborers, inventors, soldiers, artists, businessmen, educators, and ministers of African descent.[23] The commemoration of exemplary individuals in different domains—the roll call of accomplished blacks in poetry, the hall of fame of innovative blacks in science, the exhibits A, B, and C of outstanding blacks in business, and so on—became a fixture of Negro History Week celebrations. The Negro history pantheon included exceptional black men and women from all over the world. Members in good standing throughout the Negro Renaissance period included Toussaint L'Ouverture, Alexandre Dumas, Samuel Coleridge Taylor, Benjamin Banneker, Sojourner Truth, and Booker

A PAGE FROM OUR HISTORY

Published In Observance Of The 15th Anniversary Of
NEGRO HISTORY WEEK

BOOKER T. WASHINGTON

FREDERICK DOUGLASS

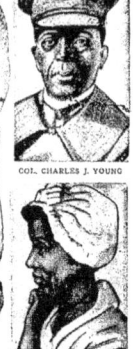
COL. CHARLES J. YOUNG

PHYLLIS WHEATLEY

TOUSSAINT L'OUVERTURE

DRED SCOTT

BERT WILLIAMS

MADAM C. J. WALKER

MRS. I. B. WELLS BARNETT

ALEXANDRE PUSHKIN

ALEXANDRE DUMAS

THE ASSOCIATION for the Study of Negro Life and History, headed by Dr. Carter G. Woodson, has designated February 11 to 18 as Negro History Week. In keeping with this observance the Chicago Defender is herewith publishing a "Page From Our History."

We are not contending that the 11 characters presented are the only men and women of achievement, but rather that they are representative of our rich heritage. In commemoration of the fifteenth anniversary of Negro History Week, we suggest that you clip this page and place it among your souvenirs.

When New York university's Hall of Fame committee meets this year Frederick Douglass, abolitionist leader and statesman, will be among those considered for a place in the chamber. Douglass was born February 9, 1817 and died February 20, 1895. As an abolitionist orator his influence was felt throughout the nation. He also edited a newspaper, "The North Star."

* * *

Booker T. Washington (1858-1915), founder of Tuskegee Institute, is credited with having revolutionized the system of education in the western hemisphere. He taught the theory that all labor should be dignified. His address at the Atlanta Exposition in 1895 sounded the keynote for both races in the southland. He graduated from Hampton Institute in 1875 and founded Tuskegee in 1881.

* * *

Col. Charles Young (1865-1919), who distinguished himself as a soldier in the Spanish-American war, was a graduate of West Point military academy. When the United States entered the World war, despite his physical fitness and military genius, he was sidetracked from going to France and instead was sent to Africa where he died of fever in 1919.

* * *

One of the greatest soldiers that the world has known was Toussaint L'Ouverture who has been called the "Black Napoleon." He liberated Haiti in a 10-year struggle against the French, Spanish, and English, and laid the foundation for the present republic. L'Ouverture was born in 1747 and died in 1803, the victim of a plot perpetrated by Napoleon.

* * *

The first American woman to win literary acclaim was Phyllis Wheatley whose poems were widely read both in America and England during the latter part of the eighteenth century. Phyllis was born in Africa and brought to America where she was sold as a slave to a Boston family. During her short lifetime of 31 years she traveled extensively in England.

* * *

Egbert Austin "Bert" Williams was one of the world's greatest comedians, whose appearances both in Europe and America won him wide acclaim. He has often been rated as the world's greatest comedian. He was able to evoke laughter from the most stolid.

* * *

Little is known about the life of Dred Scott, a Missouri slave who sued for his freedom on the grounds that he had been carried to a free state. In 1857 the United States Supreme Court handed down its famous decision, stating that Scott was not a citizen and could not sue and that he could be taken wherever his master chose. It is believed that this decision did more to hasten the Civil war than any other single act.

* * *

Mme. C. J. Walker, founder of Mme. Walker manufacturing company, makers of hair preparations and other cosmetics, was pioneer in the field of beauty culture among members of the Race. She amassed a fortune of which she gave liberally to philanthropy.

* * *

Mrs. Ida B. Wells Barnett, for whom a 10 million dollar Chicago housing project has been named was a native of Mississippi and was best known as a journalist and lecturer against lynching. When she was chased out of Memphis, Tenn., because of the stand taken by her newspaper, she came to Chicago where she continued to fight for the cause of the Race. She lectured in Europe as well as in the United States. Mrs. Barnett died in 1931.

* * *

Perhaps the greatest poet that Russia has produced was Alexander Pushkin whose works are the classics of the Soviet Union. His statue as shown at bottom left stands in the public square of Moscow.

* * *

Alexandre Dumas, the French novelist whose "The Count of Monte Cristo" has been translated into several languages, is recognized as one of the world's greatest literary figures.

The lives of the men and women mentioned on this "Page From Our History" together with hundreds of others that might be mentioned indicate the potentiality for true greatness which our group possesses, and should serve to give us courage and inspiration to carry on.

This article from the February 1940 *Chicago Defender* presented eleven "men and women of achievement," demonstrating the race's potential for "true greatness" as well as a racial consciousness that reached beyond the borders of the United States to encompass the diaspora. The newspaper editors suggested that this "Page from Our History" be clipped and displayed among readers' souvenirs.

(*Chicago Defender*)

T. Washington. Starting no later than 1927, the association sold high-quality images of these and other "distinguished Negroes," arranged by groupings such as "Negro Women of Distinction," "Negro Artists," and "Negro Statesmen."[24] In honor of the fifteenth anniversary of Negro History Week, the *Chicago Defender* printed a photo gallery of eleven men and women of achievement, including Phyllis Wheatley, Frederick Douglass, and Ida B. Wells, as well as Dumas, Pushkin, and L'Ouverture. The editors suggested that this "Page from Our History" be clipped and displayed among readers' souvenirs. The eleven figures represented the race's remarkable promise, according to the *Defender*, and "should serve to give us courage and inspiration to carry-on."[25]

Given the aim to demonstrate the race's potential for greatness, that the roster of black history "builders and heroes" included black people from across the globe should not be terribly surprising.[26] (Haiti and Liberia figured prominently in Negro history textbooks and celebrations, serving as evidence of the fitness of black people for democratic citizenship.) This wide-angle view, however, was not only intended to prove the "capability of Negro blood," as Du Bois put it in his original essay on the talented tenth. It was also meant to demonstrate the New Negro's strong diasporic consciousness, which posited that people of African descent shared a cultural heritage as well as a common struggle against white supremacy. Placing L'Ouverture side by side with Douglass, as the *Defender* did, linked the two men as comrades-in-arms, one who had waged war against a colonial power and the other who had battled slavery.

Negro History Week celebrations were not populated exclusively by the "heroes and heroines" of the race.[27] The annual celebrations included other elements that stressed a more democratic and inclusive conception of history. Starting with the 1928 celebration of Negro History Week, the association encouraged members to collect local historical records and send them to its D.C. headquarters, where they would be "preserved under fire proof protection."[28] As Woodson put it elsewhere, "In old advertisements, letters, receipts, bills of sale, deeds, wills, diaries, and the like, the history of the Negro lies buried."[29] The Negro, Woodson said, can never "make a case for himself . . . as long as he throws the facts away."[30] The association received thousands of primary source documents.[31] Those that were valuable were added to a collection that Woodson donated to the Library of Congress, now known as the Carter G. Woodson Collection of Negro Papers and Related Documents.[32] Whether or not their documents made it into the Library of Congress, those association members who participated in archival campaigns had the experience of seeing themselves as historical actors. With participants envisioning how their personal, family, and community documents might be used to record the larger story of the race, this project encouraged a historical consciousness.

It also reinforced the association's commitment to a bottom-up social history that rejected the fusty definition of history as past politics.

While the association's campaign to collect archival materials from its membership lasted only a few years, local history became a staple of Negro History Week celebrations. Based on guidelines provided by the association, students researched, wrote, and frequently performed community histories. They had the look and feel of Du Bois's Atlanta University studies in miniature, focusing on the history of a community by exploring different domains such as the "Negro in Business," the "Negro Church," and the "Negro Common School." If local histories tended to be simple and celebratory, they nevertheless encouraged students to examine their communities through a historical lens, prompting them to consider change over time and to think about the institutions that linked together the residents of their neighborhood, town, or city. Of the local histories that made it to the printing press, Woodson remarked that they "are not intended for vacation reading but they are valuable." "They may not be beautifully printed but they are printed," he continued, "and the world must take note of the facts thus made available."[33]

BROADCASTING THE RENAISSANCE

The association launched Negro History Week just as the renaissance was hitting its stride. From 1926 through the late 1930s, thousands of Negro History Week events across the country highlighted contemporary African American art, music, and literature. It was at Negro History Week events that many African Americans first encountered one of Langston Hughes's poems, first heard one of the spirituals sung by Paul Robeson, or first saw the paintings of H. O. Tanner. The association attached detailed bibliographies to its Negro History Week promotional materials, which circulated in the thousands. These bibliographies offered nearly comprehensive coverage of works pertaining to African American art, music, literature, and drama.[34]

Negro History Week celebrations were, to a large extent, patterned after the annual meetings of the association. From the inaugural meeting in 1917, the association's annual gatherings regularly featured performances of African American music, drama, and poetry as well as academic papers about the same. The typical Negro History Week program included a mix of speeches, lectures, biographical sketches, oratorical contests, poetry recitals, and music as well as dramatic performances. There was no attempt to draw bright lines among the different components of Negro History Week—history, literature, art, and drama melded together into one continuous celebration. Within a single historical pageant, for instance, there might be a reenactment of a Frederick Douglass speech, a musical rendition of a spiritual, and a reading of a Langston Hughes poem.[35]

Educators, especially women teachers, were indispensable to the success of Negro History Week.[36] (It was teachers, Woodson said, who had the "vision of reaching the youth and the masses.")[37] In their capacities as teachers, librarians, archivists, and bibliographers, African American women played vital roles as "disseminators, popularizers, researchers, and catalogers" of black history. Often working behind the scenes, African American women were "custodians of culture at the grassroots level," working with the "whole community" to "impart historical ideas and shape collective memory."[38]

The black press was instrumental in helping to popularize Negro History Week, lauding Woodson and the association while reporting on different Negro History Week programs. Urging its readers to join heartily in the inaugural Negro History Week celebration, the *Pittsburgh Courier* said that "we must have a background.... The Negro must dig into the bowels of the dead past and find for himself the records of his forefathers, long since buried beneath the tramping feet of other races." The next year the *Courier* gamely suggested that an evening spent with almost any one of the volumes published by Associated Publishers was much more entertaining than "an evening spent over a whist table, a pool table or a punch bowl."[39] The following reports from the black press provide an outline of the growth of Negro History Week and a representative sample of the ways in which the association promoted and expressed the art and energy of the renaissance from the mid-1920s to the mid-1930s.

In February 1926 Negro History Week celebrations were held under the auspices of social welfare agencies, recreational establishments, businesses, churches, and schools. They were concentrated in Washington, D.C., Maryland, Delaware, and West Virginia. Negro History Week "went over big" in Baltimore this first year, the *Afro-American* reported, with celebrations taking place in more than two dozen public schools. In school-wide assemblies across the city, students heard lectures on African American music and literature and sang spirituals as well as "Lift Every Voice and Sing." School corridors were adorned with pictures of prominent black musicians and artists as well as examples of their work. Vocational students at school no. 103 carried out a study of African life and art. At schools 113 and 115, students gathered around a Victrola phonograph to listen to the majestic voices of Marian Anderson and Roland Hayes over the occasional hiss and pop.[40]

In 1927, the *Norfolk Journal and Guide* reported that "elementary history of the Negro has become more of common knowledge among the race than at any previous time in history."[41] By the early 1930s, Negro History Week celebrations had spread as far afield as Atlanta, Boston, Detroit, Kansas City, Louisville, New York, Philadelphia, and Toledo. A large audience gathered at the Siloam Presbyterian Church in New York in 1928 for the Pi Kappa Delta–sponsored Negro History Week program dedicated to "the works of present day Negro writers and artists." At a Negro History Week event in Philadelphia that same year, Albert C. Barnes, a collector of "Negro art" from around the world, was the principal speaker. In 1932, students at David T. Howard Junior High School in Atlanta performed Georgia Douglas Johnson's play "The Plumber" in order to " illustrate the topic 'The New Negro.'"[42]

The annual association meeting in Washington, D.C., in the fall of 1933 showcased the New Negro in the nation's capital. A weeklong exhibition on Negro art at the Smithsonian was a highlight of the conference. Locke opened a session called "An Afternoon with Negro Artists" at the Smithsonian with a lecture about African art and the American Negro. Nearly five hundred people crowded into the National Museum auditorium to listen to Locke interpret the antique bronzes of Benin and the ironworks of Gambia. The Negro art exhibition, viewed by some eight thousand visitors over the next week, featured African sculpture as well as work by contemporary professional artists, including watercolors by Lois Mailou Jones and oil paintings by James Porter. It also featured artwork by the students of Atlanta and Howard Universities as well as the pupils of D.C. public schools and the Free Art Workshop and Studio of Harlem. Accompanying the artwork were two exhibits on music, one profiling African achievements in music and the other documenting black composers in America.[43] Linking the art of "the ancestors" to the efforts of contemporary artists, the exhibition reinforced the notion of blacks as a people, whose affinities reached across the Atlantic.[44] At the same time—and with the imprimatur of the Smithsonian no less—the exhibition announced that the next generation of artists was poised to make its own mark.

Outside of the Smithsonian, the meeting featured "An Evening with Negro Poets." Benjamin Brawley delivered an address titled "The Promise of Negro Literature," followed by readings by five "outstanding poets," including Sterling Brown, who had just released his sparkling collection of poems entitled *The Southern Road*. A music gala was the capstone event of the D.C. meeting. Clarence Cameron White, concert violinist, composer, and music director at the Hampton Institute, performed several pieces by Coleridge Taylor to "a whirlwind of applause" and followed that with one of his own compositions as an encore. "With grandeur [and] with proud bearing," coloratura soprano Lillian Evanti sang an aria from *La traviata*. After being called back from the wings, she sang Burleigh's "Lord I Want to Be," with "a depth of feeling [that] electrified" the audience.[45]

Galas with top-flight talent were more the exception than the rule for Negro history celebrations. Spirituals sung by the Teachers College Glee Club rounded out the special 1933 Negro History Week program broadcast from radio station WSFA in Montgomery, Alabama.[46] In 1935, the main event at the Kentucky State College Negro History Week celebration was a program called "Picture of Slavery," which featured the testimony of former slaves

In the 1930s, woodblock artist James Lesesne Wells provided prints for several books published by Associated Publishers. Originally published in the 1930 book *Plays and Pageants from the Life of the Negro*, this image was later repurposed for Negro History Week. (Historical Society of Pennsylvania)

themselves. The college library also mounted a special exhibition of books by or about Negroes as well as scenes from Negro history drawn by the art students.[47] By the mid-1930s, interest in Negro History Week had spread farther into the lower South as well as into rural areas, and Woodson would declare that the celebration was truly national in scope. Florida Normal and Industrial Institute, for example, launched an elaborate Negro History Week celebration in 1935. S. F. Johnson from the Department of Music delivered a lecture on African American singers and composers, which was followed by musical selections from the Glee Club. English instructor N. A. Ford discussed the literary contributions of authors such as Cullen, Fauset, and Brown. Miss Ruth Smith delivered a lecture focusing on the significance of the Harmon Foundation to Negro art, thereby bringing the news of Harlem to St. Augustine. Dean of the college and instructor of history R. Barney Chavis said that the institute aimed "to establish courses in Negro history with a view toward promoting racial solidarity as a means of obtaining for the Negro the rights of human beings."

According to one report, more than three-quarters of black colleges and universities offered courses in black history by 1934. Over 80 percent of them observed Negro History Week.[48] At this time, there were branches of the association—some fledgling, some thriving—in more than a dozen cities, including New York, Philadelphia, and Detroit as well as Kansas City, New Orleans, and Houston. Scores of Negro history clubs, meanwhile, sprouted up in black schools across the country, from Massachusetts to Texas. In a nod to the abolitionists who had used the term "wide awake" to describe people who were committed to ending the evil of slavery, Woodson frequently invoked the term "wide-awake Negroes" to refer to those African Americans who recognized the importance of black history in forging racial solidarity.[49] This "wide awake" contingent increased dramatically during the 1920s and 1930s, during which there was an unprecedented explosion of interest in the study of black history, its pursuit becoming "one of the central planks of black public life."[50]

While it must have been thrilling for Woodson to watch black history take hold in black communities, he sometimes fretted that its popularity would dilute the integrity of the historical content. In fact Negro History Week had become so popular by the late 1930s that Woodson felt compelled to call out the "charlatans" who were exploiting the demand for Negro History Week materials with "tawdry books supposedly bearing upon Negro history." He likewise disparaged the fashionable Negro History Week–themed dances and teas, charging them with having more flair than substance, and ridiculed local committees who pocketed the proceeds from Negro History Week events instead of donating them to "the cause."[51] Woodson lambasted a Negro History Week event he attended in 1935 where the faces of the local pastor and school principal were projected on a screen next to those of Booker T. Washington and Frederick Douglass. "History on this occasion," Woodson said, "had descended to the level of vainglory and self-admiration."[52] From Woodson's point of view, self-congratulatory or shoddy history was worse than no history at all.

At the same time that black history enjoyed unprecedented visibility, Woodson and his colleagues remained convinced that there were still far too many African Americans who were ashamed, wary, or dismissive of their own history. Woodson reserved his most acid criticism for the black educators who claimed that Negro history should not be made a part of the official curriculum or, worse still, that the Negro had no worthwhile history to begin with. "Professor Bonehead Doesn't Teach Negro History in Ham Fat University," one of Woodson's caustic newspaper subtitles from 1932 read. It was accompanied by the following byline: "Dr. Woodson Ridicules Timid and Uninformed Pedagog in a College Professor who Ignorantly Declares 'Negroes Haven't Done Much.'"[53] In 1940, the *Chicago Defender* decried the fact that "countless numbers of our own group" had read *Gone with the Wind* and other anti-Negro literature, while the historical work of Brawley, Du Bois, and Woodson was too often ignored.[54] That same year, William Pickens, journalist and director of NAACP branches, said that African Americans were reluctant to look into their own history because they had "been ignored and cheated so long in print." "They fear," he said, "they may be exposed instead of revealed."[55]

ETHIOPIA IS AWAKENING

If the parade—headed up by Civil War veterans—was the main event at the Emancipation Day celebrations of the late nineteenth century, the pageant was the marquee event at Negro history celebrations in the 1920s and 1930s. Du Bois's sprawling three-hour production *The Star of Ethiopia*, which had its debut at the National Emancipation Exposition in New York in 1913, was the "first pageant on Negro history," according to Alessandra Lorini.[56] Tracking the journey of the race from the pharaohs of Egypt to Robert Gould Shaw's Fifty-Fourth Regiment and emphasizing Negro "gifts" such as iron and fire, faith and hope, *The Star of Ethiopia* was the ur-pageant of the Negro Renaissance, serving as the basic template for the multifarious Africa-to-the-New-World dramatic productions. The Africa of Du Bois's pageant was not a dark continent but rather the very cradle of civilization. It featured a stunning historical cast, ranging from the queen of Sheba and Mohammed to L'Ouverture, David Walker, and Harriet Beecher Stowe. Reinforcing the major theme of "cultural gifts," music played a central role in the pageant, with spirituals as well as modern black compositions showcased.[57]

Star of Ethiopia and the black history pageants that followed should be understood in the context of a broader "pageantry craze." David Glassberg maintains that the historical pageant was the "characteristic form" for representing public history in the Progressive Era. Pageants were forms of "local boosterism, patriotic moralizing, and popular entertainment." Most historical pageants chronicled "local community development," and blacks were notably absent from the overwhelming majority of them. Following Du Bois's model, when blacks created their own pageants, they took an expansive view of their community, often reaching all the way back to African antiquity to locate its source. Geographical and temporal boundaries fell away, as the authors of black pageants celebrated the history of *the race* rather than the history of *a place*.[58]

Where did black history begin? In charting the past of a race, there is no clear starting point. Examining the place of Africa in race textbooks dating from the early twentieth century can help in tracking the evolving and sometimes contested ideas about the origins of black history. Most authors who wrote race textbooks in the 1910s saw Africa largely through the prism of slavery. Starting in the mid-1920s, however, Woodson and the association increasingly depicted Africa as a "cultural anchor" for African Americans.[59] Yes, Africa served as the point of embarkation for the transatlantic slave trade, but it was so much more.

C. V. Roman's *American Civilization and the Negro* (1916) barely took notice of Africa, except to lament how "anti-Negro logic" attributed to the "Americans of African descent all the savagery of Africa" but denied them "all the past glories of the civilization of that ancient and mysterious land."[60] John Cromwell's *The Negro in American History* (1914) was similarly taciturn on the subject of Africa. In the book's first chapter ("Discovery, Colonization, Slavery"), Cromwell noted that blacks served as sailors in early explorations of the New World but added that this "exception but proves the rule that the Negro came to the New World as a slave, . . . stolen from or bought on the West Coast of Africa to add to the wealth of America by his toil as bondman and laborer."[61] The first image in the body of the text was a shackled woman being branded on the Gold Coast.[62] For Cromwell, enslavement in Africa was synonymous with the origins of black history. The same was true for Benjamin Brawley, whose *A Social History of the American Negro* (1921) devoted just four short paragraphs to Africa in the book's first chapter, "The Coming of Negroes to America." The middle passage itself was crucial to Brawley's interpretation of black history, as indicated by a section of the book called "The Wake of the Slave Ship."

In contrast to Roman's, Cromwell's, and Brawley's abbreviated and murky presentations of Africa, Leila Amos Pendleton's account in *A Narrative of the Negro* (1912) was expansive, featuring some half-dozen chapters on the continent, including "Geography of Africa," "Ancient Civilization," and "Modern Africa." Pendleton presented a Janus-faced interpretation of African history; she lauded the achievements of Africa in "ancient times" and called the continent "our Motherland," but at the same time, she indicated that there was a limit to the heights of African civilization. Of the noteworthy statues that had been unearthed in Ethiopia, Pendleton wrote, "These statues were erected to the idols or gods whom the people worshipped because they did not know the *true* God." African history, in Pendleton's view, was half-charmed, half-damned, and ultimately served mostly as a prelude to the arrival of "native Africans" to Virginia in 1619.[63]

The first edition of *The Negro in Our History* (1922) included, in Woodson's own words, only a "cursory examination" of Africa. In the book's first chapter ("The Negro in Africa"), Woodson painted a picture of Africa that, recalling Pendleton's account, combined "dark continent" and "brightest Africa" discourses. For example, echoing one of the most lurid elements of travelers' accounts, Woodson asserted that "cannibalism" was practiced south of the equator, noting that Africans found "the taste of human flesh [did] not differ materially from that of other animals." Barbarism was only part of the African story, however, as Woodson also touted the glories of ancient Africa, highlighting the achievements of the "Ethiopian and Egyptian empires," as well as the "centers of civilization" that thrived in kingdoms like Ghana and Songhay. In contrast to the textbooks written by his colleagues, Woodson's account did not place quite as strong an emphasis on the importance of Africa as a staging ground for the slave trade. Instead, he stressed the extent to which African history demonstrated that "the Negro" was fit for civilization. ("It is clear," he wrote, "that African culture prior to the exploitation of the new world was in many respects like the culture of Europe.")[64]

With the release of the fourth edition of *The Negro in Our History* in 1927 (which included "four or five times as much about the Negro in Africa" as the first three editions), Woodson began to embrace African history with more vigor and sophistication.[65] He foregrounded the cultural dimensions of African life in the past and present, providing discussions of African institutions such as education, marriage, and religion, as well as of African art such as Bantu rock painting. This fourth edition also saw an injection of cultural relativism in the section on Africa, with Woodson delivering an extended refutation of the "belief that differences in culture imply superiority or inferiority."[66] This was a far cry from the values-laden language about Africa in the opening line to Woodson's first book. "Brought from the African wilds to constitute the laboring class of a pioneering society in the new world," *Education of the Negro* began, "the heathen slaves had to be trained to meet the needs of their environment."[67] Woodson had gradually developed a very different view of Africa, informed by new scholarship in history, cultural and physical anthropology, and linguistics, among other disciplines. By the mid-1930s, he no longer used the term "primitive" as a scientific term to describe African cultures and peoples. There was no such thing as "primitive art" or a "primitive people," Woodson averred. Historically-contingent, culturally-bound assumptions and standards underwrote the use of the word "primitive," assumptions that did not apply across different "races or nations."[68]

In a 1935 newspaper article, Woodson lamented that the "great achievements" of the Negro in Africa remained unknown and unacknowledged—this ignorance was fueled, according to Woodson, by the mistaken impression that black history "began in 1619 when some divinity created a handful of Negroes and loaded them on a Dutch vessel to be sold at Jamestown."[69] The central importance of Africa and African history for African Americans was consolidated—and described in great detail—in Woodson's 1936 publication, *The African Background Outlined; or, Handbook for the Study of the Negro*.[70] While this textbook repeated the vindicationist themes from *The Negro in Our History* (particularly the refrain that "the African is the father of civilization"), it concentrated much more extensively on "African survivals" and the "migration of culture."[71] One of the central arguments in *The African Background Outlined* was that "the African background of the Negro offers an explanation for much which we find today among the Negroes of the United States."[72] Woodson pointed to specific words with African roots as well as specific social roles such as the "conjure doctor." He also outlined strong links between secret societies in Africa and the various fraternal organizations developed by African Americans. American literature, Woodson claimed, was heavily "indebted to the African Negro"; myths, folktales, and fables such as the "Brer Rabbit" stories were "literary treasures" with clear African origins.[73]

After the initial burst of black historical pageants stimulated by *The Star of Ethiopia* and the multitude of semicentennial emancipation fairs and expositions held between 1913 and 1915, the fervor for black pageants subsided until it was rejuvenated by the advent of Negro History Week. Pageants created in the 1920s and 1930s expressed many of the same themes and revealed many of the same tensions found in the race textbooks, including the idea of Africa as both a homeland and launching site of a holocaust, as well as Africa as a backward continent that was simultaneously studded with evidence of glorious past civilizations. Ethiopia and Egypt were praised for their monumental cultural achievements. The unspeakable tragedy of the slave trade was never too far removed, though, from the paeans to iron smelting and regal figures like Queen Nefertari. Echoes of the "dark continent" discourse continued to reverberate—in references to "Darkest Africa," the "dusky people" of Africa, that "vast unknown land of the Sphinx" and so on—but the most powerful message was that Africa had been a home to the ancestors.[74] And that, in spite of the "sorrow and despair" associated with the middle passage, chains were not the only bonds linking African Americans to Africa.[75]

Two of the most popular pageants performed during Negro History Week were originally published in 1924—YWCA secretary Dorothy Guinn's "Out of the Dark" and African Methodist Episcopalian minister Edward McCoo's "Ethiopia at the Bar of Justice." "Out of the Dark" had four acts: "The Rape of a Continent," "Slavery," "A New Day Breaks," and "What of Today." The pageant's title not only signaled the journey from enslavement to emancipation but also the illumination of the historical record of the Negro, too often blotted out by "race hatred."[76] The last act surveyed the Negro's "gifts" to American music, art, literature, and science. After reciting Claude McKay's poem "If We Must Die," the Chronicler notes the appearance of Langston Hughes, Countee Cullen, and other promising young poets. Meta Warrick Fuller's sculpture

Ethiopia Awakening is then unveiled, symbolizing, the Chronicler explains, "the soul of this people today." "Ethiopia is awakening," the Chronicler says, "She is beginning to realize the glories of her past and the possibilities of her future."⁷⁷ A potent symbol of the broader "brightest Africa" discourse, representations of Fuller's *Ethiopia Awakening* sculpture often appeared in Negro history pageants.⁷⁸

In an informative analysis of Negro history pageants, Clare Corbould asserts that in many of them "Africa was personified specifically as Ethiopia."⁷⁹ In my reading of these pageants, however, it appears that Ethiopia is most frequently a symbol of the race, a personification of all peoples of African descent. Ethiopia was just one of the many allegorized characters in McCoo's "Ethiopia at the Bar of Justice," along with the likes of Haiti, Liberia, Opposition, Public Opinion, and Mercy. (The Declaration of Independence and the Thirteenth, Fourteenth, and Fifteenth Amendments also had starring turns.) When the play opens—"Time: Now. Place: Anywhere, Everywhere"—Opposition charges Ethiopia with drawing heavily upon the "Bank of Civilization" in spite of having nothing on deposit there. In response, Ethiopia summons History. "I am willing to rest my case upon her records," Ethiopia says. History then recites a litany of glorious African and African American deeds and contributions that overwhelm Opposition and change Public Opinion, starting with the assertion that Ethiopia was a powerful and civilized nation nearly a millennium before the birth of Jesus Christ.⁸⁰ In this litany, all people of African descent are referred to as Ethiopians.

"I am Crispus Attucks," a tall young man announces, "an Ethiopian." "My blood was the first to flow for American freedom," Attucks declares."⁸¹ "The children of men who die for their country," he continues, "should be given the opportunity to live for their country."⁸² Moments later a black veteran enters from stage left. "I represented Ethiopia in the Civil War," he says. "I am a Union soldier":

> I fought for Old Glory. Who says that Ethiopia has done nothing for civilization? When civilization was about to fail in America, Ethiopia saved it. When State after State was seceding; when the stars were falling in quick succession from our flag, I and my black comrades stepped beneath them, caught them upon the points of our bayonets and pinned them back to Old Glory!⁸³

Many scholars have identified contradictions in the ideology of the renaissance between "an emphasis on racial pride" and "a desire for integration into American society."⁸⁴ The historical plays and pageants of the renaissance era, however, demonstrate how race pride and Americanism could operate in harmony rather than in conflict. "Ethiopia at the Bar of Justice" included a remarkable array of musical selections from "John Brown's Body Lies a Mouldering in the Clay" and "Nobody Knows the Trouble I see" to the national anthems of Haiti and Liberia. After the Sorrow Songs and the paeans to the era's two black republics (which survived even though "Opposition has raged against them"), the pageant concluded with the unfurling of a large American flag, Love's exhortation to "dwell together in unity beneath the Stars and Stripes forever," and the full cast belting out the "The Star Spangled Banner."[85] McCoo simultaneously affirmed the legitimacy of black music (not to mention the pain endured by African Americans), the significance of Africa and the African diaspora, and the ultimate allegiance of African Americans to the United States.[86] For many white Americans in the 1930s, black skin excluded a person from membership in "civilization" writ large and "the Union" of the United States in particular. Black history in the association vein emphatically rejected both of these exclusions by relying on a defense that fused Ethiopia and Old Glory, race consciousness and Americanism.

The performance of plays and pageants often served as the culmination of Negro History Week celebrations at schools, colleges, and universities. While some teachers adapted published plays from the two Associated Publishers anthologies, others wrote their own, frequently in collaboration with their students. Negro history–themed productions ranged from the five-minute playlet with a single actor to the three-hour epic with a cast of dozens. One teacher reported that students became so engrossed in historical dramatizations that they "unconsciously began addressing each other by the names of characters they were representing—such as Harriet Tubman, Crispus Attucks, Booker T. Washington, or Frederick Douglass."[87] Drama has always been a significant venue for the articulation of group identity. In enacting histories of "the race," students extended and strengthened their own race consciousness.

It is helpful to think about Negro History Week celebrations in segregated black schools and communities as happening in the black counterpublic sphere or "free spaces." (Writing about the black museum movement of the 1960s and 1970s, Andrea A. Burns uses the term "free spaces" to describe locations where "marginalized groups can acquire greater self-respect, strengthen their sense of dignity and independence, and work toward a heightened sense of communal and civic identity.")[88] During Jim Crow, schools were often the lodestars of black communities, providing a place for public gatherings ranging from sporting events to voter registration campaigns. Negro History Week programs at schools obviously engaged students, teachers, and administrators but they also attracted the attention of parents, extended family, and other members of the surrounding community. As Corbould argues, by encouraging local communities to put together their own programs, Negro History Week powerfully linked "community building and the study of the past."[89] The capstone Negro History Week performances at black schools drew African American audiences in the hundreds and the thousands, frequently becoming annual highlights of a city or town's social calendar. This means that from 1926 through the late 1930s, hundreds of thousands of African Americans took part in Negro History Week celebrations at black schools.

It was not uncommon for teachers to send Woodson copies of original plays and pageants. Myrtle A. Brodie, head of the History Department at Second Ward High School in Charlotte, North Carolina, sent Woodson a copy of a pageant called "The Negro Builds a Pyramid." Several friends who had seen the pageant had urged her to have the play copyrighted, she explained to Woodson, requesting his "candid opinion" of the production. "The Negro Builds a Pyramid" was based on material collected over a three-year period by the Second Ward Woodsonian History Club. On May 6, 1935, it was performed by the entire Second Ward senior class (over one hundred students) in front of a crowd of five thousand at the Charlotte City Armory as the crowning event at commencement.[90]

When the curtains came up at the Armory, the stage was empty with the exception of a tall row of bleachers; the soft strains of "Go Down Moses" could be heard in the distance. With Father Time performing the task of narrating the history of the Negro from "ancient days" to the present, the pageant opened with six slaves collapsing at the base of the bleachers, spent from bearing the lash of the Egyptian pyramid builder Cheops.[91] "The Negro Builds a Pyramid" then raced over centuries of history from Egypt through the middle passage to the Civil War and the Negro Renaissance. The humming and then singing of Negro spirituals by the glee club interspersed each scene. A diverse cast of historical figures—including L'Ouverture, Benjamin Banneker, Madame C. J. Walker, Jack Johnson, and Du Bois—formed a steady stream onto the stage, joining the others on a tall row of bleachers to form a human pyramid. (Among the Negro Renaissance artists, musicians, and writers represented were Fauset, McKay, Cullen, Burleigh, Robeson, and Tanner.) The creation and development of black churches, black schools, and black businesses were presented as cornerstones of the structure. Singing "Tramping" and clad in "flowing gowns of pastel colors," the glee club now appeared onstage to outline the human pyramid. "Behold, the Negro builds a pyramid," Father Time announced, pointing out that "there is still much to be done to complete its construction and beautification." "Come, O children of Ethiopia and make your contribution to this massive structure." The pageant closed with the singing of "Lift Every Voice and Sing."[92]

W. Fitzhugh Brundage asserts that student participation in black history celebrations at black schools helped them to acquire "a strong sense of collective identity and responsibility that offset competing fissures of class, religious affiliation, and neighborhood *within student bodies*."[93] This same dynamic, I submit, was evident on a larger scale, with Negro History Week celebrations acting to heal cleavages of class, region, gender, politics, and so on *within the race*. Note that the pyramid formed by the Second Ward seniors included all different kinds of people of African descent—slaves and luminaries, southerners and northerners, women and men, teachers, athletes, and artists. "The Negro Builds a Pyramid" exemplified the expansive approach to contributionism that was characteristic of Negro History Week celebrations. The pageant heralded the kinds of historical figures foregrounded by nineteenth-century black history chroniclers and orators—especially religious workers, educators, abolitionists, and soldiers—while adding contemporary artists, actors, composers, and writers and accentuating their importance. Similarly, the traditional black history themes of freedom, citizenship, and progress were present in abundance but accompanied by a new emphasis on African American cultural heritage and artistic production. Both a figurative and literal expression of historical continuity and racial solidarity, "The Negro Builds a Pyramid" united African Americans under the banner of a grand narrative—an epic, arduous and not-yet-completed journey from slavery to freedom.

Like many similar pageants, "The Negro Builds a Pyramid" concluded with the audience joining the players to sing "Lift Every Voice and Sing." It was an apt selection, as it evokes a historical journey of biblical proportions and significance:

> We have come over a way that with tears has been watered
> We have come, treading our path through the blood of the slaughtered
> Out from the gloomy past, till now we stand at last
> Where the white gleam of our bright star is cast

These and other lyrics express a hard-earned racial solidarity, forged in a crucible of "bitter" suffering. The suffering, however, is accompanied by the promise of redemption: "Facing the sun of our new day begun/Let us march on till victory is won." In "Lift Every Voice" as well as epic black history pageants, the shared experience of a harrowing journey coupled with the will to persevere helped to transform black Americans into a recognizable "we." The celebration of black institutions (from churches and schools to newspapers and banks) as well as black artistic traditions also fortified the sense of African Americans as a people. In singing folk songs, hymnals, and spirituals and reciting poetry and the like, black participants in Negro History celebrations not only acknowledged but also performed their own cultural heritage.

THE *NEGRO HISTORY BULLETIN*

That the renaissance was made possible by publishers such as Knopf, Boni and Liveright, and Harcourt, Brace as well as periodicals such as *Survey Graphic*, *Crisis*, and *Opportunity* has long been recognized. The publishing wing of the association deserves to be added to this list, with its textbooks, anthologies, and watershed periodical *Journal of Negro History*.[94] Arguably the most important association publication in terms of enlivening the renaissance, though, was the *Negro History Bulletin*, a monthly magazine for schoolteachers and schoolchildren.[95] Launched in 1937, the *Negro History Bulletin* publication schedule followed the school calendar, with the first issue of every year being published in October and the last in June. The bulletin linked together a network of professional black historians and educators and served as a clearinghouse for information on the study of Negro history. It also served as the main outlet for the promotion of Negro History Week. In addition to an in-depth cover article, assorted articles about the teaching of Negro life and history, most often written by teachers themselves, and stories, pageants, and plays written by schoolchildren, each issue of the bulletin included the following regular columns: "Persons and Achievements to be Remembered," "School News," "Book of the Month," and a quiz of approximately twenty questions about the previous month's issue.[96] Within a matter of years, subscribers affectionately referred to the bulletin as "our magazine."[97]

The advent of the bulletin continued the push for more grassroots black support for the association, which had started with the creation of Negro History Week. Woodson sought to disseminate Negro history to the widest possible audience, but he also looked to Negro History Week and the bulletin with bottom-line considerations in mind. The association had received considerable financial support from the Phelps-Stokes Fund, the Carnegie Corporation, and the Laura Spelman Rockefeller Memorial fund in the 1920s, but this funding had essentially dried up by the early 1930s.[98] The bulletin was one means of attracting more association members—and with a larger membership came more financial contributions.[99] By the time the bulletin was founded, black educators were already the backbone of the association. Indeed, more than half of Virginia's thirty-nine hundred black teachers contributed to the association during a 1935 fund-raising campaign.[100] Woodson hoped that the bulletin would extend this crucial support.

From its first issue, African American women were a "dominant force" on the magazine's editorial board and comprised the majority of its writing staff.[101] Along with Woodson and Charles Wesley, Fisk graduate Florence R. Beatty, Washington, D.C., author Gertrude Parthenia McBrown, and Howard University alumna Helen A. Whiting made up the five original members of the editorial board.[102] Schoolteachers, including Boston public school teacher Wilhelmina M. Crosson, Washington, D.C., teachers (and sisters) Beatrice Fleming and Marion Jackson Pride, and Chicago schoolteacher Mavis B. Mixon, wrote regular columns for the bulletin. Howard University professor Eva Dykes contributed articles on poetry and other topics, while head librar-

THE NEGRO HISTORY BULLETIN

Published Monthly

Vol. II, No. 6 WASHINGTON, D. C. March, 1939

The Negro in Art From Africa to America

ART probably appeared first in ornaments for the body. Personal adornment, developed to the extent of becoming decorative art —decorating not only the body itself but clothing, jewelry, tools and utensils. It is difficult to think of a time when man did not appreciate the value of making a good appearance —of decorating himself and things about him so as to improve their attractiveness.

The ideas as to what was attractive and what was not differed in ancient times as they do now. Even today there are tribes which believe that it adds to personal adornment to wear heavy earrings,which pull the lobes of the ears downward and make them grow into flaps resting on the shoulders. There are women who consider it an improvement of their beauty to put large disks in their lips so that they grow wide enough to look like saucers or plates. Beauty, then, is a relative rather than an absolute term.

Among the most striking manifestations of African art are often pointed out the excellent small sculptures in stone, wood, ivory or modeling in wax, clay or metals. In all these the Negroes have shown themselves to be "ingenious workers, powerfully helped by inspiration, a sharp sense of detail and a very profound conception of the form to be given to their ideas," says Delafosse in *Negroes of Africa*.

"At the side of religious art or art for art's sake there is another main in which the Negroes are pastmasters: It is that of the industrial arts, represented by work in clay, wood, iron, copper, gold, leather, and textiles. Ornamented and glazed pottery of all forms and dimensions, finely carved spoons, gongs, staffs of command, low or high stools each one of which is a masterpiece of patience and elegant execution; harmoniously slender paddles, straight or curved knives having handles made of wood incrusted with metal, lances with multiple blades of graceful contours, axes for war or parade, small objects in molded or hammered copper; golden jewelry of filigree or made in a mold, rings and bracelets with delicately wrought openwork, cushions, saddles, boots and sheaths in supple leather diversely colored; curious boxes of oryx skin, trays and mats colored reeds, fabrics of cotton, wool or raffia that are veritable tapestries with motifs as sober as they are varied and of a very sure taste in coloring, silk or cotton embroideries of a singular richness and happy design."

It is said, however, that what we speak of as fine arts developed first in connection with architecture. In the organization of social and political institutions it became necessary to have palaces for the kings and nobles, temples for the priests, and shops for the mechanics, artisans and merchants. In the course of time, too, the lowest elements of the population, the serfs and slaves, represented in our day by the laboring classes, had to have better homes than the hovels in which the first had to live. As these buildings became more important and useful they were made more and more beautiful by decorations. This task required deep thought.

In these buildings, especially in temples, were often placed statues. By and by, as in ancient Egypt, these sculptures were changed to portrait statues to preserve for posterity the images of the deceased. In the course of time such portrait statues were used to adorn public buildings without special likeness of any individual character. This sculpture is seen as such today in the form of what is called relief. Relief here means the projection of the sculptured figures from the wall on which they are carved. If the figures project half of the circumference the sculpture is high relief. If the figures lie practically flat it is called low relief. If they are midway between the high and the low the form which they assume is called half relief. Other designations are employed for the degree of projection. When color was added to the figures lying flat on the surface on which they were made sculpture became painting. Such wall paintings were referred to later as murals.

Sculpture reached its first high level in ancient times under the Egyptians. The Sphinx near the Pyramids of Ghizeh, the Temple at Luxor, the Rock Temple at Abu-Simbel and the Obelisk show the greatness of Egyptian architecture and sculpture. Building upon what these Africans achieved in Art, the Greeks handed down through the Romans the Doric, Ionic and Corinthian styles of architecture which Europeans and Americans have modernized.

While the Egyptians were modified racially by Europeans and Asiatics who brought them some new ideas to change somewhat their way of doing things the native Africans below the Sahara and in the interior could not be reached by such influences. Yet in their way the Africans of the interior produced certain types of art which some believe passed through Egypt into the Mediterranean world to influence modern European nations and Americans of today. Some of the earliest efforts of the Africans in both architecture and sculpture appear in the fine figures of Sher-

EXPRESSING THOUGHT THROUGH SCULPTURE

Copyright 1939, by the Association for the Study of Negro Life and History, Inc.

In the late 1930s and early 1940s, Howard University painter and professor Lois Mailou Jones served as the in-house artist for the *Negro History Bulletin*. Her illustrations—such as "Expressing Thought Through Sculpture" reproduced here—often graced the magazine's cover.
(Association for the Study of African American Life and History)

ian of the Howard University Moorland-Spingarn Research Center Dorothy Porter offered her archival research skills and occasional articles.[103] Howard University painter and professor Lois Mailou Jones served on the magazine's advisory board as well as its in-house artist. Her "watercolor paintings, prints and sketches," in Pero Dagbovie's estimation, "added a sophisticated and artistic dimension to the magazine."[104]

Jones contributed numerous illustrations to volume 2 of the bulletin, which spanned the 1938–39 academic year and focused on the history of African American achievements in poetry, novel writing, drama, music, painting, and sculpture. The nine issues offered a panoramic account of the social and cultural history of African American art and artists. They also presented a virtually exhaustive "Who's Who" of the Negro Renaissance, placing the renaissance's central figures and works in a rich historical matrix. The main article of the poetry volume, entitled "Negro Poets, Singers in the Dawn," traced the history of African American poetry from the devotional poems of Phyllis Wheatley to the protest poems of Frances Ellen Watkins Harper and the blank verse of Langston Hughes. The author called on educators to develop in their children an appreciation of Negro poetry, noting that the love of reading poetry might even turn into a fondness for writing poetry.[105]

After poetry came fiction. The December 1938 edition of the bulletin focused on black novelists, noting that the rise of authors such as Jessie Fauset, Zora Neale Hurston, and Claude McKay marked "an epoch in the Negro in fiction." The feature article, "Negro Novelists—Blazing the Way in Fiction," included one- to two-paragraph synopses of the renaissance's leading works of fiction, from Hurston's *Their Eyes Were Watching God* to McKay's *Home to Harlem*.[106] Drama was the subject of the New Year's issue, which sketched the history of the Negro in drama from the minstrel tradition to the triumphant Broadway performance of Charles S. Gilpin in *Emperor Jones*. A short article on the Negro theater exhorted black communities and schools to create little theaters in order to promote the dramatic arts.

The special Negro History Week edition of the bulletin for February 1939 focused on African American music, profiling a variety of musicians, singers, and composers, including Marian Anderson, Roland Hayes, and Nathaniel Dett. Rejecting the contention that black music was merely imitative of European music forms, the author, most likely Woodson, said that only African Americans had produced novel and distinctive American music, including the "Negro spirituals, jubilee, ragtime, jazz, and blues." "The Negroes of this country are the real creators of an American art," the author declared. Although the author recognized that jazz was "novel and distinctive," he certainly did not care for it, remarking that "at its best jazz is an effort of a few Negro composers who would like to imitate the barbaric melody found among the Africans in the depths of the forest."[107]

If jazz still remained suspect to some in the talented tenth set in the late 1930s, the spirituals had been fully embraced as music of the highest caliber. In the October 1938 issue of the bulletin, Miss L. A. Duckett of Washington, D.C., described how her sixth-grade class had become interested in the history of Negro music after hearing a radio broadcast of Negro spirituals, as sung by the Howard University Glee Club. Under the guidance of Miss Duckett, the children generated a list of questions to guide a study unit about Negro musicians and their music. These questions included "How did the Spirituals arise?" "Why are Spirituals important today?" and "How much did the music of the past influence the music of today?" Among other projects, students interviewed "old persons for aid in getting information," read stories about singers such as Roland Hayes, learned to sing some of the spirituals, and wrote original stories, poems, songs, and plays, sharing their work with other children in the school. The unit culminated with the publication of a class booklet.[108]

The bulletin not only provided a forum for teachers to write in with updates about their classrooms but also supplied an outlet for students to publish their own original work. For example, "Dramatic Summary of Negro History," written by sixth graders from the Twining School in Washington, D.C., was published in the April 1940 issue of the bulletin. The printed text was a remarkably sophisticated—even poetic—summary of black history from the middle passage up to the present. Twining School students repeatedly asked their readers to imagine what it must have felt like to walk in the shoes of their ancestors. "We must try and put ourselves in their places," they wrote about newly enslaved Africans. "They must have been sick at heart, ill, weak from the voyage, starved." This kind of vicarious identification is a consistent feature of the sixth graders' writing. Of the blacks who migrated from the South to the North, the students wrote, "We now see them in offices, in homes but the homes are theirs, in churches beautifully decorated with well dressed Negroes listening to the voice of their pastor, in schools studying, trying daily to achieve, aiming, ever desiring, ever struggling, always hopeful. You see, we are these Negroes."[109] The students self-consciously identified with the trials and triumphs of black people across oceans and centuries. At the end, they even wrote themselves into the "dramatic" story they recounted. While they learned something of, in Woodson's words, what "Negroes have thought and felt and done," they also identified themselves as partners in a shared African American struggle.[110]

The Negro history movement injected the art and creative spirit of the New Negro into segregated black schools, contesting the "Old Negro" notions that blacks were an inferior race, "devoid of all the characteristics that supposedly separated the lower forms of human life from the higher forms."[111] In Nathan Huggins's estimation, despite the best efforts of teachers, early twentieth-century segregated schools could not provide black children with a "rich, dense and mysterious sense of a past like that of traditional cultures." The "sophistication and beauty of African cultures were not yet understood," and quality materials documenting black history in the United States were in short supply.[112] With the support of the association, in the 1920s and 1930s, black students were taught for the first time on a large scale that African Americans had made significant contributions to American culture, especially with respect to its expressive dimensions. In the mid-1930s, a teacher from Campbell County, Virginia, testified that students were learning to appreciate the role that African Americans played in weaving together the national fabric. They were delighted to discover, the teacher reported, that African Americans had taken part in "such things as exploration, invention, literature, music, and art." In King William County, another Virginia educator explained that it was paramount for young students to understand that "the Negro has made a contribution to something other than crime." Black history provided a platform for the New Negro credo that African Americans "would be a people rather than a problem."[113]

Through the work of the association, thousands of African Americans across the country were exposed to the art of the renaissance. Thousands more wrote poems and short stories; still others participated in the production and performances of plays and pageants. Educators, especially African American women teachers, were some of the renaissance's signal interpreters, messengers, and creators. In spite of Hughes's claims to the contrary, many "ordinary" blacks at the time no doubt had a sense of living through a period of artistic efflorescence and cultural renewal. The association's participatory attitude toward history and art was crucial in this regard. It rejected a reverential, "please-do-not-touch" approach to history and art, in which the former was confined to textbooks and the latter to museum galleries. Woodson and his colleagues wanted African Americans, especially schoolchildren, to learn to see themselves as historical actors rather than mere witnesses to history. The Africa-to-America historical narrative helped to usher along this transformation. Embedded in this narrative was the journey from slavery to freedom, the development of black institutions, especially churches and schools, and the advent of distinctive strands of African American art, ranging from poetry to music. Although it postdates the renaissance, a personal account from Angela Davis illustrates the power of black history to forge a sense of African American identity and collective solidarity. It was during Negro History Week programs at the segregated schools of Birmingham she attended as a young girl in the 1940s and 1950s that, Davis recalled, she learned about people like Frederick Douglass and Sojourner Truth who "fought for Black people as a whole." "Within this stringently segregated environment," Davis said, "we acquired a sense of 'our people,' and of freedom as our people's destiny." She credited the lessons about the black freedom struggle conveyed by Negro History Week as crucial to her "early decision to protest racism."[114]

PART THREE

RACE
1942-1956

The discursive terrain of race is constantly shifting beneath our feet—sometimes subtly, sometimes dramatically.[1] In the years spanning World War II, this terrain was rocked by tectonic shifts. Discredited by the horrors of Nazi Germany, "scientific" racism retreated, replaced by a new antiracist consensus forged in the main by anthropologists, sociologists, and psychologists. The boundaries of American whiteness expanded, as Celts, Slavs, Hebrews and others joined the "Caucasian" ranks, a transformation accelerated and signaled by the ubiquitous images of the multicultural U.S. Army platoon made up of "Protestants, Catholics, Jews, southerners, westerners, and easterners, all of whom were white."[2]

With the race concept undergoing dramatic revision, race relations likewise saw radical reconfigurations. In 1943, there were 242 race riots in forty-seven cities across the country.[3] The following year, the term "American creed" entered the national lexicon with the appearance of Gunnar Myrdal's *An American Dilemma: The Negro Problem and Modern Democracy*.[4] World War II, fought in the name of "victory over tyranny" by a segregated army, presented a stark picture of the "American dilemma." "We want," Rayford Logan said, "the same equality before a court of law that we have before an enemy's bullet."[5] By the end of the war, racial discourse in the United States had settled on a black-white fault line. If World War II was "the first shot in what came to be called the Civil Rights Revolution," this revolution saw one of its most momentous victories a decade later with the 1954 *Brown v. Board of Education* Supreme Court ruling.[6]

These three intertwined developments, the dismantling of "scientific" racism, the rise of the "Negro problem" as the country's only real race question, and a burgeoning civil rights movement, informed the work of Woodson and his colleagues during the World War II years and beyond. Although race inevitably stands front and center in accounts of Jim Crow, many historians have treated race as a kind of gravitational force that simply acts to set limits on

African American aspirations, choices, and attitudes. One leading historical study of black intellectuals, for example, is structured around the following questions: "How did racial discrimination and prejudice shape the emergence and activities of African American intellectuals? How did race define them? How did race influence individual intellectuals' life choices and attitudes?"[7] These questions are important, to be sure. Nonetheless, they ignore the fact that while race was defining African American intellectuals, these same intellectuals were also defining race. Anthony Appiah, Mia Bay, and Vernon Williams Jr. are among the small group of scholars who have investigated how African American intellectuals have interrogated the meaning of the race concept.[8] African American historians and the "Negro history" movement are effectively absent from this literature. African American intellectuals and scholars are also almost always missing from the larger body of scholarly work on the intellectual history of race and racism. If you relied on Robert Wald Sussman's recent history *The Myth of Race: The Troubling Persistence of an Unscientific Idea* (2014), for example, you might be forgiven for thinking that African American thinkers played absolutely no role at all in shaping the development of racial discourse in the United States.[9]

The two chapters that follow aim to recover the rich conversations about race questions that were stimulated by the pursuit of black history in the period from the appearance of black pathologist Julian Herman Lewis's book *The Biology of the Negro* in 1942 to the publication of two essays on the *Brown v. Board of Education* Supreme Court decision by John Hope Franklin in 1956. Chapter 5 ("A Revision of the Concept of Race and of Racism") explores how Woodson and his colleagues addressed the twin issues of race and racism in the context of a racial liberalism that privileged psychological interpretations of prejudice and discrimination. The debunking of theories of racial inequality by social scientists during World War II encouraged the association to amplify its message that racial inferiority was a dangerous myth with no scientific basis. Revising the race concept required taking a close look at the nature of *the* race. What did it mean to be "Negro"? It proved to be nearly impossible for Woodson and his colleagues to answer this question without becoming mired in the confusions and paradoxes surrounding the concept of race. Were blacks defined by their heredity, their social status, or their cultural inheritance? Regarding the nature of racism, leading social scientists offered cogent arguments for the fundamental equality of peoples and races by emphasizing that races did not differ regarding their innate cultural and intellectual capacities, but they faltered when it came to explaining the root causes of obvious racial inequalities. In his watershed 1954 book *The Negro in American Life and Thought*, Woodson collaborator and Howard University historian Rayford Logan argued that racial inequalities were a result of rampant discrimination against African Americans in the domains of government, law, and business following the end of Reconstruction. As Logan demonstrated in an extended analysis that established the basic framework for "black image in the white mind" historical scholarship, this discrimination was aided and abetted by vicious caricatures of African Americans in newspapers and magazines.

Chapter 6 ("Look to the Roots": History Lessons for the Present) examines how the association used history as a tool of both orientation and adaptation. A historical perspective helped to make sense of a racial landscape experiencing dramatic reconfigurations, allowing researchers to chart the advent of the modern civil rights movement in the context of a long black freedom struggle. Professional historians, journalists, and artists alike drew connections between the nation's "wars for freedom" and the black freedom struggle, attempting to inject a patriotic glory into civil rights battles. The unanimous *Brown* decision was a momentous victory in the modern civil rights movement. Inserting itself into the arena of racial politics as never before, the association linked its mission to the school desegregation movement, believing that a fair, racially integrated history was the best foundation for a fair, racially integrated society.

CHAPTER FIVE

"A Revision of the Concept of Race and of Racism"

"Science knows no such thing as race." This was the opening line to Carter G. Woodson's epic, rambling draft entry on race for his never-completed *Encyclopedia Africana*. Written sometime during the 1930s or early 1940s, the draft, 170 handwritten pages, oscillates wildly between refuting and reinforcing race science. On one page, referring to the classification of races by physical features, Woodson said that "scientists have tried to do what most thinkers confess to be impossible, namely determine race as a group of people who have certain well marked physical characteristics in common." On another, Woodson included a lengthy and highly technical description of the cranial index, noting that with "rare exceptions this figure ranges between 65 and 90" and offering definitions for the tongue twisting terms "dolichocephalic," "mesaticephalic," and "brachycephalic."[1]

While acknowledging that drawing on the nomenclature used to describe races in Africa was "far from a scientific approach to the problem at hand," Woodson nonetheless devoted most of his entry on race to describing the "races of Africa" on a case-by-case basis, beginning with the Bushmen and continuing on to the Hottentots, Negritos, and others. Each entry started with a detailed inventory of the race's physiognomy. The Bushman, Woodson reported, has "slightly built but well-shaped limbs and small hands and feet." "The color of his skin," Woodson continued, "is a shade of yellow or yellowish-brown and it wrinkles easily." The catalog of each race's physical characteristics was followed by National Geographic-esque descriptions of the race's diet, dress, native languages, social organization, and cultural customs, from initiation rites to burial ceremonies. The Bushmen, for example, "live on game, edible roots and vegetables." Referring to the Bushmen as "decidedly cheerful," Woodson said that this "trait they freely express in dancing."[2]

Woodson's unpublished entry is a striking illustration of the many elements both explicitly and associatively linked to the notion of race, from physical appearance and temperament to language and culture. It reveals a convoluted construction of race that drew on multiple academic disciplines, including anthropology, geography, and linguistics. While Woodson noted, for example, that language played an important part in racial classification schemes, he also stressed that it was an "an uncertain factor." Next to this he had crossed out the following line: "Pure languages are as rare as pure races."[3] Woodson's attempt to write a definitive reference entry on race may be seen as emblematic of the confusion that surrounded the race concept during this period. Scanning the draft pages, one gets a palpable sense of Woodson's mounting frustration regarding the overwhelming contradictions inherent in the race concept. Read all 170 pages and the sensation one is left with is that of watching a person desperately struggle to get out of a maze—Woodson repeatedly presses forward, only to have to turn around and retrace his steps after encountering yet another dead end.

If the scientific basis of race remained unresolved in the late 1930s and early 1940s, there was an emerging consensus among social scientists that science provided no empirical support for theories of racial inferiority. The association embraced the findings of the new antiracism, citing the work of key figures such as Franz Boas, Ashley Montagu, and Ruth Benedict. Indeed the association incorporated the social sciences–approved doctrine of racial equality into its most important public outreach efforts, including Negro History Week and the *Negro History Bulletin*. As the "Negro problem" began to eclipse any other concerns about race in the United States, Woodson and his colleagues grappled with the meaning of the term "Negro" itself. Their attempts to define "Negro" reveal some of the inherent limitations of the antiracist consensus as well as the lack of clarity about the race concept characteristic of the era. Not satisfied with the frequently abstract or schematic accounts of prejudice and discrimination offered by anthropologists, sociologists, and psychologists, Woodson and his colleagues turned to history to examine the roots of racial inequality. What, they asked, accounted for the uniquely unequal status of African Americans in the United States?

Among Woodson's coworkers in "the cause," Charles Wesley, Rayford Logan, and John Hope Franklin advanced some of the most original and compelling answers to this question. Charles Harris Wesley (1891–1987) was born in Louisville, Kentucky, the son of an undertaker and a seamstress. Handsome, charismatic, "almost artistic in mien," Wesley was a member of Fisk University's famed Jubilee Singers as an undergraduate, performing at the 1911 World's Fair in Boston. He became an ordained minister in 1919 and served as a pastor to three African Methodist Episcopal churches in Washington, D.C. One of Woodson's closest collaborators, Wesley received a PhD in history from Harvard in 1925, turning his thesis into the 1927 book *Negro Labor in the United States*. Wesley taught at Howard University from 1913 to

1942, when he left the district to become president of Wilberforce University. According to Michael Winston, he was one of the primary "shapers of Negro opinion in the 1930s and 1940s." "A marvelous speaker with a great baritone voice," Wesley was a perennial favorite at association meetings, frequently delivering the keynote address.[4] In addition to publishing pioneering histories of African American fraternal and racial uplift associations, he also was one of the first scholars to carry out extensive research on the long black freedom struggle.[5] During the 1940s and 1950s, Wesley published nine articles in the *Journal of Negro History* and six articles in the *Negro History Bulletin*. He served in the largely ceremonial post of president of the association from 1950 to 1965 and then in the more active role of executive director from 1965 to 1972.

Rayford Whittingham Logan (1897–1981) was born in Washington, D.C., the son of domestic workers (his father worked as a butler for Frederic Walcott, Republican senator from Connecticut). He attended the M Street High School, where Woodson was his teacher. "Dr. Woodson," Logan said, "gave us an appreciation of French literature and civilization, especially through Balzac's *Eugenie Grandet* and *Cousin Pons*, that stands out as one of the most memorable in [my] whole school and college life." After graduating Phi Beta Kappa from Williams in 1917, Logan served in France during World War I, earning the rank of lieutenant in the 372nd Infantry Regiment, one of only a small number of black combat units. Active in pan-Africanism as well as the NAACP during the interwar period, Logan received a PhD in history from Harvard in 1932. He worked as a research assistant to Woodson in the early 1930s, filling in as Woodson's "alter ego" when Woodson could not make a speaking engagement. Hired by Wesley, Logan had a long career at Howard, teaching history there from 1938 to 1968.[6] He was reserved and had an extremely serious demeanor, which some people interpreted as hauteur.[7] A methodical scholar, on the first day of class, he would tell his students to "hang your superlatives on this hook," gesturing to the coat hanger on the classroom door. Disciplined and exacting, he would start his day with a cigar in the morning and work until noon; after a one-martini lunch he would return to work until 6:00 p.m. on the dot.[8] A keen observer of race relations in the United States and abroad, Logan wrote frequent articles for the black press on issues ranging from discrimination in the State Department to the American military occupation of Haiti. When Woodson died in May 1950, Logan took over as interim director of the association and editor of the *Journal of Negro History*, positions he held for eighteenth months.[9] Two of Logan's watershed books are central to the analysis that follows—his 1944 edited collection *What the Negro Wants* and his 1954 monograph *The Negro in American Life and Thought: The Nadir, 1877–1901*.

Named in honor of Atlanta University president John Hope, John Hope

Franklin (1915–2009) was born in Rentiesville, Oklahoma.[10] "Lean and elegant, poised, and cosmopolitan," some of the younger black scholars that he influenced referred to him as "the Prince."[11] As a young boy, he saw his father's law office burn to the ground during the 1921 Tulsa race riot. In spite of the violence and segregation in "the American race jungle," Franklin's parents "always insisted that race was irrelevant as far as one's personal development was concerned." "They even taught me to believe that I could be," he said, "the first Negro president of the United States."[12] Franklin graduated from Fisk University in 1935 and received a PhD in history from Harvard in 1941, where he occasionally washed dishes at one of the exclusive Harvard eating clubs in exchange for a free meal. Franklin taught at Howard from 1947 to 1956, developing a close professional relationship with Logan in his time there. In 1956 he left Howard to chair the History Department at Brooklyn College, becoming the first African American historian to receive a tenured appointment at a predominantly white institution.[13] Franklin's textbook *From Slavery to Freedom: A History of American Negroes* is widely recognized as his most enduring achievement. Originally released in 1947, it is now in its ninth edition.[14] Unlike Wesley and Logan, Franklin was not one of "Woodson's boys," in the sense of being a protégé. Nonetheless, the association was pivotal to Franklin's early development as a scholar. During the 1940s and 1950s, he was a regular participant in its meetings and published five articles in the *Journal of Negro History*. After the publication of *From Slavery to Freedom*, Franklin recalled that Woodson gave him more public recognition, "graciously indicating a collegial relationship between us that was both flattering and rewarding."[15]

THE FIFTH FREEDOM

The early years of the Negro history movement coincided with the "Nordic vogue" and the push for immigration restriction by eugenicists and other advocates of 100 Percent Americanism. "Scientific" racism peaked in the mid-1920s with Madison Grant's eugenics-informed racial theories "immensely popular among academics, politicians, policy makers and the public."[16] Large-scale intelligence testing exploded during this period, accompanied by a torrent of research studies investigating the relationship between race and IQ. Carl Brigham's seminal 1923 volume *A Study of American Intelligence* concluded that the results of the massive intelligence testing conducted with army recruits during World War I supported the "race hypothesis" advanced by Grant, particularly with respect to the "superiority of the Nordic type."[17] Nineteen-twenty four saw the passage of two landmark pieces of legislation suffused with race "science": Virginia's Racial Integrity Act, which banned interracial marriage and made it a felony to falsely register one's race and the quotas-based national Immigration Restriction Act, which extended from "the conviction that the American nation was, and should remain, a white nation descended from Europe."[18]

As "scientific" racism crested, a school of thought that was intensely skeptical of "crude racial determinist thinking" was beginning to form.[19] German-American anthropologist Franz Boas was the school's mastermind and center of gravity. Boas's 1911 text *The Mind of Primitive Man* was the opening salvo in a long and protracted battle against "the idea that race and heredity were the primary sources of differences found in the mental or social capacities of human groups."[20] This battle was waged largely on the terrain defined by advocates of racial hereditarianism. Boas and his colleagues collected the same kind of anthropometric data favored by hereditarians, including measurements of skin color, lip thickness, and head length; their interpretations of this biometric evidence, however, contested some of the basic assumptions undergirding "scientific" racism such as the stability of race types. In the interwar period, papers published by scholars attempting to refute biological determinism often had titles like "Correlation of Length and Breadth of Head in American Negroes" or "Growth of Interpupillary Distance in American Negroes."[21] No matter the intentions of Boas and his colleague, their reliance on "physical traits for classification purposes" tended to reinforce the "biologically based race concept."[22] (Vernon Williams Jr. goes as far to say that Boas never fully escaped his "imprisonment in the racist paradigm of late nineteenth-century physical anthropology.")[23]

It took some twenty-five years for Boas's ideas to gain a fair hearing beyond small circles of left-leaning social scientists, intellectuals, and artists. The association was on the vanguard in this respect, as evidenced by the fact that conference meetings were held and *Journal of Negro History* articles were published that challenged "scientific" racism from a Boasian perspective starting in the early 1920s. Woodson himself had a deep appreciation for Boas's scholarship, favoring, especially, Boas's insight that "acquired cultural habits" should not be mistaken for "fixed hereditary characteristics."[24] Alain Locke and W. E. B. Du Bois were both heavily influenced by Boas as well—their frequent writings on race and culture helped to disseminate Boas's ideas to African American audiences.[25] Publications by Boas protégées Melville J. Herskovits, Ruth Benedict, and Margaret Mead made a mark inside and outside academe in the 1930s and 1940s. Their work was instrumental in terms of legitimizing and popularizing an unqualified racial egalitarianism—replacing skepticism about the veracity of specific empirical claims supporting racial inferiority with certainty that *all* of the assertions advanced by the racial inequality school were indefensible.

Starting in earnest in the mid-1920s, the association engaged in a rich, ongoing, and often critical dialogue on the topic of race "science." The *Journal of Negro History* reviewed dozens of books from this voluminous literature, including titles such as *Mongrel Virginians: A Study in Triple Race Mixture, Up from the Ape,* and *Characteristics of the American Negro*. Woodson and his colleague found that most of the books about race or the "race problem" were "unscientific production[s] composed of guesswork, hearsay, and misinformation."[26] Indeed, they hailed the occasional book that relied on "actual data" rather than "dogmatic, ex cathedra assertions," celebrating those "studies of the Negro" illuminated by the "searchlight of science."[27] Two main points came to the forefront in the *Journal*'s race literature reviews (most of which were written by Woodson himself): first, that "in the sense of pure breed there is no such thing as race" and, second, that there was no convincing evidence to support the theory that "the Negro is mentally inferior to the white man."[28]

Annual meetings of the association regularly featured panels that challenged the conventional "scientific" wisdom about race and racial hierarchies. The most frequently addressed topics were intelligence, miscegenation, and physical anthropology, which were three of the most important subjects examined by race theorists.[29] At the 1924 association convention, Hampton Institute president James E. Gregg delivered a paper called "The Question of the Superiority and Inferiority of the Races." Gregg discussed an investigation at Hampton, which aimed to test the mental capacity of "the black, the brown, the mulatto and the octoroon students." The results were "so insignificant or confusing" that no conclusions could be drawn.[30] The terms "mulatto" and "octoroon" signal a concern with so-called racial amalgamation. In 1928, Woodson presided over a session called "Negroes and Mixed Breeds," which examined the extent to which blacks had "interbreeded with the other races in America." The following year, Harvard University physical anthropologist E. A. Hooton delivered a complementary paper called "Negro White Mixtures in the New World," which argued that "race admixture of white and blacks is not biologically detrimental."[31]

At the 1930 annual meeting, Howard University sociologist W. O. Brown echoed Hooton's skepticism regarding the alleged dangers of miscegenation, proclaiming that we are all a "sort of racial hash, even the Nordics." In his talk, titled "Racial Inequality: Fact or Myth," Brown made liberal use of scare quotes, archly dismissing the "data" and "evidence" presented by proponents of what he called the "racial inequality cult." Taking a stance at odds with the association's belief in the power of education, Brown noted that it was in some ways "foolish" to try and reason with advocates of racial inferiority, given that they did not subscribe to the inequality creed "because of the compulsion of facts but rather because of emotional needs," especially the need to rationalize discriminatory practices.[32] Brown's position was a rare acknowledgment in an association forum that facts alone might not be sufficient to overcome racial bias.

At the same 1930 conference, T. Wingate Todd, a professor of anatomy, delivered a talk called "An Anthropologist's Study of Negro Life" in which he reviewed and refuted the work of early anthropologists who had found racial differences in the structure and size of the brain. Remarking that all kinds of misunderstandings resulted from "monkeying with Anthropology," Todd rejected the proposition first advanced by nineteenth-century French anatomist Louis Pierre Gratiolet that the cranium of blacks "closes itself upon the brain like a prison," interrupting normal cognitive development. Research conducted with Cleveland schoolchildren, Todd reported, proved with "overwhelming evidence" that "both races travel at the same speed" in terms of their physical development.[33] Schoolteacher Joseph Rhoads reinforced Wingate's findings, asserting in a 1933 conference talk ("Teaching the Negro Child") that there was no scientific evidence supporting the view that the "Negro race" was "distinctive" in terms of its biological makeup. Rejecting the claims of "propagators of race phobia" such as Grant and Lothrop Stoddard, Rhoads said that the Negro was emphatically not "enslaved by the absolutism of heredity or a fixed racial destiny."[34]

If the association began to challenge the notion that race set natural biological limits as early as the mid-1920s, it was not until the late 1930s that the "old guard of strict biological determinism" started to fade away among the majority of social scientists, let alone among social reformers, business leaders, politicians, and the wider American public.[35] The appearance of Jacques Barzun's pioneering *Race: A Study in Modern Superstition* in 1937 was the first antiracist text to gain widespread attention. Alarmed by Hitler's rise to power, Barzun announced that the book's main objective was to "show how equally ill-founded are the commonplace and learned views of race."[36] In 1938, the American Anthropological Association passed a resolution stating that "anthropology provides no scientific basis for discrimination against any people on the ground of racial inferiority." The same year, a leading group of scholars affiliated with the American Psychological Association released a statement that psychologists had not discovered any "inherent psychological differences" associated with race. The statement emphasized that "no conclusive evidence" had been found for racial differences in "native intelligence."[37] Nineteen forty saw the release of Ruth Benedict's *Race: Science and Politics*, and Ashley Montagu's *Man's Most Dangerous Myth: The Fallacy of Race* appeared shortly after New Year's in 1942. Both books were best sellers.

It is important to clarify the intellectual foundations of the new antiracist position that emerged in the late 1930s and early 1940s. Its two key pillars were as follows: first, there were only three primary races in the world, Caucasian, Mongoloid, and Negroid.[38] There was therefore no validity to further differentiating this grand tripartite division into smaller groups such as Jews, Irish, and Slavs (or Bushmen, Hottentots, and Negritos, for that matter). Second, while race dictated physical appearance, it did not explain psychological characteristics, intelligence, or a people's cultural capacity. "The shape of the head is a racial trait," as *Races of Mankind* explained, "but whether it is round or whether it is long, it can house a good brain." The most important feature to remark on here is that the new antiracism did not reject the idea of race itself. "In the biological sense there do, of course, exist races of mankind," Montagu wrote in *Man's Most Dangerous Myth*.[39] The "myth" of race was that there were "superior" and "inferior" races. In short, race was real but racial hierarchies were not.

World War II, "with its emphasis upon democracy and its apparent opposition to racial superiority," as Wesley put it, brought the race question to the forefront. "The Negro wants a revision of the concept of race and of racism" was the number one item in a list of seven wants that Charles Wesley spelled out in his essay for *What the Negro Wants*, the watershed 1944 compilation edited by Rayford Logan. Even though the "doctrine of racism has no scientific foundation," it was still one of the most "dangerous of dogmas," Wesley explained. "Fascist racism" was responsible for discrimination against blacks in industry, labor unions, education, and the armed forces. The *Journal of Negro Education* review of *What the Negro Wants* identified the following proposition as one of the book's main themes: "There are no fundamental differences in races." "The Negro wants that understood!" the reviewer thundered.[40] If this proposition had been a leitmotif during the association's first twenty-five years, it became an all-caps banner headline during World War II.

In the mid-1940s, Negro History Week celebrations became occasions to broadcast the message of fundamental equality among the races. The "city, State and nation were made Negro History conscious" over the course of the weeklong celebration in 1944, the *New York Amsterdam News* reported. The "brilliant, massive and splendid" enterprise that was Negro History Week served as a vital corrective to the "execrable volumes and satanic works" produced by the likes of Arthur de Gobineau, Grant, and Stoddard. So too did the work of Boas, Benedict, and Jean Finot, accomplished scholars who had "smashed the pseudo-scientific propaganda of [these] false prophets" and their "false, deceptive and hellish doctrines about the Negro."[41]

The next year in New York, Ashley Montagu delivered a special Negro History Week lecture called "The Negro's Problem: The White Man." In his talk, later printed in the *Negro History Bulletin*, Montagu asserted that race prejudice combined class prejudice with a kind of color-based caste system, contending that ruling classes always clung to "a bastion of rationalizations and myths" that convinced them of the rightness of their position. Racism, Montagu said, invoking the term for the first time in the pages of the *Negro History Bulletin*, was "a disease," an "infection of the mind" by the misguided idea that blacks were biologically inferior. In their struggle to secure citizenship rights, Montagu told his overwhelmingly black audience that "science, truth, and humanity" were on their side.[42]

Montagu's appeal to "science, truth, and humanity" reveals a natural affinity between the mission of the association and the aims of Montagu and his like-minded colleagues. Association members and the antiracist anthropologists were both devoted to debunking what they regarded as malicious propaganda. Those daring to challenge the conventions of U.S. History 101 or the "Negro problem" had to confront formidable intellectual fortresses buttressed by respected—sometimes even renowned—authorities, whether the subject was, say, the history of Reconstruction or the relationship between race and IQ. The challenge was daunting, to put it mildly, and involved reckoning with, in Wesley's words, "absurd, irrational, and emotional arguments."[43]

Antiracist messages were not only declared during Negro History Week celebrations—they were also performed. The students of Washington High School in Reidsville, North Carolina, for example, presented a play called *Meet Your Relatives* during the 1947 Negro History Week celebration. Adapted from Ruth Benedict and Gene Weltfish's famous 1943 booklet *Races of Mankind*, the play opened with students comparing race hatred in the United States to "Hitler's pet ideas on the superior, super-duper Aryan race." Some in the United States even believe that "the yellow, the black and the red races are inferior." "We are going to clear up this mess once and for all," the students announced. And they did so "scientifically," using direct quotations and examples from Benedict and Weltfish's text.[44]

Readers of the *Negro History Bulletin* in the 1940s and 1950s received a steady diet of antiracist information through articles treating the newest scholarship in the fields of anthropology, sociology, and psychology. All of these articles addressed the nature-nurture debate, stressing that research in the social sciences increasingly demonstrated the power of environmental factors over heredity. In the 1945 article "Racial Criminality: Fact or Myth?," for example, Joseph Sandy Himes Jr. set out to refute the "persistent idea" that "social behavior is causally rooted in race." Himes, president of the Columbus, Ohio, branch of the association, explained that leading social scientists now rejected the "innate racial basis of behavior, criminal or otherwise." Yes, the black crime rate was disproportionately high, he acknowledged. But this relatively high crime rate was due to two main environmental factors: first, the poor "material conditions" of blacks, including subpar educational facilities and high rates of unemployment, and second, pervasive bias in law enforcement and the judiciary. Blacks, Himes reported, were not only more likely to be arrested than whites but they also received longer sentences than whites for the same crimes. While commentators had seized on "statistics to prove their beliefs," they failed to consider the "social situation from which behavior emerges." Race, Himes, concluded was a sociological fact, not a "biological reality."[45]

On October 28, 1945, a few short months after V-E Day, with Roosevelt's booming declaration of the "four freedoms" still echoing across the country, members of the association convened to hear the keynote address for the thirtieth annual convention in Columbus, Ohio. The title, "A Fifth Freedom for the Negro," must have intrigued expectant audience members as they waited for the talk to begin. As F. D. Moon, principal of the Douglass High School in Oklahoma City and the featured speaker, explained, the fifth freedom was the freedom from the doctrine of "innate inferiority." Sketching the history of race in the United States, Moon emphasized that when blacks were first enslaved, their subjugation was not justified in terms of innate inferiority. It was only during the antebellum period amidst burgeoning antislavery sentiment that intellectuals were first enlisted in the southern cause to advance rationalizations for slavery. "Enemies of the Negro," Moon said, "left a whole crop of pseudoscientific writings in the libraries of the nation, emphasizing racial differences." These pernicious antiblack writings were no longer being churned out at even a fraction of the previous pace, but their refrains continued to worm their way into hearts and minds. As Moon put it, "The song is ended but the melody lingers on."[46]

The widespread belief in black inferiority, according to Moon, had imprisoned both black and white minds, leading blacks to suffer from a lack of self-confidence and whites from delusions of grandeur. Blacks and whites alike, Moon contended, needed to come to grips with the "revolution in scientific thought on the dogma of racial inferiority," a revolution propelled by new advances in anthropology, sociology, and social psychology. Scientific investigation showed that the evidence provided for "innate racial inferiority" could be explained by "economic and social factors." (Moon cited a line from George Bernard Shaw's *Man and Superman* to underscore this point: "The haughty American nation *makes* the Negro clean its boots and then proves the moral and physical inferiority of the Negro by the fact that he is a boot-black.")[47]

Moon's keynote address fused the work of the association with the rejection of racial hierarchies and the quest for civil rights. Without achieving the fifth freedom, there would be no "genuine emancipation." Even if granted first-class citizenship, Moon explained, African Americans would be like the goldfish released from the fishbowl into the ocean, continuing to circumscribe the same "limited radius."[48] By the early 1950s, the association had incorporated Moon's vision into its formal mission. "The program of the Association," the *Negro History Bulletin* announced in 1952, "turns to new research that will debunk ideas of the inherent inferiority of Negroes." "Promote Racial Equality through Education" became a frequent tagline gracing the pages of the *Bulletin*. Solicitations for donations to the association read as follows:

"HELP SPREAD RACIAL UNDERSTANDING!! Contribute to Advancement by Enlightenment Through Education." As a 1954 Negro History Week radio skit concluded: "The Association promotes the scientific belief in the inherent equality of all races of mankind and it explains racial differences in light of the environmental factors that have caused them."[49]

WHO AND WHAT IS "NEGRO"?

In 1938, a columnist for the *Atlanta Daily World* challenged the basic premise that black history was essential to promoting race pride, racial solidarity, and the progress of the race. "Dr. Woodson and his associates seem to be proceeding on the idea that cullud folks need a little pride in themselves, if they're to go places," Nat. D. Williams wrote. But, he claimed,

> the majority of God's chillun are part Indian (red race), part white and part black. Now, when you speak of race loyalty, it seems that somebody needs to get together and decide just which one of our grandpas we are going to honor. The issue is whether or not the word 'Negro' means a man or a condition. If it means a man . . . then what kind of man? If it means a condition, then I don't see anything so inspirational in celebrating the nasty thing.[50]

In addition to offering a trenchant critique of the logic underpinning the mission of the association, Williams's commentary posed a basic ontological question: "Who and what is 'Negro'?"[51] Williams suggested two potential answers—a *man* or a *condition*. Add a third possibility, a *people*, and the three primary responses to this question come into focus. If a man, the Negro had to display a set of essential or at the very least stable traits and characteristics, presumably biologically determined. If a condition, Negroes shared a predicament rather than a nature. And as Williams's invocation of a "nasty thing" suggests, this predicament was one of oppression. Finally, if a people, Negroes had to have a cultural heritage in common rather than merely bloodlines or social status.

In the 1940s, with the race concept in flux, Woodson and his colleagues repeatedly addressed the who and what is Negro question. Their answers were variable, as they mixed and matched elements from these three basic responses, exemplifying the profound confusion surrounding the race concept at the precise moment it was being subjected to its heaviest revision in a century. They also reveal an attempt to fashion a historical rather than a hereditary definition of "Negro."

The 1942 association annual meeting featured back-to-back presentations by two of the most eminent African Americans in the field of medicine—Julian Herman Lewis, professor of pathology at the University of Chicago, and W. Montague Cobb, professor of anatomy at Howard University. Titled "The

Physical Equipment of the Negroes to Meet the Current Emergency," Lewis's presentation focused on the differential resistance of blacks and whites to diseases.⁵² Lewis's talk appears to have been a précis of *The Biology of the Negro*, which had been published by the University of Chicago Press at the end of 1942. The book's overarching goal was to demonstrate that the "reaction to disease is no less a racial characteristic than is head form or skin color." "Anthropathology" was the term Lewis coined to describe this study of racial differences in disease expression. *The Biology of the Negro* included chapters such as "Anatomy of the Negro," "Medical Diseases," and "Obstetrics and Gynecology," along with more than a dozen tables such as "Incidence of the Sickle Cell Trait," "Racial Distribution of Gastric Carcinoma," and "Distribution of Negro Individuals with Various Amounts of Admixture with Whites and Indians."⁵³

The title of Lewis's book was an unmistakable declaration that Lewis regarded the Negro as a real biological race with distinctive physical characteristics. At the same time, however, he noted that racial differences in health outcomes were sometimes caused by environmental rather than biological factors. In the preface, he acknowledged that he used the term "race" "very loosely" and that it was a "sizeable problem" to determine who should be included under the heading "Negro." Hedging his bets, he decided the term would encompass both those individuals with "decided African origin" and, following the "one-drop" convention, those with only a small amount of "Negro blood." Regarding his selection of sources, he matter-of-factly announced that he had been forced to exclude many texts on the topic at hand because they were "so biased and so obviously propaganda."⁵⁴

Lewis's book is an extraordinary document, uneasily straddling two eras separated by more than a century. One can imagine a book with a similar title having been published in the 1840s, expressing the arch-racism of the American School of Ethnology in the vein of Samuel Morton's *Crania Americana*. (Conversely, it is hard to imagine Chicago putting out a book with the same title after 1945 and the revelation of Nazi Germany's "final solution" death camps.) While Lewis presented pioneering findings on how the incidence of sickle-cell disease varied by different populations, he also took recourse to soon-to-be-antiquated terms such as "Negro blood." Indeed the cutting-edge research he was conducting depended on a classification system that was informed more by social convention than science.

Cobb followed Lewis at the association's 1942 meeting with a lecture called "Education in Human Biology: An Essential For the Present and Future."⁵⁵ In light of the "unscientific stereotypes" and "popular misrepresentations" about biological differences between the races, Cobb maintained that the need for more education on this topic was "acute." The danger of miscegenation ranked near the top of the list of misconceptions about race and biology. Cobb therefore presented a detailed discussion of "human hybridization," attempting to overturn misguided ideas about the supposedly pernicious effects of "race crossing." Citing authorities such as Boas, E. A. Hooton, and Montagu, Cobb concluded that there was no evidence suggesting that race crossing resulted in biologically unfit offspring. Widespread ideas about racial "decay" and "deterioration" were simply unfounded.[56]

Using "lantern slides" as visual aids, Cobb explained that race was one of the four basic "human variants," along with age, sex, and body type. "Everyone," Cobb said, "represents some intergrade between the extremes of being young or old, male or female, black, yellow-brown, or white, and lean, muscular, or fat."[57] "Race is a biological reality, not a myth," Cobb continued, "and as such is a very proper object of scientific study":

> No harm can result from the objective investigation of one of the most obvious aspects of human variation and much good can be derived from the full and honest exposition of the nature and import of racial differences. These have been shown to involve much more than surface characters and no one knows their fullest extent. It is known, however, that racial traits have in themselves practically no survival value in life as man lives it today. Race as a biological [reality] is no index of physical, mental, or cultural capacity.[58]

This single paragraph is filled with so many puzzles and paradoxes it almost takes on the quality of a Zen koan. This observation is not meant to indict Cobb but rather to underline the bewildering contradictions at the heart of discourse about race in the early 1940s. We scratch our heads when we read this passage today. Did race matter or not? "Racial differences" went well beyond superficial characteristics, on the one hand; on the other, they had no "survival value." The shape of the nose, for example, according to Cobb, was a clear racial trait but variations among noses were inconsequential. "One could not infer that the Bushman could not survive in the Alps . . . because of their nasal form," Cobb explained.[59] Cobb, like many proponents of the new antiracism, was asking people to perform intellectual gymnastics of the highest difficulty—to acknowledge differences but refrain from making any qualitative judgments about them. No matter how "obvious" racial differences might be, they must not be understood in relative terms such as more and less, better and worse, or higher and lower.[60]

The relationship between race and physical appearance was simultaneously undeniable and uncertain. It was a subject so vital and so vexing, in fact, that Rayford Logan felt obliged to address it on the very first page of his 1945 book *The Negro and the Post-War World*. On the slippery meaning of the word "Negro," Logan said, the "word has been placed in quotation marks because it is very hard to tell who is a Negro." "Scientifically, it is impossible to do so, just as it is impossible to determine accurately all the members of any other 'race,'"

Logan continued, wrapping the term "race" in scare quotes as well for good measure. In Logan's estimation, it would nonetheless be foolish to deny the obvious physical differences between races when compared as large population groups. A division of Negro soldiers, he explained, would not look like a division of Indian, Chinese, or white American soldiers. "Among the Negroes," Logan said, "there would be more with a dark skin, tightly curled hair, thick lips and broad noses." On the basis of these external characteristics, this "high degree of visibility," as Logan phrased it, there were approximately two hundred million Negroes in the world.[61]

The qualifier "approximately" was key, as the numbers could change overnight. Logan described how a few years back several hundred Virginia residents had gone to bed "white" but woke up "colored" because the state had passed a law changing the basis for determining "race." While emphasizing that the individual who is classified as "Negro" by one state might well be classified as "white" in another, Logan also observed that tens of thousands of "white" residents of Latin America and North Africa would be called "Negroes" if they lived in the United States. Logan's own life was a testament to the mercurial nature of race and racial identification.[62] In his unpublished autobiography, he delineated his racial ancestry, reporting, "I am five-eighths white, two-eighths Indian, and one-eighth Negro." "Legal legerdemain," he said, "classifies me as a Negro but I had occasional difficulty convincing some persons that I am."[63] As he explained in *The Negro and the Post-War World*:

> At various times, I have been taken for an Argentine, an Australian, a Canadian, a Chinese, a French West Indian, an Irishman (freckles), a Polish Jew trying to pass for a Gentile, a Polish prince (incognito).... But the Dominican consul in Havana bestowed the full honorary degree upon me—he put me down as white without any qualification. On the other hand, when I travel south of Washington, I am usually invited to the reserved table in the dining car, the table reserved for Negroes.[64]

This last line recalls Du Bois's famous 1940 statement that "the black man is a person who must ride 'Jim Crow' in Georgia."[65] And it speaks to Logan's ultimate preference for an understanding of "Negro" as a condition. *The Negro and the Post-War World* included chapters on "the plight of Negroes" in Africa, the West Indies, the Pacific Islands, Latin America, the United States, and Canada. What justified a specific focus on "the plight of Negroes"? Noting that they accounted for about one-ninth of the world's population, Logan asserted that special attention should be paid to Negroes because most "persons of other races consider the Negro an inferior." More than their "dark skin, tightly curled hair," and so on, what connected blacks across the world was a shared history of oppression, with two pivotal historical developments forging the most important links. These were, first, the slave trade, initiated by Portuguese traders in 1442, and second, imperialism, including the "rape of Africa" and "the establishment in modern times of the domination of the white nations over the rest of the world."⁶⁶

The same year that *The Negro and the Post-War World* appeared, Woodson echoed Logan's sentiments about the Negro as a historically contingent social status, declaring, "The only thing . . . persons of African blood have in common is they are all oppressed in some way." A year later, in a column for the *Negro History Bulletin* called "Questions Answered," Woodson adopted a cultural orientation. Responding to the question of whether the Negro race had a culture, Woodson said the answer depended on the definition of the "Negro race." Observing that leading scholars questioned the scientific validity of racial categories, Woodson pointed out that "Negro" meant different things to different people—"black people who live in the dense African forests near the equator" for the European, but "anyone showing evidence of having the least blood of the black man" to the American.⁶⁷

Forging ahead in spite of the ambiguity surrounding the definition of "Negro," Woodson said that the widespread assumption that the American Negro "belongs to a race without a culture" was mistaken. It was completely wrongheaded to assert, as did some well-meaning intercultural groups, that in adapting to the New World, the "Negro has tended to become a white man with a black skin." The American Negro was no "carbon copy of the white man," Woodson insisted, in part because he never lost his connection to Africa. "Negro dialect" retained thousands of African words, according to Woodson. African folklore survived as well, and African music had provided the foundation for Negro folk music in America.⁶⁸

In his 1947 textbook *From Slavery to Freedom*, John Hope Franklin pointed to these same "Africanisms" as evidence of "the transplantation of African culture" to the United States. The role that Africa played in Franklin's landmark history is quite revealing with respect to the meaning of race in the 1940s. *From Slavery to Freedom* included three chapters on Africa ("A Cradle of Civilization," "Early Negro States of Africa," and "The African Way of Life"). Franklin's book aimed "to bring together the essential facts in the history of the American Negro from his ancient African beginnings down to the present time."⁶⁹ Many reviewers praised the "panoramic scope" of Franklin's book; one applauded it as an "epic story" that "flows along, page after page, in graceful, colorful movement."⁷⁰ At least two reviewers, however, regarded the section on Africa as one of the book's main shortcomings.⁷¹ "For some reason," one reviewer sniffed, "the American Negro writers have failed to question the validity of the argument that color and hair define a 'race.' . . . [E]very move is made to find a background for the American slaves from people who *look alike*."⁷²

With respect to the chapters on Africa, Franklin explained in the preface that "only so much of African history was considered here as evolved in the area from which the vast majority of American Negroes came and as much more as helped to shape Afro-American institutions in the Old World and the New." It was also necessary, Franklin said, to consider the Negroes of the Caribbean and Latin America because their history belonged to the "larger pattern of development of the Negro in the New World."[73] Rather than claiming a background based on family resemblances, Franklin turned to Africa and the African diaspora in order to track lines of influence. Franklin acknowledged that scholars disagreed about the extent to which African culture was preserved in the New World. Rejecting the conclusions of sociologists such as Robert E. Park, who effectively maintained that the only thing Africans brought to America was their color, Franklin endorsed the conclusions of scholars such as Woodson and Melville J. Herskovits, who insisted that "the African cultural heritage" was still evident in many facets of contemporary African American life.[74]

Intriguingly, Franklin and Woodson both imagined that personality traits could be passed along in the same way as musical or linguistic traditions. In his "Has the Negro Race a Culture?" column, Woodson averred that millions of American Negroes "still maintain certain African traits," including generosity and obedience to the law. Franklin likewise saw African Americans as especially law-abiding. Both men traced the origins of this character trait to African tribal government structures.[75] The fact that both men stressed the law-abiding nature of African Americans may have been prompted by the prevalence of the "criminal Negro" stereotype.

The African background of black Americans was not only important for cultural reasons but also for explaining the differences between American Negroes and other "minority groups." The term "minority groups" rose to prominence in the 1940s, and many black historians bristled when it was used to describe African Americans. It led, Woodson said, to the mistaken impression that blacks came to the United States during the mass immigration wave of the late nineteenth and early twentieth centuries. "Negroes are not recent immigrants into the United States," Woodson said, "and they are not here in small numbers."[76] Including blacks among the country's "minority groups" also elided the unique historical fact of slavery. If anything, blacks were, in the words of Charles Wesley, "involuntary immigrants." The physical appearance of blacks, moreover, set blacks apart from other "minority groups." As Wesley explained, it was not possible for African Americans, as it was for European immigrants, "to change [their] clothes, . . . to adopt new manners, correct pronunciations, and voice inflections, and to change their names to American ones." Because of their skin color, doors had been opened to white immigrants that remained closed to African Americans.[77]

THE BETRAYAL OF THE NEGRO

The most influential antiracist documents of the 1940s and 1950s largely ignored history. Walter A. Jackson, author of one of the most comprehensive treatments of *An American Dilemma*, said that Gunnar Myrdal's book "gave little attention to historical issues." Myrdal had a particularly low opinion of black history as a specialty, referring to it as a "waste field" in a private letter.[78] In the fifteen-point 1950 UNESCO statement on race, meanwhile, the word "history" makes a single appearance. No doubt this reflected the analytic frameworks of the anthropologists, sociologists, and psychologists who hammered out the statement.[79] When UNESCO declared that the "problem of race has its roots 'in the minds of men,'" the "psychologizing of racism," an intellectual project that took hold in the 1940s, was effectively complete. The concept of race "prejudice" had superseded the principle of race "domination." Rather than being grounded in history and political economy, racism came to be seen as "a disease."[80]

The very title of Leah Gordon's insightful 2015 monograph, *From Power to Prejudice: The Rise of Racial Individualism in Midcentury America*, distills the essence of this shift. Gordon cogently argues that encouraged by antiradicalism, the rise of behaviorism, and watershed civil rights victories in the courts, among other factors, a paradigm she calls "racial individualism" became the dominant scholarly framework for conceptualizing the "race problem" in the postwar decades. Combining "psychological individualism, rights-based individualism, and belief in the socially transformative power of education," racial individualism posited "prejudice and discrimination as the root cause of racial conflict, focused on individuals in the study of race relations, and suggested that racial justice could be attained by changing white minds and protecting African American rights." Racial individualism privileged dispositional theories that focused on individuals as the "most important causal actor and unit of analysis," placing an emphasis on discerning the "relationship between prejudiced attitudes and discriminatory behaviors." Systemic theories (which looked to social groups as the primary units of analysis, stressing the significance of large-scale social processes such as migration) and relational theories (which prioritized political economy, particularly "structures of capitalism" and the race-class nexus) receded in importance.[81]

Racial individualism, Gordon stresses, did not enjoy an uncontested reign across academe. Theoretical alternatives to dispositional accounts of the "race problem" continued to circulate in black academic networks and institutions, especially at Fisk University's Race Relations Institutes run by Charles S. Johnson and in the pages of the *Journal of Negro Education*, edited by Charles H. Thompson at Howard University. In these segregated domains, where institutional pressures incentivizing racial individualism—such as a strong preference for quantitative survey data—held less sway, the assumption that "social problems [could] be reduced to individual perpetrators and victims" was sharply contested. Many black scholars understood "prejudice as a rationalization for, not a cause of, exploitation," viewing attitudes as just "one cog in larger sociological, cultural, and political economic systems." Black sociologists, especially the likes of Johnson, Oliver Cromwell Cox, and St. Clair Drake, maintained that political oppression and labor exploitation were constitutive elements of—rather than deviations from—American democracy.[82]

Gordon's study focuses on anthropology, economics, political science, psychology, and sociology, and the field of history is largely beyond its purview. Historians such as Woodson, Franklin, and Logan, though, should be counted among the ranks of black scholars who generated multilayered analyses that could not be contained within the narrow boundaries of racial individualism. The association too should be included among the critical black intellectual sites that were committed to a holistic examination of the "race problem." Paying attention to the individual *and* society, attitudes *and* social structures as well as culture *and* capital, members of the association combined dispositional, relational, and systemic theories to fashion compelling historical narratives.

Rayford Logan's 1954 book *Negro in American Life and Thought: The Nadir, 1877–1901* is one of the best examples of this more comprehensive, integrated approach to studying race. Recognized today as Logan's "most influential book" and as "a classic work of American history," it charted the vicious erosion of black civil rights at the close of the nineteenth century.[83] Logan intended the book to fill a lacuna in scholarship on American mind and thought during the last quarter of the nineteenth century. He cited "three excellent studies" on this topic that failed to give the Negro his due: Paul Buck's Pulitzer Prize–winning *The Road to Reunion* (1937), Merle Curti's *The Growth of American Thought* (1943), and Henry Steele Commager's *The American Mind: An Interpretation of American Thought and Character Since the 1880s* (1950).[84]

The Negro in American Life and Thought was widely and favorably reviewed upon its release. The *Times* heralded Logan's book as "unusually rich in new fact and interpretation." A review in *Social Forces* called it "a much needed study, produced with such thoroughness and skill that one is tempted to characterize it as brilliant." (The same review cheerfully announced that it was "not the sort of tedious fact-grubbing that frequently passes for legitimate historical exposition.")[85] Many of the notices celebrated the fact that the book illuminated a largely neglected period in American history. Horace Mann Bond, in a glowing review in the *Journal of Negro Education*, noted that while many scholars had mined the Civil War, Reconstruction, and northward migration periods, very few had devoted any attention to "the 'dead space' now reviewed so brilliantly in Dr. Logan's book."[86] Gertrude Martin from the *Chicago Defender* remarked that it was "amazing that this period has been so long neglected."[87]

In *The Negro and the Post-War World*, Logan had written that "the fact that in most parts of the world most Negroes are in the lowliest position . . . gives some excuse for the belief in the natural inferiority of the Negro."[88] Here Logan pointed to the logic of a basic aspect of human psychology, which is the overwhelming tendency to make attributions about individuals and groups based on character traits and temperament rather than environmental factors.[89] Race prejudice thrives on this logic, where every significant difference between races, whether measured in terms of IQ scores or incarceration rates, is seized on as proof of innate deficiencies. For many whites, who looked around and saw blacks living in the most impoverished neighborhoods, attending the most dilapidated schools, working the most menial jobs, and so on, UNESCO's declaration that the "unity of mankind from both the biological and social viewpoints is the main thing" must have been unconvincing.[90] If all races were really the same, why was it always the black folks who ended up in the meanest conditions? In *The Negro in American Life and Thought*, Logan set out to demonstrate that black people were only down in a ditch because somebody had pushed them there. And, moreover, that the reason blacks struggled to get out was because somebody had a boot on their necks, pushing them down.

The signal antiracist texts produced by social scientists in the early 1940s stressed the importance of the social environment in relation to racial disparities. For example, as *Races of Mankind* explained, racial differences in IQ scores resulted from "differences in income, education, and cultural advantages."[91] But where, then, did these differences come from? The question often remained unanswered. Even Columbia University anthropologist Ruth Benedict, who paid more attention to historical issues than most of her colleagues, offered little more than generic observations regarding the root causes of racial discrepancies.[92] History showed, according to Benedict, that the racial makeup of any given society was not the primary determinant of its fate. Rather, civilizations ("whether they are Caucasian or Malay or Mongol") advanced when they were afforded sufficient political freedoms and economic opportunities. When these favorable conditions no longer obtained, "the torch soon fell from their hands," Benedict said. On the logical fallacy of attributing social progress to "eternal and biologically perpetuated" racial characteristics, Benedict wrote that "a Norman in the time of Ivanhoe could have written of the impossibility of civilizing the Saxons with much better justification than does Madison Grant of non-Nordics in the 1920's in America."[93]

Benedict was much more interested in examining the origins of racial prejudice than she was in exploring the origins of racial disparities.[94] She regarded racism as the outgrowth of an instinctual human tribalism that expressed itself in the basic psychological division of "us" versus "them." "Racism," Benedict asserted, "is essentially a pretentious way of saying that 'I' belong to the Best People." This chauvinism was inevitably linked to "political ends" and the aggrandizement of the "Best People." The "Best People," Benedict maintained, were defined in different terms, depending on the era. Tribal, religious, national, and racial definitions all held sway at one time or another. "In the eyes of history," Benedict claimed, racism was just another example of "the persecution of minorities for the advantage of those in power."[95]

Although persecution was central to Benedict's theory of racism, her conceptualization of persecution itself was notably undeveloped. Regarding African Americans, she referenced the "degrading conditions" that perpetuated black "poverty" and "ignorance" but did not take the time to analyze the nature of these conditions, nor did she explain the specific mechanisms by which they influenced outcomes such as employment and education levels.[96] In other words, she failed to provide—or even roughly sketch—a convincing account of the "persecution" of African Americans. This task, with an emphasis on black citizenship, was the crux of *The Negro in American Life and Thought*. Part 1 of the book outlined how governmental policies, Supreme Court decisions, and the activities of organized labor and big business had systematically disadvantaged blacks from 1877 to 1901. The presidents during this period paid lip service to the importance of black civil rights, but they ultimately abandoned "the poor colored people of the South" to the "honorable and influential southern whites." While Logan noted that the Freedmen's Bureau had achieved some measure of success, he maintained that the federal government had failed to provide a "long-range, comprehensive and intelligent policy of economic habilitation of the emancipated Negroes." Sharecropping had saddled many freedmen and women with crippling debt. In urban areas, meanwhile, organized labor excluded blacks, and they found themselves almost completely shut off from the boons of industrial expansion.[97]

A review of late nineteenth-century rulings concerning African Americans led Logan to conclude that equal justice under the law was likewise a sham. The *Plessy* decision marked the "descent of the Negro" to his lowest position since emancipation. For Logan, the *Plessy* decision revealed the extent to which legal segregation was primarily of symbolic importance. The "etiquette of slavery," Logan said, had permitted a slave girl to travel in the same train car as her mistress, while the "etiquette of freedom" found it intolerable that a "colored woman" paying her own fare should sit in the same coach as a white woman. The nub of the difference, Logan explained, was that after emancipation "personal contacts became social relations."[98] Without the clear racial line between the enslaved and the free, the social intercourse between blacks and whites now had to be mediated by a more explicit set of racial rules and regulations. Logan's interpretation of *Plessy* exposed the limitations of psychological theories of race contact. According to these theories (in their most elemental form), racial proximity in and of itself would reduce racial prejudice. How, then, did the psychologists explain the intimate contacts between whites and blacks during slavery?

Part 2 of *The Negro in American Life and Thought* examined white attitudes toward blacks in print media, exploring the power of racist representations. It helped build the foundations for a genre of black history that seeks to uncover and understand prejudice and discrimination.[99] We might call it, to borrow George Fredrickson's memorable phrase, the "black image in the white mind" approach to black history.[100] Drawing on over two dozen Howard University masters' theses carried out under Logan's direction, part 2 presented a more sustained and sophisticated discussion of black images and representations in print culture than had any previously published historical monograph, helping set the basic parameters of the "black image in the white mind" genre.[101] This genre of historical scholarship takes attitudes, stereotypes, prejudice, and discrimination as its main objects of inquiry. It seeks to answer the question of how representations and images of blacks both reflect and shape ideas about race (that is, racial discourses, ideologies, and hierarchies). The "black image in the white mind" approach therefore both describes instances of racism and strives to explain how it is spread and reproduced across generations.[102]

One of the abiding conceptual problems for scholars trying to explain racism is how to connect "the individual level of human experience" to "the level of society and social forces."[103] As Logan reflected, "The reciprocal effect of events on the development of attitudes and of attitudes in changing the course of events constitutes an integral, though elusive, thread in the history of mankind." While he was careful to eschew strong causal language, Logan did say that his examination of northern print media revealed that northern attitudes on the whole "endorsed the policies and approved the events that steadily reduced the Negro to a subordinate place in American life."[104] In less circumspect language Horace Mann Bond said that Logan's analysis of newspapers and literary magazines brought readers face-to-face "with the machinery by which racial stereotypes are firmly implanted in peoples, to encumber their nobler possibilities and poison the springs of national interest."[105]

The "machinery" that Bond referred to included everything from Grady's 1886 speech on the New South to cartoons depicting African cannibals. In Logan's estimation, most people made up their minds on the issues of the day on the basis of anecdotes, jokes, cartoons, and "slanted" news articles rather than "ponderous editorials." In chapters 12 ("The 'Color Line' in the 'New

North,' 1877–1901") and 13 ("The Negro as Portrayed in the Leading Literary Magazines"), Logan executed a deft cultural analysis of black representations. Starting with the conviction that popular culture is a key driving force shaping attitudes and opinions, Logan described in painstaking detail how blacks were stereotyped in terms of their physical appearance, personality traits, and the language or dialect they used. Working from newspapers and magazines, Logan constructed lexicons for "color-coded" language ("midnight black," "black as a crow," "black as a total eclipse"); appearance ("thick lips," "big ears and feet," "kinky or wooly hair"); derogatory terms ("darkey," "coon," "pickaninny"); descriptive adjectives ("stupid," "ignorant," "lazy"); and insulting nicknames ("Prince Orang Outan," "Had-a-Plenty," "Wan-na-Mo").[106] These lists taken together formed a glossary of racialization, and Logan demonstrated how the repeated invocation of certain characteristics in particular contexts had created a roster of stock black characters, including the "contented slave," the "comic Negro," and the "criminal Negro."

In an avant-garde comparison of the representations of blacks to other ethno-racial groups in the media, Logan reported that African Americans were not the only minority group that was "attacked, caricatured, and stereotyped." American Indians, for instance, were ridiculed for their "alleged fondness for 'firewater.'" The Chinese, crudely depicted with pigtails, exotic dress, and bound feet, were hopeless heathens. (Chinatowns across the country were portrayed as dangerous sites of "vice, gambling, opium-smoking, and disease," Logan observed.) Jews were "denounced" for their religion as well as their crafty filthy-lucre mercantilism. Other ethno-racial groups, including the Irish, Scottish, and Swedes, were also caricatured. In comparison to the stereotypes of African Americans, however, those of peoples of European descent were not nearly as damning. The fact that the "fighting" Irishman had gained some power in municipal politics or that the "dumb" Swede had acquired some of the most fertile farming land in the Midwest made them less "vulnerable to gibes" than African Americans, according to Logan. Moreover, caricatures of the "belligerent" Irishman or the "tight-fisted" Scotsman were less abhorrent, not to mention less all-encompassing, than the caricature of the "lazy, improvident, child-like, irresponsible, chicken-stealing, crap-shooting, policy-playing, razor-toting, immoral, and criminal" Negro.[107]

In the *Condemnation of Blackness*, Khalil Gibran Muhammad argues that black criminality became one of the preeminent justifications for prejudice, discrimination, and violence against African Americans during the Jim Crow era. The publication of the 1890 census, which included statistics on prison populations by race, marked the beginning of an era in which social scientists, race relations experts, journalists, and politicians deployed the technique of "writing crime into race," maintaining that disproportionately high black crime rates were a result of strong black criminal impulses, whether inborn or transmitted through a pathological black culture. By the 1940s, according to Muhammad, "racial crime discourse" had settled on blackness as its "sole signifier."[108]

The "criminal Negro" was the most prominent—and the most pernicious—of all the black racial stereotypes, according to Logan. Logan asserted that the quantity of articles relating to black crime, although voluminous, was less important than the "invariable racial identification of Negroes." As Logan outlined, when white people committed crimes, the race of the perpetrators was almost never mentioned. With alleged black criminals, however, racial designations were de rigueur. Logan reported that in the single month of September 1895, the *Globe-Democrat* ran more than a dozen headlines detailing black crime, including "Held Up By Masked Negroes," "Death of a Man Shot by a Dissolute Negress," and "Negro's Horse Stealing Method." The "constant repetition" of "Negro," "colored," or other racial signifiers in crime stories "helped to build up the stereotype of the criminal Negro," Logan explained. Moreover, in cases of black-on-black crime, Logan documented that a "jocular" tone of reportage was standard in mainstream newspapers and magazines. A representative headline from the *Commercial Appeal* read as follows: "Carved Her Husband. Lou Pleasant is in the city prison for too free use of a knife."[109]

If black-on-black crime was a punch line, black-on-white crime was nothing short of a crisis, especially crimes allegedly committed by black men against white women. Accusations of harassment or rape could easily lead to the formation of lynch mobs. Turn-of-the-twentieth-century media accounts of lynchings arguably comprised the most damaging instances of "writing crime into race." Logan saw the 1890s as the pivotal decade in this respect, as the news coverage of lynchings dehumanized blacks by sensationalizing the violence against them and by accepting accusations and forced "confessions" as evidence of guilt. By failing to question mob violence, newspapers and magazines helped to erode respect for the rule of law, as far as African Americans were concerned. They likewise reinforced the pernicious assumption that black people were predisposed to violent criminal behavior. Logan quoted an editorial from the *Atlanta Constitution* that decried the "horrible crimes" that provoked lynchings. "If a Negro wants to escape the danger of lynching," the newspaper asserted, "let him keep his hands off white women."[110] One would be hard-pressed to find a more succinct and distressing illustration of the "condemnation of blackness." In its most virulent form, then, the "criminal Negro" stereotype advanced the following proposition: African Americans were presumed guilty in matters of life and death.

In the fall of 1956 Logan delivered a speech to a group of black educators that might have served as a coda to *The Negro in American Life and Thought*. "One of the most shameful frauds in American history is the myth of the inherent, ineradicable inferiority of the Negro race," Logan said. Invoking the abolitionist battle to emancipate the slaves, Logan said that "you and I have the inescapable obligation to consummate their efforts by freeing the minds of men from the shameful fraud that the handicaps imposed upon Negroes constitute evidence of our racial inferiority."[111] In the 1940s and early 1950s, Logan and other association members made serious revisions to the concepts of race and racism in an attempt to liberate minds. With its proclamation that doctrines of racial inequality were not supported by science, the new antiracism formulated by social scientists proved helpful in this endeavor. At the same time, the emerging antiracist paradigm presented a paradox—if race itself was real, why were meaningful racial differences necessarily damaging fabrications? Woodson and his colleagues navigated this confusing racial landscape by attempting to define "Negro." No single designation prevailed, as meanings shifted, depending on the context. The Negro was somehow simultaneously a biological race, a sociological fact, and a people.

CHAPTER SIX

"Look to the Roots"

HISTORY LESSONS FOR
THE PRESENT

"Have we any right to expect an automatic extension of freedom as a result of this war?" So asked Charles Wesley in a January 1944 *Negro History Bulletin* article called "The Negro Citizen in Our Wars for Freedom." His answer was measured and not entirely encouraging. The participation of blacks in the War of 1812, for instance, "had little beneficial action upon their own freedom," Wesley said, noting that the "Colonization Plan" followed soon on its heels. After World War I ended, moreover, blacks found that their rousing rallying cries for freedom had fallen on deaf ears, like those of a neglected "child crying in the night." "The student of history must admit," Wesley said, that the path of freedom forged by wars was "now forward and then backward," like the upward progress along "a tortuous mountain pathway." Regarding World War II, Wesley warned his readers that many African Americans would be disillusioned if they failed to heed the "lessons of the past history of freedom's wars and face the future realistically." Nonetheless, he said that the outcome was "partly in our hands," as blacks could plan strategically to take advantage of "the days of peace" that would follow the war's conclusion, a period that often witnessed the resurgence of antiblack sentiment.[1]

How did black historians in particular and black history more broadly address the watershed events of World War II and the *Brown v. Board of Education* Supreme Court decision? As the modern civil rights movement unfolded, Woodson and his colleagues turned to history to explain and interpret a world in flux. History was a compass, a tool to gain one's bearings in the face of a rapidly shifting racial landscape. Woodson and his coworkers in the association summoned history's two most fundamental laws—constancy and change—in order to map the critical features of the here and now. Grounding their claims in the context of a long black freedom struggle, they documented relative constants (the fight for equality and justice as well as long-standing patterns of prejudice and discrimination) to render the world legible; at the same time, they charted significant shifts, transformations, and new developments (from the establishment of the Fair Employment Practices Commission to *Brown*) to demonstrate that the world was malleable. In addition to a means of orientation, the association also proposed the use of history as a method of adaptation, envisioning that the study of black history would be instrumental in ensuring the success of a new era of racial integration.

The association had never been so closely attuned to a particular social movement before. It had, as a matter of principle, refused to support or even endorse specific policy reform agendas. The death of Carter G. Woodson in 1950 likely afforded the association more latitude to engage more directly in political arenas. Whatever the case, *Brown* presented an unprecedented and apparently irresistible opportunity for the association to attempt to shape large-scale social change. From a practical perspective, history was a core academic subject taught in virtually every school across the country. Introducing black history into American history classes, at least in theory, would not require a major overhaul of the basic curriculum. For association members, then, the standard U.S. history curriculum was a nearly universal educational tool that could be wielded to promote racial understanding and racial integration. The association was not alone in holding this belief. Indeed, the fight for unbiased history textbooks was a main plank in the civil rights platform, starting in the 1940s. (In New York and Chicago, for example, the NAACP pressured school boards and state legislators to revise racist texts.) That hateful textbooks were "a chief cause" of white prejudice and discrimination as well as a "scourge upon the mental and emotional health" of blacks was a conviction shared by virtually all black activists, scholars, and intellectuals in the mid-twentieth century.[2]

Race relations were a central concern of post–World War II liberalism. After *An American Dilemma* "cast racial equality as the *telos* of American nationhood," racial progress became a litmus test of "America's claims to global leadership."[3] History, to a much greater extent than other academic disciplines, had a built-in capacity to serve as a barometer of race relations. In contrast to, say, economics, political science, or sociology, history had an essential narrative quality. Historians told stories, stories that necessarily centered on the development and transformation of the United States as a country and stories that had inescapably moral dimensions. Black history served as a running commentary on the state of the nation, with our most cherished ideals of equality, freedom, and democracy hanging in the balance. These ideals were touchstones of Cold War political rhetoric, something association members well understood. Consequently, Woodson and his colleagues touted the significance of black history as a yardstick with which to measure our progress in fulfilling the American Creed. "If from the record we can show how far we missed the mark of justice in the past," Woodson wrote in 1945, "we may be constrained to do more than ever to attain a level of equality and brotherhood in the future."⁴

"Equality" and "brotherhood" were apt words for this particular historical moment. The association's long-standing concern with combating white prejudice was an ideal fit for the reform mold of postwar racial liberalism, with its strong faith in the capacity of education to solve the country's most urgent social problems. In the Cold War world, characterized by strident anticommunism and a shift to the right in national politics, educational initiatives offered an attractive—comparatively inexpensive and uncontroversial—means through which to fight for racial justice. During the postwar decades, as Leah Gordon observes, changing "a prejudiced personality" was seen as a much more viable enterprise than attempting "to restructure a capitalist economy or reorganize an oppressive political or social system."⁵ The perception that it was easier to change a prejudiced personality did not particularly trouble association members, though, as they drew a direct line from changing racial attitudes to the transformation of society.

WHAT THE NEGRO WANTS

Released in the fall of 1944, *What the Negro Wants* pulsated with the electric energy of a nation at war. Edited by Rayford Logan and published by the University of North Carolina Press, the volume featured essays by Du Bois, Mary McLeod Bethune, and Roy Wilkins, among others. This compilation reveals the extent to which a historical perspective informed the first public reflections on the emerging civil rights movement. Most of the contributors, including several who were not professional historians, proceeded from the basic assumption that, as Wesley put it, "what the Negro wants now should be seen from the basis of his strivings in the past."⁶ The appearance of *What the Negro Wants* marked a "programmatic milestone" in the early history of the modern civil rights movement in that more than a dozen prominent African Americans of all political persuasions, southerners and northerners alike, publicly declared that Jim Crow segregation had to end.⁷ According to Kenneth Janken, the clarity, force, and unanimity of the voices featured in *What the Negro Wants* helped to "clear the ground" for the more activist next phase of the civil rights movement, providing vital ammunition "to wage a sustained assault on the system of segregation."⁸

What the Negro Wants almost never made it to the printing press. In March 1943, William T. Couch, director of the University of North Carolina Press, had solicited Logan to edit a book of personal statements on the race question by a dozen or so African Americans with different backgrounds. But after Couch received the manuscript six months later, he wrote to Logan informing him that the collection was "not publishable."⁹ The contributors, in Couch's estimation, placed far too much emphasis on white prejudice while virtually ignoring "the question of how far the Negro is responsible for his [own] condition."¹⁰ More troubling still, Du Bois, Logan, and several additional authors spoke in favor of "mixed marriages," a position that Couch found irresponsible at best and incendiary at worst, referring to the "abhorrent" practice as racial "amalgamation."¹¹ Most disturbing of all to Couch, though, was the clear consensus among all of the contributors regarding the "complete abolition of segregation." "If this is what the Negro wants," Couch wrote to Logan, "nothing could be clearer than what he needs, and needs most urgently, is to revise his wants."¹²

Couch only agreed to proceed with publication of the book after Logan threatened the press with a lawsuit and agreed to let Couch write a special publisher's introduction. The controversy surrounding the publication of the book as well as Couch's peculiar introduction helped to turn *What the Negro Wants* into "a minor literary cause célèbre."¹³ As a review in the *Journal of Negro History* noted, "Couch has allowed us to witness one of the strangest spectacles in American publishing history, of soliciting a book and then using his position and prestige to attack the book."¹⁴ Couch's introduction effectively disavowed the book's contents and conclusions, arguing that blacks were indisputably racially "inferior," pausing to note in a lengthy and convoluted footnote that whether the cause was biology or environment was beside the point, and asserting that the consequences of the complete elimination of segregation would be "disastrous."¹⁵ Reviewers writing in the black press paid special attention to the remarkable intellectual contortions Couch performed. Marjorie McKenzie, writing in the *Pittsburgh Courier*, informed her readers that Couch "is a poor creature caught in the vice of his own emotional need to believe that Negroes are inferior but dimly sensing that science has made him a fool and his ideas silly." Ben Burns, columnist for the *Chicago Defender*, saw Couch's introduction as emblematic of the impossible position taken by most white southern liberals. "To salve their conscience with their belief in democracy," Burns wrote, "they are slowly doping up fantastic formula of double-talk and jibberish on a high plane to prove that all men are not created equal [and] that Negroes are an inferior race." This highfalutin "jibberish" was nothing more than the "KKK doctrine gone intellectual."¹⁶

What the Negro Wants arrived at an opportune moment. Referring to an outpouring of books on African Americans, including Logan's edited compilation, Arthur P. Davis of the *New Journal and Guide* commented that "for the first time in many decades, the American public is doing some soul-searching on the matter of the Negro." Benjamin Mays predicted that the book would be "an eye-opener and a revelation" and that "no American should be left in doubt any longer" that blacks wanted equal rights. Echoing Mays's assessment, a reviewer in *Political Science Quarterly* declared the volume showed that "the ferment among Negro groups, already under way before the war but intensified by it, cannot be ignored, evaded or repressed."[17]

"A good deal of Negro history" appeared in the pages of *What the Negro Wants*, according to the *Pittsburgh Courier*.[18] The opening line of Logan's lead essay established the fundamental importance of a historical framework: "The Negro Problem in the United States today is a national problem spawned from two hundred forty years of slavery and the northward migration of Negroes incident to two world wars." "We have been free for eighty years," Logan continued, "one-third of the time that the Negro ancestors of most of us were slaves":

> This simple bit of arithmetic explains in large measure our third-class citizenship. It suggests also that we shall need another one hundred sixty years (approximately of course) to attain first-class citizenship, for human progress seems to require almost as long to destroy the vestiges of an institution as the institution had previously existed. This conclusion, I might observe, has been attacked by some critics as being unduly pessimistic; by others, as being incurably optimistic.[19]

There are two key interrelated ideas here with respect to viewing the "Negro problem" over time as inseparable from the larger African American historical trajectory. The first is the signal importance of coming to grips with the "vestiges" of slavery. The second relates to the question of historical progress and the possibility of change. When, if ever, would the oppressive reverberations of slavery fade into the background?

In the early 1940s, the notion that the "Negro problem" was peculiar to the South was endemic. In their respective essays for *What the Negro Wants*, both Logan and Du Bois advanced historical arguments in an attempt to overturn this conventional wisdom. Logan recounted a litany of incidents and developments in the North that demonstrated the region was not and had never been a genuine safe haven from prejudice and discrimination. To start with, the North had been complicit in the slave trade, and many northerners made their fortunes by manufacturing "slave-produced cotton." The North likewise had had its share of advocates for the forced deportation of blacks who had used "language that Hitler might have borrowed." The South had no monopoly on violence against blacks, Logan underscored, referring to the New York City "draft riots" in July 1863. There were no significant differences between southern and northern interpretations of the history of slavery, the Civil War, and Reconstruction. Indeed, southern historians had carried the day. *Gone with the Wind* was the "crowning achievement" of this victory, following a long line of books and movies that had championed the "Lost Cause." Most white people, whether they lived south or north of the Mason-Dixon Line, did "not accept the Negro as an equal," Logan concluded.[20]

While Logan briefly mentioned the importance of mercantile interests, "big business" was central to Du Bois's explanation of southern and northern complicity. As Du Bois explained, northern philanthropy, funded by the largesse of large northern corporations, forged a partnership with the retrograde forces in the South under the aegis of the Southern Education Board in order to fix blacks in a state of subservience. Schools in the Hampton and Tuskegee vein were the models for a racial philosophy designed to produce "humble, patient, hardworking" black laborers. Between 1890 and 1910, disenfranchisement laws and Jim Crow legislation passed across the southern United States and, with the tacit approval of the North, grafted "a legal caste system based on race and color" onto the U.S. Constitution.[21]

Referring to recent efforts to challenge this racial caste system, Logan wrote in his editor's preface that whites "express alarm at what they call the excessive insistence by Negroes upon a too rapid change in the *status quo*." The "double victory" campaign and the increasingly assertive calls for civil rights attendant to World War II shocked many white Americans, who perceived blacks' demands for greater equality not only as unreasonable but also as unprecedented. In her essay "Certain Unalienable Rights," Bethune observed that many people were "alarmed and bewildered" by the growing "ferment among the Negro masses," citing recent riots in Harlem, Detroit, and Los Angeles. It was vital, however, not to be misled by violent conflagrations, no matter how disturbing. To genuinely understand what the Negro wants today, Bethune said one "must look to the roots and not be confused by the branches and the leaves."[22]

Bethune's metaphor provides an apt description for the way different contributors to *What the Negro Wants* used black history to explain African American aspirations in the present. In a piece titled simply "The Negro Wants Full Equality," Roy Wilkins, assistant secretary of the NAACP and editor of the *Crisis*, clarified that African Americans were not demanding anything "new or startling"; they were not asking for anything they had not asked for before the rise of Hitler, nor were they asking for anything "inconsistent with the Constitution and the Bill of Rights." Wilkins sketched a brief history of the NAACP to prove his point, asserting that "absolute political and social equality" had been the aim of the NAACP since its founding in 1909. The perception, then, that the NAACP had "trotted out" a new World War II philosophy "to solve the race problem overnight" was completely misguided. Indeed, demands for full equality stretched back well before the NAACP years, Wilkins stressed, pointing to Frederick Douglass and Harriet Tubman as ancestors of the "complete equality school." The African American desire for freedom was not novel, Wilkins concluded, and the history of the freedom struggle was too protracted and too resilient "to admit of doubt as to the ends sought."[23]

Echoing Wilkins's analysis, Wesley titled his essay "The Negro Has Always Wanted the Four Freedoms." Wesley said that blacks had always wanted the freedom of speech, but when they expressed what they thought, many of them "were hounded, beaten and driven from their home." Blacks likewise had wanted freedom of religion, yet they had been compelled to "steal away to Jesus" and to suffer the indignation of the segregated pew. African Americans had wanted freedom from want. Instead, according to Wesley, they had been relegated largely to menial jobs and had been paid lower wages than white workers. And blacks had wanted freedom from fear, but, Wesley emphasized, "fear of bodily harm and fear for the future of self and family" had ranked near the top of African American concerns throughout American history.[24] One reviewer of *What the Negro Wants*, perhaps with Wesley's words fresh in her mind, suggested that the book's title was misleading. "It seemed to me," Marjorie McKenzie said, "to describe not so much what we want as what we have not had."[25]

After recounting how African Americans had been systematically denied the four freedoms, Wesley turned his attention to sketching the history of African American struggles for freedom and civil rights, tracing that history from the first recorded slave insurrection in 1639 to the March on Washington Movement, spearheaded by A. Philip Randolph. From the abolitionist and the convention movements to the establishment of the NAACP and the National Urban League, Wesley stressed that the paths pursued by African Americans had "varied but the objective of an improved status and an advancing standard of life have been always present in the striving."[26]

This history of "striving" was absent from mainstream history textbooks. In his foreword to the 1939 NAACP pamphlet *Anti-Negro Propaganda in School Textbooks*, Walter White said that schoolbooks were often "germ carriers of the most vicious propaganda against America's largest minority, the Negro citizen." Year after year, the pamphlet reported, a new textbook version of *Birth of a Nation* came out with its "crooning black mammies, obedient colored servants, and psalm-singing workers who tip their hats graciously to white southern plantation lords." According to the pamphlet, American historians painted an idyllic picture of slavery, arguing that it benefited the economy and the slaves themselves. This moonlight-and-magnolia myth of plantation life, of course, did not advertise slave resistance. *Anti-Negro Propaganda in School Textbooks* stated that most textbooks ignored or presented a distorted picture of the many slave revolts: "Nowhere in these books do you find the true story of the heroic roles played by Sojourner Truth, Denmark Vesey, Harriet Tubman, Nat Turner, Frederick Douglass, Gabrielle, Still, and many others." Indeed, an extensive review of over a dozen textbooks published between 1931 and 1939 carried out by Marie Carpenter in 1941 revealed that only one mentioned Harriet Tubman.[27]

In contrast, Wesley discussed and then underlined the significance of slave revolts, maintaining that these insurrections proved that claims about "the docility, the humbleness and the satisfaction" of blacks under slavery were unfounded. History proved, Wesley said, that "freedom and liberty are just as dear to the black or brown skin as to the white."[28] This was one of the fundamental lessons of *What the Negro Wants*. Couch's plea for the Negro to "revise his wants," then, was not only up against the leading black voices of the present but a chorus of black voices from the past.

"LONG CONCOURSE TO FREEDOM"

"Negro men have served their country honorably on the field of battle in every war since colonial days." So began the 1944 Negro History Week radio program produced by students from Highland Park High School in Detroit and broadcast by radio station WJBK. The "Negro Soldier in the Wars of the United States" was the special theme for the 1944 Negro History Week celebrations as well as the focus of the *Negro History Bulletin* issues for the 1943–44 school year.[29] More than two dozen articles treating the subject of war appeared in the bulletin during the World War II years. Comprehensive coverage was offered of the performance of black soldiers.[30] The legacies of all of the country's major wars were dissected.[31] The cultural and social dimensions of war were explored as well, including the eligibility of black women for membership in the Daughters of the American Revolution, the poetry of the Civil War, and the reporting of pioneering black war correspondents.[32]

The treatment of military history during World War II–era Negro History Week celebrations had quite clear vindicationist aims. "What does history say," a Highland Park student asked, about the common perception that blacks did not make "good *fighter* soldiers?" Respondents marshaled several counterexamples, including the famed World War I 369th Infantry, also known as the Harlem Hellfighters, who survived 191 days under fire in France; Navy "mess boy" Dorie Miller, who in spite of having no combat training, successfully manned an abandoned machine gun post during the Pearl Harbor attack, a feat of bravery for which he received the Navy Cross; and the 99th Pursuit squadron made up of Tuskegee airmen who flew sorties over Italy.[33] Given the sterling historical record of blacks in the military and the thousands of black soldiers on active duty in Europe, North Africa, and the South Pacific, a student concluded, "I feel that I merit my citizenship and a place in our great country fully as much as any other group."[34] Black military participation was upheld as both a badge and a credential, proof of services rendered and a pass to the body politic.

That the association trumpeted the exploits of the "Negro soldier" during World War II should not be surprising. Drawing connections between black military service and citizenship rights was a clear strategy and one with a long pedigree. A more intriguing association strategy that came to the forefront during World War II attempted to build a bridge between American "wars for freedom" and the African American freedom struggle. The history of the Negro, the *Chicago Defender* announced in the midst of Negro History Week celebrations in 1943, was the story "of a people's fight for freedom through the years." "The desire for freedom rings throughout our history," the author averred:

> In 1776 Crispus Attucks was the first to die in freedom's cause. Black men stood staunch at Lexington and Concord firing the shots that were heard all around . . . the world. Black men went through the blood and fire of Bunker Hill. Remember these names: Denmark Vesey, Nat Turner, Gabriel Prosser and many others.[35]

Those readers who did not know their black history might be forgiven for thinking that Vesey, Turner, and Prosser were black heroes of the American Revolution seeking to free Americans from the yoke of Great Britain rather than black revolutionaries seeking to free slaves from their shackles. This elision, however, was almost certainly not an error but rather a self-conscious effort to stitch together African American participation in "all American wars" with the African American struggle for civil rights. Indeed, this attempt to imaginatively fuse the narrative of American freedom with that of the black freedom struggle was a long-standing feature of black history's public discourse that reached its apex during World War II.[36] The objective was to harness the power of patriotism in order to invest the black freedom struggle with the same glory and righteousness associated with the American Revolution and other American wars for freedom.

Woodson named Gabriel, Vesey, and Turner as worthy "insurrectionists" who "took to the war path to destroy slavery" in a 1945 *Negro History Bulletin* article called "Workers for Equality and Justice." This article presents a vivid picture of the diverse individuals and groups as well as the multifarious activities and initiatives that the association regarded as constituting the black fight for "equality and justice." Woodson stressed that the recent gains in black civil rights were not chance occurrences but the result of efforts by black attorneys such as Charles Hamilton Houston, William H. Hastie, and Thurgood Marshall as well as by many other blacks, who had "risked fame, fortune, and even their lives to clear the pathway of the race toward freedom and opportunity." "The story is a long one," Woodson declared, "and thousands of actors in this drama would have to be presented to complete the portrayal of this long concourse to freedom." It started on board the ships traversing the middle passage, with those African captives who had attempted to overpower the crews that were spiriting them away to "the land of bondage." And it continued all the way to A. Philip Randolph's March on Washington Movement. It encompassed violent resistance and "moral suasion" in the nineteenth century and union organizing, campaigns against disenfranchisement, and segregated schools in the twentieth century. Leading organizations included the National Urban League, the NAACP, and the National Negro Congress.[37] As Woodson's *Negro History Bulletin* article suggests, the association's conception of the black freedom struggle was expansive and inclusive—the different backgrounds, strategies, and ideologies of black freedom fighters mattered less than the fundamental aspiration they shared to be free.

Langston Hughes, who frequently championed black history in his regular column for the *Chicago Defender*, was adroit at drawing connections between national freedom and black freedom. In a 1945 *Defender* article marking Negro History Week, Hughes listed the following individuals and groups as "freedom fighters": Crispus Attucks, Frederick Douglass, Reconstruction-era black congressmen, and the Tuskegee airmen. According to Hughes, not only had blacks fought in "every war" but they had also fought "in every good American cause," including abolition, woman's suffrage, the campaign to end the poll tax, and the movement to create the Fair Employment Practices Commission.[38] Black history was filled with "thrilling stories" that "time cannot erase," Hughes wrote in a 1951 poem called "A Ballad of Negro History":

> Crispus Attucks' blow for freedom,
> Denmark Vesey's too.
> Sojourner Truth, Fred Douglass,
> And the heroes John Brown knew—
> Before the Union Armies gave
> Black men proud uniforms of blue.[39]

This "blow for freedom" phrase was a recurring one in the black history texts that forged connections between national freedom and black emancipation during the 1940s and 1950s. To commemorate Negro History Week in 1954, the *New Journal and Guide* published an article called "Here Too for Freedom a Blow Was Struck—By Nat Turner." The article included a photograph of a roadside marker noting the place of Turner's "slave insurrection," two miles west of Courtland, Virginia, on the side of U.S. Highway 58. The *New Journal and Guide* author completed an against-the-grain reading of the inscription, which listed how many whites had died in the "insurrection" but neglected to record the death toll for the slaves. The author recorded his thoughts as he stopped to photograph the marker as follows: "As at Boston Commons, Lexington, Concord, Yorktown, Gettysburg, and Antietam, here too for freedom a blow was struck." Looking ahead to the forthcoming *Brown* ruling, the author said that if the Supreme Court outlawed segregated schools, it would be a step in the direction of securing the "free and equal citizenship" that Turner fought and died for.[40]

In 1955, Folkways Records released an LP written and narrated by Langston Hughes called *The Glory of Negro History*. Hughes dedicated the record to Woodson. Spanning the centuries all the way "from the Negro pilot who was with Columbus to Ralph Bunche at the United Nations," the album wove together historical vignettes and biographical sketches with poetry and music. The musical selections ranged from the spirituals ("Swing Low, Sweet Chariot") and the blues ("Trouble in Mind") to hot jazz (Louis Armstrong's "I'm not Rough") and swing (Ella Fitzgerald's "Organ Grinder's Swing"). Hughes himself called *The Glory of Negro History* a "pageant." (Listening to this recording likely offers the closest available approximation of what it would have been like to attend a Negro History Week pageant in person in the mid-1950s.)[41]

If Hughes's record captured the tenor of Negro History Week celebrations, it was also an exemplary depiction of black history as a long black freedom struggle. From the beginning of U.S. history, Hughes explained, blacks had wanted "a world in which all men" would "walk together as equals and with dignity." The theme of black resistance recurs throughout *The Glory of Negro History*. "No man wanted to be a slave," Hughes told his listeners, who heard a song called "Ol' Riley" about a slave who escaped "like a turkey through the corn," trailed by a bloodhound who could not pick up his scent. Hughes introduced his listeners to Nat Turner, Sojourner Truth, and Harriet Tubman. Frederick Douglass was a central figure as well, and Hughes quoted Douglass's famed Fourth of July speech in which he called for "the storm, the whirlwind, and the earthquake." Among twentieth-century developments, Hughes extolled the virtues of the NAACP and its fights against restrictive real estate covenants, segregation in interstate travel, and segregated schools. Hughes turned to a musical analogy to describe the character of black history, comparing it to the blues, "with pools of prejudice and segregation at the doorstep but with hope and determination always there."[42] Resistance invariably accompanied oppression: the unrelenting desire to be free was one of black history's most important lessons.

"A FOUNDATION FOR INTEGRATION"

The *Negro History Bulletin* offered extensive analysis of the topic of school desegregation in the lead up to and wake of the *Brown* decision. The relevant previous court cases were reviewed; case studies and recent scholarship on school desegregation were presented, including an official release from the American Psychological Association called "Desegregation: An Appraisal of the Evidence," which summarized the research findings of Kenneth Clark; and editorials speculated on the likely effects of school desegregation, including whether black schools would have to close their doors.[43]

The association not only felt obligated to cover integration as an important topic of discussion and analysis. More ambitiously, it believed it had an important role to play in the process of integration as well. The theme for Negro History Week celebrations in 1954 was "Negro History—A Foundation for Integration." "Firm Foundations," a Negro History Week radio skit, captured the spirit of this particular year's celebrations. Featured on the popular "Americans All" program broadcast over WOOK, a station out of Washington, D.C., "Firm Foundations" was written by Mrs. Charlotte K. Brooks, a teacher at Banneker Junior High School, which sat perched on the hilltop next to Howard University. The skit opened with a jangling schoolbell, placing listeners inside Mrs. Brooks's social studies classroom, where students were set to discuss how "a real understanding of the history of the Negro" could serve as a positive basis for integration. A student called Phyllis ventured that "biased history" was the root cause of racial prejudice and discrimination. "Sad but true," all the students cried in unison. One of the main tasks of black history, the students therefore determined, was to expose damaging "propaganda masquerading as history."[44]

Looking ahead to the imminent verdict in the *Brown* case, the students proclaimed, "The Supreme Court decision can end the fact of segregation, but education through Negro history must end prejudice and hatred based upon ignorance and fear."[45] This is a concise statement of the association's overarching approach to the looming issue of integration. "Ridding the public of misinformation," as Charles Wesley put it, was just as important as supplying new information.[46] The "ugly stereotypes" that fueled racial prejudice needed to be challenged.[47] So too did the larger framework for discussions of the "Negro problem" in which white voices who "knew best" drowned out or silenced those of blacks. "Our good friends who say they know the Negro are just plain ignorant," John B. Henderson of the *New Journal and Guide* wrote in a 1954 Negro History Week article. "They think they know the Negro but really know absolutely nothing about him, neither his past nor his present," Henderson concluded. For precisely this reason, Richard V. Moore, president of Bethune-Cookman College, thought that black history was pregnant with possibilities for better understanding between the races. Many whites, he explained in a statement prepared for Negro History Week in 1954, had no knowledge of African American life apart from some kind of variation on the basic master-slave relationship. They had only ever approached blacks "from the perspective of boss over hired help, mistress of the house over maid" or as "patrons for entertainment [and] landlords of squalor huts and run-down tenements."[48]

Genuine understanding and exchange could not proceed on this uneven footing. As Albert Brooks, secretary-treasurer of the association and editor of the *Negro History Bulletin*, explained in 1954, "The acceptance of Negroes as equals by other Americans is the key to integration in this country."[49] Black history proponents regarded integration as about much more than "moving into the same schools or jobs or houses or social circles."[50] It was, as an author for the *Atlanta Daily World* said, "a process which must be based upon mutual respect for the dignity, the inherent worth and the personality of all human beings." Similarly, D.C. teacher Colston Stewart Jr. said integration "means acceptance of each other, it means love and respect of fellowman, it means an open smile and a will to friendship." In addition to this spirit of generosity and brotherhood, true integration required the "free flow of ideas" and the "blending" rather than the "clashing" of cultures. It had to be built on a foundation of genuine reciprocity. No group should be forced to abandon its "worthwhile mental and spiritual possessions," the *Philadelphia Tribune* opined.[51] Likewise, the pursuit of integration, Howard University public relations director James Nabrit Jr. explained during a 1955 Negro History Week event in Los Angeles, did not indicate that "we wish to lose our identity as Negroes."[52]

Opponents of integration maintained that racial prejudice was a "natural human urge or emotion." In the mid-1950s, one of the association's core messages was that prejudice was a learned rather than an instinctual response to the "fact of difference."[53] The song "You've Got to Be Carefully Taught" from the 1949 Rodgers and Hammerstein musical *South Pacific* was a favorite of association members in this regard. James Egert Allen, the program coordinator of the New York branch of the association, quoted the song lyrics at length during a 1954 Negro History Week radio address out of White Plains, New York. Some of the "stirring lines" he cited were as follows:

> You've got to be taught to hate and fear,
> You've got to be taught from year to year . . .
> You've got to be taught to be afraid,
> Of people whose eyes are oddly made;
> And people whose skin is a different shade.[54]

The association's bedrock belief that the pursuit of black history would only encourage the process of racial integration was not universally accepted and was often debated in the pages of the black press. Indeed, the observance of Negro History Week in the mid-1950s saw an annual February rush of essays, articles, and commentaries dedicated to the question of whether "Negro history" hindered the struggle for "the integration of the Negro in American life." Negro History Week was "offensive to certain frustrated members of the race who like to feel that integration is just around the corner," the *New York*

Amsterdam News reported in February 1954.⁵⁵ When the *Pittsburgh Courier* conducted an informal poll of nine black college presidents on this question, however, none of them concluded that the annual celebration was an impediment to integration. M. W. Curry Jr., president of Bishop College, summed up the consensus as follows: until the day came when "American historians decide[d] to tell the whole story without prejudice against any group because of its race, creed or color," Negro History Week would still be necessary.⁵⁶

Fisk president Charles S. Johnson agreed with Curry but then took his position one dramatic step further. Negro History Week would no longer be necessary, according to Johnson, as soon as "the study of Negro history" was accepted as an integral part of the study of American history" and as soon as integration was "really achieved." Underscoring this last point, Johnson explained, Negro History Week would continue to serve a worthwhile purpose just as long as blacks remained "a segregated and oppressed group within American society."⁵⁷ There is a dramatic difference, obviously, between integrating a textbook and integrating a society. But nothing short of the latter was the ultimate goal of the association in the mid-1950s. As Albert Brooks said in 1954, "The need for Negro history will endure as long as a Caucasian will caress a black dog but shrink away from a black man."⁵⁸

Brooks's statement is key to understanding the association's position on the larger purpose and potential of black history. From the association's point of view, "prejudice and segregation" were direct outgrowths of a "polluted history."⁵⁹ Woodson and his colleagues invested extraordinary power in the formal history curriculum and public outreach efforts such as Negro History Week. As a 1955 Negro History Week circular announced, the association "has taught and still insists that cold-blooded facts of history speak for themselves to men and women of illwill and goodwill."⁶⁰ Integrating our national history was the most surefire way to integrate the nation, according to the association. Transform the content and narrative of U.S. history and one would cut off the main source of prejudice and discrimination, like turning off a tap. The association never seemed to acknowledge in a serious way that history lessons provided just one of many sources of racial hatred and fear. Young people arguably learned just as much about race sitting at the kitchen table as they did seated at a school desk. Race lessons were presented, however informally, in multiple institutions and across multiple media, ranging from the family and the church to the comics and movies. No matter how sophisticated the association program for transforming the way U.S. history was learned, it could not bear the burden of the task it was assigned.

In his chapter for *What the Negro Wants*, Sterling Brown wrote about the importance of the "cheering signpost," which indicated that some important "mileage [had] been covered on the long journey" toward equal rights.⁶¹ The

Brown decision was the ultimate signpost, instantly recognized as a decision for the ages. When Negro History Week was celebrated in 1955, less than a year later, the Supreme Court decision had already been added to special Negro History–themed calendars as well as to lists such as "Fifteen Red Letter Days in Negro History."[62] Negro History Week in 1955 was an especially noteworthy occasion, as participants tried to make sense of the epochal ruling. On the one hand, there were more positive signs than ever before, indicating that "the long struggle for full equality of the Negro in American life will become a reality."[63] In addition to *Brown*, there had been the 1944 Supreme Court ruling *Smith v. Allwright*, which had outlawed white primaries. The executive branch had been more responsive to black concerns as well: in 1941, Roosevelt issued Executive Order 8802 to establish the Fair Employment Practices Commission, and in 1948, Truman issued Executive Order 9981 to desegregate the armed forces. The optimism of Negro History Week's 1955 celebrants was not unbounded, however. It was tempered by the recognition of rampant historical inequalities that were far from being fully rectified. "The millennium has not arrived yet," one of the year's special Negro History Week speakers warned.[64] Another noted that while the "future is bright," blacks needed to remain cognizant of continuing racial disparities and work as hard as they could to eliminate them.[65]

"DESEGREGATION: THE SOUTH'S NEWEST DILEMMA"

Rayford Logan and John Hope Franklin wrote extensively about the *Brown* decision. Their interest must have been due at least in part to the fact that they both worked as part of the Legal Defense Fund's crack historical research team that helped to prepare for *Brown*'s second round of arguments. In the fall of 1953, Franklin, Logan, and a handful of other historians including C. Vann Woodward, Howard Beale, and Alfred Kelly were tasked with researching the relationship between the Fourteenth Amendment and segregated schools.[66] Thurgood Marshall recruited Logan not so much by asking him as by telling him that he would be a part of the team. He was a hard man to say no to—after meeting him for the first time, Logan noted in his diary that "someone ought to do a 'profile' of him for *The New Yorker*. Tall, handsome, cool, he is a real 'character.'"[67] At regular meetings in New York, Franklin said that the legal counsel looked to the historians to answer many of the questions that the court had raised. "Whenever we [historians] so much as opened our mouths," Franklin recalled, "they said, 'be quiet, the historians are talking.'"[68] Although Franklin claimed that the *Brown* decision involved historians as no other event of the civil rights struggle, psychology proved to be more decisive in moving the court, Kenneth and Mamie Clark's famous doll studies trumping the complex and ultimately "inconclusive" historical briefs on the Fourteenth Amendment.[69]

With the *Brown* verdict, Logan said that the South had "suffered a defeat second only to that in the Civil War."[70] The decision, Logan reported, had provoked widespread discussion of practically every aspect of race relations in the United States from intermarriage and "the nature and susceptibility to cure of race prejudice" to "the morals, economic status, and intelligence of Negroes" and gradualism versus the "fell-swoop."[71] Logan himself was particularly interested in the test that *Brown* would pose to sociologist William Graham Sumner's famous and remarkably durable dictum that "stateways cannot change folkways."[72] In the immediate aftermath of *Brown*, Logan published two essays that examined the ruling in light of Sumner's axiom. While Logan noted that Prohibition was the favorite example for those trying to prove Sumner right, he maintained that Sumner's assertion was "too sweeping," citing a number of recent examples from history to support his point of view. The 1944 Supreme Court case *Smith v. Allwright* had resulted in a significant increase in voting by southern blacks, Logan noted, in spite of threats that blood would flow in the streets if the court ruled in the Negro's favor. Other examples that Logan presented included the integration of the armed forces and the effectiveness of the Fair Employment Practice Commission laws in helping blacks to secure jobs.[73]

In his autobiography, Franklin recalled staying up to the "wee hours of the morning" to celebrate the "sweet victory" of *Brown*. "We would not know until later," Franklin said, "that the decision's many opponents were also awake that night and already plotting its reversal."[74] On September 8, 1955, as massive resistance against *Brown* was ramping up, BBC London broadcast Franklin's reflections on the *Brown* decision in a segment called "Desegregation—The South's Newest Dilemma." The transcript later appeared in the *Journal of Negro Education*. Franklin asserted that the *Brown* decision had to be understood in the context of a century of southern dilemmas, all of which hinged on black-white relations. Much to its detriment, Franklin said, the South had carved out a clear pattern regarding race relations. When faced with the vexing problem of slavery before the Civil War, for example, the South chose secession. Likewise, when faced with the question of black citizenship after Reconstruction, the South chose disenfranchisement and segregation statutes. White southerners, Franklin argued, had made it a habit to confuse their needs with their wants. Consequently they "got what they wanted most of all: Negro domination."[75]

Regarding the significance of *Brown*, Franklin explained to the BBC listening audience that segregated schools had been the "cornerstone" of the southern way of life for more than two generations. He emphasized that segregated schools had made possible not only the diversion of the lion's share of public funds to schools for whites but had also helped to strengthen the argument for segregation. "As inadequately prepared Negroes emerged from inadequately supported schools," Franklin observed, "the whites could point to them as examples of the inability of the Negro to assimilate learning." Uneducated blacks, Franklin noted, in the South's "curious way of reasoning," were proof that they should be segregated and should not have equal opportunities. We return here to the faulty argument that the constraints imposed on African Americans supplied evidence of their natural inferiority. Franklin was worried that the burgeoning mobilization against school desegregation signaled that the South would once again hamstring itself on the question of race. And in a prescient remark, Franklin speculated that the South might have to be "dragged, kicking and screaming, into a state of legal obedience."[76]

Less than a year after his BBC address, Franklin contributed an essay to a special issue of the *Annals of the American Academy of Political and Social Science* on racial desegregation. Entitled "History of Racial Segregation in the United States," the essay clearly drew on the scholarship of Franklin's friend C. Vann Woodward for inspiration. Franklin read the first drafts of the celebrated lectures that Woodward delivered at the University of Virginia in the summer of 1954, lectures that turned into the pathbreaking book *The Strange Career of Jim Crow* the following year.[77] Martin Luther King Jr. would later say that *Strange Career* gave people the "heart to fight."[78] The opening line of the book provides a clue as to why: "The people of the South should be the last Americans to expect indefinite continuity of their institutions and social arrangements."[79] As E. Franklin Frazier noted in his review of *Strange Career*, Woodward had demonstrated that "the race problem was *made* and that men can *unmake* it."[80] Of the many Americans unable to remember a time before Jim Crow, Woodward said, "they have naturally assumed that things have 'always been that way.'" Jim Crow, in other words, had taken on a powerful "illusion of permanency."[81]

The first line of Franklin's "History of Racial Segregation" essay alluded to this "illusion of permanency" idea, proclaiming that the "enactment of state segregation statutes is a relatively recent phenomenon in the history of race relations in the United States." Franklin noted that they did not appear on the books until the last quarter of the nineteenth century and that, moreover, it was not until the twentieth century that these statutes became "a major apparatus for keeping the Negro 'in his place.'" Segregation statutes were a legacy of the slave regime, Franklin said, and received their inspiration from a basic assumption of black inferiority. Franklin recounted some of the more extravagant segregation initiatives, including one in Oklahoma calling for segregated telephone booths and one in New Orleans calling for an ordinance to keep black and white prostitutes separate. He also shared an anecdote about a white fisherman who would put his fishing rod across the boat to separate himself from his black companion while they were eating lunch. While Franklin did not deny that the wall of segregation was "formidable," he also pointed out that "the pattern of segregation was as irregular as it was complex."[82] As such, in a Woodward-esque argument, he highlighted the fact that segregation was a human invention, thereby suggesting that, contrary to beliefs held by many white southerners, it was neither natural nor ordained by God.

To understand the shifting racial landscape in the United States from the early 1940s to the mid-1950s, Woodson and his colleagues turned to history. The historical record revealed an American "tradition" of racial prejudice and discrimination.[83] But it also uncovered a prolonged and energetic black freedom struggle. The emerging civil rights movement could only be properly understood by stepping back to view new developments from a historical perspective. Otherwise, one might be overwhelmed or misled by the continuous, unfolding drama of the present. It was especially important to keep in mind that there was a long legacy of activism that had provided the scaffolding for monumental civil rights victories like *Brown*. It was also important to remain vigilant in the wake of celebrating milestones in racial progress. History showed that black gains would be contested, that white prejudice was resilient, and that structures of institutional discrimination were often reconfigured rather than completely dismantled.

With the *Brown* decision, the association believed that the study of black history provided an answer to the challenge posed by the nascent movement toward racial integration. As bias and discrimination disappeared from history classrooms, so too would bias and discrimination disappear from society. This expectation was predicated on an almost evangelical faith in the power of history. As John Hope Franklin proclaimed in 1944, a scientific history devoted to the "whole truth" would inexorably lead to history "as a force in the construction of a more perfect society."[84] For members and friends of the association, it was history that would connect truth and justice, history that would turn the wheels of progress forward. If we could just get our history right, all would be right in the world.

Epilogue

The Smithsonian's National Museum of African American History and Culture (NMAAHC) opened its doors on September 24, 2016, just over a century after Carter G. Woodson founded the Association for the Study of Negro Life and History.[1] The $540 million building is sited "at the geographic center of American civic identity," nestled between the Washington Monument and the Museum of American History on the National Mall.[2] The building itself—a "triple, inverted pyramid form," decorated with thirty-six hundred panels of "shimmering, bronze filigree"—nods to both Yoruba art from West Africa and the fine ironwork made by black craftsmen in cities like New Orleans and Charleston.[3] The museum's lower-level history galleries are organized chronologically around three thematic exhibitions, starting seventy feet below the ground with "Slavery and Freedom," followed by "Defending Freedom, Defining Freedom: Era of Segregation 1876–1968" and "A Changing America: 1968 and Beyond." On the upper floors are the community and culture galleries, which feature exhibitions such as "Sports: Leveling the Playing Field," "Double Victory: The African American Military Experience," and "Musical Crossroads."[4]

Established by an act of Congress in 2003, the museum holds some forty thousand artifacts, many of which were collected during an "Antiques Roadshow"-style campaign called "Save Our African American Treasures" that traveled to fifteen cities across the country.[5] Among the thirty-five hundred objects on display when the museum opened were the following: remnants from the São José, a Portuguese slave ship that sank off the coast of South Africa, a set of shackles fit for a child, Nat Turner's bible, Frederick Douglass's cane, Emmett Till's empty coffin, Rosa Parks's mug shot, Muhammad Ali's boxing gloves, Klan hoods, an Angola Prison tower, and the twelve-hundred-pound aluminum "Mothership" stage prop used by Parliament-Funkadelic in their live concerts.

The museum opened to overwhelmingly positive, even rapturous, reviews.

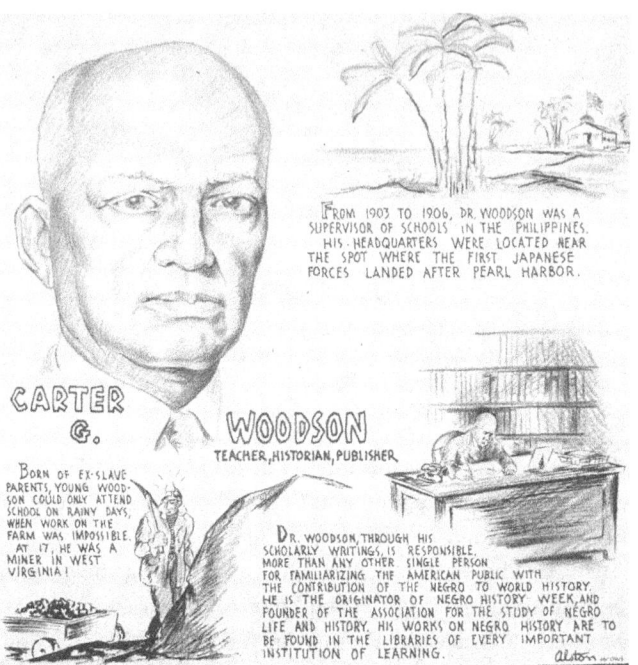

1943 cartoon depicting Woodson's journey from the coalmines of West Virginia to leader of the "Negro History" movement.
(Charles Henry Alston, National Archives, item no. 535622, Records of the Office of War Information)

"It's here at last, here at last," the *Times* enthused, riffing on the famous concluding lines from Martin Luther King Jr.'s "I Have a Dream" speech.[6] The museum is, in many respects, a monumental vindication of the association's pathbreaking work. It embodies, with resources and reach beyond Woodson's wildest imagination, the robust black archive that the association envisioned and began to construct. The museum also ratifies the claims that black history and black culture are integral to the American experience, propositions that were revolutionary when they were advanced by Woodson and his colleagues. The stories that the museum tells have virtually the same protagonists, plotlines, and morals as those crafted by Woodson and his coworkers. They include accounts of the horrifying trauma of slavery and the "unending bitterness and violence" of Jim Crow, as well as the trajectory of the long black freedom struggle and the evolution of remarkable black cultural achievements in music, literature, drama, and the fine arts.[7]

"African-American history is not somehow separate from our larger American story" but is "central to the American story."[8] So said President Obama in remarks delivered at the museum's opening. From the 1960s to the present, black history has progressively moved from the margins to the center with respect to academic history, popular history, public history, and schoolbook history. African American history has been a vibrant specialty of U.S. history for decades now, attracting scholars of all ethno-racial backgrounds. Books, monuments, and movies pertaining to black history have enjoyed a high degree of visibility and acclaim in recent years. Isabel Wilkerson's 2010 book *The Warmth of Other Suns: The Epic Story of America's Great Migration*, for example, was a *New York Times* best seller and won the National Book Critics Circle Award. The last major construction project on the National Mall before the NMAAHC was the King Memorial, which opened in 2011. The 2013 period drama *12 Years a Slave*, meanwhile, was a box office smash and won the Academy Award for Best Picture. In terms of the school curriculum, as Jonathan Zimmerman concludes, "thanks to several generations of grassroots black activists, students of every color now learn as much (if not more) about Frederick Douglass, Booker T. Washington, and Martin Luther King, Jr. as they do about Andrew Jackson, Theodore Roosevelt, or John F. Kennedy."[9] A survey conducted in 2004–5, which was featured in the *Journal of American History*, asked high school students to write down the "names of the most famous Americans in history," excluding presidents. The top three names were Martin Luther King Jr., Rosa Parks, and Harriet Tubman.[10] In the realm of arts and letters, some of the most frequently assigned texts in English literature courses are by black authors, including Zora Neale Hurston's *Their Eyes Were Watching God*, Ralph Ellison's *Invisible Man*, and Toni Morrison's *Beloved*.[11] Not only Hurston but many of the other writers first championed in renaissance-era anthologies—including Langston Hughes, Claude McKay, and Jean Toomer—have been inducted into the American literary canon. Regarding music, the spirituals, blues, jazz, and hip-hop are acknowledged as national treasures.[12]

Woodson and his colleagues were among the first professional historians to challenge the narrative of U.S. history as one of continuously expanding freedom and opportunity. They demonstrated that, as far as blacks were concerned, progress happened in fits and starts and generally followed the principle of one step forward, two steps back. Black history—the likes of Benjamin Brawley, John Hope Franklin, Rayford Logan, Leila Amos Pendleton, and Woodson all maintained—was characterized by pendulum swings driven by powerful dialectics such as slavery and freedom, oppression and resistance, heartbreak and triumph. NMAAHC founding director Lonnie Bunch said that the "tension between moments of pain and stories of resiliency" is at the heart of the museum's experience, a view reinforced by the first waves of museum visitors. The "complex narrative" conveyed by the museum, the *Times* reported, puts "uplift and tragedy" on a "collision course." It is filled, the *New Yorker* said, with both "treasures" and "traumas." "The tone, throughout, is a shifting mix of sadness and celebration," the *Washington Post* testified, a "juxtaposition of promise with sorrow," according to the *Atlantic*.[13]

The tenor of the museum reflects the association's belief that the "whole truth" must be told about the American past, especially with respect to the hard truths of racial terrorism. "A great nation does not hide its history," George W. Bush said at the museum's opening ceremony. "This museum," he continued, "tells the truth that a country founded on the premise of liberty held millions in chains. That the price of our union was America's original sin."[14] According to Bunch, one of the museum's fundamental objectives is "to harness the power of memory to help America illuminate all the dark corners of its past."[15] One cannot understand black history, Bunch explained, without addressing "the pain of slavery, segregation, or racial violence."[16] Regarding the museum's head-on approach to confronting the country's "tortured racial past," one visitor said approvingly that "you just have to face the reality. It [slavery] was brutal. And it should not be sugarcoated."[17] Beyond the museum, the nation's disturbing history of racial violence is included as a matter of course in today's leading U.S. history survey textbooks. Students learn in detail about everything from slave whippings and lynchings to race riots and church bombings. It is not uncommon for textbooks to include even the most grisly of images, such as a photograph of the charred body of seventeen-year-old Jesse Washington, lynched in Waco, Texas, on May 15, 1916.[18]

The history taught in schools, museums, mass media, and popular culture approaches the association's ideal curriculum oriented around the "unvarnished truth."[19] There is no longer a yawning gap between the "facts" of black history and the stories that we tell about black history—between "what has *actually* happened and what those who have written the history have *said* has happened."[20] In short, the association's vision of justice in history has arguably been achieved. But if schoolbooks are more racially integrated than they have ever been before, our schools themselves are increasingly segregated. Almost three-quarters of blacks attend majority nonwhite schools, while 15 percent attend so-called apartheid schools, where whites make up less than 1 percent of the enrollment.[21] And at the same time that the vexed history of race is depicted fairly and accurately (from the point of view of Woodson and his colleagues), a Washington Post–ABC News poll taken in the summer of 2016 indicated that "pessimism about race relations in America is higher than it has been in nearly a generation."[22]

Less than a week before the museum's gala opening, Keith Lamont Scott, a forty-three-year old black man, was shot and killed by a police officer in Charlotte, North Carolina. His death followed two years of protests and controversies over police killings of African Americans (especially young African American men), sparked by the fatal shooting of Michael Brown in Ferguson, Missouri, and invigorated by the Black Lives Matter movement. African Americans represent almost one-third of the people shot by police, a disproportionate ratio that is more than double the percentage of African Americans in the general population.[23] Significant racial disparities, revealed by mountains of empirical data, are clearly evident across a wide range of domains, reflected in high unemployment and poverty levels, lower levels of educational attainment, lower life expectancy, and higher incarceration rates.[24]

How would Woodson and his coworkers make sense of today's racial landscape, which remains rife with racial inequalities? Many of the most original, challenging, and contested ideas advanced by the association in the age of Jim Crow have become part of our collective, conventional wisdom. There is a conundrum here that speaks to the limitations of historical representation and commemoration. Obama put his finger on it in his NMAAHC address. In a speech that was largely a paean to the wonder and power of black history, the president paused to offer the following observation:

> A museum alone will not alleviate poverty in every inner city or every rural hamlet. It won't eliminate gun violence from all our neighborhoods, or immediately ensure that justice is always colorblind. It won't wipe away every instance of discrimination in a job interview or a sentencing hearing or folks trying to rent an apartment. Those things are up to us, the decisions and choices we make. It requires speaking out, and organizing, and voting, until our values are fully reflected in our laws and our policies and our communities.[25]

History, even one as long, terrifying, and inspiring as that of African Americans, can only carry you so far.

NOTES

INTRODUCTION

1. Hurston, *Dust Tracks on a Road*, 140.
2. Litwack, *How Free Is Free?*, 30.
3. On Woodson, see Goggin, *Carter G. Woodson*; Dagbovie, *The Early Black History Movement, Carter G. Woodson, and Lorenzo Johnston Greene*, pt. 1; Meier and Rudwick, *Black History and the Historical Profession*, chs. 1 and 2; and Thorpe, *Black Historians*, ch.5. See also Du Bois, "A Portrait of Carter G. Woodson"; Franklin, "The Place of Carter G. Woodson in American Historiography"; Greene and Strickland, *Working with Carter G. Woodson, the Father of Black History*, and *Selling Black History for Carter G. Woodson*; Hughes, "When I Worked for Dr. Woodson"; Lindsay, "Dr. Carter G. Woodson as a Teacher"; Logan, "Carter G. Woodson," and "Carter G. Woodson: Mirror and Molder of His Time"; Reddick, "Carter G. Woodson"; Wesley, "Carter G. Woodson."
4. Quoted in Dagbovie, *The Early Black History Movement, Carter G. Woodson, and Lorenzo Johnston Greene*, xi.
5. Goggin, "Carter Godwin Woodson."
6. Quoted in Winston, "Through the Back Door," 693.
7. The work of scholars such as Julie Des Jardins (*Women and the Historical Enterprise in America*), Robert B. Townsend (*History's Babel*), and Michel-Rolph Trouillot (*Silencing the Past*) has demonstrated the merits of taking a broad view of the historical enterprise.
8. During the interwar period, the intercultural education movement introduced black history to small numbers of white schoolchildren, most notably in progressive schools in the New York metropolitan era. On intercultural education, see Selig, *Americans All*.
9. Whereas "Negro" or "black" history appeared in the headlines of 51 *New York Times* articles from 1915 through 1960, "Negro" or "black" history made the *Times* headlines 253 times from 1961 to 1971. "With the sit-ins, marches and demonstrations," the *Negro History Bulletin* reported, "there came ... the requests and the demands for black history." All of the major civil rights organizations from the NAACP to the National Urban League and the Congress on Race Equality "entered the textbook arena" in the early 1960s, calling for an end to racial bias and stereotypes in American history textbooks. In 1965, California passed a law requiring history textbooks to "correctly

portray the role and contribution of the American Negro and members of other ethnic groups." School desegregation provoked vigorous debates about "integrated" textbooks and black history in the curriculum (for the first time in U.S. history, white children would learn more than the rudiments about the African American experience). See "Teaching Black History," 5; Zimmerman, *Whose America?*, 112, 107, 111.

10. Johnson, "The Dilemma of the Negro Author," my italics. "Situated as his own race is amidst and amongst them [white people]," Johnson said, "their influence is irresistible." "I judge there is not a single Negro writer who is not, at least secondarily impelled by the desire to make his work have some effect on the white world for the good of his race" (267).

11. Anderson, *The Education of Blacks in the South*, 148, 181, 153, 274.

12. On the introduction of black history into the curriculum at black colleges and universities at the turn of the twentieth century, see Hall, *A Faithful Account of the Race*, ch.6. See also Winston, *Howard University Department of History*.

13. Gaines, *Uplifting the Race*, xxi, 4, 1, 3. On the gendered dimensions of racial uplift, see Mitchell, *Righteous Propagation*.

14. Van Wyck Brooks coined the term "usable past" in his 1918 essay "On Creating a Usable Past."

15. Woodson, "Jim Crow's Profits and Prophets," *Atlanta Daily World*, June 30, 1932.

16. Woodson, "Annual Report of the Director" (1946), 388.

17. Woodson, "Future Task of Race History Is Outlined," *Chicago Defender*, September 7, 1935; Bethune, "Clarifying Our Vision with the Facts," 15.

18. Franklin, "The New Negro History," 41, italics in original. Michel-Rolph Trouillot describes the nub of this issue as the difference between "the facts of the matter" and "a narrative of those facts" (*Silencing the Past*, 2).

19. Bethune, "The Association for the Study of Negro Life and History," 406–7.

20. Ibid., 407.

21. As Woodson remarked in a 1926 issue of the *Journal of Negro History*, "The Negro race has done as much good as any other race but neither the Negroes nor the whites generally know it. To have a record which we suffer to remain hidden away in the past means a loss of prestige, a loss of social status and a possible loss of existence" ("Notes," 423).

22. Woodson, "Negro History Week—the Eighth Year," 126.

23. Woodson, "Negro History Week—the Fifth Year," 127.

24. Woodson, "Negro History Week—the Third Year," 123–24; Woodson, "Annual Report of the Director" (1938), 414; Woodson, "Notes" (1928), 110.

25. Woodson, *The African Background Outlined*, 5; Du Bois, *Darkwater*, 1.

26. Franklin, "The New Negro History," 48, italics in original.

27. Quarles, "Black History's Diversified Clientele," 204.

28. Woodson, *The Miseducation of the Negro*, 93; Woodson, "Proceedings of the Eighth Annual Meeting of the Association for the Study of Negro Life and History," 103–4.

29. See, for example, Woodson, "Annual Report of the Director" (1943), 377.

30. Logan, "Our European Heritage and Our African Heritage," Rayford Logan Papers, box 181-15, folder 18.

31. Woodson, "Notes" (1928), 111.

32. Bethune, "The Association for the Study of Negro Life and History," 409.

33. Woodson, "Notes" (1928), 111; Woodson, "Annual Report of the Director" (1945), 254–55; Woodson, "Annual Report of the Director" (1946), 388; Woodson, "Annual Report of the Director," (1945), 255; Woodson, "Future Task of Race History is Outlined."

34. Franklin, "The Dilemma of the Negro Scholar," 306.

35. Woodson also predicted that radical groups seemingly friendly to the Negro would "drop him" as soon as their own short-term goals had been achieved (*Miseducation of the Negro*, 90-91). For more on Woodson's politics, see Goggin, *Carter G. Woodson*, ch.5.

36. Holloway, *Confronting the Veil*, 15.

37. Thompson, "The Education of the Negro in the United States," 947.

38. Woodson, "Test Yourself to See If You Are a Segregationist," *New York Amsterdam News*, July 27, 1932; Woodson, "Dr. Carter Woodson Thinks He Would Like to Live Way Down in Atlanta, Ga.," *Baltimore Afro-American*, December 3, 1932; Woodson, "A Rejoinder to Dr. Tobias," *Chicago Defender*, July 30, 1932.

39. Woodson, *Miseducation of the Negro*, 54. These quotes from Woodson prefigure the statements Du Bois made regarding segregation in the last essay he wrote as editor of *Crisis* in June 1934: "Use segregation. Use every bit that comes your way and transmute it into power. Power that will some day smash all race separation" ("Postscript," 183–84.)

40. Frederick Douglass, quoted in Logan, *The Betrayal of the Negro, from Rutherford B. Hayes to Woodrow Wilson*, 3.

41. Ibid., 315.

42. Holloway and Keppel, introduction, 2. The black academy was an overwhelmingly male preserve. Black women who were interested in academe faced the double stigma of race and gender, which translated into formidable obstacles with respect to funding graduate studies and securing employment. It was not until 1940 that Marion Thompson became the first African American woman to earn the history PhD in the United States. Merze Tate, the first female member of the Howard History Department, was appointed in 1942. On why so few African American women entered the historical profession in the first half of the twentieth century, see White, introduction; see also Wilson, *The Segregated Scholars*, ch. 3.

43. Quoted in Winston, "Through the Back Door," 702.

44. Quoted in Wilson, *The Segregated Scholars*, 81.

45. Winston, "Through the Back Door," 702; Hine, "Carter G. Woodson, White Philanthropy, and Negro Historiography," 406.

46. Wilson, *The Segregated Scholars*, 2.

47. Franklin, "The Dilemma of the Negro Scholar," 303.

48. Woodson himself maintained contacts with a handful of prominent white historians, including Edward Channing, Albert Bushnell Hart, and J. Franklin Jameson, who would vouch for the quality of the association's scholarship when Woodson was attempting to secure grants from foundations and philanthropies.

49. Meier and Rudwick, *Black History and the Historical Profession*, xii.

50. Holloway and Keppel, introduction, 2; Holloway, *Confronting the Veil*, 19.

51. Franklin, "The Dilemma of the Negro Scholar," 304.

52. Des Jardins, *Women and the Historical Enterprise in America*, 93, 109–10.

53. Ibid., 267.

54. Robin D. G. Kelley argues that black history has maintained a cosmopolitan focus from its inception and that black scholars such as Woodson, Wesley, and Logan were some of the first historians to write transnational history. "The consensus among scholars of African American history," Kelley says, "was that there is no United States history outside of world affairs" ("'But a Local Phase of a World Problem,'" 1076).

55. Holloway and Keppel, introduction, 12.

56. Woodson, *The Negro in Our History*, 2nd ed., 267.

57. Woodson, "Why We Should Publish Truth in Self-Defense," *New York Amsterdam News*, November 9, 1932.

58. Franklin, "The New Negro History," 45, italics in original.

59. Hall, *A Faithful Account of the Race*, 19–20.

60. Franklin, "The Dilemma of the Negro Scholar," 302, 299, italics in original.

61. Hall, *A Faithful Account of the Race*, 9.

62. Litwack, *How Free is Free?*, 4.

63. Woodson, "Prophets and Profits of Racial Segregation," *New York Amsterdam News*, June 29, 1932.

64. Quoted in Litwack, *How Free is Free?*, 8.

65. Meier and Rudwick, *Black History and the Historical Profession*, 47.

PART ONE. THE COLOR LINE

1. Douglass, "The Color Line," 573, 575, 568.

2. See, for example, Du Bois's *The Souls of Black Folk* (1903), William Benjamin Smith's *The Color Line* (1905) and Ray Stannard Baker's *Following the Color Line* (1908).

3. Franklin and Higginbotham, *From Slavery to Freedom*, 261, 266–67, 282.

4. Litwack, *How Free Is Free?*, 14.

5. Meier and Rudwick, *Black History and the Historical Profession*, 2.

6. Gates, "The Trope of a New Negro and the Reconstruction of the Image of the Black," 149–50; Hale, *Making Whiteness*, 164. On the mammy figure and the invention of Aunt Jemima, see McElya, *Clinging to Mammy*.

7. Hale, *Making Whiteness*, 160.

8. Smethurst, *The African American Roots of Modernism*, 16.

9. Litwack, *How Free Is Free?*, 14. Indeed even the most liberal whites generally shared two basic beliefs with the most rabid Negrophobes: first, that blacks were inferior, whether by blood or by circumstances, and second, that they were not 100 percent American. On the core white supremacist propositions "acceptable to almost all shades of white opinion" from the 1840s through the 1910s, see Fredrickson, *The Black Image in the White Mind*, 321.

10. Novick, *That Noble Dream*, 76–77.

11. See Goggin, "Countering White Racist Scholarship"; Logan, "Carter G. Woodson" (1973); Novick, *That Noble Dream*, esp. ch.3; and Wilson, "Racial Consciousness and Black Scholarship."

12. Meier and Rudwick, *Black History and the Historical Profession*, 2; Dagbovie, *Early Black History Movement*, 1; Goggin, *Carter G. Woodson*, xv.

13. On "internalist" versus "externalist" approaches to intellectual history, see Novick, *That Noble Dream*, 9–10.

14. Gates, "The Trope of a New Negro and the Reconstruction of the Image of the Black," 131, 136-37.

15. See Yellin, *Racism in the Nation's Service*.

16. Woodson, review of *American Negro Slavery*, 103.

17. See, for example, Dagbovie, *Early Black History Movement, Carter G. Woodson, and Lorenzo Johnston Greene*, 1, 114; Goggin, *Carter G. Woodson*, 67; Meier and Rudwick, *Black History and the Historical Profession*, 10; Hall, *A Faithful Account of the Race*, 169, 217, 224-25; Zimmerman, "'Each 'Race' Could Have Its Heroes Sung,'" esp. 103-5, and *Whose America?*, 8, 33.

CHAPTER ONE. "THE CAUSE"

1. Woodson, "My Recollections of Veterans of the Civil War," 103-4; Goggin, *Carter G. Woodson*, 3-4.

2. Carter G. Woodson, "Notes" (1942), 243-44; Cade, "Out of the Mouths of Ex-Slaves," 306; Woodson, "My Recollections of Veterans of the Civil War," 104.

3. Woodson, "My Recollections of Veterans of the Civil War," 116.

4. Ibid.

5. Ibid. *Men of Mark* was a sprawling "collective biography," running to 1,138 pages with entries on more than 175 individuals, "the most comprehensive biographical catalog published during this period" (Hall, *A Faithful Account of the Race*, 171).

6. Wilson, dedication, *The Black Phalanx*, n.p.; Williams, *A History of the Negro Troops in the War of the Rebellion*, xiv.

7. Brundage, *The Southern Past*, 71. The newspapers that Woodson read in his twenties (such as the *Richmond Planet*) regularly reported on emancipation day celebrations.

8. Ibid., 59, 75, 60, 64.

9. Ibid., 95, 90; see also Kachun, *Festivals of Freedom*, 235.

10. Kachun, *Festivals of Freedom*, 13-14.

11. Woodson, "My Recollections of Veterans of the Civil War," 117.

12. Carter G. Woodson, transcript, Harvard University Archives; Harvard Courses of Instruction, 1908-9, HUC 8500.16, Harvard University Archives; Joyce, "Edward Channing."

13. Goggin, *Carter G. Woodson*, 21-22; Woodson, "The George Washington Bicentennial Eliminates March 5th, Crispus Attucks Day," *New York Age*, January 2, 1932; Williams, *History of the Negro Troops in the War of the Rebellion*, 103; Woodson, "Camden, N.J., School Music Dept. Found New Reason to Bar Pupils from Opera," *Baltimore Afro-American*, April 7, 1934.

14. Townsend, *History's Babel*, 15.

15. Ibid.

16. On Woodson's experience as a student at Harvard, see Goggin, *Carter G. Woodson*, 20-26. The three seminars he took with Channing were "Selected Topics in the Historical Development of American Institutions—The Opposition to England, 1760-1775," "Selected Topics in the Historical Development of American Institutions—The Formation of the Constitution, 1775-1789," and "The Literature of American History" (Woodson transcript, Harvard University Archives; Harvard Courses of Instruction, 1908-9, HUC 8500.16, Harvard University Archives).

17. Higham, quoted in Novick, *That Noble Dream*, 72.

18. Whelan, "Albert Bushnell Hart," *American National Biography*; Buck and Church, *Social Sciences at Harvard*, 141. Hart was exceptionally prolific, publishing more than nine hundred articles and authoring or editing about one hundred books.

19. Joyce, "Edward Channing"; Channing, *A History of the United States*, vi. The first edition of Channing's *A Student's History of the United States* was published in 1898; by 1924, the book had gone through five editions.

20. Bogue, "Frederick Jackson Turner." On the place of "the frontier" in Woodson's scholarship, see Goggin, *Carter G. Woodson*, 200–202.

21. Novick, *That Noble Dream*, 71.

22. Hoffer, *Past Imperfect*, 14; Hofstadter, *The Progressive Historians*, 27.

23. Channing, *A Student's History of the United States*, 599–600.

24. The full quote is as follows: "The English colonists who came to the most vigorous and permanent colonial life had also an obstinate belief in the English principles of personal freedom, local self-control, representative government, and the traditional common law, which are the common inheritance of all the members of the Anglo-Saxon race" (Channing, Hart, and Turner, *Guide to the Study and Reading of American History*, 2).

25. Hart, *The Southern South*, 105; Novick, *That Noble Dream*, 75; Hart, *School History of the United States* (1918), 109. Hart served on the Howard University Board of Trustees for over two decades, from 1920 to 1943.

26. Lewis, *W. E. B. Du Bois: Biography of a Race*, 112. In a 1916 letter to the editor of the *American Historical Review*, Channing recommended Woodson as a "very good man," committed to "doing thorough work." "I think you can trust him as fully as you can trust any colored man," Channing said, "but he has, of course, the defects of his color." Quoted in Wilson, "Racial Consciousness and Black Scholarship," 77. Channing and Hart did not think of their black students as "pure blooded" Africans (as Channing's use of the term "colored" suggests)—and they would have dismissed as out of hand the notion that Du Bois, Woodson, and Channing represented the potential of the "Negro race." Writing to Charles Wesley in August 1925, Channing exhorted him to "try to realize that Du Bois, Woodson and yourself are much more white than negro" (reprinted in Harris, "Charles Harris Wesley, Educator and Historian," 192). In another letter to Wesley, Channing had written that "I cannot think of you and your little daughter as anything but essentially white people, a few of whose ancestors were negroes" (ibid., 193).

27. Turner, quoted in Newby, "Historians and Negroes," 39.

28. Lewis, *W. E. B. Du Bois: Biography of a Race*, 112; Buck and Church, *Social Sciences at Harvard*, 133.

29. Goggin, *Carter G. Woodson*, 24–29; Logan, "Carter G. Woodson" (1973), 8.

30. Channing, Hart, and Turner, *Guide to the Study and Reading of American History*, 7.

31. On racism in the Wilson administration, see Yellin, *Racism in the Nation's Service*.

32. Logan, review of *The Secret City*, 219; Holloway, *Confronting the Veil*, 36, 40.

33. McHenry, *Forgotten Readers*, 154.

34. On the Bethel Literary and Historical Society and other African American literary societies, see McHenry, *Forgotten Readers*, esp. ch. 3. On the American Negro Academy, see Moss, *The American Negro Academy*. On the Negro Society for Histori-

cal Research, see Sinnette, *Arthur Alfonso Schomburg: Black Bibliophile and Collector*, esp. ch. 2.

35. McHenry, *Forgotten Readers*, 141, 174; Gatewood, *Aristocrats of Color*, 216; Goggin, *Carter G. Woodson*, 28; Brundage, *The Southern Past*, 147.

36. Moss, *The American Negro Academy*, 1, 249–50, 119, 245; "Election of Officers Is Feature of Session," *Evening Star*, December 29, 1914.

37. Moss, *The American Negro Academy*, 298; Hall, *A Faithful Account of the Race*, 159.

38. Moss, *The American Negro Academy*, 299, 291. In an even more damning assessment of the ANA's limited influence, Jonathan Scott Holloway describes it as "limp[ing] along quietly for thirty-three years" (*Confronting the Veil*, 23).

39. Goggin, *Carter G. Woodson*, 142–43; "Villard's Criticism Stings Secretary of the Treasury," *Baltimore Afro-American*, November 1, 1913; Du Bois, "Another Open Letter to Woodrow Wilson," 233; Woodson, *The Negro in Our History*, 327.

40. Stokes, *D. W. Griffith's "The Birth of a Nation"*, 111; Rogin, "'The Sword Became a Flashing Vision,'" 152; *Birth of a Nation* intertitles, excerpted from *History of the American People*, quoted in Stokes, *D. W. Griffith's "Birth of a Nation"*, 199.

41. Quoted in Stokes, *D. W. Griffith's "Birth of a Nation"*, 173. For Griffith's views on history, see Stokes, ch. 7. "The time will come," Griffith said in a 1915 interview, "when the children in the public schools will be taught practically everything by moving pictures. Certainly they will never be obliged to read history again" (ibid., 172).

42. Franklin, *"The Birth of a Nation,"* 18; Reinhart, *Abraham Lincoln on Screen*, 58.

43. Peter Novick, *That Noble Dream*, 77.

44. Hale, *Making Whiteness*, 80. Dunning's two most important publications were *Essays on the Civil War and Reconstruction* (1897) and *Reconstruction, Political and Economic, 1865–1877* (1907).

45. Novick, *That Noble Dream*, 14.

46. Quoted in Newby, *Jim Crow's Defense*, 66. One or another variation of this statement found its place into textbooks for decades to come. For example, in the 1911 edition of his best-selling textbook, David Muzzey wrote: "Since their emancipation fifty years ago they [blacks] have made considerable progress; but still they are, as a race, far, perhaps centuries, behind the whites in civilization" (*An American History*, 619).

47. Rogin, "'Sword Became a Flashing Vision,'" 153, 174.

48. Woodson, *The Negro in Our History*, 4th ed., 490; Woodson, unpublished *Birth of a Nation* encyclopedia entry, Carter G. Woodson and the Association for Negro Life and History Papers, reel 10, frame 220; Woodson, "Negro Life and History in Our Schools," 274.

49. "Lincoln Jubilee and National Half-Century Anniversary Exposition," *Chicago Defender*, May 22, 1915. It was the Lincoln Jubilee that took place in Chicago that summer, not the "Exposition of Negro Progress," as Stamps remembered and Jacqueline Goggin and many other scholars have subsequently reported. For more background information on the Lincoln Jubilee, see Wilson, *Negro Building*, 160–71.

50. Goggin, *Carter G. Woodson*, 32; Stokes, *D. W. Griffith's "The Birth of a Nation"*, 150–53.

51. Stokes, *D. W. Griffith's "The Birth of a Nation"*, 153.

52. "'America's Greatest Problem: The Negro': Three Students of the Subject View

the Racial Question from Different Angles and Offer Suggestions for Its Solution," *New York Times*, July 18, 1915.

53. Shufeldt, *America's Greatest Problem*, 276. Regarding his competence to address the "Negro problem," Shufeldt pointed to his familiarity with "the lives of the slaves of Cuba and the free negroes in Hayti," his visits to every southern state in the Union, his knowledge of "the sciences of anatomy, physiology, anthropology, ethnology, psychology, medicine and organic evolution," and his experience "dissect[ing] males, females, and young of both Negroes and mulattoes" (ibid., 2–3).

54. Ibid., 3–4, 253.

55. "'America's Greatest Problem: The Negro': Three Students of the Subject View the Racial Question from Different Angles and Offer Suggestions for Its Solution," *New York Times*, July 18, 1915; "Negro Fellowship League," *Chicago Defender*, July 24 and August 7, 1915.

56. Woodson, *The Education of the Negro*, iv.

57. Ibid., 170, 9, 206–7.

58. Ibid., 89–90.

59. Here and elsewhere, Woodson was quick to acknowledge the positive contributions of white philanthropists to black education. For instance, he introduced readers to Baltimore's William Crane, who donated $20,000 to erect a well-appointed school for blacks in the center of the city (ibid., 133, 144).

60. Ibid., 82–83.

61. Among the primary sources excerpted were: "Benjamin Fawcett's Address to the Christian Negroes in Virginia About 1755"; "Address to the Free People of Color by the American Convention for Promoting the Abolition of Slavery, 1819"; and the anonymously published "Education of Colored People, 1854."

62. Wilson, *Negro Building*, 145.

63. "Lincoln Jubilee Album: 50th Anniversary of Our Emancipation," compiled by John H. Ballard, Lincoln Jubilee official photographer, 1915.

64. Stamps, "Fifty Years Later," 31; "Lincoln Jubilee Is a Big Success," *Chicago Defender*, August 28, 1915; "Lincoln Jubilee to End Next Week," *Chicago Defender*, September 11, 1915.

65. On African American responses to the Columbian Exposition in Chicago, including the protest led by Ida B. Wells, see Lorini, *Rituals of Race*, 42–51.

66. Wilson, *Negro Building*, 31, 28.

67. Ibid., 82.

68. Ibid., 82–83.

69. Blight, *Race and Reunion*, 329.

70. Wilson, *Negro Building*, 62.

71. Blight, *Race and Reunion*, 198.

72. Brundage, "Meta Warrick's 1907 'Negro Tableaux,'" 1390, 1368, 1393, 1396–97, 1391.

73. Wilson, *Negro Building*, 141–43, 167, 189, 154–55, 166.

74. Ibid., 170, 8. Bridget R. Cooks, for example, demonstrates that some of the first formal museum exhibitions of African and African American art in the 1920s and 1930s embraced an "anthropological" approach to black art, treating black artistic production as a curiosity and assessing its value in relation to a white aesthetic "norm" (*Exhibiting Blackness*, 1). According to Cooks, a quintessential example of this anthro-

pological approach to curating black art was the 1937 exhibition of William Edmondson's sculptures at the Museum of Modern Art.

75. "'America's Greatest Problem': Three Students of the Subject View the Racial Question from Different Angles and Offer Suggestions for Its Solution," *New York Times*, July 18, 1915.

76. Carter G. Woodson to Jesse Moorland, August 24, 1915, Jesse Moorland Papers, box 126-34, folder 695.

77. James Stamps quoted in Romero, "Carter G. Woodson," 92. Present at the initial meeting in Chicago were Washington, D.C., schoolteacher William B. Hartgrove, Dr. George Cleveland Hall, physician to Booker T. Washington, executive secretary of the YMCA Alexander L. Jackson and Jackson's assistant, James Stamps. On the circumstances surrounding the founding of the association in Chicago, see Goggin, *Carter G. Woodson*, 33–35; Jackson, "Reminiscences, Greetings, Challenges"; Stamps, "Fifty Years Later"; Wesley, "Our Fiftieth Year."

78. Wesley, "Our Fiftieth Year," 173; Goggin, *Carter G. Woodson*, 35; Woodson, "Ten Years of Collecting and Publishing the Records of the Negro," 600.

79. Quoted in Winston, "Through the Back Door," 693. See also Hall, *A Faithful Account of the Race*, 218.

80. *Boston Herald*, quoted in "How the Public Received the *Journal of Negro History*," 230; Joel E. Spingarn, quoted in ibid., 225.

81. Novick, *That Noble Dream*, 268, 2.

82. Smith, *The Gender of History*; Des Jardins, *Women and the Historical Enterprise in America*.

83. Des Jardins, *Women and the Historical Enterprise in America*, 25, my italics.

84. See, for example, Woodson, "Annual Report of the Director" (1949), 387–88; Woodson, "Annual Report of the Director" (1941), 416; and Woodson, "Annual Report of the Director" (1933), 363.

85. Novick, *That Noble Dream*, 231–32.

86. "Editorial Comment."

87. "Notes" (1928), 112; "Negro History Week—the Eighth Year," 108. In a review of Davis Saville Muzzey's textbook *An American History*, Woodson said: "When a reader in quest of the truth has read this text-book of American history . . . he will be compelled to ask the question as to why there appears throughout this volume references to the achievements of all groups influencing the history of this country, and there is no mention of what the Negroes, constituting a tenth of the population of the United States, have thought and felt and done." Muzzey, Woodson declared, had not written a "balanced and unprejudiced account of the rise and progress of the United States" but rather "a story as conforms with the biased minds of pseudo-American historians who do not desire to publish to posterity the achievements of all the people of this country" (377).

88. Laurie F. Maffly-Kipp applies this phrase to Du Bois (*Setting Down the Sacred Past*, 8), but it is similarly applicable to Woodson.

89. Hall, *A Faithful Account of the Race*, 216.

90. Woodson, *The Education of the Negro*, bibliography.

91. Woodson, *The Mind of the Negro as Reflected in Letters Written during the Crisis*, 328; Pennington, *A Textbook of the Origin and History of the Colored People*, 6–7. Referring to antebellum black historians, Benjamin Quarles said they "hoped to reach

some whites, particularly those who were influential. . . . But it was even more imperative to reach their fellow blacks, ignorance of the black past not being confined to whites. Uncounted numbers of blacks knew little or nothing about the Afro-American past" ("Black History's Antebellum Origins," 94).

92. Douglass, quoted in Kachun, *Festivals of Freedom*, 54; Williams, *History of the Negro Race in America*, vi.

93. Booker T. Washington, *The Story of the Negro*, v–vi.

94. Smith, *The Gender of History*, 128.

95. Maffly-Kipp, *Setting Down the Sacred Past*, 9.

96. The subheadings of chapter 1 ("The Unity of Mankind") of *History of the Negro Race* exemplify the biblically inflected character of Williams's scholarship: "The Biblical Argument.—One Race, One Language.—One Blood.—The Curse of Canaan." As late as 1908, the study of the Old Testament appeared as a junior-year history course at Hampton (Hall, *A Faithful Account of the Race*, 208). In addition to eschewing religious interpretations of history, Woodson also distanced himself from historical accounts written by, in Arthur Schomburg's disparaging words, "the rash and rabid amateur who has glibly tried to prove half of the world's geniuses to have been Negroes" ("The Negro Digs Up His Past," 236). One would count among these "amateurs" the journalist John E. Bruce, who wrote under the nom de plume "Bruce Grit"; intellectual, radical political activist, and unsurpassed Harlem soapbox orator Hubert Harrison; and J. A. Rogers, author of a regular column in the *Pittsburgh Courier* called "Your History" as well as the 1931 book *World's Greatest Men of African Descent*.

97. See, for example, Rush, *A Short Account of the Rise and Progress of the African ME Church in America*; Tanner, *An Outline of Our History and Government for African Methodist Churchmen*; and Wright, *Centennial Encyclopedia of the African Methodist Episcopal Church*.

98. Kachun, *Festivals of Freedom*, 111. On the religious interpretations of emancipation by black authors in the postbellum era, see Maffly-Kipp, *Setting Down the Sacred Past*, 211–16.

99. Rudavsky, "Charles Victor Roman"; Cobb, "Medical History," 301–3.

100. Woodson, "The First Biennial Meeting of the Association for the Study of Negro Life and History at Washington," 443.

101. Quoted in Woodson, *Negro Orators and Their Orations*, 646, italics in original.

102. Roman, *American Civilization and the Negro*, vii, v, 3, italics in original.

103. Goggin, "Countering White Racist Scholarship," 361.

104. See, for example, Pendleton, "Our New Possessions"; Lynch, "Some Historical Errors of James Ford Rhodes"; Terrell, "History of the High School for Negroes in Washington"; Dunbar-Nelson, "People of Color in Louisiana," pt. 1, and "People of Color in Louisiana," pt. 2.

105. Woodson, "The First Biennial Meeting of the Association for the Study of Negro Life and History at Washington," 443, 446; Logan, "Carter G. Woodson" (1945), 320; Greene, *Working with Carter G. Woodson, the Father of Black History*, 176; Meier and Rudwick, *Black History and the Historical Profession*, 19; Carter G. Woodson to A. A. Taylor, March 1923, Carter G. Woodson and the Association for Negro Life and History Papers, reel 2, frame 228. Woodson could also be insulting in person as well. Lorenzo Johnston Greene recalled one dispute that Woodson had with Wesley. "It was evident to me that Wesley was being worsted," Greene wrote in his diary. "Woodson

dominated the conference," he continued, "his voice, exultant, boomed out his sentences, acrid with sarcasm and irony, and pungent with evil" (*Working with Carter G. Woodson, the Father of Black History*, 192).

106. Quoted in Wilson, *The Segregated Scholars*, 142.

107. Logan, "Carter G. Woodson" (1945), 320.

108. Greene, *Working with Carter G. Woodson, the Father of Black History*, 193, 376.

109. Hughes, "When I Worked for Dr. Woodson," 188.

110. Greene, *Working with Carter G. Woodson, the Father of Black History*, 158; Logan, "Carter G. Woodson" (1945), 321.

111. At the first annual meeting, Kelly Miller read a paper called "The Place of Negro History in our Schools" (Woodson, "The First Biennial Meeting of the Association for the Study of Negro Life and History at Washington," 448).

112. Meier and Rudwick, *Black History and the Historical Profession*, 99; Wilson, *The Segregated Scholars*, 171.

113. Meier and Rudwick, *Black History and the Historical Profession*, 75.

114. On Lorenzo Johnston Greene (field representative and research assistant to Carter G. Woodson, professor of history at Lincoln University and author of the 1942 monograph *The Negro in Colonial New England*), see Dagbovie, *Early Black History Movement, Carter G. Woodson, and Lorenzo Johnston Greene*; Greene, *Working with Carter G. Woodson, the Father of Black History*, and *Selling Black History for Carter G. Woodson*; Meier and Rudwick, *Black History and the Historical Profession*, 79–83; and Thorpe, *Black Historians*, 176–77. On Luther Porter Jackson (professor of history at Virginia State College and highly effective fund-raiser for both the Association and the NAACP), see Brundage, *The Southern Past*, ch. 4; Dennis, *Luther P. Jackson and a Life for Civil Rights*; and Meier and Rudwick, *Black History and the Historical Profession*, 85–89. On James Hugo Johnston (professor at Virginia State College), see Meier and Rudwick, *Black History and the Historical Profession*, 84–85. On Rayford Logan (professor at Howard University and author of the pioneering 1954 monograph *The Negro in American Life and Thought: The Nadir, 1877–1901*), see Janken, *Rayford W. Logan and the Dilemma of the African-American Intellectual*; and Meier and Rudwick, *Black History and the Historical Profession*, 89–92. On W. Sherman Savage (professor at Lincoln University and expert on the history of blacks on the western frontier), see Greene, "W. Sherman Savage"; and Meier and Rudwick, *Black History and the Historical Profession*, 83–84. On Alrutheus Ambush Taylor (association investigator, author of two pathbreaking monographs about Reconstruction published in the mid-1920s and professor and then dean at Fisk University), see Franklin, "Alrutheus Ambush Taylor"; Hall, "'Research as Opportunity'"; Meier and Rudwick, *Black History and the Historical Profession*, 75–77; and Thorpe, *Black Historians*, 178–79. On Charles Wesley (professor at Howard University and one of Woodson's closest collaborators), see Aptheker, "Charles H. Wesley"; Harris, "Charles Harris Wesley, Educator and Historian" and "Woodson and Wesley "; Meier and Rudwick, *Black History and the Historical Profession*, 77–79; Miller, "Historiography of Charles H. Wesley as Reflected through the *Journal of Negro History*"; Wilson, "Racial Consciousness and Black Scholarship" and *The Segregated Scholars*, esp. ch. 4; and Winston, *Howard University Department of History*, esp. 27–35.

115. Quoted in Logan, *Howard University*, 249.

116. Bethune served in the "largely ceremonial" role of association president from 1936 to 1952 (Dagbovie, *Early Black History Movement, Carter G. Woodson, and Lorenzo Johnston Greene*, 96).

117. Jackson, "The First Twenty-Five Volumes of the *Journal of Negro History* Digested," 432.

118. Woodson, *The Education of the Negro*, 8.

119. Woodson, *A Century of Negro Migration*, v, 180, 186.

120. Woodson conveyed this same lesson in many of his books, articles, and speeches; in his discussion of the World War in *The Negro in Our History*, for example, he described how the army exported Jim Crow practices to France, providing French officers with a kind of tutorial on proper racial etiquette with publications such as *Secret Information concerning Black American Troops* (*The Negro in Our History*, 4th ed., 528–30).

121. See, for example, *The Negro in Our History*, 45–50. A précis of the article also appeared in the *Baltimore Afro-American*. See "Family Skeletons," December 13, 1918.

122. Woodson, "The Beginnings of the Miscegenation of Whites and Blacks," 335.

123. For Grant and Stoddard, race was literally *the* key to history. "A better reading of history," Stoddard wrote in *The Rising Tide of Color against White World-Supremacy*, "must bring home the truth that the basic factor in human affairs is not politics, but race" (5). According to Grant and Stoddard the "divisions of social cleavage" followed racial lines (Grant, *The Passing of the Great Race*, xv). The subtitle to Grant's 1916 book *The Passing of the Great Race* was "The Racial Basis of European History." Part 2 of *Passing*, entitled "European Races in History," provided historical sketches of the "Alpine," "Nordic" and "Mediterranean" races, among many others.

124. Grant, *The Passing of the Great Race*, 55–56.

125. Woodson, "The Beginnings of the Miscegenation of Whites and Blacks," 350, 352, 351.

126. "Leading Article in *Journal of Negro History*," *Norfolk Journal and Guide*, February 26, 1921; Woodson, "Notes" (1921), 259; "Fifty Years of Negro Citizenship as Qualified by the United States Supreme Court," 1, 48, 2–3, 4–5.

127. Woodson, "Fifty Years of Negro Citizenship as Qualified by the United States Supreme Court," 6, 10, 52, 53.

128. On the privileged backgrounds of historians at the turn of the twentieth-century, see Novick, *That Noble Dream*, 68.

129. Turner, quoted in Hofstadter, *The Progressive Historians*, 53. The original quote ("America is another word for opportunity") comes from Ralph Waldo Emerson.

CHAPTER TWO. REVERSE THE STAGE

1. Locke, *The New Negro*, 3; Reddick, "Racial Attitudes in American History Textbooks of the South," 235.

2. Morton, *Disfigured Images*, 24.

3. Novick, *That Noble Dream*, 229. In 1929, Phillips published another influential monograph about slavery, *Life and Labor in the Old South*.

4. Woodson, review of *American Negro Slavery* (*Journal of Negro History*), 103.

5. Ibid.

6. Woodson, "Negro Life and History in Our Schools," 277.

7. Trouillot, *Silencing the Past*, 29, 26, 48, 52.

8. Smith, *The Gender of History*, 149; Des Jardins, *Women and the Historical Enterprise in America*, 21.

9. Fitzpatrick, *History's Memory*, 3, 96–97; Goggin, "Carter G. Woodson and the Collection of Source Materials for Afro-American History," 262.

10. The first issue of the *Journal of Negro History* featured two collections of documents, "What the Negro Was Thinking during the Eighteenth Century" (which included several essays about slavery written by free blacks) and "Letters Showing the Rise and Progress of the Early Negro Churches of Georgia and the West Indies" (see the January 1916 issue, 49–92).

11. Hall, *A Faithful Account of the Race*, 217.

12. "Eighteenth Century Slaves as Advertised by Their Masters"; "Travelers' Impressions of Slavery in America from 1750 to 1800"; "Letters of George Washington Bearing on the Negro"; "Thomas Jefferson's Thoughts on the Negro," pt. 1.

13. Jackson, "The First Twenty-Five Volumes of the *Journal of Negro History* Digested," 434.

14. Townsend, *History's Babel*, 18; Smith, *The Gender of History*, 103.

15. Trouillot, *Silencing the Past*, xix; Dagbovie, *Early Black History Movement, Carter G. Woodson, and Lorenzo Johnston Greene*, xi; Hall, *A Faithful Account of the Race*, 218.

16. Trouillot, *Silencing the Past*, 48.

17. Woodson, *The Mind of the Negro as Reflected in Letters Written during the Crisis*, v. Letters constituted some of the most valuable primary source documents published in the *Journal of Negro History*. See, for example, "Letters Showing the Rise and Progress of the Early Negro Churches of Georgia and the West Indies"; "Some Letters of Richard Allen and Absalom Jones to Dorothy Ripley"; "Letters of Anthony Benezet"; "Letters of Negro Migrants of 1916–1918"; "More Letters of Negro Migrants of 1916–1918"; "Letters, Addresses, and the Like Throwing Light on the Career of Lott Cary"; "Letters to the American Colonization Society, parts 1–6"; "Letters to Antislavery Workers and Agencies"; "Letters of Negroes, Largely Personal and Private."

18. Woodson, *The Mind of the Negro as Reflected in Letters Written during the Crisis*, v.

19. Berlin, *The Making of African America*, 18, 31, 19.

20. Theodore Stephens, "The Bookshelf," *Chicago Defender*, September 4, 1926; "Brief Reviews," *New York Times*, October 24, 1926, 1–2.

21. Woodson, *The Mind of the Negro as Reflected in Letters Written during the Crisis*, 1, 2, 116.

22. Ibid., 15, 12, 16, 22–23, 26–27, 42, 47.

23. Ibid., 159.

24. Ibid., 260, 267.

25. Ibid., 555.

26. Ibid., 537–39.

27. "Letters of Negro Migrants of 1916–1918," 290.

28. Anonymous letter dated May 13, 1917, "More Letters of Negro Migrants of 1916–1918," 440; anonymous letter dated May 12, 1917, ibid., 439.

29. Anonymous letter dated June 7, 1917, ibid., 413.

30. Woodson, foreword to *Negro Orators and Their Orations*, n.p.

31. D. W. Johnson, "The Bookshelf," *Chicago Defender*, February 27, 1926; Woodson, *Negro Orators and Their Orations*, 11.

32. The color line is the vital subject of both of these speeches, with Douglass protesting, "I am not within the pale of this glorious anniversary!" and Washington famously declaring that "in all things that are purely social we can be as separate as the fingers, yet one as the hand in all things essential to mutual progress."

33. Woodson, *Negro Orators and Their Orations*, 2–5.

34. See Woodson, *The Mind of the Negro as Reflected in Letters Written during the Crisis*, 539–44.

35. Du Bois, *The Souls of Black Folk*, 3.

36. See, for example, Brown's *The Rising Son; or, The Antecedents of the Colored Race* (1874); Anna Julia Cooper's *A Voice from the South* (1892); and Crogman's *Progress of the Race; or, The Remarkable Advancement of the Afro-American Negro* (1897). On race histories, see Hall, *A Faithful Account of the Race*, 158–165; and Maffly-Kipp, *Setting Down the Sacred Past*, ch. 5.

37. Advertisement for *The Negro in Our History* serialization, *Chicago Defender*, November 25, 1922; unsigned review of *The Negro in Our History* in *Baltimore Afro-American*, July 14, 1922.

38. In 1920, the circulation of the *Defender* was 230,000 (Borucki, "The *Chicago Defender*").

39. Woodson, "Ten Years of Collecting and Publishing the Records of the Negro," 605; "Negro History in More Than 100 Schools," *Norfolk Journal and Guide*, October 31, 1925. For an excellent account of the campaign to promote black history in black schools during the 1920s and 1930s, see Zimmerman, *Whose America?*, ch. 2.

40. "It has actually remolded the attitude of the popular mind, especially among Negroes, as to the place and importance of the Negro in American history," Locke said (Locke, review of *The Negro in Our History*, 100–101).

41. Gould, review of *The Negro in Our History*, 212.

42. Tuttle, "Four Books on the Negro," 259.

43. Ibid.

44. See Berlin, *Many Thousands Gone*.

45. Hall, *A Faithful Account of the Race*, 210; Novick, *That Noble Dream*, 71. Leila Amos Pendleton (1868–1938) was a D.C. resident who worked for some years as a schoolteacher, assisted her husband with his printing business, the R. L. Pendleton Printing Company, and took an active part in the clubwoman movement. One of the first individuals to become a lifetime member of the association, Pendleton contributed an article on the Danish West Indies to an early volume of the *Journal of Negro History*. See Woodson, "Notes" (1939), 136; and Dagbovie, "Black Women Historians from the late 19th Century to the Dawning of the Civil Rights Movement," 249. See also Pendleton, "Our New Possessions." John Bach McMaster (1852–1932) was born in Brooklyn, the son of a former Mississippi plantation owner. Trained as a civil engineer, McMaster was not a professional historian, according to *Encyclopedia Britannica* online. David Saville Muzzey (1870–1965), "the most popular history-textbook author of the first half of the twentieth century," was a Columbia-trained PhD who taught at Barnard College (Moreau, *Schoolbook Nation*, 89). Lawton B. Evans (1862–1934), Emory

graduate, son of a Confederate army officer, not a PhD-credentialed historian, was the longtime superintendent of the Richmond County, Georgia, school district ("Dr. Lawton B. Evans," *New York Times*, April 7, 1934).

46. See, for example, Moreau, *Schoolbook Nation*, esp. ch. 4; Morton, *Disfigured Images*, esp. chs. 2 and 3; and Novick, *That Noble Dream*, esp. ch. 3.

47. See, for example, Dagbovie, *Early Black History Movement, Carter G. Woodson, and Lorenzo Johnston Greene*; Des Jardins, *Women and the Historical Enterprise in America*, esp. chs. 4 and 5; Goggin, "Countering White Racist Scholarship"; and Hall, "'Research as Opportunity.'"

48. Review of *The Negro in American History*, 94.

49. Review of *A Social History of the American Negro*, 114–15.

50. See also, Woodson, review of *The Negro Trail Blazers of California*.

51. The initial reviews of *The Negro in Our History* praised Woodson for his objectivity. Tuttle wrote that Woodson told his story "coolly [and] exhaustively" ("Four Books on the Negro," 259.) *The Negro in Our History*, according to Joseph Gould in the *Crisis*, was remarkable both "for its scholarship and its impartiality" (212.) Henry Sherwood in the *Mississippi Valley Historical Review*, meanwhile, concluded that "Dr. Woodson has used the principles of historical investigation which safeguard accuracy, proportion and judgment to record in a sympathetic way the story of his race" (421).

52. Eugene Kinckle Jones, review of *The Negro in Our History*, *Messenger* 5 (May 1923), 704; "prognoses for future improvement" were key features of the race histories produced between 1867 and 1920, according to Maffly-Kipp (*Setting Down the Sacred Past*, 203).

53. Woodson, *The Negro in Our History*, 105.

54. Cromwell, *The Negro In American History*, 19

55. Woodson quoted the free Negroes of Hartford, Connecticut, as follows: "Why should we leave this land so dearly bought by the blood, groans and tears of our fathers? This is our home; here let us live and let us die" (*The Negro in Our History*, 162).

56. Hart, *School History of the United States* (1920), xxxi, 359; Pendleton, *A Narrative of the Negro*, 98.

57. Muzzey, *An American History* (1920), 257.

58. Ibid., 321; Hart, *School History of the United States* (1920), 321; Brawley, *A Social History of the American Negro*, 237.

59. Rhodes, *History of the United States from the Compromise of 1850 to the McKinley-Bryan Campaign of 1896*, 335. As late as World War II, mainstream historical accounts blamed Jezebel for miscegenation during slavery. Wilbur Cash's 1941 *The Mind of the South*, for example, described the black woman slave as follows: "Torn from her tribal restraints and taught an easy compliance . . . she was to be had for the taking. . . . [Hence] efforts to build up a taboo against miscegenation made little real progress" (quoted in Morton, *Disfigured Images*, 33).

60. Brawley, *A Social History of the American Negro*, 403; Woodson, *The Negro in Our History*, 112.

61. Cromwell, *The Negro in American History*, 193; Brawley, *A Social History of the American Negro*, 216; Pendleton, *A Narrative of the Negro*, 204; Woodson, *The Negro in Our History*, 259.

62. Brawley, *A Social History of the American Negro*, 295; Woodson, *The Negro in Our History*, 260.

63. Cromwell, *The Negro in American History*, 193.

64. Pendleton, *A Narrative of the Negro*, 179; see "In the Interpreter's House," 222–23.

65. Evans, *The Essential Facts of American History*, 418, 448.

66. Muzzey, *American History* (1920), 338; Brawley, *A Social History of the American Negro*, 273.

67. Woodson, *The Negro in Our History*, 269–70.

68. See, for example, Brundage, "Meta Warrick's 1907 'Negro Tableaux' and (Re)Presenting African American Historical Memory"; Maffly-Kipp, *Setting Down the Sacred Past*, 209–10; and Zimmerman, "Each 'Race' Could Have Its Heroes Sung," 110–11.

69. "Eminent, Progressive and Rising" is the subtitle to W. J. Simmons's 1887 book *Men of Mark*.

70. Woodson, *The Negro in Our History*, 280, 283–84; Cromwell, *The Negro in American History*, 72.

71. Pendleton, *A Narrative of the Negro*, 168; Cromwell, *The Negro in American History*, 122, 170, 206.

72. Woodson, *The Negro in Our History*, 276; Pendleton, *A Narrative of the Negro*, 196.

73. Brawley, *A Social History of the American Negro*, 295, 301; Woodson, *The Negro in Our History*, 270; Brawley, *A Social History of the American Negro*, 340; Pendleton, *A Narrative of the Negro*, 178; Cromwell, *The Negro in American History*, 72; Woodson, *The Negro in Our History*, 261.

74. Smethurst, *The African American Roots of Modernism*, 76.

75. *A Social History of the American Negro* and *A Narrative of the Negro* did not include appendices.

76. Woodson, *The Negro in Our History*, 350.

77. Smethurst, *The African American Roots of Modernism*, 73, 75, 93.

78. Pendleton, *A Narrative of the Negro*, 178; Brawley, *A Social History of the American Negro*, 357.

79. Brawley, *A Social History of the American Negro*, 274, 345; Woodson, *The Negro in Our History*, 326, 313, 334.

80. Woodson, *The Negro in Our History*, 327.

81. Evans, *The Essential Facts of American History*, 349; McMaster, *A School History of the United States*, 96; Hart, *School History of the United States* (1920), 83, 201, 317, 359.

82. "Dr. Woodson's Negro History Confiscated in Oklahoma," *Baltimore Afro-American*, August 1, 1925.

PART TWO. CULTURE

1. See, for example, Singal, "Towards A Definition of American Modernism."

2. Brundage, "Working in the 'Kingdom of Culture,'" 4.

3. See, for instance, Hutchison, *The Harlem Renaissance in Black and White*, ch. 2. As Hutchison notes, "Boasian concepts became bedrock assumptions among 'New Negro' authors of virtually every persuasion" (62).

4. Gilkeson, "The Domestication of 'Culture' in Interwar America," 167.

5. Ibid., 159, 168; Cook and Glickman, "Twelve Propositions for a History of U.S. Cultural History," 12.

6. Baker, *Modernism and the Harlem Renaissance*; Douglas, *Terrible Honesty*; Hutchinson, *Harlem Renaissance in Black and White*.

7. Hutchinson, *Harlem Renaissance in Black and White*, 35 ("attempt to explain America to itself" is Cornel West's phrase.) "In the 1920s, for the first time in American history," Ann Douglas maintains, "many blacks and some whites viewed the black tradition in the arts not as a slight and inferior tributary to white culture but as a dominant influence on it and as a separate tradition with a complex identity and history of its own" (*Terrible Honesty*, 303).

8. Bourne, "Trans-National America," 182.

9. Kallen, "Democracy versus the Melting-Pot," pt. 1, 200.

10. Bourne, "Trans-National America," 183.

11. Corbould, *Becoming African Americans*, 42.

12. Kallen, "Democracy versus the Melting-Pot," pt. 2, 220.

13. On the different varieties of cultural pluralism, see Hollinger, *Postethnic America*, esp. ch.4.

14. Jones, *In Search of Brightest Africa*, 2.

15. Ibid., 3, 18. After 1919, as Clare Corbould explains, "What had for a long time been a marginal pursuit—the telling and retelling of Africa's glorious history—became instrumental in the development of black civic life" (*Becoming African Americans*, 127).

16. Holt, *Children of Fire*, 199–200.

17. Locke, "The Negro's Contribution to American Art and Literature," 235.

18. Von Eschen, *Race against Empire*, 11.

19. Lewis, preface xvi; Baker, *From Savage to Negro*, 177.

20. The following books also included significant coverage of Africa: the revised fourth edition of *The Negro in Our History* (1927), *Negro History in Thirteen Plays* (1935), *Negro Art, Music, and Rhyme* (1938), *Negro Folk Tales for Pupils* (1938), and *Plays and Pageants from the Life of the Negro* (1938).

21. Sherwood, "The Redemption of Africa"; Jones, "American Opposition to Slavery in Africa"; Bunche, "French and British Imperialism in West Africa."

22. Work, *Folk Song of the American Negro*, 118.

23. Locke, "The Negro Poets of the United States," 422–23.

24. Du Bois, writing in his 1940 autobiography, *Dusk of Dawn*, said that the "greatest single accomplishment" of the "artistic movement among American Negroes" was Carter G. Woodson's Negro History Week (702).

CHAPTER THREE. HERITAGE

1. Rampersad, introduction, ix. On the curious history of the term "New Negro," see Gates, "The Trope of a New Negro and the Reconstruction of the Image of the Black."

2. Lewis, "The Harlem Renaissance."

3. Schomburg, "The Negro Digs Up His Past," 231, 236–237. On Schomburg, see Hoffnung-Garskof, "The Migrations of Arturo Schomburg"; Holton, "Decolonizing History"; Sinnette, *Arthur Alfonso Schomburg, Black Bibliophile and Collector*; and Thorpe, *Black Historians*, 145–46.

4. Douglas, *Terrible Honesty*, 331.

5. Early, introduction, 33; Edwards, *The Practice of Diaspora*, 43. For background information on African American anthologies, I have relied on Edwards, *Practice of Diaspora*, esp. ch. 1; Kinnamon, "Anthologies of African-American Literature from 1845 to 1994"; Lash, "The Anthologist and the Negro Author"; and Mason, "The African-American Anthology."

6. Frank, quoted in Douglas, *Terrible Honesty*, 331; Kaplan, *Miss Anne in Harlem*, 17. Between 1917 and 1934, the *Journal of American Folklore* published more than a dozen "Negro Numbers" devoted to black folklore (Baker, *From Savage to Negro*, 144).

7. Parker, "Benjamin Brawley," 18.

8. See, for example, Brawley's "Lorenzo Dow"; "Three Negro Poets"; "Elizabeth Barrett Browning and the Negro"; and "The Promise of Negro Literature."

9. See Woodson, review of *The Negro in Literature and Art*; review of *Women of Achievement*; and review of *A Social History of the American Negro*.

10. Woodson, "The First Biennial Meeting of the Association for the Study of Negro Life and History at Washington," 448.

11. On Johnson's life and work, see Lewis, *When Harlem Was in Vogue*, 143–49; and Franklin, *Living Our Stories, Telling Our Truths*, ch. 3.

12. Woodson, "Proceedings of the Annual Meeting of the Association Held in Cleveland, Ohio, October 26–30, 1930," 2.

13. Philosopher Tommy L. Lott is a notable exception in this regard. Lott maintains that Locke should be considered a cultural historian, pointing to Locke's *Negro Art—Past and Present* and *The Negro and His Music* (both published in 1936) as sterling examples of cultural history. Lott does not, however, link Locke to the association and to the larger Negro history enterprise ("Alain Leroy Locke").

14. In the late 1920s, Locke taught two classes—"African Art and Culture" and "The Negro in Recent Literature"—for the association's ambitious and short-lived Home Study Department, which offered adult education correspondence courses. Locke reviewed no fewer than five of Woodson's own books. His many reviews of Negro history surveys, textbooks, and Associated Publishers monographs appeared in the *Journal of Negro History*, *Survey Graphic*, the *Nation*, the *Saturday Review of Literature*, and the *New York Herald Tribune Books*, among other publications (Carter G. Woodson and the Association for Negro Life and History Papers, reel 25, frames 816–22).

15. Hegel, quoted in Singh, *Black Is a Country*, 76.

16. Hegel, *Lectures on the Philosophy of World History*, 177.

17. See Fredrickson, *The Black Image in the White Mind*, esp. ch. 10.

18. Schomburg, "The Negro Digs Up His Past," 237.

19. Edwards, *The Practice of Diaspora*, 44.

20. Ibid., 45.

21. The transcription of spirituals dates back to the 1867 collection *Slave Songs of the United States*. See Cruz, *Culture on the Margins*, 150–57.

22. On Work's life and career, see Singleton, "John Wesley Work, Sr."

23. Harris, *The Rise of Gospel Blues*, 69, 113; Du Bois, quoted in Anderson, *Deep River*, 80. Writing in 1936, Woodson said of *Folk Song of the American Negro* that "this small but epoch-making volume awakened new interest in the Negroes' musical background and served as the key to a new interpretation of the soul of the race" (*The African Background Outlined*, 451).

24. Work, *Folk Song of the American Negro*, 6.

25. Ibid., 90, 18.

26. Ibid., 16–17, 29, 18, 98.

27. Ibid., 118.

28. *Folk Song of the American Negro*, for example, is not mentioned in the major renaissance studies written by Nathan Huggins (1971), David Levering Lewis (1979), or George Hutchinson (1996). On Work's efforts to preserve the spirituals, see Anderson, *Deep River*, 78–81; Harris, *The Rise of Gospel Blues*, 112–14; and Spencer, *New Negroes and Their Music*, 63–64.

29. Cruz, *Culture on the Margins*, 191, 22.

30. See Locke, "Beauty Instead of Ashes."

31. Mary White Ovington, "Book Chat," *Philadelphia Tribune*, November 7, 1925.

32. "New Book of Negro Spirituals," *New York Amsterdam News*, October 14, 1925.

33. "Brief Reviews," *New York Times*, December 19, 1926.

34. "The Bookshelf," *Chicago Defender*, March 20, 1926. "If so," Frankenstein had remarked, "that renaissance will have as a cornerstone a glowing, glittering slab, wrung from the strivings and yearnings of a race" ("New Book on Spirituals Wins Praise," *Chicago Defender*, October 24, 1925).

35. Johnson, *The Book of American Negro Spirituals*, 12–13, 17, 20. Brown, review of *The Book of American Negro Spirituals*, 221–222.

36. Johnson, *The Book of American Negro Spirituals*, 14–17.

37. Mary White Ovington, "Book Chat," *Philadelphia Tribune*, November 7, 1925.

38. Quoted in Kachun, *Festivals of Freedom*, 151.

39. Johnson, *The Book of American Negro Spirituals*, 49–50.

40. Scarborough, *On the Trail of Negro Folk Songs*, 281. Scarborough described how she gathered material from many different sources, including "teachers, preachers, plantation owners, musicians [and] writers." "I have received," she reported, "songs written in the trembling hand of age and in the cramped scrawl of childhood." "I visited my kitchen acquaintances, offering to help shell peas or dry dishes, if I might but listen to songs," she said. "I loafed on back steps, I hung guilefully over garden fences, I broiled myself beside cook stoves and ironing boards" (ibid., 31, 10).

41. Odum and Johnson, *The Negro and His Songs*, v, 8.

42. Review of *The Negro and His Songs*, 775.

43. Locke, "The Negro Spirituals," 199–200, 210.

44. Frederick Law Olmsted, quoted in Cruz, *Culture on the Margins*, 46.

45. Brawley, preface, n.p.

46. Woodson, review of *The Negro in Literature and Art in the United States*, 329.

47. Brawley, *The Negro in Literature and Art in the United States*, 4, 7.

48. Ibid., 7–9.

49. Schomburg, *A Bibliographic Checklist of American Negro Poetry*.

50. "Book of American Negro Poetry," *Baltimore Afro-American*, April 21, 1922.

51. Mary White Ovington, "Book Chat," *New Journal and Guide*, May 6, 1922. The *Journal of Negro History* even reviewed Johnson's book, noting that a "review of a book of poetry is out of place in an historical magazine unless, like the volume before us, it has an historical significance." The biographical index of the authors in the appendix was especially valuable, the *Journal of Negro History* reported, with "entirely new information," appearing "here in print for the first time" (review of *The Book of American Negro Poetry*, 347).

52. "The public, generally speaking, does not know that there are American Negro

poets," Johnson announced in the preface. "To supply this lack of information is, alone, a work worthy of somebody's effort" (426).

53. Review of *The Book of American Negro Poetry*, 347.

54. Johnson, preface, 443, 430, 428, 431.

55. Ibid., 431.

56. See Lewis, *W. E. B. Du Bois: The Fight for Equality and the American Century*, ch. 5; Lewis, introduction, xxiii.

57. Du Bois, *The Souls of Black Folk*, 9.

58. Johnson, preface, 433.

59. "The Book Shelf," *Chicago Defender*, February 18, 1922.

60. Curry, introduction, xi.

61. Ibid, xi, v.

62. A second edition of *Negro Poets and Their Poems* followed in 1935 that included an additional sixteen writers and thirty-six new selections.

63. Fuller herself said that the sculpture depicted "humanity weeping over her suddenly freed children, who, beneath the gnarled fingers of Fate, step forth into the world, unafraid" (http://publicartboston.com/content/emancipation.)

64. Kerlin, *Negro Poets and Their Poems*, 1, 62–63.

65. Woodson, review of *Negro Poets and Their Poems*, 91.

66. Kerlin, *Negro Poets and Their Poems*, 52, 5–6, xv.

67. White and Jackson, introduction, iii, x; White and Jackson, "Editorial Note," 24.

68. Review of *An Anthology of Verse by American Negroes*, 372, 371.

69. Locke, *Four Negro Poets*.

70. Cullen, foreword, ix–x.

71. Locke, *Four Negro Poets*, 5.

72. Cullen, foreword, xi, xiv.

73. Locke, *Four Negro Poets*, 6.

74. Brawley, *Early Negro American Writers*, v, 4–5, 8.

75. William Bayless, "Book Chat," *New Journal and Guide*, January 28, 1928.

76. Locke, introduction, n.p.

77. William Bayless, in his *New Journal and Guide* review of *Plays of Negro Life* (January 28, 1928), saw fit to highlight Paul Green for "special mention": "Green, a southern white man, appears to fully understand the Negro and knows how to turn his observations of actual Negro life into dramatic material which is unoffensive to Negro readers."

78. Locke, "The Contribution of Race to Culture," 202, 206.

79. Locke, "The High Cost of Prejudice," 503.

80. Montgomery Gregory, "A Chronology of the Negro Theatre," 417.

81. Locke, "The High Cost of Prejudice," 504.

82. Ibid.

83. Gray, introduction, vii.

84. Review of *Plays and Pageants from the Life of the Negro*, 264.

85. Richardson, introduction, xliii.

86. Quoted in Gray, introduction, xix–xx. Other regular "Saturday Nighters" at Johnson's northwest D.C. "halfway house" ("I'm halfway between everything and everybody and I bring them together," she said) included Locke, Hughes, Toomer and Jessie Fauset (Parascandola, "Georgia Douglas Johnson.") On Douglas's salon, see McHenry, *Forgotten Readers*, ch. 5.

87. Richardson, introduction, xliii.

88. Ibid., xxxii–xxxiv.

89. Woodson, introduction, v.

90. Woodson, "Noted Historian Discusses the Dramatization of Negro Life and History," *New Journal and Guide*, December 14, 1935.

91. Woodson, review of *Negro History in Thirteen Plays*, 75–76.

92. Kinnamon, "Anthologies of African-American Literature from 1845 to 1994," 475.

93. Schuyler, "Negro Art Hokum," 97–98.

94. Ibid., 96.

95. Ibid., 99.

96. Du Bois, *The Souls of Black Folk*, 167. The Negro folk song, Du Bois averred, was the "singular spiritual heritage of the nation and the greatest gift of the Negro people" (168).

97. Locke, *The Negro in America*, 48–49.

98. Here Locke gives a nod to the fears of Horace Kallen and Randolph Bourne regarding the degrading effects of American commercial culture.

99. Locke, "The Negro Poets of the United States," 422, 425.

100. Bay, *The White Image in the Black Mind*, 50, 54, 9, 72.

101. Discussions of "Negro art" and "Negro genius" could easily slip into crude stereotypes, as Schuyler had warned. In a positive notice of Locke and Gregory's *Plays of Negro Life* in the *New York Times*, for example, the reviewer advanced a series of claims that had no doubt disturbed Locke and Gregory when they read the review. The "American negro is a primitive creature," the author declared. "His lack of complexity," the reviewer continued, "makes him essentially dramatic material." O'Neill's *Emperor Jones*, the review contended, used "in a manner that is fiendishly clever the negro's egotism, his credulity and his cowering fear born of superstition" ("Two Books Which Show the American Negro as He Is," *New York Times*, January 1, 1928).

102. Locke, "The Negro Poets of the United States," 422.

103. Channing, Hart, and Turner, *Guide to the Study and Reading of American History*, 2.

104. Locke, "The Negro Poets of the United States," 422–23.

105. Brown, Davis and Lee, preface, v.

CHAPTER FOUR. THE NEW NEGRO GOES TO SCHOOL

1. Hughes, *The Big Sea*, 228.

2. Baldwin, introduction, 19. For examples of scholarship that widen the scope beyond Harlem, see Ogbar, ed., *The Harlem Renaissance Revisited*; and Baldwin and Makalani, eds., *Escape From New York*.

3. Fabre and Feith, *Temples for Tomorrow*, 13, 26.

4. From Harold Cruse's blistering opening salvo in *The Crisis of the Negro Intellectual* (1967) to the recently published *Miss Anne in Harlem: The White Women of the Black Renaissance* (2013) by Carla Kaplan, there has been a vigorous debate about the question of black-white relations in the renaissance. Nathan Huggins, for instance, asserts that Harlem in the 1920s was no less a game of masks than the traditional minstrel show, with black artists pandering to white audiences and renaissance art necessarily suffering as a result. Tony Martin echoes Huggins's assessment, calling the

renaissance a "transient fad... propelled largely by a white bohemian desire for the sensual and the exotic" (*Literary Garveyism*, 158). In contrast, George Hutchinson (*The Harlem Renaissance in Black and White*) and Kaplan (*Miss Anne in Harlem*) argue that black-white exchanges were substantive, reciprocal, and in the main positive. This concern with interracial dynamics, however vital, has obscured the importance of the renaissance in shaping a distinctive African American identity. Clare Corbould's penetrating *Becoming African Americans* is a noteworthy exception in this regard.

5. Previous recipients included the biologist Ernest E. Just, the actor Charles S. Gilpin, and Mary B. Talbert, president of the National Association of Colored Women.

6. Du Bois to John Hope, March 25, 1925, in Aptheker, *The Correspondence of W. E. B. Du Bois*, 312.

7. Hughes, "The Negro Artist and the Racial Mountain," 95; Du Bois, "Criteria of Negro Art," 511.

8. J. Blaine Poindexter, "Crowd Mass Meeting of NAACP," *Chicago Defender*, July 3, 1926; Du Bois, "Criteria," 510; Holmes, "On Presenting the Spingarn Medal," 232-33.

9. Woodson, "Negro History Week," 238.

10. A "thought which emerged from the mind of the Director," as he put it (Woodson, "Annual Report of the Director" [1926], 551).

11. Smith, *Sick and Tired of Being Sick and Tired*, 33.

12. Romero, "Carter G. Woodson," 148-49; Wright, "Educational Programs for the Improvement of Race Relations," 359.

13. Reddick, "Twenty-Five Negro History Weeks," 178.

14. On Negro History Week, see Corbould, *Becoming African Americans*, 106-11; Dagbovie, *The Early Black History Movement, Carter G. Woodson, and Lorenzo Johnston Greene*, 47-53; Dennis, *Luther P. Jackson and a Life for Civil Rights*, 54-60; Goggin, *Carter G. Woodson*, 84-85, 119-20; and Selig, *Americans All*, 208-12.

15. Goggin, "Carter G. Woodson and the Movement to Promote Black History," 28. See, for example, Oliver Randolph, "Big Celebration in Washington: Mu-So-Lit Club Devotes Evening to Lincoln and Douglass," *Baltimore Afro-American*, March 4, 1911; and "Lincoln and Douglass Jointly Honored," *Baltimore Afro-American*, February 24, 1912.

16. Woodson, "Negro History Week," 239-40.

17. Woodson, "National Negro History Week Celebration from February 6 to 13," *New York Amsterdam News*, February 2, 1927.

18. Woodson, "Negro History Week," 240.

19. See, for example, Woodson, "Negro History Week—The Tenth Year," 127.

20. Woodson, *The Miseducation of the Negro*, 7.

21. Woodson, "The Celebration of Negro History Week, 1927," 105. Questions about the wisdom of setting aside a special time to commemorate black history have a surprisingly long history. An editorial in the *Baltimore Afro-American* dated February 25, 1933, for example, introduced readers to "little Johnny" who asked his teacher why they did not get Negro history in their "regular history." "We are at heart uncompromisingly opposed to the Negro History Week observance because of the idea of separation that it sets up," the editors wrote. "We are in hearty accord with little Johnny—we'll take our Negro history along with the rest." Debates about the merit of Black History Month in the twenty-first century are now perennial. See, for instance, McWhorter, "Black History Month Is Over"; and Zimmerman, "Let's End Black History Month."

22. Woodson, "Negro History Week from Different Points of View," *New York Amsterdam News*, December 7, 1932; Woodson, *The Miseducation of the Negro*, 67.

23. Woodson, "Negro History Week," 241.

24. "Pictures of Distinguished Negroes" flyer, library of Carter G. Woodson, box 1, folder 3, n.d.

25. "Negro History Week," *Pittsburgh Courier*, January 29, 1927; "Negro History Week Celebration Popular," *Pittsburgh Courier*, February 4, 1928; "A Page from Our History," *Chicago Defender*, February 10, 1940. Remarks by Mary McLeod Bethune at the association's twentieth anniversary meeting in 1935 capture this aspirational quality of history in the Woodson vein. At the height of the Roman Empire, the highways of Romans were "studded with the statues of their illustrious men," Bethune noted. These statues were erected, according to Bethune, so that the Roman youth, "gazing upon their faces, might be stimulated to greater achievement and accomplishment," and the association, she noted, served a similar function for Negro youth. The study of black history, Bethune maintained, would push young black men and women "forward toward their destinies." While some truths "inform our minds," others "feed our spirits," Bethune observed ("The Association for the Study of Negro Life and History," 407–8).

26. The phrase "builders and Heroes" comes from Benjamin Brawley's 1937 book *Negro Builders and Heroes*.

27. Woodson, "The Celebration of Negro History Week, 1927," 104.

28. Woodson, "Negro History Week-the Fifth Year," 126.

29. "Timely Suggestions for Negro History Week," 12.

30. Woodson, "Negro History Week—the Eleventh Year," 106.

31. Woodson, "Annual Report of the Director" (1930), 398.

32. In 1929, Woodson donated his first set of documents to the Library of Congress ("Annual Report of the Director" [1929], 369). After Woodson made his final donation in 1938, the library had approximately five thousand items in its collection of "Negro Papers" ("Annual Report of the Director" [1944], 259).

33. "Timely Suggestions for Negro History Week," 12.

34. One Negro History Week circular listed more than a half dozen works under "The Negro Poet," including Countee Cullen's *Caroling Dusk* and Paul Laurence Dunbar's *Life and Works*. Well over a dozen references appeared in the same circular under "The Negro in Art," including *The New Negro*, James Weldon Johnson's *Book of American Negro Spirituals* and Benjamin Brawley's *The Negro in Literature and Art in the United States* (1934 Negro History Week pamphlet).

35. The pioneering anthologies and critical studies produced by Woodson and his colleagues provided invaluable source material here. Douglass's speeches, for example, were available in Woodson's *Negro Orators and Their Orations*. The sheet music for dozens of spirituals, meanwhile, could be found in James Weldon Johnson's *Book of American Negro Spirituals*. Locke's *Four Negro Poets* contained a wide selection of Hughes's poems.

36. See Dagbovie, "Black Women, Carter G. Woodson, and the Association for the Study of Negro Life and History," 30, 34–37. In Dagbovie's judgment, "Without the practical work of women, Woodson's efforts at popularizing African and African American history would not have been nearly as successful" (ibid., 29).

37. Woodson, "What's behind the *Negro History Bulletin*," 16, 18.

38. Des Jardins, *Women and the Historical Enterprise in America*, 147, 175, 146, 148.

39. "Negro History Week," *Pittsburgh Courier*, January 29, 1927; "Negro History Week Celebration Popular," *Pittsburgh Courier*, February 4, 1928.

40. "Negro History Week Is Observed in Public Schools," *Baltimore Afro-American*, February 20, 1926.

41. Quoted in Woodson, "The Celebration of Negro History Week, 1927," 106.

42. "Pi Kappa Delta Holds 'Negro History Week' Program," *New York Amsterdam News*, February 8, 1928; "Armstrong Association Plans Negro History Week Program," *Philadelphia Tribune*, February 9, 1928; "David T. Studes [sic] Celebrate Negro History Week," *Atlanta Daily World*, February 10, 1932.

43. "8,000 View Works of Negro Artists In the Nat'l Gallery Of Art," *Pittsburgh Courier*, November 11, 1933; "Negro Session Exalts African World of Art," *Washington Post*, October 29, 1933; "Exhibition of Works by Negro Artists at National Gallery of Art," pamphlet, Alain Locke Papers, box 164–176, folder 9; and Woodson, "Proceedings of the Annual Meeting of the Association, 1933," 6.

44. Locke believed that African art would have a "galvanizing influence" on African American artists, showing them that "the Negro is not a cultural foundling without his own inheritance." "If the forefathers could so adroitly master [sculpture, painting, and the decorative arts], why not we?" ("The Legacy of the Ancestral Arts," 256).

45. Woodson, "Proceedings of the Annual Meeting, 1933," 7; Lulu Randall, "Artists, Composers Score in Brilliant D.C. Recital," *Baltimore Afro-American*, November 11, 1933.

46. "Trenholm Broadcasts on 'Negro History Week' in Southland," *Pittsburgh Courier*, February 25, 1933. Radio was a part of Negro History Week almost from the start. Floyd Galvin broadcast a message from Woodson over WCGU New York on January 26, 1928. Radio programming would become an increasingly important component of Negro History Week celebrations through the 1930s and 1940s. In 1939, the New York branch of the association arranged for more than a dozen broadcasts ("Dr. Woodson to Open Negro History Week on CBS Chain," *New York Amsterdam News*, February 4, 1939).

47. "At Virginia Union," *Baltimore Afro-American*, February 22, 1930; "KY State Plans Elaborate Negro History Week Program Featuring Many Artists," *Atlanta Daily World*, February 4, 1935. Following Woodson's suggestion, many schools and public libraries prepared special Negro History Week book exhibitions. A 1928 exhibit at the New Jersey Avenue branch of the Atlantic City public library, for example, displayed a full run of Woodson's textbooks next to the following signal renaissance titles: Alain Locke's *The New Negro*, Langston Hughes's *Weary Blues* and Walter White's *Fire in the Flint*. In Baltimore in 1937, the Negro History Club at Frederick Douglass Junior and Senior High School mounted a window display at the Enoch Pratt public library. Entitled "The Negro Surveys His Past," the display featured books, photographs, and illustrations, all artfully arranged around a lion-maned bust of Frederick Douglass ("Northside News," *Atlantic City New Jersey Union*, February 9, 1928; "School News," October 1937, 7–8).

48. Dabney, "The Study of the Negro," 303, 282.

49. See, for example, Woodson, "Negro History Week—the Twelfth Year," 141.

50. Corbould, *Becoming African Americans*, 13.

51. Woodson, "Negro History Week" (1926), 241, 238; Woodson, "Negro History Week—the Third Year," 125; Woodson, "A Negro History Week Warning to Seekers

after the Whole Truth," 74; Woodson, "History Week Is 'Used' by Society," *Pittsburgh Courier*, February 10, 1940.

52. Woodson, "The Horizon," *New York Amsterdam News*, February 1, 1936.

53. Woodson, "Teachers Accept Assignment Ofays Give Negro," *Baltimore Afro-American*, April 30, 1932.

54. "Negro History Week," *Chicago Defender*, February 17. 1940. Woodson occasionally noted that it was difficult to get African Americans interested in their own history when Americans, in general, were apathetic toward historical study. See, for example, Woodson, "Annual Report of the Director" (1928), 403.

55. William Pickens, "Negro History Week," *Atlanta Daily World*, February 6, 1940.

56. Lorini, "'The Spell of Africa Is upon Me,'" 165.

57. On the production and reception of "Star," see Glassberg, *American Historical Pageantry*, 132–33; Lewis, *W. E. B. Du Bois: Biography of a Race*, 459–63; Lorini, *Rituals of Race*, 221–24; and Wilson, *Negro Building*, 156–60.

58. Glassberg, *American Historical Pageantry*, 1, 285, 4, 202.

59. Moses, *Afrotopia*, 38.

60. Roman, *American Civilization and the Negro*, 40.

61. Cromwell, *The Negro in American History*, 2.

62. An image of the Boston Massacre appeared in the book's frontispiece.

63. Pendleton, *A Narrative of the Negro*, 18, 5, 13, 81, my italics.

64. Woodson, *The Negro in Our History*, 2nd ed., 1, 4, 11–12.

65. Ibid., 5th ed., preface, n.p.

66. Ibid., 7. Woodson explained that we too often mistake "advance in culture with brain improvement," asserting that environmental factors rather than racial factors were responsible for cultural development (ibid., 9).

67. Woodson, *The Education of the Negro*, 1.

68. "No word has been more extensively misused than the word 'primitive,'" Woodson declared (*The African Background Outlined*, 435).

69. Woodson, "Noted Historian Discusses the Dramatization of Negro Life and History," *New Journal and Guide*, December 14, 1935.

70. Part 1 of *The African Background Outlined* related "the story of the Negro from the preliterate period in Africa through the fascinating drama of the rise and fall of the great mediaeval kingdoms there to the latest rape of Africa in the name of civilization by Mussolini" (Logan, review of *The African Background Outlined*, 322). Part 2 featured annotated reading lists on different topics such as the Negro in art. An ambitious book, *The African Background Outlined* is also uneven in quality; for example, there are several chapters that are stitched together out of long extracts from the work of other scholars. "The material is detailed and prosy," a review in the *Journal of Southern History* concluded, "and suffers from a lack of interpretation, tending indeed to become a recital of battles, kingdoms and empires which have little reality for the Western mind" (Glunt, review of *African Background Outlined*, 359).

71. Woodson, *The Negro in Our History*, 5th ed., 22; Woodson, *The African Background Outlined*, 170. On "African survivals," see Woodson, *The African Background*, ch. 12.

72. Woodson, *The African Background Outlined*, 168.

73. Ibid., 169–72.

74. McCoo, "Ethiopia at the Bar of Justice," 313, 311.

75. Ibid., 358.

76. Ibid., 311.

77. Guinn, "Out of the Dark," 322–33.

78. Ater, *Remaking Race and History*, 129. Fuller's *Ethiopia* sculpture was displayed at the 1921 America's Making Exposition in New York, which focused on the contributions that immigrants had made to the country. In the section titled "Americans of Negro Lineage" in the exposition's official book, Fuller's sculpture is described as "a Symbolic Statue of the EMANCIPATION of the NEGRO RACE" (ibid., 125).

79. Corbould, *Becoming African Americans*, 36.

80. McCoo, "Ethiopia at the Bar of Justice," 354.

81. Ibid., 353, 347, 358.

82. Ibid., 359.

83. Ibid., 360.

84. Fabre and Feith, *Temples of Tomorrow*, 5. See also Bay, *The White Image in the Black Mind*, esp. ch. 6.

85. Hutchinson, *Harlem Renaissance in Black and White*, 42; McCoo, "Ethiopia at the Bar of Justice," 373, 366.

86. Du Bois, "The Talented Tenth," 44.

87. "The Problem of Teaching Negro History in the Elementary School," 36.

88. Burns, *From Storefront to Monument*, 5.

89. Corbould, *Becoming African Americans*, 109.

90. Myrtle A. Brodie to Woodson, June 1, 1935, Carter G. Woodson and the Association for Negro Life and History Papers, reel 5, frames 825, 828.

91. Crawford, "The Negro Builds a Pyramid," 29.

92. Ibid., 29–31.

93. Brundage, *Southern Past*, 175, my italics.

94. The *Journal of Negro History* took notice of the literary renaissance, printing no fewer than eighteen reviews of key Negro Renaissance books including works by Arna Bontemps, Sterling Brown, Langston Hughes, James Weldon Johnson, and Zora Neale Hurston. Associated Publishers even published novels, including *Veiled Aristocrats* (1923) by Gertrude Sanborn (1923) and *Princess Malah* (1933) by John H. Hill.

95. On the advent of the *Negro History Bulletin*, see Dagbovie, *The Early Black History Movement, Carter G. Woodson, and Lorenzo Johnston Greene*, 55–60; and Goggin, *Carter G. Woodson*, 114–15.

96. Among other books on black arts and letters, the first four volumes of the *Negro History Bulletin* (1937–41) spotlighted the following titles: *To Make a Poet Black*, by J. Saunders Redding; *Black Labor Chant and Other Poems*, by David Wadsworth Cannon; *The Negro and the Drama*, by F. W. Bond, *Negro Poets and Their Poems*, by Robert T. Kerlin; *American Negro Songs*, by John W. Work; and *The Negro in Art*, by Alain Locke.

97. Woodson, "What's behind the *Negro History Bulletin*," 16.

98. On philanthropic support for the association, see Goggin, *Carter G. Woodson*, ch. 3, and Hine, "Carter G. Woodson, White Philanthropy, and Negro Historiography." After 1933, no white foundations made substantial monetary contributions to the association (Goggin, *Carter G. Woodson*, 94).

99. Goggin, *Carter G. Woodson*, 84.

100. Jackson, "The Work of the Association and the People," 395.

101. Dagbovie, "Black Women Historians from the Late 19th Century to the Dawn-

ing of the Civil Rights Movement," 34; Des Jardins, *Women and the Historical Enterprise*, 159.

102. See the front matter of the first issue.

103. See, for example, Crosson, "Wilhelmina M. Crosson Reports on Intercultural Education in Mexico"; Fleming, "Angelo Solimann," "Luiz Gama," and "America's First Woman Bank President"; Pride, "Negroes in Guatemala" and "Henry Ward Beecher"; Mixon, "I Am a Negro" and "Color"; Dykes, "William Cullen Bryant," "Democracy and Walt Whitman" and "The Poetry of the Civil War"; and Porter, "Negro Women in Our Wars."

104. Dagbovie, "Black Women Historians from the Late 19th Century to the Dawning of the Civil Rights Movement," 36. On Jones, see Benjamin, "Lois Mailou Jones."

105. "Negro Poets, Singers in the Dawn," 15. Many of the *Negro History Bulletin* articles, especially the features, were unsigned. If the unsigned articles and reviews in the *Journal of Negro History* are any guide, however, the unattributed essays in the *Bulletin* were in all likelihood written by Woodson.

106. "Negro Novelists—Blazing the Way in Fiction," 22.

107. "The Negro Theater," 31; "Negro History Week to Feature Musicians and Their Music," 33–34.

108. Duckett, "A Method for Studying Negro Contributions to Progress," 3–4.

109. "A Dramatic Summary of Negro History by Mrs. A. B. Finlayson's Pupils of the Twining School, D.C.," 109.

110. Woodson, review of *American Negro Slavery* (*Journal of Negro History*), 102–3.

111. Gates and Jarrett, introduction, 3.

112. Huggins, *Harlem Renaissance*, 63.

113. Jackson, "The Work of the Association and the People," 392; Huggins, *Harlem Renaissance*, 60.

114. Davis, quoted in Zack, *Women of Color and Philosophy*, 135–36.

PART THREE. RACE

1. On the slippery nature of the race concept, see Fields, "Slavery, Race, and Ideology in the United States of America"; Hodes, "The Mercurial Nature and Abiding Power of Race"; and Jones, *A Dreadful Deceit*.

2. Gerstle, *American Crucible*, 204. On the retreat of "scientific racism" during World War II, see Baker, *From Savage to Negro*, ch. 9; Barkan, *The Retreat of Scientific Racism*; Fredrickson, *Racism*, esp. ch. 3; Gershenhorn, *Melville J. Herskovits and the Racial Politics of Knowledge*, ch. 2; and Gossett, *Race*, esp. ch. 16. On the enlargement of whiteness and the narrowing of race relations in the United States to a black-white divide, see Burkholder, "From 'Wops and Dagoes and Hunkies' to 'Caucasian'"; Jacobson, *Whiteness of a Different Color*; and Painter, *The History of White People*.

3. Litwack, *How Free is Free?*, 84.

4. Of course, generations of African American intellectuals and activists from Benjamin Banneker and Frederick Douglass to Ida B. Wells and W. E. B. Du Bois had argued that a critical gap existed between the theory and practice of American democracy. But it was the publication of *An American Dilemma* that first brought the theory-practice gap to the nation's attention on a mass scale. Financed by the Carnegie Corporation, with forty-five chapters totaling 1,024 pages, ten appendices of over 100 pages and over 250 pages of footnotes, *An American Dilemma* endowed the study

of race relations with a powerful imprint of mainstream respectability and placed the "American Creed" at the heart of the nation's lexicon. Ralph Ellison's brilliant review of *An American Dilemma* referred to the "sense of alienation and embarrassment that the book might arouse by reminding him [the American Negro] that it is necessary in our democracy for a European scientist to affirm the American Negro's humanity" (http://teachingamericanhistory.org/library/index.asp?document=554). On the epochal influence of *An American Dilemma*, see Jackson, *Gunnar Myrdal and America's Conscience*; and Singh, *Black Is a Country*, esp. ch. 4.

5. Logan, "The Negro Wants First-Class Citizenship," 7.

6. Litwack, *How Free Is Free?*, 91.

7. Banks, *Black Intellectuals*, xv.

8. See, for example, Appiah, "The Uncompleted Argument"; Bay, *The White Image in the Black Mind*, esp. ch. 6; and Williams, *The Social Sciences and Theories of Race*.

9. See Sussman, *The Myth of Race*.

CHAPTER FIVE. "A REVISION OF THE CONCEPT OF RACE AND OF RACISM"

1. Woodson, draft encyclopedia entry on "race," Carter G. Woodson Papers and the Association for Negro Life and History Papers, reel 15, frames 5, 3.

2. Ibid., frames 101, 107, 110–11, 117.

3. Ibid., frame 102.

4. Greene, *Working with Carter G. Woodson, the Father of Black History*, 14; Winston, *Howard University Department of History*, 33; Michael R. Winston, interview with the author, Washington, D.C., July 13, 2009.

5. With respect to fraternal and racial uplift associations, see, for instance, Wesley's *The History of Alpha Phi Alpha*; *History of Sigma Pi Phi*; and *The History of the National Association of Colored Women's Clubs*. With respect to the black freedom struggle, see, for example, his "The Negroes of New York in the Emancipation Movement"; "The Negro in the Organization of Abolition"; "The Participation of Negroes in Anti-Slavery Political Parties"; "The Negro's Struggle for Freedom in Its Birthplace"; and "Negro Suffrage in the Period of Constitution-Making."

6. Logan, "Carter G. Woodson" (1945), 320; Janken, *Rayford W. Logan and the Dilemma of the African-American Intellectual*, 86.

7. Winston, interview with the author, Washington, D.C., July 13, 2009. As Logan wrote in his unpublished autobiography, "I am a bit standoffish, particularly because of an innate shyness and partly because I have a horror of being accused of pushing myself into situations where I am not wanted" (Rayford Logan Papers, box 166–32, folder 8, IX-7-IX-8).

8. Winston, interview with the author, Washington, D.C., July 13, 2009.

9. Janken, *Rayford W. Logan and the Dilemma of the African-American Intellectual*, 214–15. In the early 1950s, Logan published four articles in the *Negro History Bulletin*.

10. On Franklin, see Faust, "John Hope Franklin"; Jarrett, *Tributes to John Hope Franklin*; and the "Legacy of Dr. John Hope Franklin" special issue of the *Journal of African American History* 94 (Summer 2009). See also Franklin's autobiography, *Mirror to America*.

11. Gates, "John Hope, the Prince Who Refused the Kingdom."

12. Franklin, *Mirror to America*, 374.

13. Franklin had a long and storied career, comprised of a remarkable string of firsts and capped by a flurry of laurels and accolades, including the Presidential Medal of Freedom, which he received in 1995. With respect to "firsts," he was, for example, the first black president of the Southern Historical Association (1969–70), the Organization of American Historians (1974–75) and the American Historical Association (1978–79).

14. As of 2005, *From Slavery to Freedom* had sold 3.5 million copies (see the inside of the dust jacket of *Mirror to America*). Franklin said that you could chart the progress of the civil rights movements by tracking the sales of his textbook—what began as a trickle with the first two hardcover editions turned into a deluge when the first paperback edition came out in 1969. According to Franklin, "In September 1969, the first paperback edition of *From Slavery to Freedom* finally appeared, and purchasers snapped it up as though they had been waiting for it for years.... My publishers, however, seemed not to understand what was happening. One had to be rather close to the civil rights movement to understand the great demand for a book that related the way the African American story was inextricably woven into the history of the United States. Consequently, the paperback of the third edition went rapidly into a second and third printing (*Mirror to America*, 246).

15. Franklin, *Mirror to America*, 136.

16. Sussman, *Myth of Race*, 303, 168.

17. Quoted in Sussman, *Myth of Race*, 97.

18. Ibid., 74; Ngai, *Impossible Subjects*, 27.

19. Williams, *The Social Sciences and Theories of Race*, 32.

20. Sussman, *Myth of Race*, 164.

21. See Herskovits, "Correlation of Length and Breadth of Head in American Negroes"; and "Growth of Interpupillary Distance in American Negroes."

22. Gershenhorn, *Melville J. Herskovits and the Racial Politics of Knowledge*, 44.

23. Williams, *The Social Sciences and Theories of Race*, 18.

24. Here is how Woodson summed up the significance of Boas's career: "Franz Boas was one of the great scientists of his time.... Dr. Boas was among the first in this country to take the position that there is nothing in anthropology or psychology to support the claim of superiority or inferiority of races. He disproved, therefore, the prevailing theories of race and demonstrated that there is no pure race and showed how acquired cultural habits are mistaken for fixed hereditary characteristics" (review of *Race and Democratic Society*, 231).

25. Hutchinson, *Harlem Renaissance in Black and White*, 63.

26. Review of *The American Race Problem*, 560.

27. Woodson, review of *The Myth of the Negro Past*, 116.

28. Review of *Christianity and the Race Problem*, 102. See also review of *Up from the Ape*; and Woodson, review of *Characteristics of the American Negro*.

29. Woodson clearly kept abreast of research on "the Negro" in physical anthropology, mentioning relevant citations in the "Notes" section of the *Journal of Negro History*. In the January 1935 issue, for example, Woodson cited several articles in this vein, including "Septal Apertures in the Humerus of American Whites and Negroes," "Patterns of the Aortic Arch in American White and Negro Stocks with Comparative Notes on Certain other Animals" and "The Calcification of the First Costal Cartilage among Whites and Negroes" (103).

30. Woodson, "Proceedings of the Ninth Annual Meeting of the Association for the Study of Negro Life and History," 110–11. At an association convention ten years later, professor R. O. Lanier of Houston College discussed the attitude of psychologists toward the Negro, highlighting the serious limitations of the mental tests that had purportedly shown the Negro to be intellectually inferior (Woodson, "Proceedings of the Annual Meeting of the Association Held in Houston, Texas, from November 10–14, 1934," 7–8).

31. Woodson, "Proceedings of the Annual Meeting of the Association Held in St. Louis, Missouri, October 21 to 25, 1928," 7; Woodson, "Proceedings of the Annual Meeting of the Association Held in Washington, D.C., October 27–31, 1929," 11.

32. Brown, "Racial Inequality", 54, 45, 44, 56.

33. Woodson, "Proceedings of the Annual Meeting of the Association Held in Cleveland, Ohio, October 26–30, 1930," 3–4; Todd, "An Anthropologist's Study of Negro Life," 36–37, 40.

34. Rhoads, "Teaching the Negro Child," 15, 18–19.

35. Sussman, *The Myth of Race*, 197.

36. Barzun, quoted in Fredrickson, *Racism*, 163.

37. Benedict, *Race*, 260–61, 263. Nazi Germany provided a major impetus to anthropologists and psychologists to go on record regarding the meaning of "race." The former, for example, stressed that the terms "Aryan" and "Semitic" had no "racial significance whatsoever." The latter asserted that the "Nazi theory that people must be related by blood in order to participate in the same cultural or intellectual heritage has absolutely no support from scientific findings" (ibid., 260, 262).

38. On the advent of this tripartite framework, see Baum, *The Rise and Fall of the Caucasian Race*, ch. 5.

39. Benedict and Weltfish, *The Races of Mankind*, 7; Montagu, *Man's Most Dangerous Myth*, 2.

40. Wesley, "The Negro Has Always Wanted the Four Freedoms," 107; Nelson, review of *What the Negro Wants*, 68.

41. "Negro History Week Observed," *New York Amsterdam News*, February 19, 1944.

42. Montagu, "The Negro's Problem," 177–79, 188.

43. Wesley, "The Concept of Negro Inferiority in American Thought," 559.

44. "Washington High Observes History Week," *New Journal and Guide*, March 1, 1947; Burkholder, *Color in the Classroom*, 3–4.

45. Himes, "Racial Criminality," 140. On the past and present misuse of racial statistics, see Zuberi, *Thicker Than Blood*.

46. Moon, "A Fifth Freedom for the Negro," 66–67.

47. Ibid.

48. Ibid., 67.

49. Brooks, "Segregation and Gradualism," 151; *Negro History Bulletin* 19 (October 1955), 23; *Negro History Bulletin* 18 (October 1954), 20; Brooks, "Firm Foundations," 131.

50. Nat. D. Williams, "Down on Beale," *Atlanta Daily World*, February 15, 1938. Earl Thorpe, the first historian to write a monograph on the development of Negro history as a field, also rejected the principle that "a glorious and wonderful past is necessary for racial achievement," but for different reasons. "This motivating idea," Thorpe said, "is suspect simply because there is no convincing proof of its truthfulness. . . .

There is even evidence that the reverse position from that taken by Woodson and others is true, that is, that the possession of a 'history' negates the possibility of future achievement and survival of a race or peoples by causing them to 'rest on their oars'" (*Black Historians*, 18-19).

51. This was the title to Alain Locke's "Literature of the Negro" review for 1942. See Locke, "Who and What Is 'Negro'?"

52. Woodson, "Proceedings of the Annual Meeting of the Association, Held in Washington, D.C., October 30-November 1, 1942," 2.

53. Lewis, *The Biology of the Negro*, ix, x.

54. Ibid., xii-xiii.

55. Cobb's lecture was printed under the same title in the April 1943 issue of *Journal of Negro History*. Cobb was the first African American to receive a doctorate in physical anthropology. On his life and career, see Rankin-Hill and Blakey, "W. Montague Cobb (1904-1990): Physical Anthropologist, Anatomist and Activist"; and Watkins, "Knowledge from the Margins: W. Montague Cobb's Pioneering Research in Biocultural Anthropology."

56. Cobb, "Education in Human Biology," 124, 122, 143.

57. Ibid., 120.

58. Ibid., 142.

59. Ibid., 139.

60. Benedict, like Cobb, was somewhat mystified that there was so much "confusion between race and racism." "It is no paradox," Benedict explained, "that a student may have at his tongue's end a hundred racial differences and still be no racist." "Race is a matter for careful scientific study," Benedict averred. "Racism is an unproven assumption of the biological and perpetual superiority of one human group over another" (*Race*, v-vi).

61. Logan, *The Negro and the Post-War World*, 1-2.

62. Logan's diaries are filled with observations—brimming with an almost ethnographic attention to fine-grained detail—about race and the color line not only in the United States but also in Cuba, Latin America, Europe, and Africa. See also Logan's 1927 essay "The Confessions of an Unwilling Nordic."

63. Autobiography, Rayford Logan Papers, box 133-31, folder 1, I-1-I-2.

64. Logan, *The Negro and the Post-War World*, 1.

65. Quoted in Jacobson, *Whiteness of a Different Color*, 110.

66. Logan, *The Negro and the Post-War World*, vi, viii, 3, 6-7.

67. Woodson, "The Cooperation of Persons of African Blood," 96; Woodson, "Has the Negro Race a Culture?," 15.

68. Woodson, "Has the Negro Race a Culture?," 16.

69. Franklin, *From Slavery to Freedom*, 39-41, vii.

70. Quarles, "The Road We Trod," 173; Himes, review of *From Slavery to Freedom*, 487.

71. Lofton, review of *From Slavery to Freedom*, 225-26; Streator, review of *From Slavery to Freedom*.

72. Streator, review of *From Slavery to Freedom*, italics in original.

73. Franklin, *From Slavery to Freedom*, vii. On Herskovits's analysis of the African influence on African Americans, see Gershenhorn, *Melville J. Herskovits and the Racial Politics of Knowledge*, esp. ch. 4.

74. Franklin, *From Slavery to Freedom*, 39-40.

75. Woodson, "Has the Negro Race a Culture?," 16; Franklin, *From Slavery to Freedom*, 39. Regarding generosity, Woodson said the Negro American was "generous to a fault because in the tribal life in Africa all things are held in common" ("Has the Negro Race a Culture?," 16).

76. Wesley, "Why We Fight for First-Class Citizenship," *Pittsburgh Courier*, September 4, 1954; Woodson, "A Misleading Term," 48.

77. Wesley, "Why We Fight for First-Class Citizenship," *Pittsburgh Courier*, September 4, 1954. Noting that competition for jobs often increased animosity between immigrants and blacks, Wesley said that many immigrants "yielded to the prejudice of older Americans in order that they might advance themselves and their interests." He relayed the story of the Jewish immigrant who opened a theater and relegated Negroes to a special section, thus showing how the "persecuted can become the persecutors."

78. Jackson, *Gunnar Myrdal and America's Conscience*, 112. In a short section of *An American Dilemma* called "Negro History and Culture," this dismissive point of view is evident, even if Myrdal's language is more circumspect. Negro history, Myrdal reported in *American Dilemma*, was largely a response to the anti-Negro bias characteristic of the standard historical accounts written by white historians. While acknowledging that the research carried out by Woodson and his colleagues was of the highest quality, Myrdal asserted that "there has been a definite distortion in the emphasis and the perspective given the facts." "Mediocrities have been expanded into 'great men,'" Myrdal said, and "cultural achievements which are no better—and no worse—than any others are placed on a pinnacle; minor historical events are magnified into crises." The association, according to Myrdal, combined "propagandistic activities" with scholarly ones. "In spite of all scholarly pretenses and accomplishments," Myrdal concluded, "this movement is basically an expression of the Negro protest" (752).

79. Among the experts who drafted the UNESCO statement were E. Franklin Frazier, Claude Levi-Strauss, and Ashley Montagu. The text was revised in light of criticism from, among others, Otto Klineberg and Gunnar Myrdal.

80. *UNESCO and Its Programme*; Von Eschen, *Race against Empire*, 153–9.

81. Gordon, *From Power to Prejudice*, 2, 8–9.

82. Ibid., 180–81, 34.

83. Meier and Rudwick, *Black History and the Historical Profession*, 92; Foner, introduction, xi.

84. Logan, *The Betrayal of the Negro, from Rutherford B. Hayes to Woodrow Wilson*, 168–69. In 1965, Logan released an expanded edition of the book with a new title, *The Betrayal of the Negro, from Rutherford B. Hayes to Woodrow Wilson*. I refer throughout to the 1997 Da Capo Press reprint of *The Betrayal of the Negro*. The text and pagination are the same as in the 1954 original.

85. Bell I. Wiley, "As the North Yielded," *New York Times*, February 14, 1954; Bradley, review of *The Negro in American Life and Thought*, 297–8.

86. Bond, review of *The Negro in American Life and Thought*, 470.

87. Gertrude Martin, review of *The Negro in American Life and Thought*, *Chicago Defender*, March 6, 1954.

88. Logan, *The Negro and the Post-War World*, 7.

89. In the jargon of social psychology, this is called the fundamental attribution error, and it is one of the field's most robust findings.

90. *UNESCO and Its Programme*, 8.

91. Benedict and Weltfish, *Races of Mankind*, 280.

92. According to Benedict, unlike race, which could be "scientifically investigated," racism was a "dogma" that had to be "studied historically." "We must investigate," Benedict wrote, "the conditions under which it arises and the uses to which it has been put" (*Race*, 153–54).

93. Benedict, *Race*, 143, 133, 199.

94. See ibid., esp. chs.7 and 8.

95. Ibid., 154, 216, 234.

96. Ibid., 242–43.

97. Logan, *The Betrayal of the Negro, from Rutherford B. Hayes to Woodrow Wilson*, 35, 119, 125, 13.

98. Ibid., 116, 83, 107.

99. Foner, introduction, xiii.

100. See Fredrickson, *Black Image in the White Mind*. The "black image in the white mind" analytic approach pioneered by Logan was not widely embraced until the late 1960s and early 1970s when it rose to prominence with the release of Winthrop Jordan's *White Over Black: American Attitudes Toward the Negro, 1550–1812* and Fredrickson's *The Black Image in the White Mind*. Fredrickson cites *The Betrayal of the Negro* on numerous occasions, especially in his ninth chapter. More recent examples include Guterl, *Seeing Race in Modern America*; Hale, *Making Whiteness*; and McElya, *Clinging to Mammy*. The field of literary history has also adopted this genre of scholarship. See, for instance, Gates, "Trope of a New Negro and the Reconstruction of the Image of the Black."

101. "Where Logan really broke new ground," Foner said of *The Negro in American Life and Thought*, "was in the second part, a comprehensive analysis of the *images* of blacks in newspapers, magazines, popular literature, and other cultural forums" (introduction, xiv, italics in original). Logan acknowledged the pioneering work of Sterling Brown on the stereotyping of blacks in literature, citing his seminal article on how white writers perceived Negro character in the *Journal of Negro Education*. See Brown, "Negro Character as Seen by White Authors."

102. Along these lines Logan's "black image" framework drew on both psychological and cultural paradigms. Perhaps most importantly, his approach shares several key assumptions of the cultural model. First, racism cannot be reduced to the effect of a different variable such as class. Second, racism does not exist outside of time (it is "not exogenous" to the culture). And third, racism is "simultaneously a product of that culture and producing that culture" (Holt, "Explaining Racism in American History," 115).

103. Holt, "Explaining Racism in American History," 108.

104. Logan, *The Betrayal of the Negro, from Rutherford B. Hayes to Woodrow Wilson*, 159.

105. Bond, review of *The Negro in American Life and Thought*, 470. Logan's biographer agreed with Bond, noting that the American press's denial of the humanity of African Americans "was an essential part of the climate of violence against blacks and the ideological preparation for their disenfranchisement and segregation" (Janken, *Rayford W. Logan and the Dilemma of the African-American Intellectual*, 241).

106. Logan, *The Betrayal of the Negro, from Rutherford B. Hayes to Woodrow Wilson*, 216, 241, 240, 242, 241.

107. Ibid., 159–61.

108. Muhammad, *The Condemnation of Blackness*, 4, 86, 5.

109. Logan, *The Betrayal of the Negro, from Rutherford B. Hayes to Woodrow Wilson*, 217–18, 302, 295.

110. Ibid., 265, 220–25, 292, 288.

111. Rayford Logan, "Socio-Economic Factors in the Apparent Differences Between Negroes and Whites," speech delivered September 23, 1956, Rayford Logan Papers, box 166-43, folder 25, 1, 4.

CHAPTER SIX. LOOK TO THE ROOTS

1. Wesley, "The Negro Citizen in Our Wars for Freedom," 78, 93, 83, 94.
2. Zimmerman, "*Brown*-ing the American Textbook," 53, 52, 48.
3. Singh, *Black Is a Country*, 135, 140, italics in original.
4. Woodson, "History as It Is," 168.
5. Gordon, *From Power to Prejudice*, 8, 118.
6. Wesley, "The Negro Has Always Wanted the Four Freedoms," 92.
7. Janken, introduction, vii. As sociologist Charles S. Johnson remarked, "the logic of democracy made all the conclusions identical" (review of *What the Negro Wants*, 245).
8. Janken, introduction, xxix.
9. Logan, introduction to the 1969 reprint, xxxi.
10. Couch, quoted in Janken, introduction, xviii.
11. Logan, "The Negro Wants First-Class Citizenship," 28; Couch, publisher's introduction, xxii.
12. Quoted in Janken, introduction, xix.
13. Logan, introduction to the 1969 reprint, xxxi.
14. Holmes, review of *What the Negro Wants*, 91. For more on this "strange spectacle," see Holloway, *Jim Crow Wisdom*, 29–33.
15. Couch, publisher's introduction, xx.
16. Marjorie McKenzie, "Pursuit of Democracy," *Pittsburgh Courier*, November 4, 1944; Ben Burns, "Books," *Chicago Defender*, November 4, 1944.
17. Arthur P. Davis, "With a Grain of Salt," *New Journal and Guide*, August 18, 1945; Mays, "Minority Mandates," 387, 389; Stern, review of *What the Negro Wants*, 306.
18. Marjorie McKenzie, "Pursuit of Democracy," *Pittsburgh Courier*, November 4, 1944; Janken, introduction, vii–viii; Johnson, review of *What the Negro Wants*, 245.
19. Logan, "The Negro Wants First-Class Citizenship," 1.
20. Ibid., 5–7. "The picture of an undivided North militantly fighting for the rights of the Negro," Logan said, "is as great a myth as the specter of a South in which every man, woman and child is adamant in his determination to deny to the Negro any opportunity for progress" (Ibid., 5).
21. Du Bois, "My Evolving Program for Negro Freedom," 51–52.
22. Logan, *What the Negro Wants*, vii, italics in original; Bethune, "Certain Unalienable Rights," 250.
23. Wilkins, "The Negro Wants Full Equality," 116, 118, 128–29.
24. Wesley, "The Negro Has Always Wanted the Four Freedoms," 91–2.
25. "It is a litany chanted over and over again," McKenzie continued, "of what the white man has kept us from having—the security of our persons and homes, the ballot, education, decent housing and jobs, health" ("Pursuit of Democracy," *Pittsburgh Courier*, November 4, 1944).

26. Wesley, "The Negro Has Always Wanted the Four Freedoms," 90.

27. *Anti-Negro Propaganda in School Textbooks*, 3, 9, 12, 10; Carpenter, *The Treatment of the Negro in American History School Textbooks*, 99.

28. Wesley, "The Negro Has Always Wanted the Four Freedoms," 90, 92–3.

29. "Proclamation to Spur Negro History Week," *New York Amsterdam News*, February 5, 1944.

30. See, for example, "Military Service in Colonial America"; Browning, "The Negro in the Hispanic-American Wars of Independence"; and Woodson, "The Negro in the First World War."

31. See, for instance, Wesley, "The Negro Citizen in Our Wars"; "What did the Civil War Settle?"; and "What did the First World War Accomplish?".

32. Woodson, "Negro Women Eligible to Be Daughters of the American Revolution"; Dykes, "The Poetry of the Civil War"; and Williams, "A Tribute to the Negro War Correspondent."

33. "Negro History Week Program," Carter G. Woodson Papers and the Association for Negro Life and History, reel 20, frames 903, 907–9.

34. Ibid., 907–8. As Woodson put it, "The record [of black military participation] itself will be the Negroes' greatest claim for recognition as full-fledged citizens" ("Why Negroes Fight in this War," 170).

35. Margaret T. Goss, "Billikens Observe Negro History Week," *Chicago Defender*, February 13, 1943.

36. Woodson, "The Negro Looks for Democracy," 72.

37. Woodson, "Workers for Equality and Justice," 125–28, 141, 143.

38. Langston Hughes, "Here to Yonder," *Chicago Defender*, February 10, 1945.

39. Hughes, "A Ballad of Negro History," 92.

40. "Here Too for Freedom a Blow Was Struck—By Nat Turner," *New Journal and Guide*, February 13, 1954.

41. *Glory of Negro History* liner notes, Folkways Records, Library of Congress Catalogue Card No. R 58–520, 1958, n.p.

42. Ibid.

43. See, for example, Rosenbaum, "The Origin of Judicial Sanction of Educational Segregation"; Crawford, "Some Aspects of Preparation for Desegregation in the Public Schools of Louisville"; and Brooks, "Equality and Educational Policy."

44. Brooks, "Firm Foundations," 128–30.

45. Ibid., 130.

46. Wesley, "The Association and the Public," 75.

47. Brooks, "Negro History," 96.

48. John B. Henderson, "Negro History Week Meets a Great Need," *New Journal and Guide*, February 6, 1954; "Why 'Negro History Week'? College Presidents Answer Question of Integrationists," *Pittsburgh Courier*, February 13, 1954.

49. Brooks, "Reconstruction Period and Integration," n.p.

50. Stewart, "A Negro History Week Oration," 82. On historiographical debates about the contested meaning of "integration," see Gaines, "Whose Integration Was It?"

51. "Cites Text Book Deficiencies In Treating History of America," *Atlanta Daily World*, February 11, 1954; Stewart, "Negro History Week Oration," 82; "Negro History Week," *Philadelphia Tribune*, February 1, 1955.

52. Howard Aide Sparks History Week Program," *LA Sentinel*, February 16, 1956.

53. Brooks, "Negro History," 94.

54. Egert, "Building Foundations for Integration," 196.

55. "Why Negro History Week?," *New York Amsterdam News*, February 13, 1954.

56. "Why 'Negro History Week'? College Presidents Answer Question of Integrationists," *Pittsburgh Courier*, February 13, 1954.

57. Ibid.

58. Brooks, "Negro History," 94.

59. Ibid., 90.

60. "Negro History Week," *LA Sentinel*, February 10, 1955.

61. Brown, "Count Us In," 334.

62. See, for example, "Milestones in Negro History," *New York Amsterdam News*, February 12, 1955.

63. Douglass, "Contemporary Trends in Negro History," 23.

64. "Clark Prof. E. F. Sweat Speaks for Negro History Week at M'Brown," *Atlanta Daily World*, February 20, 1955.

65. Douglass, "Contemporary Trends in Negro History," 23.

66. More specifically, "What evidence was there that the Congress that passed the Fourteenth Amendment and the state legislature and conventions that ratified it understood that the amendment would abolish segregation in the public schools?" (Franklin, *Mirror to America*, 156).

67. Autobiography, Rayford Logan Papers, box 166-34, folder 9, II-4-2.

68. Ballard oral history interview, audiocassette listening copy 36, John Hope Franklin Papers.

69. John Hope Franklin, "Historians and the Black Movement," ibid., box W10; Patterson, *Brown v. Board of Education*, 66. On the role that history played in *Brown*, see Patterson, *Brown v. Board of Education*, esp. 63–64.

70. Logan, "Public School Desegregation," 9.

71. Logan, "The Realities and Ethics of Desegregation," 398.

72. Logan defined Sumner's dictum as follows: "It is futile for government to seek through judicial, legislative or executive means to overcome deeply rooted attitudes and behavior" ("The Realities and Ethics of Desegregation," 308).

73. Ibid., 308–9. On the lecture circuit in the early 1950s, Logan regularly fielded questions about whether stateways could change folkways. His standard response was that "Americans were going to drink and smoke despite laws to the contrary," that "in some aspects of civil rights such as voting in some southern states, laws were changing folkways," and finally that "there was a twilight zone about which men of good will might differ" (Autobiography, Rayford Logan Papers, box 166-34, folder 5, II-2-4.)

74. Franklin, *Mirror to America*, 159.

75. Franklin, "Desegregation," 96.

76. Ibid., 97–98, 100.

77. Franklin, *Mirror to America*, 328.

78. Quoted in ibid., 177–78.

79. Woodward, *The Strange Career of Jim Crow*, 3.

80. Quoted in Novick, *That Noble Dream*, 354.

81. Woodward, *The Strange Career of Jim Crow*, vii, 8.

82. Franklin, "History of Racial Segregation in the United States," 1, 9.

83. Woodson, "American and Un-American Activities," 74.

84. Franklin, "History," 258.

EPILOGUE

1. On the tortuous effort to establish the NMAAHC, see Burns, *From Storefront to Monument*, ch. 6; Wilson, *Negro Building*, 306–10; and Wilson, *Begin with the Past*.
2. Kate Taylor, "The Thorny Path to a National Black Museum," *New York Times*, January 22, 2011.
3. Shapiro and Pao, "Mission Of African-American Museum Writ Large in Its Very Design."
4. Wilson, *Begin with the Past*, 16.
5. Graham Bowley, "How the Fight for a National African-American Museum Was Won," *New York Times*, September 4, 2016.
6. Holand Cotter, "The Smithsonian African American Museum Is Here at Last, and It Uplifts and Upsets," *New York Times*, September 15, 2016.
7. Brawley, *A Social History of the American Negro*, 340.
8. "Remarks by the President at the Dedication of the National Museum of African American History and Culture," September 24, 2016, www.whitehouse.gov/the-press-office/2016/09/24/remarks-president-dedication-national-museum-african-american-history.
9. Zimmerman, *Whose America?*, 3.
10. More than two-thirds of respondents mentioned King, while only a third mentioned the highest-ranked white name on the list, Susan B. Anthony (Wineburg and Monte-Sano, "'Famous Americans,'" 1190.)
11. See the "text rankings" in English at the Open Syllabus Explorer: http://explorer.opensyllabusproject.org.
12. Hip-hop received a stamp of official approval when Yale University Press released the *Anthology of Rap* in 2010, which featured a foreword by none other than the reigning dean of African American life and culture, Henry Louis Gates Jr. See Bradley and DuBois, eds., *The Anthology of Rap*.
13. Bunch, "The Definitive Story of How the National Museum of African American History and Culture Came to Be"; Cotter, "The Smithsonian African American Museum Is Here at Last, and It Uplifts and Upsets," *New York Times*, September 15, 2016"; Cunningham, "Making a Home for Black History"; Philip Kennicott, "The African American Museum Tells Powerful Stories—but Not as Powerfully as It Could," *Washington Post*, September 14, 2016; Van R. Newkirk, "How a Museum Reckons with Black Pain," *Atlantic*, September 23, 2016.
14. Emily Yahr, "Read George W. Bush's Speech at the African American Museum, 13 Years after Signing the Bill to Build It," *Washington Post*, September 24, 2016.
15. Bunch, "The Definitive Story of How the National Museum of African American History and Culture Came to Be."
16. Krissah Thompson, "Painful but Crucial: Why You'll See Emmett Till's Casket at the African American Museum," *Washington Post*, August 18, 2016.
17. Lonnie Bunch, quoted in Clare Foran, "Allowing America to Confront Its Tortured Racial Past," *Atlantic*, September 28, 2016; Dhakkiyyah Lee quoted in Melena Ryzik, "Pride and Pain on Opening Day at a Museum of African-American History," *New York Times*, September 26, 2016.
18. This assessment is based on an analysis of the flagship U.S. history high school textbooks from three of the educational publishing giants—McGraw Hill, Pearson, and

Prentice Hall. The titles are Appleby, McPherson, et al., *United States History and Geography*, Carnes and Garraty, *The American Nation: A History of the United States* and Davidson and Stoff, *America: History of Our Nation*, respectively. I conducted a thorough content analysis of these three books with respect to their treatments of African American history, paying especially close attention to whether and how they addressed the topic of racial violence. Photograph of Jesse Washington in *The American Nation*, 493.

19. George Washington Williams, quoted in Franklin, *George Washington Williams*, 43.

20. Franklin, "The New Negro History," 2.

21. Orfield, Kucsera and Siegel-Hawley, *E Pluribus . . . Separation*.

22. Krissah Thompson and Scott Clement, "Poll: Majority of Americans Think Race Relations Are Getting Worse," *Washington Post*, July 16, 2016.

23. Sendhil Mullainathan, "Police Killing of Blacks: Here Is What the Data Say," *New York Times*, October 16, 2015.

24. See, for example, Nicholas Kristof's multipart *New York Times* series "When Whites Just Don't Get It": August 31, 2014; September 7, 2014; October 12, 2014; November 16, 2014; November 30, 2014; April 2, 2016; and October 1, 2016.

25. "Remarks by the President at the Dedication of the National Museum of African American History and Culture," September 24, 2016, www.whitehouse.gov/the-press-office/2016/09/24/remarks-president-dedication-national-museum-african-american-history.

BIBLIOGRAPHY

MANUSCRIPT COLLECTIONS

Alain Locke Papers, Moorland-Spingarn Research Center, Howard University, Washington, D.C.

Carter G. Woodson and the Association for the Study of Negro Life and History Papers, Washington, D.C., Library of Congress.

Carter G. Woodson Collection of Negro Papers and Related Documents, Washington, D.C., Library of Congress.

Jesse Edward Moorland Papers, Moorland-Spingarn Research Center, Howard University, Washington, D.C.

John Hope Franklin Papers, Rare Book, Manuscript and Special Collections Library, Duke University, Durham, N.C.

Library of Carter G. Woodson, Manuscript, Archives and Rare Book Library, Emory University, Atlanta, Ga.

Rayford Logan Papers, Moorland-Spingarn Research Center, Howard University, Washington, D.C.

NEWSPAPERS AND PERIODICALS

Atlanta Daily World
Baltimore Afro-American
Chicago Defender
Crisis
Journal of Negro History

Negro History Bulletin
New York Amsterdam News
New York Times
Norfolk Journal and Guide
Pittsburgh Courier

PRINTED PRIMARY SOURCES

Allen, James Egert. "Building Foundations for Integration." *Negro History Bulletin* 17, no. 8 (1954): 195–97.

Allen, Richard, and Absalom Jones. "Some Letters of Richard Allen and Absalom Jones to Dorothy Ripley." *Journal of Negro History* 1, no. 4 (1916): 436–43.

Anti-Negro Propaganda in School Textbooks. New York: NAACP, 1939.

Aptheker, Herbert, ed. *The Correspondence of W. E. B. Du Bois.* Vol. 1. Amherst: University of Massachusetts Press, 1973.

Benedict, Ruth. *Race: Science and Politics*. New York: Modern Age Books, 1940.

Benedict, Ruth, and Gene Weltfish. *The Races of Mankind*. New York: Public Affairs, 1943.

Benezet, Anthony. "Letters of Anthony Benezet." *Journal of Negro History* 2, no. 1 (1917): 83–95.

Bethune, Mary McLeod. "Certain Unalienable Rights." In *What the Negro Wants*, edited by Rayford Logan. Notre Dame, Ind.: University of Notre Dame Press, 2001.

———. "Clarifying Our Vision with the Facts." *Journal of Negro History* 23, no. 1 (1938): 10–15.

———. "The Association for the Study of Negro Life and History: Its Contribution to Our Modern Life." *Journal of Negro History* 20, no. 4 (1935): 406–10.

Bond, Horace Mann. Review of *The Negro in American Life and Thought: The Nadir, 1877–1901*, by Rayford W. Logan. *Journal of Negro Education* 23, no. 4 (1954): 469–70.

Bourne, Randolph. "Trans-National America." 1916. In *The American Intellectual Tradition: A Sourcebook*, edited by David A. Hollinger and Charles Capper. New York: Oxford University Press, 2001.

Bradley, H.C. Review of *The Negro in American Life and Thought: The Nadir, 1877–1901*, by Rayford W. Logan. *Social Forces* 33 (1955): 297–98.

Brawley, Benjamin. *A Social History of the American Negro*. New York: Macmillan, 1921.

———, ed. *Early Negro American Writers: Selections with Biographical and Critical Introduction*. Chapel Hill: University of North Carolina Press, 1935.

———. "Elizabeth Barrett Browning and the Negro." *Journal of Negro History* 3 (January 1918): 22–28.

———, "Lorenzo Dow." *Journal of Negro History* 1, no. 3 (1916): 265–75.

———. *Negro Builders and Heroes*. Chapel Hill: University of North Carolina press, 1937.

———. Preface to *Early Negro American Writers: Selections with Biographical and Critical Introduction*, edited by Benjamin Brawley. Chapel Hill: University of North Carolina Press, 1935.

———. *The Negro in Literature and Art in the United States*. 1918. New York: Duffield, 1921.

———. "The Promise of Negro Literature." *Journal of Negro History* 19, no. 1 (1934): 53–59.

———. "Three Negro Poets: Horton, Mrs. Harper, and Whitman." *Journal of Negro History* 2, no. 4 (1917): 384–92.

Brooks, Albert N. D. "Equality and Educational Policy." *Negro History Bulletin* 16, no. 8 (1953): 191–92.

———. "Negro History—a Foundation for Integration." *Negro History Bulletin* 17, no. 4 (1954): 96.

———. "Reconstruction Period and Integration." *Negro History Bulletin* 17, no. 5 (1954): n.p.

———. "Segregation and Gradualism." *Negro History Bulletin* 15, no. 7 (1952): 151–52.

Brooks, Charlotte K. "Firm Foundations: A Radio Skit for Negro History Week." *Negro History Bulletin* 23, no. 7 (1960): 157–60.

Brooks, Van Wyck. "On Creating a Usable Past." *Dial*, April 11, 1918, 337–41.

Brown, Lawrence. Review of *The Book of American Negro Spirituals*, edited by James Weldon Johnson. *Journal of Negro History* 11, no. 1 (1926): 221–22.

Brown, Sterling. "Count Us In." In *What the Negro Wants*, edited by Rayford Logan. Notre Dame, Ind.: University of Notre Dame Press, 2001.

———. "Negro Character as Seen by White Authors." *Journal of Negro Education* 2, no. 2 (1933): 179–203.

Brown, Sterling A., Arthur Paul Davis, and Ulysses Lee, eds. *The Negro Caravan: Writings by American Negroes*. New York: Dryden Press, 1941.

———. Preface to *The Negro Caravan: Writings by American Negroes*. New York: Dryden Press, 1941.

Brown, W. O. "Racial Inequality: Fact or Myth." *Journal of Negro History* 16, no. 1 (1931): 43–60.

Brown, William Wells. *The Rising Son; or, The Antecedents and Advancement of the Colored Race*. Boston: A. G. Brown, 1876.

Browning, James B. "The Negro in the Hispanic-American Wars of Independence." *Negro History Bulletin* 7, no. 4 (1944): 77, 94.

Bunche, Ralph J. "French and British Imperialism in West Africa." *Journal of Negro History* 21, no. 1 (1936): 31–46.

Burnaby, Andrew, et al. "Travelers' Impressions of Slavery in America from 1750 to 1800." *Journal of Negro History* 1, no. 4 (1916): 399–435.

Cade, John B. "Out of the Mouths of Ex-Slaves." *Journal of Negro History* 20, no. 3 (1935): 294–337.

Camp, Abraham, et al. "Letters to the American Colonization Society." Pt. 1. *Journal of Negro History* 10, no. 2 (1925): 154–80.

Carpenter, Marie Elizabeth Ruffin. *The Treatment of the Negro in American History School Textbooks*. Menasha, Wis.: George Banta Publishing Company, 1941.

Channing, Edward. *A History of the United States*. New York: MacMillan, 1905.

———. *A Student's History of the United States*. New York: Macmillan, 1913.

Channing, Edward, Albert Bushnell Hart, and Frederick Jackson Turner. *Guide to the Study and Reading of American History*. Boston: Ginn and Company, 1912.

Cobb, W. Montague. "Education in Human Biology: An Essential for the Present and Future." *Journal of Negro History* 28, no. 2 (1943): 119–55.

Cooper, Anna J. *A Voice from the South*. Xenia, Ohio: Aldine Printing House, 1892.

Couch, William T. Publisher's introduction to *What the Negro Wants*, edited by Rayford Logan. Notre Dame, Ind.: University of Notre Dame Press, 2001.

Crawford, Myrtle Brodie. "Some Aspects of Preparation for Desegregation in the Public Schools of Louisville." *Negro History Bulletin* 20, no. 4 (1957): 79–82.

———. "The Negro Builds a Pyramid." *Social Studies* 32, no. 1 (1941): 27–31.

Crogman, W. H. *Progress of the Race; or, The Remarkable Advancement of the Afro-American Negro*. Atlanta, Ga: J. L. Nichols, 1897.

Cromwell, John Wesley. *The Negro in American History: Men and Women Eminent in the Evolution of the American of African Descent*. Washington, D.C.: American Negro Academy, 1914.

Crosson, Wilhelmina M. "Wilhelmina M. Crosson Reports on Intercultural Education in Mexico." *Negro History Bulletin* 10, no. 3 (1946): 55–60, 68–71.

Cullen, Countee, ed. *Caroling Dusk: An Anthology of Verse by Negro Poets*. New York: Harper and Brothers, 1927.

———. Foreword to Caroling Dusk: *An Anthology of Verse by Negro Poets*, edited by Countee Cullen. New York: Harper and Brothers, 1927.

Curry, Walter Clyde. Introduction to *Negro Folk Rhymes: Wise and Otherwise*, ed. Thomas Talley. New York: Macmillan, 1922.

Dabney, Thomas L. "The Study of the Negro." *Journal of Negro History* 19, no. 3 (1934): 266–307.

Douglass, Frederick. "The Color Line." *North American Review* 132, no. 295 (1881): 567–77.

Douglass, Joseph Henry. "Contemporary Trends in Negro History." *Negro History Bulletin* 19, no. 1 (1955): 20–24.

"A Dramatic Summary of Negro History by Mrs. A. B. Finlayson's Pupils of the Twining School, D.C." *Negro History Bulletin* 3, no. 7 (1940): 107–9.

Du Bois, W. E. B. "Another Open Letter to Woodrow Wilson." *Crisis* 6, no. 5 (1913): 232–36.

———. "Criteria of Negro Art." 1926. In *Du Bois: A Reader*, edited by David Levering Lewis. New York: Henry Holt, 1995.

———. *Darkwater: Voices from within the Veil*. 1920. Mineola, NY: Dover Publications, 1999.

———. "Dusk of Dawn: An Essay toward an Autobiography of a Race Concept." In *W. E. B. Du Bois: Writings*, edited by Nathan Huggins. New York: Library of America, 1986.

———. "My Evolving Program for Negro Freedom." In *What the Negro Wants*, edited by Rayford Logan. Notre Dame, Ind.: University of Notre Dame Press, 2001.

———. "Postscript." *Crisis* 41, no. 6 (1934): 182–84.

———. *The Souls of Black Folk*. 1903. Oxford: Oxford University Press, 2014.

———. "The Talented Tenth." In *The Negro Problem: A Series of Articles by Representative American Negroes of To-Day*, 1903, edited by Booker T. Washington. New York: Arno Press, 1969.

Duckett, L. A. "A Method for Studying Negro Contributions to Progress." *Negro History Bulletin* 2, no. 1 (1938): 3–4, 7–8.

Dunbar-Nelson, Alice. "People of Color in Louisiana." Pt. 1. *Journal of Negro History* 1, no. 4 (1916): 361–76.

———. "People of Color in Louisiana." Pt. 2. *Journal of Negro History* 2, no. 1 (1917): 51–78.

Dykes, Eva B. "Democracy and Walt Whitman." *Negro History Bulletin* 6, no. 8 (1943): 175–77.

———. "The Poetry of the Civil War." *Negro History Bulletin* 7, no. 5 (1944): 105–6, 14–15.

———. "William Cullen Bryant: Apostle of Freedom." *Negro History Bulletin* 6, no. 2 (1942): 29–31.

"Editorial Comment." *Mississippi Valley Historical Review* 12, no. 4 (1926): 622–34.

"Eighteenth Century Slaves as Advertised by Their Masters." *Journal of Negro History* 1, no. 2 (1916): 163–216.

Evans, Lawton B. *The Essential Facts of American History*. New York: Benjamin H. Sanborn, 1922.

Fleming, Beatrice J. "America's First Woman Bank President." *Negro History Bulletin* 5, no. 4 (1942): 75, 95.

———. "Angelo Solimann." *Negro History Bulletin* 4, no. 3 (1940): 55–56.
———. "Luiz Gama." *Negro History Bulletin* 4, no. 5 (1941): 103–4.
Franklin, John Hope. "Desegregation—the South's Newest Dilemma." *Journal of Negro Education* 25, no. 2 (1956): 95–100.
———. *From Slavery to Freedom: A History of American Negroes*. New York: Knopf, 1947.
———. "History of Racial Segregation in the United States." *Annals of the American Academy of Political and Social Science* 304 (1956): 1–9.
———. "History—Weapon of War and Peace." *Phylon* 5, no. 3 (1944): 249–59.
———. *Mirror to America: The Autobiography of John Hope Franklin*. New York: Farrar, Straus and Giroux, 2005.
———. "*The Birth of a Nation*: Propaganda as History." 1979. In John Hope Franklin, *Race and History: Selected Essays, 1938–1988*. Baton Rouge: Louisiana State University Press, 1989.
———. "The Dilemma of the Negro Scholar." 1963. In John Hope Franklin, *Race and History: Selected Essays, 1938–1988*. Baton Rouge: Louisiana State University Press, 1989.
———. "The New Negro History." 1957. In John Hope Franklin, *Race and History: Selected Essays 1938–1988*. Baton Rouge: Louisiana State University Press, 1989.
Garraty, Mark C., and John A Carnes. *The American Nation: A History of the United States*. Vols. 1 and 2. New York: Pearson, 2016.
Glunt, James D. Review of *The African Background Outlined; or, Handbook for the Study of the Negro*, by Carter G. Woodson. *Journal of Southern History* 3, no. 3 (1937): 359–60.
Gould, Joseph. Review of *The Negro in Our History*, 2nd ed., by Carter G. Woodson. *Crisis* 26 (1923): 212–13.
Grant, Madison. *The Passing of the Great Race; or, The Racial Basis of European History*. New York: Scribner, 1916.
Greene, Lorenzo Johnston, and Arvarh E. Strickland. *Selling Black History for Carter G. Woodson: A Diary, 1930–1933*. Columbia: University of Missouri Press, 1996.
———. *Working with Carter G. Woodson, the Father of Black History: A Diary, 1928–1930*. Baton Rouge: Louisiana State University Press, 1989.
Gregory, Montgomery. "A Chronology of the Negro Theatre." In *Plays of Negro Life: A Sourcebook of Native American Drama*, edited by Alain Locke and Montgomery Gregory. New York: Harper, 1927.
Guinn, Dorothy. "Out of the Dark." In *Plays and Pageants from the Life of the Negro*, 1930, edited by Willis Richardson. Jackson: University Press of Mississippi, 1993.
Hart, Albert Bushnell. *School History of the United States*. New York: American Book Company, 1918.
———. *School History of the United States*. New York: American Book Company, 1920.
———. *The Southern South*. New York: Association Press, 1911.
Hegel, Georg Wilhelm Friedrich. *Lectures on the Philosophy of World History*. Cambridge: Cambridge University Press, 1975.
Herskovits, Melville J. "Correlation of Length and Breadth of Head in American Negroes." *American Journal of Physical Anthropology* 9 (1926): 87–97.
———. "Growth of Interpupillary Distance in American Negroes." *American Journal of Physical Anthropology* 9 (1926): 467–70.

Himes, Joseph Sandy. "Racial Criminality: Fact or Myth?" *Negro History Bulletin* 8, no. 6 (1945): 140–41.

———. Review of *From Slavery to Freedom*, by John Hope Franklin. *Social Forces* 26, no. 4 (1948): 486–87.

Holmes, Eugene. Review of *What the Negro Wants*, edited by Rayford Logan. *Journal of Negro History* 30, no. 1 (1945): 90–92.

Holmes, John Haynes. "On Presenting the Spingarn Medal." *Crisis* 32, no. 5 (1926): 232–33.

"How the Public Received the *Journal of Negro History*." *Journal of Negro History* 1, no. 2 (1916): 225–32.

Hughes, Langston. "A Ballad of Negro History." *Negro History Bulletin* 15, no. 5 (1952): 92.

———. *The Big Sea*. 1940. New York: Hill and Wang, 1993.

———. "The Negro Artist and the Racial Mountain." In *The Portable Harlem Renaissance Reader*, edited by David Levering Lewis. New York: Viking, 1995.

———. "When I Worked for Dr. Woodson." *Negro History Bulletin* 13, no. 8 (1950): 188.

Hurston, Zora Neale. *Dust Tracks on a Road: An Autobiography*. New York: Harper Collins, 1942.

"In the Interpreter's House." *American Magazine* 63, no. 1 (1906): 220–24.

Jackson, A. L. "Reminiscences, Greetings, Challenges." *Negro History Bulletin* 28, no. 8 (1965): 181–82.

Jackson, Luther P. "The First Twenty-Five Volumes of the *Journal of Negro History* Digested." *Journal of Negro History* 25, no. 4 (1940): 432–39.

———. "The Work of the Association and the People." *Journal of Negro History* 20, no. 4 (1935): 385–96.

Jefferson, Thomas. "Thomas Jefferson's Thoughts on the Negro." Pt. 1. *Journal of Negro History* 3, no. 1 (1918): 55–89.

Johnson, Charles S. Review of *What the Negro Wants*, edited by Rayford Logan. *American Sociological Review* 11, no. 2 (1946): 244–45.

Johnson, James Weldon. Preface to *The Book of American Negro Poetry*. 1922. In *The New Negro: Readings on Race, Representation, and African American Culture, 1892–1938*, edited by Henry Louis Gates Jr. and Gene Andrew Jarrett. Princeton, N.J.: Princeton University Press, 2007.

———. *The Book of American Negro Spirituals*. 1925. New York: Da Capo Press, 1969.

———. "The Dilemma of the Negro Author." In *Black Scholars on the Line: Race, Social Science, and American Thought in the Twentieth Century*, edited by Jonathan Scott Holloway and Ben Keppel. Notre Dame, Ind.: University of Notre Dame Press, 2007.

Jones, Eugene Kinckle. Review of *The Negro In Our History*, 2nd ed., by Carter G. Woodson. *Messenger* 5 (1923): 704.

Jones, R. L. "American Opposition to Slavery in Africa." *Journal of Negro History* 16, no. 3 (1931): 266–86.

Kallen, Horace. "Democracy versus the Melting-Pot." Pt. 1. *Nation*, February 18, 1915, 190–94.

———. "Democracy versus the Melting-Pot." Pt. 2. *Nation*, February 25, 1915, 217–20.

Kerlin, Robert Thomas. *Negro Poets and Their Poems*. Washington, D.C.: Associated Publishers, 1923.

Lewis, Julian Herman. *The Biology of the Negro*. Chicago: University of Chicago Press, 1942.

Liele, George, et al. "Letters Showing the Rise and Progress of the Early Negro Churches of Georgia and the West Indies." *Journal of Negro History* 1, no. 1 (1916): 69–92.

Lindsay, Arnett G. "Dr. Carter G. Woodson as a Teacher." *Negro History Bulletin* 13, no. 8 (May 1950): 183, 91.

Locke, Alain. "Beauty Instead of Ashes." *Nation*, April 18, 1928, 432–34.

———, ed. *Four Negro Poets*. New York: Simon and Schuster, 1927.

———, ed. *The New Negro*. 1925. New York: Touchstone, 1997.

———. Introduction to *Plays of Negro Life: A Sourcebook of Native American Drama*, edited by Alain Locke and Montgomery Gregory. New York: Harper, 1927.

———. *Negro Art—Past and Present*. Washington, D.C.: Associates in Negro Folk Education, 1936.

———. Review of *The Negro in Our History*, 4th ed., by Carter G. Woodson. *Journal of Negro History* 12, no. 1 (1927): 99–101.

———. "The Contribution of Race to Culture." 1930. In *The Philosophy of Alain Locke: Harlem Renaissance and Beyond*, edited by Leonard Harris. Philadelphia: Temple University Press, 1989.

———. "The High Cost of Prejudice." *Forum* (October 1927): 500–510.

———. "The Legacy of the Ancestral Arts." In *The New Negro*, edited by Alain Locke. 1925. New York: Touchstone, 1997.

———. *The Negro and His Music*. Washington, D.C.: The Associates in Negro Folk Education, 1936.

———. "The Negro's Contribution to American Art and Literature." *Annals of the American Academy of Political and Social Science* 140 (1928): 234–47.

———. *The Negro in America*. Chicago: American Library Association, 1933.

———. "The Negro Poets of the United States." 1926. In *The New Negro: Readings on Race, Representation, and African American Culture, 1892–1938*, edited by Henry Louis Gates Jr. and Gene Andrew Jarrett. Princeton, N.J.: Princeton University Press, 2007.

———. "The Negro Spirituals." 1925. In *The New Negro: Readings on Race, Representation, and African American Culture, 1892–1938*, edited by Henry Louis Gates Jr. and Gene Andrew Jarrett. Princeton, N.J.: Princeton University Press, 2007.

———. "Who and What Is 'Negro'?" *Opportunity* 20, no. 2 (1942): 36–41.

Locke, Alain, and Thomas Montgomery Gregory, eds. *Plays of Negro Life: A Sourcebook of Native American Drama*. New York: Harper, 1927.

Lofton, Williston H. Review of *From Slavery to Freedom*, by John Hope Franklin. *Journal of Negro History* 33, no. 2 (1948): 225–26.

Logan, Rayford, ed. *What the Negro Wants*. Notre Dame, Ind.: University of Notre Dame Press, 2001.

———. Introduction to 1969 reprint. In *What the Negro Wants*. Notre Dame, Ind.: University of Notre Dame Press, 2001.

———. "Public School Desegregation." *Williams Alumni Review* (1954): 8–9.

———. Review of *The African Background Outlined; or, Handbook for the Study of the Negro*, by Carter G. Woodson. *Journal of Negro History* 21, no. 3 (1936): 322–24.

———. Review of the *Secret City: A History of Race Relations in the Nation's Capital*, by Constance McLaughlin Green. *Annals of the American Academy of Political and Social Science* 374 (1967): 219–20.

———. *The Betrayal of the Negro, from Rutherford B. Hayes to Woodrow Wilson*. 1965. New York: Da Capo Press, 1997.

———. "The Confessions of an Unwilling Nordic." 1927. In *The Negro Caravan: Writings by American Negroes*, edited by Sterling A. Brown, Arthur Paul Davis, and Ulysses Lee. New York: Dryden Press, 1941.

———. *The Negro and the Post-War World*. Washington, D.C.: Minorities Publishers, 1945.

———. "The Negro Wants First-Class Citizenship." In *What the Negro Wants*, edited by Rayford Logan. Notre Dame, Ind.: University of Notre Dame Press, 2001.

———. "The Realities and Ethics of Desegregation." *Antioch Review* 14, no. 4 (1954): 398–404.

Lynch, John R. "Some Historical Errors of James Ford Rhodes." *Journal of Negro History* 2, no. 4 (1917): 345–68.

Mays, Benjamin E. "Minority Mandates." Review of *What the Negro Wants*, edited by Rayford Logan. *Phylon* 5, no. 4 (1944): 387–89.

McCoo, Edward. "Ethiopia at the Bar of Justice." In *Plays and Pageants from the Life of the Negro*, 1930, edited by Willis Richardson. Jackson: University Press of Mississippi, 1993.

McMaster, John Bach. *A School History of the United States*. New York: American Book Company, 1917.

"A Method for Studying Negro Contributions to Progress." *Negro History Bulletin* 2, no. 1 (1938): 3–4, 7–8.

"Military Service in Colonial America." *Negro History Bulletin* 7, no. 1 (1943): 3–4.

Mixon, Mavis B. "'Color,' a Poem." *Negro History Bulletin* 5, no. 2 (1941): 37.

———. "I Am a Negro." *Negro History Bulletin* 4, no. 6 (1941): 140.

Montagu, Ashley. *Man's Most Dangerous Myth: The Fallacy of Race*. 1942. New York: Columbia University Press, 1945.

———. "The Negro's Problem: The White Man." *Negro History Bulletin* 8, no. 8 (1945): 177–79, 88.

Moon, Frederick D. "A Fifth Freedom for the Negro." *Negro History Bulletin* 9, no. 3 (1945): 65–68.

Muzzey, David. *An American History*. New York: Ginn, 1911.

———. *An American History*. New York: Ginn, 1920.

Myrdal, Gunnar. *An American Dilemma: The Negro Problem and Modern Democracy*. New York: Harper and Brothers, 1944.

Nathaniel, Paul, et al. "Letters to Antislavery Workers and Agencies." Pt. 1. *Journal of Negro History* 10, no. 3 (1925): 343–67.

"Negro History Week to Feature Musicians and Their Music." *Negro History Bulletin* 2, no. 5 (1939): 33–34, 45–47.

"The Negro Looks for Democracy." *Negro History Bulletin* 7, no. 3 (1943): 72.

"Negro Novelists—Blazing the Way in Fiction." *Negro History Bulletin* 2, no. 3 (1938): 17-18, 22-23.

"Negro Poets, Singers in the Dawn." *Negro History Bulletin* 2, no. 2 (1938): 9-10, 14-15.

"The Negro Theatre." *Negro History Bulletin* 2, no. 4 (1939): 28, 31.

Nell, William C., et al. "Letters of Negroes, Largely Personal and Private." Pt. 6. *Journal of Negro History* 11, no. 1 (1926): 186-214.

Nelson, William Stuart. Review of *What the Negro Wants*, edited by Rayford Logan. *Journal of Negro Education* 14 (1945): 67-68.

Odum, Howard Washington, and Guy Benton Johnson. *The Negro and His Songs: A Study of the Typical Negro Songs in the South*. Chapel Hill: University of North Carolina Press, 1925.

Pendleton, Leila Amos. *A Narrative of the Negro*. Washington, D.C.: R. L. Pendleton, 1912.

———. "Our New Possessions—the Danish West Indies." *Journal of Negro History* 2, no. 3 (1917): 267-88.

Pennington, James W. C. *A Textbook of the Origin and History of the Colored People*. Hartford, Conn.: L. Skinner, 1841.

Porter, Dorothy B. "Negro Women in Our Wars." *Negro History Bulletin* 7, no. 9 (1944): 195-96, 215.

Pride, Marion Jackson. "Henry Ward Beecher: The War Preacher." *Negro History Bulletin* 6, no. 9 (1943): 197, 208.

———. "Negroes in Guatemala." *Negro History Bulletin* 4, no. 5 (1941): 109-10.

"The Problem of Teaching Negro History in the Elementary School." *Negro History Bulletin* 3, no. 3 (1939): 35-36, 39-41.

Quarles, Benjamin. "The Road We Trod." *Phylon* 9, no. 2 (1948): 172-73.

Reddick, Lawrence D. "Racial Attitudes in American History Textbooks of the South." *Journal of Negro History* 19, no. 3 (1934): 225-65.

———. "Twenty-Five Negro History Weeks." *Negro History Bulletin* 13, no. 8 (1950): 178-79, 88.

Review of *The American Race Problem*, by E. B. Reuter. *Journal of Negro History* 12, no. 3 (1927): 559-61.

Review of *An Anthology of Verse by American Negroes*, edited by Newman Ivey White, Walter Clinton Jackson, and James Hardy Dillard. *Journal of Negro History* 9, no. 3 (1924): 371-73.

Review of *The Book of American Negro Poetry*, edited by James Weldon Johnson. *Journal of Negro History* 8, no. 3 (1923): 347-48.

Review of *Christianity and the Race Problem*, by J. H. Oldham. *Journal of Negro History* 10, no. 1 (1925): 101-2.

Review of *The Negro and His Songs*, by Howard W. Odum and Guy B. Johnson. *Journal of Negro History* 10, no. 4 (1925): 775-76.

Review of *The Negro in American History*, by John W. Cromwell. *Journal of Negro History* 1, no. 1 (1916): 94.

Review of *Negro Poets and Their Poems*, edited by Robert T. Kerlin. *Journal of Negro History* 9, no. 1 (1924): 90-91.

Review of *The Negro Trail Blazers of California*, by Delilah L. Beasley. *Journal of Negro History* 5, no. 1 (1920): 128-29.

Review of *Plays and Pageants from the Life of the Negro*, edited by Willis Richardson. *Journal of Negro History* 15, no. 2 (1930): 263–64.

Review of *A Social History of the American Negro*, by Benjamin Brawley. *Journal of Negro History* 7, no. 1 (1922): 114–15.

Review of *Up from the Ape*, by Ernest Albert Hooton. *Journal of Negro History* 16, no. 4 (1931): 478–79.

Review of *Women of Achievement*, by Benjamin Brawley. *Journal of Negro History* 4, no. 3 (1919): 345–46.

Rhoads, Joseph J. "Teaching the Negro Child." *Journal of Negro History* 19, no. 1 (1934): 15–31.

Rhodes, James Ford. *History of the United States from the Compromise of 1850 to the Mckinley-Bryan Campaign of 1896*. New York: Macmillan, 1920.

Richardson, Willis, ed. Introduction to *Plays and Pageants from the Life of the Negro*, 1930, edited by Willis Richardson. Jackson: University Press of Mississippi, 1993.

———. *Plays and Pageants from the Life of the Negro*. 1930. Jackson: University Press of Mississippi, 1993.

Richardson, Willis, and May Miller, eds. *Negro History in Thirteen Plays*. Washington, D.C.: Associated Publishers, 1935.

Roman, C. V. *American Civilization and the Negro: The Afro-American in Relation to National Progress*. Philadelphia: F. A. Davis, 1916.

Rosenbaum, Solomon. "The Origin of Judicial Sanction of Educational Segregation." *Negro History Bulletin* 18, no. 4 (1955): 75–78, 80.

Rush, Christopher. *A Short Account of the Rise and Progress of the African ME Church in America*. New York: J. J. Zuille, 1866.

Scarborough, Dorothy. *On the Trail of Negro Folk Songs*. Cambridge, Mass.: Harvard University Press, 1925.

Schomburg, Arthur. *A Bibliographic Checklist of American Negro Poetry*. New York: Hartman, 1916.

———. "The Negro Digs up His Past." In *The New Negro*, edited by Alain Locke. 1925. New York: Touchstone, 1997.

Schuyler, George. "Negro Art Hokum." 1926. In *The Portable Harlem Renaissance Reader*, edited by David Levering Lewis. New York: Viking, 1995.

"School News." *Negro History Bulletin* 1, no. 1 (1937): 7–8.

Scott, Emmett J. "Letters of Negro Migrants of 1916–1918." *Journal of Negro History* 4, no. 3 (1919): 290–340.

———. "More Letters of Negro Migrants of 1916–1918." *Journal of Negro History* 4, no. 4 (1919): 412–65.

Sherwood, Henry Noble. Review of *The Negro in Our History*, 3rd ed., by Carter G. Woodson. *Mississippi Valley Historical Review* 14, no. 3 (1927): 420–21.

———. "The Redemption of Africa." *Journal of Negro History* 8, no. 2 (1923): 167–73.

Shufeldt, R. W. *America's Greatest Problem: The Negro*. Philadelphia: F. A. Davis, 1915.

Stamps, James E. "Fifty Years Later: A Founding Associate Reminisces." *Negro History Bulletin* 29, no. 2 (1965): 31–32.

Staughton, Williama, et al. "Letters, Addresses, and the Like Throwing Light on the Career of Lott Cary." *Journal of Negro History* 7, no. 4 (1922): 427–48.

Stern, Bernhard J. Review of *What the Negro Wants*, edited by Rayford Logan. *Political Science Quarterly* 60, no. 2 (1945): 306–7.

Stewart, Colston R., Jr. "A Negro History Week Oration." *Negro History Bulletin* 18, no. 4 (1955): 81–83.

Stoddard, Lothrop. *The Rising Tide of Color against White World-Supremacy*. New York: Scribner, 1921.

Stoff, James West Davidson, and Michael B. *America: History of Our Nation*. New York: Prentice Hall, 2014.

Streator, George. Review of *From Slavery to Freedom*, by John Hope Franklin. *Commonweal* 47 (1947): 76.

Talley, Thomas W. *Negro Folk Rhymes: Wise and Otherwise*. New York: Macmillan, 1922.

Tanner, Benjamin Tucker. *An Outline of Our History and Government for African Methodist Churchmen*. Philadelphia: Grant, Faires and Rodgers, 1884.

"Teaching Black History." *Negro History Bulletin* 32, no. 3 (1969): 4–6.

Terrell, Mary Church. "History of the High School for Negroes in Washington." *Journal of Negro History* 2, no. 3 (1917): 252–66.

Thompson, Charles H. "The Education of the Negro in the United States." In *The Negro Caravan: Writings by American Negroes*, edited by Sterling A. Brown, Arthur Paul Davis, and Ulysses Lee. New York: Dryden Press, 1941.

"Timely Suggestions for Negro History Week." *Negro History Bulletin* 1, no. 5 (1938): 11.

Todd, T. Wingate. "An Anthropologist's Study of Negro Life." *Journal of Negro History* 16, no. 1 (1931): 36–42.

Tuttle, Worth. "Four Books on the Negro." *New Republic* 32 (1922): 259–60.

UNESCO and Its Programme: The Race Question. Paris: United Nations Educational, Scientific, and Cultural Organization, 1950.

Washington, Booker T. *The Story of the Negro: The Rise of the Race from Slavery*. New York: Doubleday, Page, 1909.

Washington, George. "Letters of George Washington Bearing on the Negro." *Journal of Negro History* 2, no. 4 (1917): 411–22.

Wesley, Charles. *History of Sigma Pi Phi: First of the Negro-American Greek Letter Fraternities*. Washington, D.C.: Association for the Study of Negro Life and History, 1954.

———. "The Association and the Public." *Negro History Bulletin* 17, no. 4 (1954): 75–78, 80.

———. "The Concept of Negro Inferiority in American Thought." *Journal of Negro History* 25, no. 4 (1940): 540–560.

———. *The History of Alpha Phi Alpha*. Washington, D.C.: Howard University Press, 1929.

———. *The History of the National Association of Colored Women's Clubs: A Legacy of Service*. Washington, D.C.: Mercury, 1954.

———. "The Negro Citizen in Our Wars for Freedom." *Negro History Bulletin* 7, no. 4 (1944): 78–84, 93–94.

———. "The Negro Has Always Wanted the Four Freedoms." In *What the Negro Wants*, edited by Rayford Logan. Notre Dame, Ind.: University of Notre Dame Press, 2001.

———. "The Negro in the Organization of Abolition." *Phylon* 2, no. 3 (1941): 223–35.

———. "The Negroes of New York in the Emancipation Movement." *Journal of Negro History* 24, no. 1 (1939): 65–103.

———. "The Negro's Struggle for Freedom in Its Birthplace." *Journal of Negro History* 30, no. 1 (1945): 62–81.

———. "Negro Suffrage in the Period of Constitution-Making, 1787–1865." *Journal of Negro History* 32, no. 2 (1947): 143–168.

———. "Our Fiftieth Year." *Negro History Bulletin* 28, no. 8 (1965): 172–73, 95.

———. "The Participation of Negroes in Anti-Slavery Political Parties." *Journal of Negro History* 29, no. 1 (1944): 32–74.

"What Did the Civil War Settle?" *Negro History Bulletin* 7, no. 5 (1944): 120.

"What Did the First World War Accomplish?" *Negro History Bulletin* 7, no. 7 (1944): 146.

White, Newman Ivey, and Walter Clinton Jackson. *An Anthology of Verse by American Negroes*. Durham, N.C.: Trinity College Press, 1924.

———. "Editorial Note." In *An Anthology of Verse by American Negroes*, edited by Newman Ivey White and Walter Clinton Jackson. Durham, N.C.: Trinity College Press, 1924.

———. Introduction to *An Anthology of Verse by American Negroes*, edited by Newman Ivey White and Walter Clinton Jackson. Durham, N.C.: Trinity College Press, 1924.

Wilkins, Roy. "The Negro Wants Full Equality." In *What the Negro Wants*, edited by Rayford Logan. Notre Dame, Ind.: University of Notre Dame Press, 2001.

Williams, Ethel L. "A Tribute to the Negro War Correspondent." *Negro History Bulletin* 8, no. 5 (1945): 110–16, 18–19.

Williams, George Washington. *A History of the Negro Troops in the War of the Rebellion, 1861–1865*. New York: Harper and Brothers, 1888.

———. *History of the Negro Race in America*. Vol. 1. New York: G. P. Putnam's Sons, 1883.

Wilson, Joseph T. *The Black Phalanx: A History of the Negro Soldiers of the United States in the Wars of 1775–1812, 1861–'65*. Hartford, Conn.: American Publishing Company, 1890.

Woodson, Carter G. *A Century of Negro Migration*. Washington, D.C.: Association for the Study of Negro Life and History, 1918.

———. "A Misleading Term." *Negro History Bulletin* 11, no. 2 (1947): 47–48.

———. "A Negro History Week Warning to Seekers after the Whole Truth." *Negro History Bulletin* 3, no. 5 (1940): 74–75, 77.

———. "American and Un-American Activities." *Negro History Bulletin* 13, no. 4 (1950): 74.

———. "Annual Report of the Director." *Journal of Negro History* 11, no. 4 (1926): 547–55.

———. "Annual Report of the Director." *Journal of Negro History* 13, no. 4 (1928): 403–12.

———. "Annual Report of the Director." *Journal of Negro History* 14, no. 4 (1929): 361–70.

———. "Annual Report of the Director." *Journal of Negro History* 15, no. 4 (1930): 391–400.

———. "Annual Report of the Director." *Journal of Negro History* 18, no. 4 (1933): 355–68.

———. "Annual Report of the Director." *Journal of Negro History* 23, no. 4 (1938): 409–19.

———. "Annual Report of the Director." *Journal of Negro History* 26, no. 4 (1941): 413–20.

———. "Annual Report of the Director." *Journal of Negro History* 28, no. 4 (1943): 373–80.

———. "Annual Report of the Director." *Journal of Negro History* 29, no. 3 (1944): 251–59.

———. "Annual Report of the Director." *Journal of Negro History* 30, no. 3 (1945): 251–59.

———. "Annual Report of the Director." *Journal of Negro History* 31, no. 4 (1946): 385–91.

———. "Annual Report of the Director." *Journal of Negro History* 34, no. 4 (1949): 383–90.

———. Introduction to *Negro History in Thirteen Plays*, edited by Willis Richardson and May Miller. Washington, D.C.: Associated Publishers, 1935.

———. "Fifty Years of Negro Citizenship as Qualified by the United States Supreme Court." *Journal of Negro History* 6, no. 1 (1921): 1–53.

———. "Has the Negro Race a Culture?" *Negro History Bulletin* 10, no. 1 (1946): 15–16.

———. "History as It Is." *Negro History Bulletin* 8, no. 7 (1945): 168.

———. "My Recollections of Veterans of the Civil War." *Negro History Bulletin* 7 (1944): 103–4, 115–18.

———. "Negro History Week." *Journal of Negro History* 11, no. 2 (1926): 238–42.

———. "Negro History Week—the Eighth Year." *Journal of Negro History* 18, no. 2 (1933): 107–13.

———. "Negro History Week—the Eleventh Year." *Journal of Negro History* 21, no. 2 (1936): 105–10.

———. "Negro History Week—the Fifth Year." *Journal of Negro History* 16, no. 2 (1931): 125–31.

———. "Negro History Week—the Tenth Year." *Journal of Negro History* 20, no. 2 (1935): 123–30.

———. "Negro History Week—the Third Year." *Journal of Negro History* 13, no. 2 (1928): 121–25.

———. "Negro History Week—the Twelfth Year." *Journal of Negro History* 22, no. 2 (1937): 141–47.

———. "Negro Life and History in Our Schools." *Journal of Negro History* 4, no. 3 (1919): 273–80.

———. *Negro Orators and Their Orations*. 1925. New York: Russell and Russell, 1969.

———. "Negro Women Eligible to Be Daughters of the American Revolution." *Negro History Bulletin* 7, no. 2 (1943): 36, 39.

———. "Notes." *Journal of Negro History* 6, no. 2 (1921): 259–59.

———. "Notes." *Journal of Negro History* 11, no. 2 (1926): 423–24.

———. "Notes." *Journal of Negro History* 13, no. 1 (1928): 109–19.

———. "Notes." *Journal of Negro History* 20, no. 1 (1935): 100–22.

———. "Notes." *Journal of Negro History* 24, no. 1 (1939): 128–36.

———. "Notes." *Journal of Negro History* 27, no. 2 (1942): 238–46.

———. "Proceedings of the Annual Meeting of the Association for the Study of Negro Life and History Held in Houston, Texas, from November 10 to 14, 1934." *Journal of Negro History* 20, no. 1 (1935): 1–12.

———. "Proceedings of the Annual Meeting of the Association for the Study of Negro Life and History Held in St. Louis, Missouri, October 21 to 25, 1928." *Journal of Negro History* 14, no. 1 (1929): 1–11.

———. "Proceedings of the Annual Meeting of the Association for the Study of Negro Life and History Held in Washington D.C., October 27–31, 1929." *Journal of Negro History* 15, no. 1 (1930): 1–13.

———. "Proceedings of the Annual Meeting of the Association for the Study of Negro Life and History Held in Washington, D.C., from October 29 to November 1, 1933." *Journal of Negro History* 19, no. 1 (1934): 1–14.

———. "Proceedings of the Annual Meeting of the Association Held in Cleveland, Ohio, October 26–30, 1930." *Journal of Negro History* 16, no. 1 (1931): 1–8.

———. "Proceedings of the Annual Meeting of the Association, Held in Washington, D.C., October 30–November 1, 1942." *Journal of Negro History* 28, no. 1 (1943): 1–9.

———. "Proceedings of the Eighth Annual Meeting of the Association for the Study of Negro Life and History, Held in Atlanta, Georgia, October 24, 25, and 26, 1923." *Journal of Negro History* 9, no. 1 (1924): 101–6.

———. "Proceedings of the Ninth Annual Meeting of the Association for the Study of Negro Life and History Held at Richmond, Virginia, September 29 and 30, 1924." *Journal of Negro History* 10, no. 1 (1925): 107–11.

———. Review of American Negro Slavery, by Ulrich Bonnell Phillips. *Journal of Negro History* 4, no. 1 (1919): 102–3.

———. Review of *American Negro Slavery*, by Ulrich Bonnell Phillips. *Mississippi Valley Historical Review* 5, no. 4 (1919): 480–82.

———. Review of *An American History*, by Davis Saville Muzzey. *Journal of Negro History* 6, no. 3 (1921): 376–77.

———. Review of *Characteristics of the American Negro*, by Otto Klineberg. *Journal of Negro History* 29, no. 2 (1944): 233–36.

———. Review of *Negro History in Thirteen Plays*, edited by Willis Richardson and May Miller. *Journal of Negro History* 21, no. 1 (1936): 73–76.

———. Review of *Race and Democratic Society*, by Franz Boas. *Journal of Negro History* 31, no. 2 (1946): 231–32.

———. Review of *The Myth of the Negro Past*, by Melville J. Herskovits. *Journal of Negro History* 27, no. 1 (1942): 115–18.

———. Review of *The Negro in Literature and Art*, by Benjamin Brawley. *Journal of Negro History* 3, no. 3 (1918): 329–30.

———. "Ten Years of Collecting and Publishing the Records of the Negro." *Journal of Negro History* 10, no. 4 (1925): 598–606.

———. *The African Background Outlined; or, Handbook for the Study of the Negro*. Washington, D.C.: The Association for the Study of Negro Life and History, 1936.

———. "The Beginnings of the Miscegenation of the Whites and Blacks." *Journal of Negro History* 3, no. 4 (1918): 335–53.

——. "The Celebration of Negro History Week, 1927." *Journal of Negro History* 12, no. 2 (1927): 103–9.
——. "The Cooperation of Persons of African Blood." *Negro History Bulletin* 8, no. 4 (1945): 96.
——. *The Education of the Negro*. 1915. Salem, N.H.: Ayer, 1986.
——. "The First Biennial Meeting of the Association for the Study of Negro Life and History at Washington." *Journal of Negro History* 2, no. 4 (1917): 442–48.
——. *The Mind of the Negro as Reflected in Letters Written during the Crisis, 1800–1860*. Washington, D.C.: Association for the Study of Negro Life and History, 1926.
——. *The Miseducation of the Negro*. 1933. Radford, Va.: Wilder, 2008.
——. *The Negro in Our History*. 2nd ed. Washington, D.C.: Associated Publishers, 1922.
——. *The Negro in Our History*. 4th ed. Washington, D.C.: Associated Publishers, 1927.
——. *The Negro in Our History*. 5th ed. Washington, D.C.: Associated Publishers, 1928.
——. "The Negro in the First World War." *Negro History Bulletin* 7, no. 7 (1944): 147–48, 167.
——. "The Negro Looks for Democracy." *Negro History Bulletin* 7, no. 3 (1943): 72.
——. "What's behind the *Negro History Bulletin*." *Negro History Bulletin* 7, no. 1 (1943): 16–20.
——. "Why Negroes Fight in This War." *Negro History Bulletin* 7, no. 8 (1944): 170.
——. "Workers for Equality and Justice." *Negro History Bulletin* 8, no. 6 (1945): 125–28, 41, 43.
Woodward, C. Vann. *The Strange Career of Jim Crow*. New York: Oxford University Press, 1955.
Work, John Wesley. *Folk Song of the American Negro*. Nashville, Tenn.: Fisk University Press, 1915.
Wright, Marion Thompson. "Educational Programs for the Improvement of Race Relations: Negro Advancement Organizations." *Journal of Negro Education* 13, no. 3 (1944): 349–60.
Wright, Richard R. *Centennial Encyclopedia of the African Methodist Episcopal Church*. Philadelphia: Book Concern of the AME Church, 1916.

SECONDARY SOURCES

Anderson, James D. *The Education of Blacks in the South, 1860–1935*. Chapel Hill: University of North Carolina Press, 1988.
Anderson, Paul Allen. *Deep River: Music and Memory in Harlem Renaissance Thought*. Durham, N.C.: Duke University Press, 2001.
Appiah, Anthony. "The Uncompleted Argument: Du Bois and the Illusion of Race." *Critical Inquiry* 12, no. 1 (1985): 21–37.
Appleby, Joyce, and James M. McPherson et al. *United States History and Geography*. New York: McGraw Hill, 2013.
Aptheker, Herbert. "Charles H. Wesley: Some Memories." *Journal of Negro History* 83, no. 2 (1998): 153–54.

Ater, Renée. *Remaking Race and History: The Sculpture of Meta Warrick Fuller.* Berkeley: University of California Press, 2011.

Baker, Houston A. *Modernism and the Harlem Renaissance.* Chicago: University of Chicago Press, 1987.

Baker, Lee D. *From Savage to Negro: Anthropology and the Construction of Race, 1896–1954.* Berkeley: University of California Press, 1998.

Baldwin, Davarian L. Introduction to *Escape from New York: The New Negro Renaissance Beyond Harlem,* edited by Davarian L. Baldwin and Minkah Makalani. Minneapolis: University of Minnesota Press, 2013.

Baldwin, Davarian L., and Minkah Makalani, eds. *Escape from New York: The New Negro Renaissance Beyond Harlem.* Minneapolis: University of Minnesota Press, 2013.

Banks, William M. *Black Intellectuals: Race and Responsibility in American Life.* New York: Norton, 1996.

Barkan, Elazar. *The Retreat of Scientific Racism: Changing Concepts of Race in Britain and America between the World Wars.* Cambridge: Cambridge University Press, 1991.

Baum, Bruce David. *The Rise and Fall of the Caucasian Race: A Political History of Racial Identity.* New York: New York University Press, 2006.

Bay, Mia. *The White Image in the Black Mind: African-American Ideas About White People, 1830–1925.* New York: Oxford University Press, 2000.

Benjamin, Tritobia Hayes. "Lois Mailou Jones: The Decorative Patterns of Her Life." *American Visions* 8 (1993): 16–20.

Berlin, Ira. *Many Thousands Gone: The First Two Centuries of Slavery in North America.* Cambridge, Mass.: Harvard University Press, 1998.

———. *The Making of African America: The Four Great Migrations.* New York: Viking, 2010.

Blight, David W. *Race and Reunion: The Civil War in American Memory.* Cambridge, Mass.: Harvard University Press, 2001.

Bogue, Allan G. "Frederick Jackson Turner." *American National Biography.*

Borucki, Wesley. "The *Chicago Defender.*" *Encyclopedia of African American History 1896 to the Present,* edited by Paul Finkelman. Oxford: Oxford University Press, 2009.

Bradley, Adam, and Andrew DuBois, eds. *The Anthology of Rap.* New Haven, Conn.: Yale University Press, 2010.

Brundage, W. Fitzhugh. "Meta Warrick's 1907 'Negro Tableaux' and (Re)Presenting African American Historical Memory." *Journal of American History* 89, no. 4 (2003): 1368–400.

———. *The Southern Past: A Clash of Race and Memory.* Cambridge, Mass.: Harvard University Press, 2005.

———. "Working in the 'Kingdom of Culture': African Americans and American Popular Culture, 1890–1930." In *Beyond Blackface: African Americans and the Creation of American Popular Culture,* edited by W. Fitzhugh Brundage. Chapel Hill: University of North Carolina Press, 2011.

Buck, Paul Herman, and Robert L. Church. *Social Sciences at Harvard, 1860–1920: From Inculcation to the Open Mind.* Cambridge, Mass.: Harvard University Press, 1965.

Bunch, Lonnie. "The Definitive Story of How the National Museum of African American History and Culture Came to Be." *Smithsonian Magazine* (September 2016).

Burkholder, Zoë. *Color in the Classroom: How American Schools Taught Race, 1900-1954*. New York: Oxford University Press, 2011.

———. "From 'Wops and Dagoes and Hunkies' to 'Caucasian': Changing Racial Discourse in American Classrooms During World War II." *History of Education Quarterly* 50, no. 3 (2010): 324-58.

Burns, Andrea A. *From Storefront to Monument: Tracing the Public History of the Black Museum Movement*. Amherst: University of Massachusetts Press, 2013.

Campbell, James T. *Middle Passages: African American Journeys to Africa, 1787-2005*. New York: Penguin Press, 2006.

Cobb, W. Montague. "Medical History." *Journal of the National Medical Association* 45, no. 4 (1953): 301-4.

Cooks, Bridget R. *Exhibiting Blackness: African Americans and the American Art Museum*. Amherst: University of Massachusetts Press, 2011.

Cook, James W., and Lawrence B. Glickman. "Twelve Propositions for a History of U.S. Cultural History." In *The Cultural Turn in U.S. History*, edited by James W. Cook, Lawrence B. Glickman, and Michael O'Malley. Chicago: University of Chicago Press, 2008.

Corbould, Clare. *Becoming African Americans: Black Public Life in Harlem, 1919-1939*. Cambridge, Mass.: Harvard University Press, 2009.

Cruse, Harold. *The Crisis of the Negro Intellectual*. New York: Morrow, 1967.

Cruz, Jon. *Culture on the Margins: The Black Spiritual and the Rise of American Cultural Interpretation*. Princeton, N.J.: Princeton University Press, 1999.

Cunningham, Vinson. "Making a Home for Black History." *New Yorker*, August 29, 2016.

Dagbovie, Pero Gaglo. "Black Women, Carter G. Woodson, and the Association for the Study of Negro Life and History, 1915-1950." *Journal of African American History* 88, no. 1 (2003): 21-41.

———. "Black Women Historians from the Late 19th Century to the Dawning of the Civil Rights Movement." *Journal of African American History* 89, no. 3 (2004): 241-61.

———. *The Early Black History Movement, Carter G. Woodson, and Lorenzo Johnston Greene*. Urbana: University of Illinois Press, 2007.

Dennis, Michael. *Luther P. Jackson and a Life for Civil Rights*. Gainesville: University Press of Florida, 2004.

Des Jardins, Julie. *Women and the Historical Enterprise in America: Gender, Race, and The Politics of Memory, 1880-1945*. Chapel Hill: University of North Carolina Press, 2003.

Douglas, Ann. *Terrible Honesty: Mongrel Manhattan in the 1920s*. New York: Farrar, Straus and Giroux, 1995.

Du Bois, W. E. B. "A Portrait of Carter G. Woodson." *Masses and Mainstream* 3 (1950): 19, 21, 23, 24.

Early, Gerald Lyn, ed. *My Soul's High Song: The Collected Writings of Countee Cullen*. New York: Doubleday, 1991.

Edwards, Brent Hayes. *The Practice of Diaspora: Literature, Translation, and the Rise of Black Internationalism*. Cambridge, Mass.: Harvard University Press, 2003.

Fabre, Geneviève, and Michel Feith. *Temples for Tomorrow: Looking Back at the Harlem Renaissance*. Bloomington: Indiana University Press, 2001.

Faust, Drew Gilpin. "John Hope Franklin: Race and the Meaning of America." *New York Review of Books*, December 7, 2015.

Fields, Barbara J. "Slavery, Race, and Ideology in the United States of America." *New Left Review* 181 (1990): 95–118.

Fitzpatrick, Ellen F. *History's Memory: Writing America's Past, 1880–1980*. Cambridge, Mass.: Harvard University Press, 2002.

Foner, Eric. Introduction to *The Betrayal of the Negro, from Rutherford B. Hayes to Woodrow Wilson*, by Rayford Logan. New York: Da Capo Press, 1997.

Franklin, John Hope. "Alrutheus Ambush Taylor." *Journal of Negro History* 39, no. 3 (1954): 240–42.

———. *George Washington Williams: A Biography*. Durham, N.C.: Duke University Press, 1998.

———. "The Place of Carter G. Woodson in American Historiography." *Negro History Bulletin* 13, no. 8 (1950): 174–76.

Franklin, John Hope, and Evelyn Brooks Higginbotham. *From Slavery to Freedom: A History of African Americans*. New York: McGraw-Hill, 2011.

Franklin, V. P. *Living Our Stories, Telling Our Truths: Autobiography and the Making of the African-American Intellectual Tradition*. New York: Scribner, 1995.

Fredrickson, George M. *Racism: A Short History*. Princeton, N.J.: Princeton University Press, 2002.

———. *The Black Image in the White Mind: The Debate on Afro-American Character and Destiny, 1817–1914*. New York: Harper and Row, 1971.

Gaines, Kevin. *Uplifting the Race: Black Leadership, Politics, and Culture in the Twentieth Century*. Chapel Hill: University of North Carolina Press, 1996.

———. "Whose Integration Was It? An Introduction." *Journal of American History* 91, no. 1 (2004): 19–25.

Gates, Henry Louis, Jr. "John Hope, the Prince Who Refused the Kingdom." *Root*, April 1, 2009.

———. "The Trope of a New Negro and the Reconstruction of the Image of the Black." *Representations* 24 (1988): 129–55.

Gates, Henry Louis, Jr., and Gene Andrew Jarrett. Introduction to *The New Negro: Readings on Race, Representation, and African American Culture, 1892–1938*, edited by Henry Louis Gates Jr. and Gene Andrew Jarrett. Princeton, N.J.: Princeton University Press, 2007.

Gatewood, Willard B. *Aristocrats of Color: The Black Elite, 1880–1920*. Bloomington: Indiana University Press, 1990.

Gershenhorn, Jerry. *Melville J. Herskovits and the Racial Politics of Knowledge*. Lincoln: University of Nebraska Press, 2004.

Gerstle, Gary. *American Crucible: Race and Nation in the Twentieth Century*. Princeton, N.J.: Princeton University Press, 2001.

Gilkeson, John S., Jr. "The Domestication of 'Culture' in Interwar America, 1919–1941." In *The Estate of Social Knowledge*, edited by JoAnne Brown and David K. Van Keuren. Baltimore, Md.: Johns Hopkins University Press, 1991.

Glassberg, David. *American Historical Pageantry: The Uses of Tradition in the Early Twentieth Century*. Chapel Hill: University of North Carolina Press, 1990.

Goggin, Jacqueline Anne. "Carter Godwin Woodson." In *American National Biography*.
———. "Carter G. Woodson and the Collection of Source Materials for Afro-American History." *American Archivist* 48, no. 3 (1985): 261–71.
———. *Carter G. Woodson: A Life in Black History*. Baton Rouge: Louisiana State University Press, 1993.
———. "Carter G. Woodson and the Movement to Promote Black History." PhD diss., University of Rochester, 1984.
———. "Countering White Racist Scholarship: Carter G. Woodson and the *Journal of Negro History*." *Journal of Negro History* 68, no. 4 (1983): 355–75.
Gordon, Leah N. *From Power to Prejudice: The Rise of Racial Individualism in Mid-century America*. Chicago: University of Chicago Press, 2015.
Gossett, Thomas F. *Race: The History of an Idea in America*. New York: Oxford University Press, 1997.
Gray, Christine R. Introduction to *Plays and Pageants from the Life of the Negro*, 1930, edited by Willis Richardson. Jackson: University Press of Mississippi, 1993.
Greene, Lorenzo J. "W. Sherman Savage." *Journal of Negro History* 66, no. 1 (1981): 80–84.
Guterl, Matthew Pratt. *Seeing Race in Modern America*. Chapel Hill: University of North Carolina Press, 2013.
Hale, Grace Elizabeth. *Making Whiteness: The Culture of Segregation in the South, 1890–1940*. New York: Pantheon, 1998.
Hall, Stephen G. *A Faithful Account of the Race: African American Historical Writing in Nineteenth-Century America*. Chapel Hill: University of North Carolina Press, 2009.
———. "'Research as Opportunity': Alrutheus Ambush Taylor, Black Intellectualism, and the Remaking of Reconstruction Historiography, 1893–1954." *UCLA Historical Journal* 16 (1996): 39–60.
Harris, Janette Hoston. "Charles Harris Wesley, Educator and Historian, 1891–1947." PhD diss., Howard University, 1975.
———. "Woodson and Wesley: A Partnership in Building the Association for the Study of Afro-American Life and History." *Journal of Negro History* 83, no. 2 (1998): 109–19.
Harris, Michael W. *The Rise of Gospel Blues: The Music of Thomas Andrew Dorsey in the Urban Church*. New York: Oxford University Press, 1992.
Hine, Darlene Clark. "Carter G. Woodson, White Philanthropy, and Negro Historiography." *History Teacher* 19, no. 3 (1986): 405–25.
Hodes, Martha. "The Mercurial Nature and Abiding Power of Race: A Transnational Family Story." *American Historical Review* 108, no. 1 (2003): 84–118.
Hoffer, Peter Charles. *Past Imperfect: Facts, Fictions, Fraud—American History from Bancroft and Parkman to Ambrose, Bellesiles, Ellis, and Goodwin*. New York: Public Affairs, 2004.
Hoffnung-Garskof, Jesse. "The Migrations of Arturo Schomburg: On Being Antillano, Negro, and Puerto Rican in New York, 1891–1938." *Journal of American Ethnic History* 21, no. 1 (2001): 3–49.
Hofstadter, Richard. *The Progressive Historians: Turner, Beard, Parrington*. New York: Knopf, 1968.

Hollinger, David. *Postethnic America: Beyond Multiculturalism*. New York: Basic Books, 1995.

Holloway, Jonathan Scott. *Confronting the Veil: Abram Harris Jr., E. Franklin Frazier, and Ralph Bunche, 1919–1941*. Chapel Hill: University of North Carolina Press, 2002.

———. *Jim Crow Wisdom: Memory and Identity in Black America since 1940*. Chapel Hill: University of North Carolina Press, 2013.

Holloway, Jonathan Scott, and Ben Keppel, eds. *Black Scholars on the Line: Race, Social Science, and American Thought in the Twentieth Century*. Notre Dame, Ind.: University of Notre Dame Press, 2007.

———. Introduction to *Black Scholars on the Line: Race, Social Science, and American Thought in the Twentieth Century*, edited by Jonathan Scott Holloway and Ben Keppel. Notre Dame, Ind.: University of Notre Dame Press, 2007.

Holt, Thomas. *Children of Fire: A History of African Americans*. New York: Hill and Wang, 2011.

———. "Explaining Racism in American History." In *Imagined Histories: American Historians Interpret the Past*, edited by Anthony Molho and Gordon S. Wood. Princeton, N.J.: Princeton University Press, 1998.

Holton, Adalaine. "Decolonizing History: Arthur Schomburg's Afrodiasporic Archive." *Journal of African American History* 92, no. 2 (2007): 218–38.

Huggins, Nathan Irvin. *Harlem Renaissance*. New York: Oxford University Press, 1971.

Hutchinson, George. *The Harlem Renaissance in Black and White*. Cambridge, Mass.: Harvard University Press, 1995.

Jackson, Walter A. *Gunnar Myrdal and America's Conscience: Social Engineering and Racial Liberalism, 1938–1937*. Chapel Hill: University of North Carolina Press, 1990.

Jacobson, Matthew Frye. *Whiteness of a Different Color: European Immigrants and the Alchemy of Race*. Cambridge, Mass.: Harvard University Press, 1998.

Janken, Kenneth Robert. Introduction to *What the Negro Wants*, edited by Rayford Logan. Notre Dame, Ind.: University of Notre Dame Press, 2001.

———. *Rayford W. Logan and the Dilemma of the African-American Intellectual*. Amherst: University of Massachusetts Press, 1993.

Jarrett, Beverly, ed. *Tributes to John Hope Franklin: Scholar, Mentor, Father, Friend*. Columbia: University of Missouri Press, 2003.

Jones, Jacqueline. *A Dreadful Deceit: The Myth of Race from the Colonial Era to Obama's America*. New York: Basic Books, 2013.

Jones, Jeannette Eileen. *In Search of Brightest Africa: Reimagining the Dark Continent in American Culture, 1884–1936*. Athens: University of Georgia Press, 2011.

Jordan, Winthrop D. *White over Black: American Attitudes toward the Negro, 1550–1812*. Chapel Hill: University of North Carolina Press, 1968.

Joyce, Davis D. "Edward Channing." *American National Biography*.

Kachun, Mitchell A. *Festivals of Freedom: Memory and Meaning in African American Emancipation Celebrations, 1808–1915*. Amherst: University of Massachusetts Press, 2003.

Kaplan, Carla. *Miss Anne in Harlem: The White Women of the Black Renaissance*. New York: Harper, 2013.

Kelley, Robin D. G. "'But a Local Phase of a World Problem': Black History's Global Vision, 1883–1950." *Journal of American History* 86, no. 3 (1999): 1045–77.

Kinnamon, Kenneth. "Anthologies of African-American Literature from 1845 to 1994." *Callaloo* 20, no. 2 (1997): 461–81.

Lash, John S. "The Anthologist and the Negro Author." *Phylon* 8, no. 1 (1947): 68–76.

Lewis, David Levering. Introduction to *The Portable Harlem Renaissance Reader*. New York: Viking, 1994.

———. "The Harlem Renaissance: Vogue of the New Negro." In *Africana: The Encyclopedia of the African and African American Experience*, edited by Kwame Anthony Appiah and Henry Louis Gates Jr. Oxford: Oxford University Press, 2004.

———, ed. *The Portable Harlem Renaissance Reader*. New York: Viking, 1994.

———. Preface to James Campbell, *Middle Passages: African American Journeys to Africa, 1787–2005*. New York: Penguin Press, 2006.

———. *W. E. B. Du Bois: Biography of a Race, 1868–1919*. New York: Henry Holt, 1993.

———. *W. E. B. Du Bois: The Fight for Equality and the American Century, 1919–1963*. New York: Henry Holt, 2000.

———. *When Harlem Was in Vogue*. New York: Penguin, 1997.

Litwack, Leon F. *How Free Is Free? The Long Death of Jim Crow*. Cambridge, Mass.: Harvard University Press, 2009.

Logan, Rayford W. "Carter G. Woodson." *Phylon* 6, no. 4 (1945): 315–321.

———. "Carter G. Woodson: Mirror and Molder of His Time, 1875–1950." *Journal of Negro History* 58, no. 1 (1973): 1–17.

———. *Howard University: The First Hundred Years, 1867–1967*. New York: New York University Press, 1969.

Lorini, Alessandra. *Rituals of Race: American Public Culture and the Search for Racial Democracy*. Charlottesville: University Press of Virginia, 1999.

———. "'The Spell of Africa Is upon Me': W. E. B. Du Bois's Notion of Art as Propaganda." In *Temples for Tomorrow: Looking Back at the Harlem Renaissance*, edited by Geneviève Fabre and Michel Feith. Bloomington: Indiana University Press, 2001.

Lott, Tommy L. "Alain Leroy Locke: African American Cultural Historian." In *Key Writers On Art: The Twentieth Century*, edited by Chris Murray. New York: Routledge, 2002.

Maffly-Kipp, Laurie F. *Setting Down the Sacred Past: African-American Race Histories*. Cambridge, Mass.: Harvard University Press, 2010.

Martin, Tony. *Literary Garveyism: Garvey, Black Arts, and the Harlem Renaissance*. Dover, Mass.: Majority Press, 1983.

Mason, Theodore O. "The African-American Anthology: Mapping the Territory, Taking the National Census, Building the Museum." *American Literary History* 10, no. 1 (1998): 185–98.

McElya, Micki. *Clinging to Mammy: The Faithful Slave in Twentieth-Century America*. Cambridge, Mass.: Harvard University Press, 2007.

McHenry, Elizabeth. *Forgotten Readers: Recovering the Lost History of African American Literary Societies*. Durham, N.C.: Duke University Press, 2002.

McWhorter, John. "Black History Month Is Over—Very Over." *Root*, March 3, 2011.

Meier, August, and Elliott M. Rudwick. *Black History and the Historical Profession, 1915–1980*. Urbana: University of Illinois Press, 1986.

Miller, M. Sammye. "Historiography of Charles H. Wesley as Reflected through the *Journal of Negro History*, 1915–1969." *Journal of Negro History* 83, no. 2 (1998): 120–26.

Mitchell, Michele. *Righteous Propagation: African Americans and the Politics of Racial Destiny after Reconstruction*. Chapel Hill: University of North Carolina Press, 2004.

Moreau, Joseph. *Schoolbook Nation: Conflicts over American History Textbooks from the Civil War to the Present*. Ann Arbor: University of Michigan Press, 2003.

Morton, Patricia. *Disfigured Images: The Historical Assault on Afro-American Women*. New York: Praeger, 1991.

Moses, Wilson Jeremiah. *Afrotopia: The Roots of African American Popular History*. New York: Cambridge University Press, 1998.

Moss, Alfred A. *The American Negro Academy: Voice of the Talented Tenth*. Baton Rouge: Louisiana State University Press, 1981.

Muhammad, Khalil Gibran. *The Condemnation of Blackness: Race, Crime, and the Making of Modern Urban America*. Cambridge, Mass.: Harvard University Press, 2010.

Newby, I. A. "Historians and Negroes." *Journal of Negro History* 54, no. 1 (1969): 32–47.

———. *Jim Crow's Defense: Anti-Negro Thought in America, 1900–1930*. Baton Rouge: Louisiana State University Press, 1965.

Ngai, Mae M. *Impossible Subjects: Illegal Aliens and the Making of Modern America*. Princeton, N.J.: Princeton University Press, 2004.

Novick, Peter. *That Noble Dream: The "Objectivity Question" and the American Historical Profession*. Cambridge: Cambridge University Press, 1988.

Ogbar, Jeffrey O. G., ed. *The Harlem Renaissance Revisited*. Baltimore, Md.: Johns Hopkins University Press, 2010.

Orfield, Gary, John Kucsera, and Genevieve Siegel-Hawley. *E Pluribus . . . Separation: Deepening Double Segregation for More Students*. Civil Rights Project, 2012.

Painter, Nell Irvin. *The History of White People*. New York: Norton, 2010.

Parascandola, Louis J. "Georgia Douglas Johnson." *American National Biography*.

Parker, John W. "Benjamin Brawley—Teacher and Scholar." *Phylon* 10, no. 1 (1949): 15–24.

Patterson, James T. *Brown v. Board of Education: A Civil Rights Milestone and Its Troubled Legacy*. New York: Oxford University Press, 2001.

Quarles, Benjamin. "Black History's Antebellum Origins." *Proceedings of the American Antiquarian Society* 89, no. 1 (1979): 89–122.

———. "Black History's Diversified Clientele." In *Black Mosaic: Essays in Afro-American History and Historiography*, edited by Benjamin Quarles. Amherst: University of Massachusetts Press, 1988.

Rampersad, Arnold. Introduction to Alain Locke, *The New Negro*. New York: Touchstone, 1997.

Rankin-Hill, Lesley M., and Michael L. Blakey. "W. Montague Cobb (1904–1990): Physical Anthropologist, Anatomist, and Activist." *American Anthropologist* 96, no. 1 (1994): 74–96.

Reddick, L. D. "Carter G. Woodson (1875–1950): An Appreciation." *Phylon* 11, no. 2 (1950): 177–79.

Reinhart, Mark S. *Abraham Lincoln on Screen: A Filmography of Dramas and Documentaries, Including Television*. Jefferson, N.C.: McFarland, 1999.

Rogin, Michael. "'The Sword Became a Flashing Vision': D. W. Griffith's the *Birth of a Nation*." *Representations* 9 (1985): 150–95.

Romero, Patricia Watkins. "Carter G. Woodson: A Biography." PhD diss., Ohio State University, 1971.

Roper, John Herbert, ed. *C. Vann Woodward: A Southern Historian and His Critics*. Athens: University of Georgia Press, 1997.

Rudavsky, Shari. "Charles Victor Roman." *American National Biography*.

Selig, Diana. *Americans All: The Cultural Gifts Movement*. Cambridge, Mass.: Harvard University Press, 2008.

Shapiro, Ari, and Maureen Pao. "Mission of African-American Museum Writ Large in Its Very Design." NPR.org. September 15, 2016.

Singal, Daniel Joseph. "Towards a Definition of American Modernism." *American Quarterly* 39, no. 1 (1987): 7–26.

Singh, Nikhil Pal. *Black Is a Country: Race and the Unfinished Struggle for Democracy*. Cambridge, Mass.: Harvard University Press, 2005.

Singleton, Velma. "John Wesley Work, Sr." *Negro History Bulletin* 5, no. 5 (1942): 115–16.

Sinnette, Elinor Des Verney. *Arthur Alfonso Schomburg, Black Bibliophile and Collector: A Biography*. Detroit, Mich.: Wayne State University Press, 1989.

Smethurst, James Edward. *The African American Roots of Modernism: From Reconstruction to the Harlem Renaissance*. Chapel Hill: University of North Carolina Press, 2011.

Smith, Bonnie G. *The Gender of History: Men, Women, and Historical Practice*. Cambridge, Mass.: Harvard University Press, 2000.

Smith, Susan Lynn. *Sick and Tired of Being Sick and Tired: Black Women's Health Activism in America, 1890–1950*. Philadelphia: University of Pennsylvania Press, 1995.

Spencer, Jon Michael. *New Negroes and Their Music: The Success of the Harlem Renaissance*. Knoxville: University of Tennessee Press, 1997.

Stokes, Melvyn. *D. W. Griffith's "The Birth of a Nation": A History of "the Most Controversial Motion Picture of All Time."* New York: Oxford University Press, 2007.

Sussman, Robert W. *The Myth of Race: The Troubling Persistence of an Unscientific Idea*. Cambridge, Mass.: Harvard University Press, 2014.

Thorpe, Earl E. *Black Historians: A Critique*. New York: Morrow, 1971.

Townsend, Robert B. *History's Babel: Scholarship, Professionalization, and the Historical Enterprise in the United States, 1880–1940*. Chicago University of Chicago Press, 2013.

Trouillot, Michel-Rolph. *Silencing the Past: Power and the Production of History*. Boston: Beacon Press, 1995.

Von Eschen, Penny M. *Race against Empire: Black Americans and Anticolonialism, 1937–1957*. Ithaca, N.Y.: Cornell University Press, 1997.

Watkins, Rachel, J. "Knowledge from the Margins: W. Montague Cobb's Pioneering Research in Biocultural Anthropology." *American Anthropologist* 109, no. 1 (2007): 186–96.

Wesley, Charles H. "Carter G. Woodson—as a Scholar." *Journal of Negro History* 36, no. 1 (1951): 12–24.

Whelan, Michael. "Albert Bushnell Hart." *American National Biography*.

White, Deborah G. Introduction to *Telling Histories: Black Women Historians in the Ivory Tower*, edited by Deborah G. White. Chapel Hill: University of North Carolina Press, 2008.

Williams, Vernon J. *The Social Sciences and Theories of Race*. Urbana: University of Illinois Press, 2006.

Wilson, Francille Rusan. "Racial Consciousness and Black Scholarship: Charles H. Wesley and the Construction of Negro Labor in the United States." *Journal of Negro History* 81, no. 1 (1996): 72–88.

———. *The Segregated Scholars: Black Social Scientists and the Creation of Black Labor Studies, 1890–1950*. Charlottesville: University of Virginia Press, 2006.

Wilson, Mabel O. *Begin with the Past: Building the National Museum of African American History and Culture*. Washington, D.C.: Smithsonian Books, 2016.

———. *Negro Building: Black Americans in the World of Fairs and Museums*. Berkeley: University of California Press, 2012.

Wineburg, Sam, and Chauncey Monte-Sano. "'Famous Americans': The Changing Pantheon of American Heroes." *Journal of American History* 94, no. 4 (2008): 1186–202.

Winston, Michael R. *Howard University Department of History, 1913–1973*. Washington, D.C.: Howard University Department of History, 1973.

———. "Through the Back Door: Academic Racism and the Negro Scholar in Historical Perspective." *Daedalus* 100, no. 3 (1971): 678–719.

Yellin, Eric Steven. *Racism in the Nation's Service: Government Workers and the Color Line in Woodrow Wilson's America*. Chapel Hill: University of North Carolina Press, 2013.

Zack, Naomi. *Women of Color and Philosophy: A Critical Reader*. Malden, Mass.: Blackwell, 2000.

Zimmerman, Jonathan. "*Brown*-ing the American Textbook: History, Psychology, and the Origins of Modern Multiculturalism." *History of Education Quarterly* 44, no. 1 (2004): 46–69.

———. "'Each 'Race' Could Have Its Heroes Sung': Ethnicity and the History Wars in the 1920s." *Journal of American History* 87, no. 1 (2000): 92–111.

———. "Let's End Black History Month." *Education Week*, March 17, 2010.

———. *Whose America? Culture Wars in the Public Schools*. Cambridge, Mass.: Harvard University Press, 2002.

Zuberi, Tukufu. *Thicker Than Blood: How Racial Statistics Lie*. Minneapolis: University of Minnesota Press, 2001.

INDEX

abolitionists, 23, 49–51, 54, 59–60, 78, 87, 104, 112, 146, 153
activists, 7–8, 39, 41, 54, 75, 148, 149, 164, 167, 180n96, 197n4
Africa, 14, 28–29, 31, 73, 94, 187n20, 195n70, 201n62, 202n75; art or music from or influenced by, 71, 72, 75, 77–79, 86, 90, 101, 102, 107, 137, 165; black emigration to (see American Colonization Society; colonization movement); black views of, 70–71, 106–8, 136–38, 187n15; colonialism or imperialism in, 70, 71, 137; as cradle of civilization or culture, 38, 70–71, 105, 108; "dark" or "bright," 38, 70, 71, 105, 107–9; denigrations of, 24, 75; in expositions or pageants, 31–32, 72, 105, 110; races in, 123; and slave trade, 106, 107; Woodson on (see under Woodson). See also Egypt; Ethiopia; Liberia
African Americans: in antebellum period, 29–30, 46, 87, 132; caricatures or stereotypes of (see stereotypes); as collective, 11, 12, 69, 72, 74, 79, 81, 94–95, 112, 133, 146; military service by, 64, 125, 147, 154–56, 161, 162, 205n34 (see also Civil War: veterans of); nineteenth-century historical writings by, 17, 20, 36, 37–38, 44; police killings of, 168–69; scholars, 9–11, 25, 35, 40, 120, 140, 174n54; and white immigrants, 138, 144, 202n77
African Methodist Episcopal Church, 1, 26, 80; bishops, 25, 71; ministers or preachers, 38, 80, 108, 124
Alabama, 53, 102, 117
Ali, Muhammad, 165
Amenia ideal, 8
American Colonization Society, 49–51, 59
"American creed," 119

American Historical Association, 10, 21, 22, 199n13
American Historical Review, 10, 22, 34, 176n26
American Negro Academy, 1, 25–26, 37, 177n38
Anderson, Jourdon, 52
Anderson, Marian, 101, 115
anthologies, 14, 110, 113, 167; bibliographies or appendices to, 82, 89; compilers of, 74, 76, 85, 86, 91, 92; compulsion or obsession of, 74, 76; cultural credentialing by, 82, 92; and Harlem/Negro Renaissance, 72, 74, 76, 78; as historical documents, 76, 92; prefaces to, 76–77; Woodson's, 2, 17, 54, 72, 84–85, 93, 193n35. See also under art or artists; dramas; literature; music; poetry; spirituals
antislavery movement, 50–51, 63, 132
Appiah, Anthony, 120
archives, 13–14, 17, 26, 35, 92, 99; black, 45, 47–49, 55, 66, 166; National, 166
art or artists, 2, 62, 79, 81, 117, 121, 127, 178n74, 187n7, 187n24, 191n4, 194n44; anthologized, 14, 72, 74, 76, 86; Brawley on, 82–84, 167; Du Bois on, 95; "group character" of, 85–87; Johnson on, 84; in *Negro History Bulletin*, 114–15; in Negro History Week, 97, 99, 100, 101, 102; social change or transformation, 84, 88. See also "Negro art"
Associated Publishers, 2, 10, 17, 37, 47, 71, 101, 103, 188n14, 196n94; anthologies from, 85, 89, 110
Association for the Study of Negro Life and History: achievements or contributions of, 10–11, 17, 48, 95, 117; activism of, 7–8,

233

Association for the Study of Negro Life and
  History: (*continued*)
  121, 148–49, 202n78; anthologies of, 74,
  84; branches of, 104, 131, 159, 194n46;
  and civil rights movement, 14, 121, 132,
  147–48, 156; conferences or meetings of, 2,
  37, 38, 40, 75, 100, 102, 126, 127, 128–29,
  132–33, 181n111, 193n25, 200n30; finances
  of, 34, 113, 173n48, 181n114, 196n98;
  founding of, 1, 2, 13, 16, 33–34, 36, 44,
  165, 179n77; goals or mission of, 5, 7, 11,
  17, 34, 36–37, 133, 160; Harlem/Negro
  Renaissance and, 95, 101, 113, 117; Home
  Study Department, 188n14; leaders of, 125,
  131, 148, 159, 182n116; membership of,
  40–41, 126, 131, 147, 184n45; NAACP and,
  8; Negro History Week and, 14, 37, 96–97,
  101, 124; NMAAHC and, 166; primary
  sources collected by, 99–100; race concept
  challenged by, 14, 120, 124, 127–31, 146;
  values of, 5; whites and, 3, 10, 41, 173n48
Atlanta, 31–32, 40, 54, 64, 101, 102
Attucks, Crispus, 21–22, 59, 89, 109, 110, 155,
  156

Banneker, Benjamin, 30, 97, 111, 197n4
Barzun, Jacques, 129
Bay, Mia, 91, 120
Beale, Howard, 161
Beatty, Florence R., 113
Benedict, Ruth, 124, 127, 129, 142, 200n37;
  201n60, 203n92; *Races of Mankind*, 130,
  131, 141, 200
Berlin, Ira, 49–50, 56
Bethel Literary and Historical Society (BLHS),
  25, 37, 96
Bethune, Mary McLeod, 5–7, 41, 149, 152,
  182n116, 193n25
Bibb, Henry, 52
Birth of a Nation, 16, 17, 26–28, 33, 153,
  177n41
black history: Africa in, 71, 106, 107; and
  American history, 2–3, 10, 18, 56, 62,
  148, 160, 166–67, 192n21, 199n14; and
  "black intellectual reconstruction," 16–17;
  as cause or movement, 2, 3, 5, 14, 16–17,
  39, 75; celebration of, 1, 72, 111 (*see also*
  Negro History Week); contributors
  to, 2, 94; denigration of, 139; elite vs.
  popular interest, 26, 37, 38, 94, 104, 113,
  171–72n9, 195n54; essential feature of, 6; in
  expositions, 31–32; and Harlem or Negro

Renaissance, 14, 71–74, 92, 95, 97–98, 117;
  in *New Negro*, 73; and NMAAHC, 167–68;
  in official curriculum, 2, 14, 40, 56, 104,
  148, 160, 167, 172n9; opposition to week
  or month for, 159–60, 192n21; power of
  study of, 7, 104, 116–17, 148, 160, 164, 169,
  193n25; as professional field, 2, 38, 48,
  200n50; and race pride, 17, 25, 36, 74,
  133; in Sixties, 9; taught in colleges and
  universities, 4, 56, 104, 172n12; taught in
  schools, 40, 56, 66, 94, 104, 116, 167; and
  transnational history, 173n54; and white
  audiences, 22, 37, 158–59, 171n8, 172n9,
  179–80n91
Black Lives Matter movement, 168
Black Power movement, 3
black pride, 17, 36. *See also* race pride
blues, 90, 115, 157, 167
Boas, Franz, 41, 69, 124, 127, 130, 135, 186n3,
  199n24
Bond, Horace Mann, 140–41, 143
Bontemps, Arna, 86, 196n94
Boston, 56, 101, 113, 124
Bourne, Randolph, 70, 191n98
Brawley, Benjamin, 41, 57–58, 60–65, 72, 93,
  102, 105, 167, 193n26; biographical details,
  74–75; *Early Negro American Writers*, 87;
  Negro in Literature and Art, 74, 75, 82–84,
  193n34; reviews of, 82; *Social History of the
  American Negro*, 106
Brigham, Carl, 126
Brooks, Albert, 159, 160
Brown v. Board of Education, 14, 119, 120, 121,
  147, 148, 156–58, 161–62, 164
Brown, John, 60, 109, 156
Brown, Michael, 168
Brown, Sterling, 41, 69, 93, 102, 103, 160,
  196n94, 203n101. See also *Negro Caravan,
  The*
Brown, W. O., 128
Brown, William Wells, 55
Brundage, W. Fitzhugh, 69, 111
Buck, Paul, 140
Bunch, Lonnie, 167–68
Bunche, Ralph, 8, 25, 41, 157
Burleigh, Harry T., 72, 102, 111
Burns, Andrea A., 110
Bush, George W., 168

California, 172n9
Caribbean, 32, 138
Carpenter, Marie, 153

Channing, Edward, 21, 34, 45, 92, 173n48, 175n16, 176n26; *Guide to the Study and Reading of American History*, 24, 176n24; *Student's History of the United States*, 22, 23, 176n19

Chicago, 2, 5, 29, 64, 148, 178n65, 179n77. *See also* Lincoln Jubilee

Chicago Defender, 4, 28, 53, 105, 155, 189n34; circulation of, 184n38; Hughes column in, 156; Johnson's book reviewed in, 79; Logan's books reviewed in, 141, 150; "men and women of achievement" in, 98–99; "wars for freedom" in, 155–56; Woodson's books reviewed in, 50, 54, 55–56

Christianity, 71, 78, 79

churches, 1–2, 25, 30, 40, 51, 77, 117; bombed, 160; and Negro History Week, 101, 111

citizenship, 4, 7, 11, 27, 37, 42, 49, 99, 142, 157, 162; and freedom, 13, 63–64; and freedom festivals, 21; and military service, 154–55, 205n34; as Negro History Week theme, 112; second- or third-class, 132, 151; Supreme Court rulings on black, 13, 43–44

civic groups, 2

Civil Rights Act (1875), 15

civil rights movement, 2, 3, 119, 121, 147–49, 164, 199n14

Civil War: Appomattox, 19, 27; and *Brown* decision, 162; historical representations of, 16, 21, 32, 38, 141, 151; in pageants or plays, 109, 111; veterans of, 19–21, 32, 59, 63, 105, 109

Clark, Kenneth and Mamie, 158, 162

class, socioeconomic, 5, 8, 23, 47

Cobb, W. Montague, 41, 133–35, 201n55, 201n60

Cold War, 148–49

colleges, 1, 4, 40, 56, 62, 85, 104, 110, 172n12; Atlanta Baptist (Morehouse), 41, 74; Bethune-Cookman, 158; Brooklyn, 126; Kentucky State, 102–3; presidents of black, 160. *See also* universities

colonies, American, 30, 31, 42, 154, 176n24

colonization movement, 42, 50–51, 58–59, 87, 147

color line, 3, 50, 184n32, 201n62; Du Bois on, 15; and freedom, 66; history's role in, 16; invention of, 13; as key theme, 12–13, 18, 42; Woodson on, 42–44, 65, 66

Commager, Henry Steele, 140

Constitution, U.S., 63, 109, 152, 161–62, 206n66

"contributionist" histories or historiography, 18, 20, 44, 112

Coolidge, Calvin, 79, 81

Cooper, Anna Julia, 55

Corbould, Clare, 109–10, 187n15, 192n4

Cotton States and International Exposition (Atlanta, 1895), 31–32, 54

Couch Jr., William, 90, 149–50, 154

Cox, Oliver Cromwell, 140

Crogman, William H., 26, 55

Cromwell Sr., John Wesley, 25, 38, 57–59, 61–64, 106

Crosson, Wilhelmina M., 113

Crummell, Alexander, 26, 76

Cruz, Jon, 78

Cuffe, Paul, 59

Cullen, Countee, 71, 73, 86, 91, 103, 108, 111, 193n34

cultural associations, 25, 26

culture: black and American, 70, 72, 79, 83, 90–91, 117; defined, 69–70; and history or heritage, 32, 76; as key theme, 12; and race, 72, 77, 137

Curti, Merle, 140

Dagbovie, Pero, 114

Davis, Angela, 117

Davis, Arthur P., 93, 150

Davis, John W., 41

Delany, Martin, 87

Delaware, 101

democracy, 5, 7, 9, 23, 26, 88, 130, 140, 148, 150, 197–98n4

desegregation, 121, 149, 150, 157–59, 161–63, 172n9

Des Jardins, Julie, 10, 35, 171n7

Detroit, 52, 101, 104, 152, 154

Dett, Nathaniel, 115

Dillard, James, 41

disenfranchisement, 9, 13, 63, 152, 156, 162, 203n105. *See also* voting

Dixon Jr., Thomas, 27, 33, 62, 75

Douglas, Aaron, 71, 86, 87

Douglas, Ann, 69, 187n7

Douglass, Frederick, 37, 51, 93, 96, 99, 100, 104, 117, 152, 156, 157, 165, 184n32, 194n47, 197n4; anthologized, 54, 55, 83, 193n35; "Color Line" essay, 15; in pageants or plays, 89, 110; philosophy of history of, 36–37; in textbooks (or not), 58, 59, 153, 167; and Woodson, 30–31, 59

Drake, St. Clair, 140

dramas, 25, 72, 74, 115, 166, 167; anthologized, 87–90, 93, 190n77; historical, 89, 110; during Negro History Week, 94, 100, 105, 110
Dreer, Herman, 41
Du Bois, W. E. B., 11, 23, 45, 55, 111, 176n26, 197n4; ANA member, 26; anthologized or in textbooks, 62, 83, 149–52; on art, 95; *Darkwater*, 6; exposition or congress organizer, 33, 71, 105; on folk songs or spirituals, 77, 91, 191n96; and Johnson, 84; *The Negro*, 28; as scholar, 9, 10, 11, 40, 100, 105, 127, 151; on segregation or Jim Crow, 136, 152, 173n39; *Souls of Black Folk*, 15, 91; *Star of Ethiopia* pageant, 105, 108; and Woodson, 8, 34, 40, 44, 95, 187n24
Dumas, Alexander, 97, 98, 99
Dunbar, Paul Laurence, 31, 61, 62, 83, 84–85, 91, 193n34
Dunbar-Nelson, Alice, 39
Dunning, William Archibald, 27, 46, 177n44
Dykes, Eva, 113

Easton, Hosea, 37
educators, 25, 72, 85, 94, 112, 115, 117, 145; and Association, 2, 37, 41, 113; and Negro History Week, 97, 101, 104
Edwards, Brent Hayes, 76–77
Egypt, 32, 33, 105, 107, 108, 111
Ellison, Ralph, 167
Emancipation, 19, 21, 37, 49–50, 80, 142, 156, 177n46; celebrations or commemorations, 20, 28, 31–32, 105, 108, 175n7;
Emancipation Proclamation, 20, 33
equality: as American ideal, 11, 148–49; legal, 23, 119; political, 13, 152; racial, 14, 35, 91, 120, 124, 130, 132, 133, 148 (*see also* inequality); social, 13, 152; struggle for, 7, 19, 64, 147, 152, 155, 161
Ethiopia, 71, 89, 106, 107, 109, 110, 111
Evans, Lawton B., 57, 59–60, 65, 184–85n45
expositions, 15, 28, 31–33, 44, 54, 105, 108, 177n49, 196n78

facts, 5–7, 29, 34–36, 49, 172n18. *See also* objectivity
Fair Employment Practices Commission, 148, 156, 161, 162
Fauset, Arthur Huff, 73
Fauset, Jessie, 84, 103, 111, 115, 190n86
Finot, Jean, 130
Fleetwood, Christian A., 32

Fleming, Beatrice, 113
Florida, 53, 103–4
folklore, 10, 48, 74, 78, 81, 108, 137, 188n6
folk songs or music, 77–78, 80–81, 112, 137, 191n96. *See also* spirituals
Forten, James, 54
foundations, 4, 104, 113, 173n48, 196n98
Frank, Waldo, 74
Franklin, John Hope, 8, 9, 10, 12, 124, 167, 199n13; biographical details, 125–26; on *Brown*, 120, 161–64; *From Slavery to Freedom*, 56, 126, 137–38, 199n14; and Woodson, 11, 126, 138, 140
fraternal organizations, 1, 25, 108, 125, 198n5
fraternities, 1, 4, 96
Frazier, E. Franklin, 8, 41, 163, 202n79
Fredrickson, George, 121, 143, 203n100
freedom festivals, 17, 20–21, 31, 37
freedom struggle, 47, 117, 125, 152–53, 164, 166; and "wars for freedom", 121, 147, 155–57
Fugitive Slave Law (1850), 44, 87
Fuller, Meta Warrick, 32, 71, 83, 85, 108–9, 190n63, 196n78

Garnet, Henry Highland, 36, 54
Garrison, William Lloyd, 51, 93
Garvey, Marcus, 71
gender, 5, 10, 35, 112, 173n42
Georgia, 65–66, 81, 136. *See also* Atlanta
Gilpin, Charles S., 115, 192n5
Gordon, Leah, 139, 140, 149
Grant, Madison, 43, 90, 92, 126, 129, 130, 141, 182n123
Great Britain, 20, 22, 155
Great Depression, 8
Great Migration, 42, 47, 50, 53, 167
Greene, Lorenzo Johnston, 39, 40, 180n105, 181n114
Gregg, James E., 128
Gregory, Montgomery, 87–88, 191n101
Griffith, D. W., 16, 17, 26–28, 33, 177n41
Grimké, Archibald, 41, 54
Grimké, Francis J., 26
Guinn, Dorothy, 89, 108

Haiti, 42, 99, 109, 110, 125, 178n53
Hall, Stephen, 36, 48
Hammon, Jupiter, 85, 87
Harlem Renaissance, 2, 14, 75, 94; scholars on, 69, 187n7. *See also* Negro Renaissance
Harper, Frances E. W., 87, 115
Harris, Abram, 8

Hart, Albert Bushnell, 22–24, 41, 45, 92, 173n48, 176n18, 176nn24–26; *School History*, 57, 59–61, 65–66

Harvard University, 1, 9, 74, 128; history PhDs from, 40, 124, 125, 126 (*see also* Woodson: at Harvard)

Hastie, William H., 155

Hayes, Roland, 101, 115, 116

Haynes, George Edmund, 4, 41

Hegel, G. W. F., 75–76

Henderson, John B., 158

heritage, 20, 32, 72, 79, 91–92, 94, 112, 133, 200n37; African, 71, 73, 83, 86, 99, 138; and history, 72, 74, 76; invention of, 82

Herskovits, Melville J., 41, 127, 138

Hill, Leslie Pinckney, 85

Himes Jr., Joseph Sandy, 131–32

historians, 160, 174n54, 179n87; amateur or lay, 2, 35, 73, 180n96, 184n45; antebellum black, 179n91; black or segregated, 9–10, 35, 40, 113, 120–21, 138, 147; blacks as seen by, 49; *Brown* research by, 161–62; culture as seen by, 69; professional, 2, 16, 17, 35, 40, 58, 62, 46–49, 113, 121, 149, 167, 199n13; race as seen by, 119–21, 140; role of, 7, 24, 35, slavery as seen by, 46, 153; southern, 151; violence as seen by, 65; white, 14, 23, 27, 173n48, 202n78; women, 10, 173n42

historical societies or clubs, 17, 25, 37, 96, 104, 111

historiography: American, 23; "contributionist," 18, 20; modern, 38, 47, 59; racist, 16, 17, 58; Reconstruction, 17, 27; slavery, 46

history: biased (*see* propaganda); bottom-up social, 48, 100; as discipline or profession, 16, 22, 34–35, 48; disciplinary margins of, 10; mainstream accounts of, 17, 62 (*see also* textbooks: biased or mainstream); narratives of, 47, 49, 117, 148, 160; pageants, 17, 33, 72, 89, 105, 108–9, 112; and present time, 5, 24, 41, 121, 147, 149; scientific or as science, 17, 22, 24, 34–35, 38, 164 (*see also* facts; objectivity)

holidays, 20

Holloway, Jonathan Scott, 11, 177n38

Holmes, John Haynes, 95–96

Holt, Thomas, 71

Hooton, E. A., 128, 135

Hope, John, 95

Houston, Charles Hamilton, 155

Howard University, 1, 4, 25, 32, 89, 158; alumni or students, 102, 113, 143; faculty, staff, or trustees, 9, 25, 40, 41, 113–15, 120, 124, 125, 126, 128, 133, 139, 159, 173n42, 176n25, 181n114; Founders Library, 62; Glee Club, 116; Law School, 44; Moorland-Spingarn Research Center, 115

Huggins, Nathan, 116–17, 189n28

Hughes, Langston, 69, 72, 75, 86, 100, 108, 115, 190n86, 196n94; album, 157; anthologized, 73, 86, 167, 193n35; "Ballad of Negro History," 156; *Big Sea*, 94; *Chicago Defender* column, 156; "Negro Artist," 95, 117; and Woodson, 39, 157

Hurston, Zora Neale, 1, 73, 75, 115, 167, 196n94

Hutchinson, George, 69, 189n28, 191n4

Illinois, 4, 28

Immigration Restriction Act, 126

inequality, 14, 88, 120, 124, 127, 128, 146

integration, 5, 9, 14; of armed forces, 162; defined, 159, 205n50; and history, 18, 121, 148, 158–160, 164; of society, 109, 121, 160; of textbooks, 160, 168, 172n9

Jackson, Luther Porter, 8, 40, 48, 181n114

Jackson, Walter A., 139, 148

Jackson, Walter Clinton, 85–86

Jamestown, 77, 107

Jamestown Tercentennial Exhibition, 32

Janken, Kenneth, 149

jazz, 115–16, 157, 167

Jefferson, Thomas, 43, 48, 66

Jews, 119, 129, 144

Jim Crow, 119, 136, 166, 182n120; black institutions during, 8, 110; cracks in or end of, 14, 149; as era, 1, 4, 10, 26, 144, 169; features of, 13, 16; fight against, 11; "illusion of permanency" of, 163; impact on artists, 83; impact on scholars, 9–12, 17, 120; impact on Woodson, 15, 17; legislation, 152; lexicon of, 12–13; and racial uplift ideology, 4

Johnson, Charles S., 41, 139–40, 160, 204n7

Johnson, Fenton, 84

Johnson, Georgia Douglas, 87, 89, 102, 190n86

Johnson, Jack, 111

Johnson, James Weldon, 3, 54, 62, 74, 76, 93, 172n10, 196n94; biographical details, 75; *Book of American Negro Poetry*, 71, 83, 85, 189nn51–52; *Book of American Negro Spirituals*, 79–82, 193nn34–35;

Johnson, James Weldon, (continued)
  "Lift Every Voice and Sing," 75, 82, 101, 111, 112; "Negro's Creative Genius," 83–85; as poet, 85, 86
Johnson, Mordecai, 41, 54
Johnston, James Hugo, 40, 181n114
Jones, Eugene Kinckle, 58
Jones, Jeannette Eileen, 70
Jones, Lois Mailou, 102, 114
Jones, Oliver, 19–20
journalists, 2, 39, 105, 121, 144, 180n96
Journal of Negro Education, 1, 130, 139–40, 162, 203n101
Journal of Negro History, 4, 113, 127, 184n45; articles about Africa in, 71; and Association, 2, 37; contributors to, 38–41, 125, 126; editors of, 125; first issue of, 34, 183n10; primary sources in, 17, 47–48, 50, 53, 55, 183n17; reviews in, 46, 75, 79, 81, 83, 85, 86, 90, 128, 150, 188n14, 189n51, 196n94, 197n105; Woodson articles or "Notes" in, 42, 44, 46, 48–49, 58, 82, 85, 90, 172n21, 199n29
Just, Ernest Everett, 25, 192n5

Kallen, Horace, 70, 191n98
Kansas City, 101, 104
Kelly, Alfred, 161
Kentucky, 41, 52, 101, 102
Keppel, Ben, 11
Kerlin, Robert T., 41, 85, 93, 190n62, 196n96
King Jr., Martin Luther, 163, 166, 167, 207n10
Ku Klux Klan, 16, 61, 65, 90, 150, 165

Lee, Ulysses, 93
letters, 12, 30, 55, 75, 84, 93, 99; to ACS, 49–51; from former slaves, 51–53, 92; in *Journal of Negro History*, 48–49, 183n10, 183n17; from migrants, 53–54; from or about Woodson, 39, 95, 176n26
Lewis, David Levering, 73, 84, 88, 189n28
Lewis, Julian Herman, 120, 133–34
liberalism, 120, 148–49
Liberia, 51, 99, 109, 110
librarians, 2, 101, 113
libraries, 9, 26, 75, 103, 194n47
Library of Congress, 24, 50, 92; Carter G. Woodson Collection in, 99, 193n32
Lincoln, Abraham, 20, 27, 96
Lincoln Jubilee, 28, 31–33, 177n49
literacy, 3–4, 15, 26, 44, 82
literary magazines, 143–44

literary societies, 17, 25, 26, 37, 94, 96
literature, 14, 29, 100, 108, 125; anthologies of, 72, 74, 75, 85–87, 93; and Association, 41; canons of, 167; celebration of black, 71, 82–84, 86, 96, 100–102, 117; concept of black, 72, 93; folk, 73; and identity, 25; racist or anti-Negro, 105; Reconstruction-era, 63; renaissance-era, 86, 94; slave narratives as protest, 87; stereotypes in, 203n101
Litwack, Leon, 1, 16
Locke, Alain, 1, 9, 25, 33, 56, 69, 78, 190n86, 194n44; anthologies edited by, 72–76, 86–88, 191n101, 193n35; on art, music, or poetry, 75, 81, 91, 196n96; as Association member, 41, 75, 188n14; on culture or cultural pluralism, 70, 84, 88, 91–92, 97, 127, 191n98, 188n13; and Harlem/Negro Renaissance, 69, 70, 75; *New Negro*, 46, 72, 73–74, 76, 81, 89, 93, 193n34, 194n47; reviews by, 184n40, 188n14, 201n51; Smithsonian lecture, 102
Logan, Rayford, 8, 10, 119, 124, 167, 174n54, 198n7, 198n9, 201n62, 204n20, 206nn72–73; *Betrayal of the Negro*, 202n84, 203n100; biographical details, 125, 136, 181n114; and "black image in the white mind" scholarship, 120–21, 203nn100–102; on *Brown*, 161–62; *Negro and the Post-War World*, 135–37, 141; *Negro in American Life and Thought*, 9, 15, 120–21, 140–46, 203n101; *What the Negro Wants*, 125, 130, 149–54, 160, 204n7; and Woodson, 24, 40, 125–26, 137, 195n70
Lorini, Alessandra, 105
Louisiana, 15, 53, 56, 80
L'Ouverture, Toussaint, 97, 99, 105, 111
Lynch, John R., 38, 54
lynchings, 6, 9, 13, 15, 16, 60–61, 96, 145, 168

Mann, Bureel W., 50–51
March on Washington Movement, 153, 156
marriage, interracial, 13, 126, 150, 162
Marshall, Thurgood, 155, 161
Martin, Gertrude, 141
Marx, Karl, 8
Maryland, 101
Mays, Benjamin, 150
McBrown, Gertrude Parthenia, 113
McCoo, Edward J., 89, 108–110
McKay, Claude, 71, 73, 84–86, 108, 111, 115, 167

McMaster, John Bach, 57, 59–61, 65, 184n45
Mead, Margaret, 74, 127
Meier, August, 10, 16
Miller, Dorie, 154
Miller, Kelly, 1, 11, 25, 40, 89, 181n111
Miller, May, 89
miscegenation, 13, 29, 42–43, 58, 60, 128, 134, 185n59
Mississippi, 14, 15, 31, 39, 64, 81, 83, 184n45
Mississippi Valley Historical Review, 34, 35, 46, 185n51
Missouri, 41, 64, 101, 168
Mixon, Mavis B., 113
Montagu, Ashley, 124, 129, 130, 131, 135, 202n79
Moon, F. D., 132
Moore, Richard V., 158
Moorland, Jesse, 33, 39, 41
Morrison, Toni, 167
Morton, Samuel, 134
Moton, Robert Russa, 54
Muhammad, Khalil Gibran, 144–45
mulattoes, 22, 43, 128, 178n53
Murphy, Beatrice M., 87
museums, 75, 110, 117, 165–67, 178–79n74
music, 14, 21, 25, 28, 40, 62, 70, 89, 90, 110, 115–16, 157, 167, 207n12; anthologized, 72, 77–83
Muzzey, David Saville, 57, 59–61, 65, 177n46, 179n87, 184n45
Myrdal, Gunnar, 119, 139, 148, 197–98n4, 202nn78–79

NAACP, 28, 156, 157; and Association members, 8; founded, 4, 152, 153; fundraisers for, 39, 181n114; members or leadership of, 26, 75, 105, 125, 152; Spingarn Medal awarded by, 95–96; textbook activism by, 148, 153, 171n9
National Association of Colored Women, 4, 25, 41, 192n5
National Museum of African American History and Culture (NMAAHC), 165–67
National Negro Business League, 4
National Negro Congress, 8, 156
National Urban League, 4, 41, 58, 153, 156, 171n9
Nebraska, 64
"Negro": definitions of, xi, 124, 133, 135–37, 146; "the," xi, 45, 72, 75–76, 91, 94, 97, 107, 199n29
"Negro art," 72, 77, 88, 95, 102, 104, 188n13, 191n101; Schuyler vs. Du Bois or Locke on, 90–92
Negro Caravan, The, 71–72, 92–93
"Negro genius," 77, 82–85, 90–92, 191n101
Negro History Bulletin, 124, 171n9, 196n96; antiracist articles in, 130–32; contributors to or editors of, 113–15, 125, 159; on desegregation, 156–57; war in, 137, 147, 154–55
Negro History Week, 2, 3, 10, 40, 95–101, 154, 187n24; bibliographies for, 100, 193n34; and collective identity, 111–12; at colleges and universities, 75, 103–4, 110; date of, 96; equality of races stressed in, 130, 131, 133; and local history, 100; and music, 75, 100, 101, 102, 103, 115, 157; and *Negro History Bulletin*, 113; pageants for, 71, 72, 100, 105, 108, 110–11, 131; pamphlets for, 35, 96–97, 193n34; radio programs for, 102, 133, 154, 158, 159, 194n46; in schools, 14, 75, 101, 110–11, 194n47; start or spread of, 14, 37, 72, 96, 101–4; themes or messages of, 130, 154, 158
"Negro literature," 93
"Negro mind," 17, 46–49, 54, 84
"Negro problem," 5, 33, 34, 58–59, 119, 124, 131, 151, 158, 178n53
Negro Renaissance, 81, 92, 194n47; and Africa, 70; and anthologies, 72, 73, 74, 76–79, 84–86, 167; and Association, 95, 101, 113, 117; and black history, 14, 71–74, 92, 95, 97–98, 117; extent of participation in, 94, 117; key contemporary figures of, 41, 69, 73, 84, 86, 111, 115, 167, 194n47, 196n94; key historical figures for, 97–99; name of, 69; and Negro History Week, 72, 94, 100–101; pageants or plays of, 105, 109, 111; and periodicals or publishers, 112–13; philosophy of, 94–95; scholars on, 14, 69, 73, 78, 94, 109, 187n7, 189n28, 191–92n4; in schools, 72, 94; start of, 73, 79; Woodson's role in, 75. *See also* Harlem Renaissance
networks, academic or professional, 2, 10, 37, 113, 139
New Negro, 69–72, 74–76, 85, 92, 94, 96, 99, 102, 116–17, 186n3, 187n1. *See also* Locke: *New Negro*
New Orleans, 104, 163, 165
newspapers and periodicals, 70, 75, 175n7; Atlanta, 133, 145, 159; *Baltimore Afro-American*, 1, 25, 56, 83, 101, 182n21; bias or prejudice in, 60, 121, 143–45, 203n101,

newspapers and periodicals, (*continued*) 203n105; black, 3, 20, 25, 33, 71, 83, 101, 112, 150; *Boston Herald*, 34; Chicago, 28 (see also *Chicago Defender*); *Colored American*, 25; *Crisis*, 1, 11, 26, 56, 95, 112, 152, 173n39, 185n51; *Globe-Democrat*, 145; *Liberator*, 51; *New Journal and Guide*, 83, 87, 150, 156, 158, 190n77; *New Republic*, 56; *New York Amsterdam News*, 79, 130, 160; *New York Globe*, 27; *New York Times*, 28–29, 33, 50, 140, 166, 167, 171n9, 191n101; *Norfolk Journal and Guide*, 44, 101; *Opportunity*, 56, 89, 112; *Philadelphia Tribune*, 79, 159; *Pittsburgh Courier*, 101, 150, 151, 160, 180n96; as primary sources, 30; *Social Forces*, 140; *Southern Workman*, 34; *Survey Graphic*, 112; *Washington Bee*, 25; *Washington Post*, 168

New York, 25, 53, 54, 88, 130, 148; Association branches or meeting in, 75, 104, 159; expositions in, 32, 33, 105, 196n78; National Guard regiment, 64; Negro History Week in, 101, 130, 159; riots in, 151, 152

Novick, Peter, 27, 34–35, 46

Obama, Barack H., 166, 169
objectivity, 17, 34–36, 185n51. *See also* facts; history: scientific or as science
Ohio, 52, 64, 101, 131, 132
Oklahoma, 66, 126, 163
"one-drop rule," 13, 43, 134
O'Neill, Eugene, 87–88, 191n101
Ovington, Mary White, 80

pamphlets, 2, 26, 35, 42, 44, 93, 96, 97, 153, 193n34
pan-Africanism, 71, 125
parades, 20–21, 105
Park, Robert E., 41, 138
Parks, Rosa, 165
Payne, Daniel A., 25
Pendleton, Leila Amos, 38, 57–58, 61–64, 106-7, 167, 184n45
Pennington, James W. C., 36–37
Philadelphia, 101, 102, 103, 104
philanthropy, 4, 41, 152, 173n48, 178n59, 196n98
Phillips, U. B., 46–47, 51–52, 182n3
plays. *See* dramas
pluralism: ethnic, 32; cultural, 69–70, 84, 97
poetry, 21, 25, 102, 113, 115, 117, 157, 189n51; anthologized, 71, 72, 74, 75, 83–87, 93; in Negro History Week, 72, 94, 97, 100, 108, 112; Negro poets vs. Negro, 86, 91; nineteenth-century black, 63, 154
political organizations, 26
poll tax, 15, 156
Popular Front, 8
Porter, Dorothy, 114
Porter, James, 102
Pride, Marion Jackson, 113
primary sources, 12–14, 29–31, 47–49, 55, 77, 92, 99, 178n61, 183n17. *See also* letters; *see also under* Woodson
"primitives," 70, 76, 107, 191n101, 195n68
progress, 22–24, 26, 33, 40; black, 21, 32, 62, 167; challenge to U.S. narrative, 13, 45, 47, 62, 65–67, 167; of "the race," 133; of racial equality, 148
propaganda, 6, 28, 35, 36, 62, 73, 95, 130–31, 134, 153, 158
Prosser, Gabriel, 42, 155
Protestants, 31, 38, 119
psychologists, 14, 119, 124, 129, 131, 132, 139, 143, 157, 161, 199n24, 200n30
Pushkin, Alexander, 98, 99

race: Aryan, 131, 200n37; biological or "scientific" view of, 12–13, 14, 120, 123, 126–30, 134–35; and biometric measurements, 123, 127, 129–30; Caucasian, 22–23, 43, 45, 119, 90, 92, 119, 128–29, 134, 141, 176n24, 182n123; and class, 5, 8; cultural or sociological view of, 12–13, 92, 120, 124, 127, 132; definitions or terminology of, xi, 43, 119–20, 123–24, 128, 133–37, 146; historians' role in debates on, 120, 140; and intelligence or IQ, 126, 128–31, 141; key theme, 12; Mongoloid, 129; "mulatto hypothesis," 22; Negro, 23, 24, 26, 36, 39, 76, 90, 95, 129, 137, 138, 147, 172n21, 176n26, 196n78; reality of, 130, 132, 135, 146; "soul of the," 78–79, 82, 188n23; "the," 11, 12, 69, 81–82, 91, 120, 105; UNESCO statement on, 139, 202n79
race consciousness, 72, 80, 94–95, 98, 110
"race histories," 38, 55, 57, 58, 62, 73, 76, 105, 185n52
race pride, 5, 14, 25, 94, 109, 133. *See also* black pride
"race women or men," 2, 54, 95
racial inferiority doctrine, 16, 23–24, 80, 130, 150, 174n9, 200n30; anthropologists on, 127, 129, 199n24; art or literature

challenges, 84; Association challenges, 35, 120, 128; "fifth freedom" from, 132; Franklin on, 11–12, 163; Logan on, 136, 146; *Negro History Bulletin* challenges, 130, 132; in schools or textbooks, 6, 97, 116, 131; science and, 97, 120, 124, 132; Woodson on, 107

racial uplift, 29, 41, 59, 65, 95; associations, 4, 8, 125, 198n5; ideology, 4–5, 38

racism: in academe, 45, 134; in American society, 5, 12, 17, 44, 70, 121; vs. black history, 1, 12, 117; concept of, 130, 145, 146; and culture, 203n102; in historical profession, 12, 16, 17; history of, 119–20, 139, 203n92; images and artifacts of, 16; individualist vs. systemic, 139–40, 142–43; "liberal," 24, 174n9; in print media or textbooks, 143, 148; and race, 120, 201n60, 203n92; vs. race vindication, 11–12; vs. racial uplift, 5; "scientific," 14, 16, 43, 119, 126–27

ragtime, 83, 90, 115

Rainey, Joseph H., 54

Randolph, A. Philip, 8, 153, 156

Rapier, James T., 54

Reconstruction, 13, 49, 58, 66, 141, 162, 181n114; black congressmen during, 61, 76, 156; racist histories of, 6, 16–17, 27, 57, 76, 131, 151; Woodson on, 44–45, 60

Reconstruction Amendments, 13, 15

Renaissance. *See* Harlem Renaissance; Negro Renaissance

Revolutionary War, 21, 29, 59, 155, 156

Rhoads, Joseph J., 41, 129

Rhodes, James Ford, 60

Richardson, Willis, 89

riots, 4, 27, 64–65, 119, 126, 151, 152, 168

Robeson, Paul, 100, 111

Roman, C. V., 38, 106

Roosevelt, Franklin D., 41, 132, 161

Rosenwald, Julius, 4, 41

Rudwick, Elliott, 10, 16

Saint-Gaudens, Augustus, 66

Savage, W. Sherman, 40, 181n114

Scarborough, Dorothy, 80–81, 189n40

Schomburg, Arthur, 25, 73–74, 76, 83, 180n96

schools: black history in 40, 56, 66, 94, 104, 116, 167; black, 2, 30, 33, 40, 41, 44, 72, 104, 111, 116, 141, 158, 163, 178n59; and black communities, 110, 117; common, 4, 29, 100; desegregated (*see* desegregation); Harlem or Negro Renaissance in, 95, 101, 113, 117; M Street High School, 24, 125; and *Negro History Bulletin*, 113, 116, 154; Negro history clubs in, 104, 194n47; Negro History Week in, 14, 75, 101, 110–11, 194n47; *Negro in Our History*'s use or confiscation in, 56, 66; performances in, 89, 102, 110, 111, 131; Piney Woods, 31; public, 25, 42, 101, 102, 177n41, 206n66; racial inferiority doctrine taught in, 6; Rosenwald, 41; segregated, 1, 2, 3, 8, 14, 25, 42, 72, 94, 110, 116, 117, 142, 156–58, 161–63, 168, 206n66

Schuyler, George, 90–92, 191n101

Scott, Keith Lamont, 168

segregation, 16, 33, 67, 96, 126, 149–150, 160, 164, 168, 203n105; of army, 64, 119, 161; in buses or trains, 136, 142, 157; of businesses or workplaces, 25, 26; of churches, 25, 153; in public accommodations, 13; of scholars, 9–11, 25, 139; of schools (*see under* schools); statutes or legislation, 162, 163; "used to kill segregation," 8, 173n39

Shaw, Robert Gould, 105

Shufeldt, R. W., 28–29, 33, 43, 178n53

Simmons, W. J., 20, 175n5

slave revolts, 42, 60, 153–54, 156

slavery, 19–21, 25, 31, 44, 73, 99, 136, 138, 153–55, 162, 185n59; and Africa, 106–7, 111; and art, literature, music, 78–80, 82–83, 86, 87, 183n10; dramas or pageants about, 89–90, 116; and education, 29–30, 42; Negro History Week depictions of, 102; personal vs. economic dimensions of, 52–53; primary sources about, 12, 30–31, 47–53; representations of, 7, 12, 24, 46–49, 55–60, 63, 65–66, 106, 132, 151, 153; and segregation or color line, 13, 15, 142–43, 163; "vestiges" of, 151; violence of, 52–53, 60, 61, 166, 168

Smethurst, James, 63

Smith, Bonnie, 35

Smith, Lucy Harth, 41

Social Darwinists, 9, 17

social welfare groups, 2

sociologists, 14, 40, 119, 124, 131, 132, 138, 139, 140, 148, 162

solidarity, 5, 8, 21, 104, 112, 117, 133

South Carolina, 27, 44, 74

spirituals, 105, 116, 157: African (or European) influences on, 77–80; in American canons or culture, 74, 167; approaches to study of, 78; Johnson's anthology of, 79–80, 82, 193n35;

spirituals, (continued)
  Locke on, 81; and Negro History Week, 100–102, 105, 111–12, 115; transcriptions of, 77, 80–82, 188n21; white anthologists of, 80–81; Work's anthology of, 77–79
statistics: about black history, 56, 104, 171n9, 207n10; about black progress, 62; about general education or literacy, 4; about historians or history departments, 22, 40; about lynchings, 15, 60; about police violence, 169; U.S. Census, 43, 144
stereotypes, 12, 17, 27, 36, 46–47, 49, 53, 65, 76, 94, 121, 138, 158, 191n101; "contented slave," 12, 55, 57, 144; "criminal Negro," 57, 138, 144–45; in literature, 203n101; in print media, 143–45, 153; in textbooks (see textbooks: biased or mainstream)
Steward, Theophilus G., 80
Stoddard, Lothrop, 43, 88, 90, 92, 129, 130, 182n123
Stowe, Harriet Beecher, 105
Sumner, William Graham, 162, 206n72
Supreme Court, U.S., 13, 15, 33, 43–44, 142; *Brown*, 14, 119, 120, 121, 147, 148, 156–58, 161–62, 164; *Dred Scott*, 44; *Plessy v. Ferguson*, 13, 15, 44, 142–43; *Smith v. Allwright*, 161, 162
Sussman, Robert Wald, 120

Taft, William Howard, 63
"talented tenth," 4–5, 90, 99, 73
Talley, Thomas, 84
Tanner, Henry O., 83, 100, 111
Taylor, Alrutheus Ambush, 39, 40, 181n114
Taylor, Samuel Coleridge, 97
teachers, 2, 25, 94, 101, 110–11, 113, 116, 117, 158, 159. *See also* educators
Tennessee, 52, 64
Terrell, Mary Church, 4, 25, 39
Texas, 80, 104, 168
textbooks, 3, 37, 71, 113, 117, 160, 188n14, 207–8n18; Africa in, 106; agency vs. oppression in, 65; appendices to, 63; biased or mainstream, 46, 55, 57–59, 65–66, 97, 148, 153, 171–72n9, 177n46, 179n87; black history, 56, 71, 99, 126, 137; "celebratory" or progress narratives in, 22–23, 45, 62; free blacks in, 58–59; images in, 46, 56–57, 62, 65–66, 168; race, 57, 58, 106, 108; racial violence in, 17–18, 58, 63–65, 168, 208n18; Woodson's, 2, 56, 107, 108, 194n47 (*see also* Woodson: *Negro in Our History*)

Thompson, Charles H., 139
Till, Emmett, 168
Tillman, Benjamin, 62
Todd, T. Wingate, 129
Toney, Jack, 19
Toomer, Jean, 73, 86, 87, 167, 190n86
Torrence, Ridgley, 88
Trouillot, Michel-Rolph, 47–49, 171n7, 172n18
Truman, Harry S., 161
Truth, Sojourner, 31, 59, 89, 99, 117, 153, 156, 157
Tubman, Harriet, 4, 59, 110, 152, 153, 157, 167
Turner, Frederick Jackson, 22–24, 34, 44–45, 92, 176n24
Turner, Henry McNeal, 71
Turner, Mary, 64
Turner, Nat, 42, 60, 153, 155–57, 165
Tuskegee University, 4, 31, 41, 62, 152; airmen, 154, 156
Tuttle, Worth, 56

Union Army, 19, 21, 59, 109, 156
Universal Negro Improvement Association, 71
universities, 9, 75; Atlanta, 4, 95, 100, 102, 125; black history taught in, 4, 56, 104, 172n12; black, 1, 4, 40, 104, 172n12; Chicago, 2, 9, 40, 74, 133; Clark, 26; Columbia, 9, 22, 27, 40, 141, 184n45; Cornell, 4; Fisk, 77, 84, 113, 124, 126, 139, 160, 181n114; German, 22; Hampton, 4, 31, 128, 152, 180n96; Johns Hopkins, 22; Lincoln, 181n114; Negro History Week at, 75, 103–4, 110; Virginia, 163; Wilberforce, 1, 31, 62, 125. *See also* colleges; Harvard University; Howard University; Tuskegee University

Vesey, Denmark, 42, 153, 155–56
vindicationism, 11–12, 26, 30, 108, 154
violence, 1, 13, 18, 58, 61, 63–65, 126, 144–45, 151–52, 156, 166, 168, 169, 203n105. *See also* lynchings; riots; slavery: violence of; women: violence against
Virginia, 2, 19–21, 50, 66, 106, 113, 117, 136, 156; Racial Integrity Act, 126
voting, 15, 44, 61, 110, 162

Walker, David, 87
Walker, Madame C. J., 98, 111
Washington, Booker T., 4, 15, 58, 62, 93, 96, 99, 104, 167, 179n77, 184n32; anthologized, 83; "Atlanta Compromise" speech, 31–32,

54; in pageants or plays, 89, 110; *Story of the Negro*, 37
Washington, D.C., 24–26, 64–66, 101, 102, 116
Washington, George, 48, 59, 84
Washington, Jesse, 168
Wells, Ida B., 4, 29, 98, 99, 178n65, 197n4
Wells, James Lesesne, 89, 103
Weltfish, Gene, 131
Wesley, Charles, 10, 39, 40, 113, 138, 147, 158, 174n54, 202n77; biographical details, 124–25, 181n114; and Channing, 176n26; *What the Negro Wants* essay, 130–31, 149, 153–54; and Woodson, 180n105
West Indies, 20, 37, 136, 184n45
West Virginia, 2, 19–20, 24, 101, 166
Wheatley, Phyllis, 30, 76, 83–84, 87, 91, 93, 98, 99, 115
White, Clarence Cameron, 102
White, Newman Ivey, 85–86
White, Walter, 153
white supremacy doctrine, 13, 16, 21, 63, 88, 92, 99, 174n9
Whiting, Helen A., 113
Wilkerson, Isabel, 167
Wilkins, Roy, 149, 152–53
Williams Jr., Vernon, 120, 127
Williams, George Washington, 20, 21, 36–38, 55, 180n96
Williams, Nat. D., 133
Wilson, Francille Rusan, 9
Wilson, J. T., 20
Wilson, Mabel, 33
Wilson, Woodrow, 17, 25–27, 66, 96
Winston, Michael, 125
women, 10, 28, 35, 43, 47–48, 62, 97, 99, 154, 156, 185n59, 193n36; in academe, 173n42; educators, 72, 94, 101, 117; and *Negro History Bulletin*, 113; organizations or clubs of, 4, 25, 31; violence against, 60, 64, 145
Woodson, Carter Godwin: anthologies edited by, 2, 17, 54, 72, 84–85, 93, 193n35; Africa or *African Background Outlined*, 6, 71, 106–8, 138, 188n23, 195n68, 195n70; ANA member, 25–26; biographical details, 2; birth, childhood, or adolescence of, 2, 15, 19; cartoon of, 166; *Century of Negro Migration*, 42; character of, 5, 39, 44, 95, 180n105; in Chicago, 2, 28, 31, 33, 95; and civil rights movement, 119, 147, 155, 164; death of, 148; education as theme, 29; *Education of the Negro*, 28–31, 36, 42, 107; *Encyclopedia Africana*, 123; as "father of black history," 36; at Harvard, 2, 17, 21–22, 24, 92, 175n16; *History of the Negro Church*, 38; Hughes's record dedicated to, 157; *Journal of Negro History* articles or "Notes," 42–44, 172n21, 199n29; *Mind of the Negro*, 17, 50, 55, 49, 84–85; *Miseducation of the Negro*, 8, 173n35; and NAACP, 8, 26, 39, 95–96; *Negro History in Thirteen Plays* introduction, 89–90; *Negro History Bulletin* articles or editorial committee, 113, 115, 137, 155, 156, 197n105; and Negro History Week, 96–97, 101, 103–4, 111, 113, 160, 187n24, 194n47; *Negro in Our History*, 11, 17, 38, 43, 55–64, 66, 106–8, 182n120, 184n40, 185n51, 185n55, 187n20; *Negro Orators*, 17, 54, 84–85, 193n35; newspaper articles by, 2, 11, 90, 105, 107; parents or family of, 2, 17, 19, 39; primary sources important for, 12, 17, 24, 29–31, 47–48, 99–100; protégés of, 40, 125–26; publications by, 2; on race or racism, 97, 120, 123, 127–28, 133, 137, 146, 199n24; reviews by, 2, 46–47, 51, 58, 83, 85, 89, 128, 179n87, 199n24; reviews of, 28–29, 50, 54, 55–56, 105n51, 188n14, 195n70; scholarship on, 16, 171n3; on segregation, 13, 164; as teacher, 7, 24, 117, 125; in Washington, D.C., 24–26, 64–65; in West Virginia, 2, 19–20
Woodson, James Henry, 19, 21
Woodward, C. Vann, 161, 163
Work, John Wesley, 74, 77–79, 81, 84, 188nn22–23, 196n96
Work, Monroe, 10, 41
World's Columbian Exposition (Chicago, 1893), 31, 44, 178n65
World War I, 40, 126, 147, 182n120; black migration during, 42, 53, 151; black units in, 125, 154
World War II, 119, 130, 147, 152, 154–55

YMCA or YWCA, 1, 33, 39, 40, 41, 5, 108, 179n77

Zimmerman, Jonathan, 167

www.ingramcontent.com/pod-product-compliance
Lightning Source LLC
Chambersburg PA
CBHW052231230426
43666CB00035B/2638